CAPOTOSTO'S
WOODWORKING
TECHNIQUES AND PROJECTS

A Popular Science Book

CAPOTOSTO'S

WOOD

WORKING
TECHNIQUES AND PROJECTS

Rosario Capotosto

Drawings by Michael Capotosto

POPULAR SCIENCE BOOKS

VAN NOSTRAND REINHOLD COMPANY
NEW YORK   CINCINNATI   TORONTO   LONDON   MELBOURNE

Copyright © 1982 by Rosario Capotosto

Published by
Popular Science Books
Times Mirror Magazines, Inc.
380 Madison Avenue
New York, NY 10017

Distributed to the trade by
Van Nostrand Reinhold Company
135 West 50th Street
New York, NY 10020

Brief quotations may be used in critical articles and reviews.
For any other reproduction of the book, however, including
electronic, mechanical, photocopying, recording, or other
means, written permission must be obtained from the publisher.

Library of Congress Catalog Card Number: 82-50648
ISBN: 0–442–21497–9

Library of Congress Cataloging in Publication Data

Capotosto, Rosario.
    Capotosto's Woodworking techniques and projects.

    Includes index.
    1. Woodwork.   I. Title.   II. Title: Woodworking techniques
and projects.
TT180.C363   1982   684.1′042   82-50648
ISBN 0-442-21497-9

Fourth Printing, 1983

Manufactured in the United States of America

To Jennie, Michael, Raymond, August, Susan and Emily
for their moral support.

CONTENTS

PART III   ON YOUR OWN: FURNITURE PLANS

PART IV   JIGS, AIDS AND SPECIAL TECHNIQUES

Acknowledgments

The bulk of the project concepts in this book were designed and built by the author. Many originally appeared in national publications such as *Mechanix Illustrated, Popular Mechanics, Popular Science,* and *Workbench.*

Numerous projects were rebuilt to achieve some refinement of design.

Special thanks must be given to Michael Capotosto who patiently measured and made new drawings of all project plans to suit the format of this book.

Also thanks to Furniture Designs for permission to adapt their Rolltop Desk plan for inclusion in this book.

Grateful appreciation is extended to Henry Gross for his advice and assistance in the preparation of the book, and to William Gray, Natasha Sylvester, and Jeff Fitschen for their design and layout.

INTRODUCTION

Among the numerous hobbies and leisure activities, woodworking is easily the most popular, having become for many people an established way of life. The raw material is second to none in terms of natural beauty, workability, durability, and availability. Working with wood offers great opportunity for creative as well as profitable use of leisure time. In transforming raw wood into decorative accessories, comfortable furniture, and attractive home improvements, you will not only save money but, perhaps more important, enjoy the deep satisfaction of accomplishment. Fortunately, skill in woodworking is not an inborn talent but is a knack that can be acquired.

Woodworking demands two kinds of skills: manual skills for using hand tools and technical skills for using power tools. With certain hand tools, you must develop a feel for control and accuracy which comes only after long experience, trial and error. Most power tools, on the other hand, have control and accuracy built in. They enable you to perform fine work easier, faster, and with greater precision than by hand-tool methods—provided, of course, that you have learned to use them properly.

Woodworking machines are not automatic, nor can they think. To achieve precise, predicted results you must know how to set them up, and how to use special jigs and devices.

This book assumes that you have rudimentary woodworking skills. Nevertheless, the first part provides a review of the basics; use it as a refresher to update your working methods.

The second part provides practical "on-the-job training" through a series of project chapters. Ranging from the simple to the complex, these projects have been selected to provide well-rounded experience in woodworking. Each project chapter consists of a photo of the finished piece, a detailed plan of the project, complete instructions on how to build it, and step-by-step photos that show every phase of construction.

The third part consists of plans for twelve large furniture projects accompanied by a photo of the finished project and an explanatory text. With experience acquired building some of the projects in Part II, you should be able to tackle any of these pieces on your own.

Part IV includes a collection of jigs, aids, and special techniques that will expand the scope and utility of your tools.

Since practical experience is often the best teacher, it is hoped that by building the projects in this book you will gradually enlarge your knowledge of woodworking techniques and develop your skills with hand and power tools. And the results of your work will be apparent to everyone: handsome furniture and accessories to decorate your home.

PART I

BRUSH-UP ON BASICS

1

Working with Plans

You may be dissuaded from building an otherwise appealing project because its style does not suit your taste or fit in with the decor of your home. This need not be a deterrent. Often a few minor exterior changes can transform the piece to another style while the basic design and function remain unchanged.

The examples shown, of projects in this book, illustrate the possibilities. It should be noted that in some situations the kind of wood and type of hardware may have to be changed to suit the altered style. For example, knotty pine and rustic, wrought-iron hardware, appropriate for a colonial piece, would be out of place on a contemporary design.

You may also find it desirable to alter the dimensions of a project to suit your own particular requirements. If the change is a minor one you need only to revise the measurements in the plan. But if you contemplate a major change, it is advisable first to make a revised drawing of the general outline to scale—that is, in exact proportion to full size. This will enable you to make an accurate visual appraisal of the new proportional relationship of the components to each other and in overall appearance. Pleasing proportion is an important element of design so this aspect should be carefully considered.

Style of a piece can easily be transformed with only superficial changes. The basic form is identical in both versions.

This is another example of how you can dramatically change the appearance of a project to suit a particular preference.

The easiest way to make a drawing according to scale is with an architect's scale or by drawing on graph paper. If you work with the scale rule, select one of the common scales which will be appropriate for the size of the object and the paper. For example, if the original object is a rectangle measuring 4 by 5 feet, a scale of 1½ inches = 1 foot will produce an outline that measures 6 by 7½ inches on your paper. This is a reasonable size that would be easy to see and to work with. On the other hand, if a scale of ¼ inch = 1 foot were used, the resultant outline would measure only 1 by 1¼ inches. This obviously would be of little value for the purpose at hand. In making the scale drawing with graph paper that is ruled with ¼ inch squares you would let six squares represent 1 foot.

If you decide to use a material different from that which is indicated in the plan, you may have to

Make scale drawings when revising a plan in order to assure pleasing proportions. A scale rule simplifies the task, or you can use graph paper.

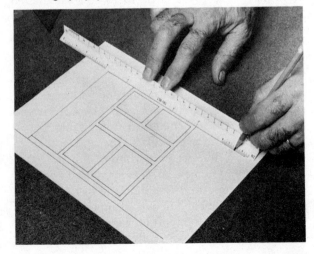

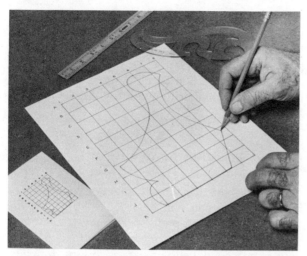

Irregular designs in a small drawing are enlarged to full size by working on a grid of squares. Key points on the small drawing are simply drawn in the corresponding positions on the larger, grid-ruled paper. A French curve is used to smooth the freehand drawing.

revise dimensions. For example, if the plan calls for the use of ¾-inch plywood and you prefer to use solid hardwood in a standard stock size instead, all thickness dimensions would probably have to be changed. This is because the nearest equivalent to ¾ inch in hardwood standard stock is $^{13}/_{16}$ inch thick. Note that solid hardwood is available in exact ¾-inch thickness, but not readily.

Another consideration when contemplating dimension changes in both solid lumber or plywood constructions: Try to keep within standard stock dimensions for reasons of economy. For example, if you were to redesign a softwood bookcase so the new dimensions would call for a number of 97-inch-long shelves, you would be forced to buy a lot of expensive waste for a mere 1 inch. Lumber stock sizes are 8, 10, 12 feet, etc. Since your 97 inches is over the 8-foot length, you would have to buy 10-foot boards and commit 23-inch leftovers to the scrap pile. By the same token, bear in mind that most lumber dealers will gladly cut and sell modular parts of a 4 × 8 plywood panel such as 2 by 8 feet or 4 by 4 feet. If you require a panel 8 feet by 25 inches you would most likely be obligated to buy the cut-off waste from a full panel.

Project plans found in books or magazines are normally drawn in reduced size because of page size limitations. This means that any irregular-shaped parts that are contained in a plan must be enlarged to full size. The resultant pattern is used to transfer the outline to the work for cutting.

The contoured outline in the plan is usually drawn over a grid of small squares and includes a notation as to the size of the full-scale squares to be used for enlarging the drawing. The procedure, called "enlarging with squares," is simple and effective.

In the example shown, 1 inch is indicated for each square. To make the full-size pattern, lay out a grid of 1 inch squares on a sheet of paper or thin cardboard to equal the number of squares in the small drawing. To avoid confusion it is advisable to number and letter the vertical and horizontal lines in both the small and large grids so they correspond. Referring to a square on the small drawing, lightly draw a matching line in the corresponding large square. Continue the process until the full pattern is outlined. The lines can be darkened and smoothened with the aid of French curves. If the pattern is drawn on paper it can be traced onto the work with carbon paper. A pattern made on cardboard is cut out with a knife and is used as a template to trace the outline on the work.

Full-size patterns are particularly useful for determining the most advantageous cutting plan for lumber and plywood with respect to grain direction and economy. Correct grain orientation frequently is especially important in terms of strength when dealing with solid lumber parts of irregular shape. Structurally unsound end-grain sections in critical areas can be avoided by careful positioning of a full-size pattern on the wood when making the cutting layout. The illustration shows this clearly.

In plywood constructions which are to be painted, grain direction is not particularly important since the material is equally strong in all directions. Here the patterns can be juxtapositioned to yield the greatest number of parts with minimal waste.

Use full-size patterns to trace irregular cutting lines onto the stock. Careful positioning will result in the most economical yield and proper grain orientation.

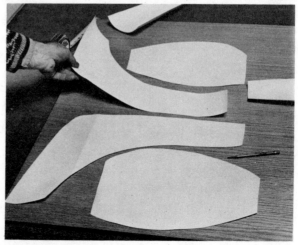

End-grain across narrow dimensions of solid lumber results in a weak cross section and should be avoided where structural soundness is important. Use full-size patterns to lay out the work for the best grain orientation.

With fine face-veneer plywood which is to be clear finished, the patterns play a somewhat different role. Here grain direction should be planned with the aim of obtaining an overall harmony in the finished product. While it may not be possible to realize maximum utilization of a veneer panel when the concentration is on grain direction, judicious placement of the patterns can result in a compromise.

Planning grain direction applies equally to regular as well as to irregular cutting layouts. However, when only regular shapes such as squares and rectangles are involved, small reduced-scale templates will serve the purpose. Use the scale rule to draw both the template patterns and the representation of the panel to the correct proportions. Or you can use graph paper for the latter. Be sure to indicate the desired grain direction on all patterns or templates regardless of whether they are full size or reduced scale.

MAKING WORKING DRAWINGS

Working on projects from prepared plans like the ones in this book has the advantage of convenience, but eventually you will be eager to strike out on your own, designing projects from scratch.

When you have developed an idea for a project, your first step will be to prepare a working drawing. While it need not be of fine artistic quality, it will have to be professional with respect to content. It must show the size and shape of the project and its component parts.

The complexity of the project will determine the number of drawings required. A multiview, reduced-scale drawing—two-dimensional straight-on views of the front, top, and side—will usually suffice. In addition, detail and section views may also be needed.

Start with a freehand sketch which shows what the project will look like when finished. This is preferably done in perspective to show three faces in one view. The next step is to make decisions about the type and size of wood and the kinds of joints, fasteners, and hardware to be used. Now make the drawing using graph paper for simplicity. Select a ratio scale that will result in a drawing that will show

Reduced-scale templates are drawn with the aid of a scale rule.

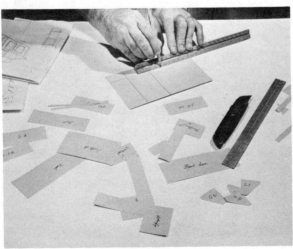

Using the templates to determine the best cutting plan for a plywood project. The bold outlines on the paper represent 4' × 8' panels.

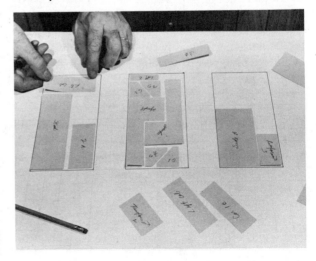

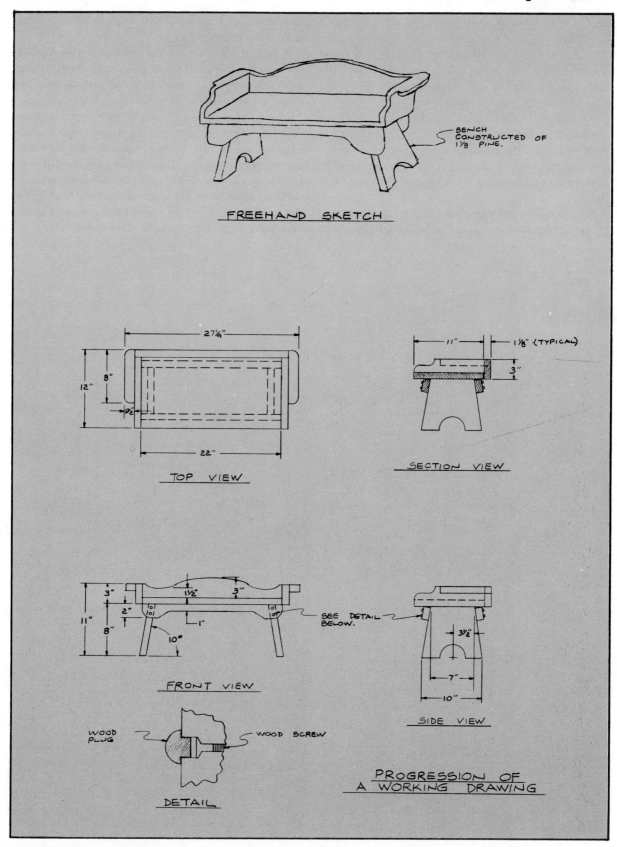

FREEHAND SKETCH

TOP VIEW

SECTION VIEW

FRONT VIEW

SIDE VIEW

DETAIL

PROGRESSION OF A WORKING DRAWING

A good working drawing provides all the information needed to permit construction of a project without further explanation.

details clearly and permit dimensioning without crowding.

Draw the major visible outlines of each view using a solid heavy line. Add broken lines for those outlines that cannot be seen from the surface, making sure to indicate clearly all joints.

Next draw in dimension lines for all parts. These are long lines broken at the center and terminated at each end with arrowheads. Insert the precise dimension for each part in the center space. Use extension lines to carry dimension lines beyond the main outlines.

Detail views are required for interior parts and those parts that are too small to be accurately drawn on the exterior views. These are drawn to a larger scale than the main views.

A section view shows the interior of the object as if it were cut apart. This is used when there is considerable interior detail that would be too confusing to be shown with broken (hidden) lines.

Many professionally made working drawings contain exploded perspective views which show some or all of the parts separated and in proper assembly relationship, thus making construction details very clear. Complicated constructions are very difficult to draw in this manner and are best left to the professional. But you may have reasonable success with exploded views of simple projects.

2
Selecting Wood

Since wood is the raw material of woodworking, there are some basic facts you should know about it to enable you to select it wisely and to use it effectively and efficiently.

Wood is commonly classified as either softwood or hardwood according to the species of tree from which it is derived. Softwoods come from needle-bearing evergreen trees such as pine, spruce, and redwood. Hardwoods are cut from broad-leaved trees—those that shed their leaves—such as cherry, maple, and oak. This method of classification can be somewhat misleading, however, because some softwoods are harder than some hardwoods. For example, balsa is the softest of all woods, yet it is classified as a hardwood by virtue of the fact that it comes from a broadleaf tree. On the other hand, yellow pine, a so-called softwood, is considerably harder than a number of hardwoods.

Both softwoods and hardwoods offer certain advantages for shop work and home-improvement projects. As a general rule hardwood is stronger and more attractive than softwood with respect to grain pattern and color. But softwood is more easily worked and is less expensive than hardwood. The accompanying table lists several properties of some of the common species of woods which are suitable for general woodwork. Refer to it to assess the utility of a species for the job at hand. From a practical standpoint, you need to know the relative hardness of a wood in terms of its workability and resistance to wear; for outdoor projects, you need to know its resistance to decay as well.

EXOTIC WOODS

There is ample variety among the native woods and the more common imported species that are normally obtainable from local sources. But on occasion you may want to use a special wood for a special project. Highly prized rare and exotic species are available to you. Strikingly beautiful woods such as rosewood, teak, and zebrawood can do much to give your project an outstanding, out-of-the-ordinary look. However, inasmuch as they're relatively expensive and too infrequently purchased, the average lumber retailer normally doesn't stock them. These woods, in solid lumber and veneer, are available from mail-order woodworker's supply houses. Several are listed in the back of this book.

Species	Hardness	Hand Tool Workability	Nailability	Decay Resistance	Clear Finishing
Softwoods					
Cedar, white	soft	medium	good	good	poor
Cypress	soft	medium	good	good	poor
Fir, Douglas	soft	medium	poor	medium	poor
Fir, white	soft	easy	poor	poor	poor
Pine, northern	soft	easy	good	medium	medium
Pine, ponderosa	soft	easy	good	poor	medium
Pine, sugar	soft	easy	good	medium	poor
Pine, yellow	hard	hard	poor	medium	medium
Redwood	soft	easy	good	good	poor
Spruce	soft	medium	medium	poor	medium
Hardwoods					
Ash	hard	hard	poor	poor	medium
Basswood	soft	easy	good	poor	medium
Beech	hard	hard	poor	poor	good
Birch	hard	hard	poor	poor	good
Butternut	soft	easy	good	medium	medium
Cherry	hard	hard	poor	medium	good
Chestnut	medium	medium	medium	good	poor
Cottonwood	soft	medium	good	poor	poor
Elm, soft	medium	hard	good	medium	medium
Hickory	hard	hard	good	medium	medium
Mahogany	medium	good	good	good	medium
Maple, hard	hard	hard	poor	poor	good
Maple, soft	hard	hard	poor	poor	good
Oak, red	hard	hard	medium	poor	medium
Oak, white	hard	hard	medium	good	good
Poplar	soft	easy	good	poor	good
Sycamore	medium	hard	good	poor	good
Walnut	hard	medium	medium	good	good
Willow	soft	easy	good	poor	medium

Characteristics of common softwoods and hardwoods.

Redwood has natural resistance to decay and insect damage. This fence, made of heart redwood, will probably outlast the house.

A well-designed walkway and patio adds beauty and value to any backyard. Wolmanized pressure-treated lumber is used for this project.

TREATED WOOD

Wood is naturally very durable. If kept continuously dry, it will last indefinitely. In some applications where alternate wetting and drying conditions are inevitable, or where wood is in direct ground contact, however, it deteriorates. It decays, sometimes quite rapidly, due to attack by bacteria and fungi, which thrive in damp wood.

Some species of wood are naturally resistant to decay, as indicated in the table. Use them for projects which will be exposed to moisture. Redwood, cypress, and the cedars, in that order, have particularly high decay resistance. But it should be noted that only the heartwood enjoys this reputation. The sapwood of substantially all species has low decay resistance. In addition to its high decay-resistance

characteristics, heart redwood is particularly resistant to termites.

Another way to avoid problems of decay and insect damage is to use treated lumber. Pressure-injected wood preservatives are commonly used in house construction. The most widely known brand name is Wolman, the trademark of Koppers Company. This is used in the production of Wolmanized wood, which is available at most lumberyards. This lumber costs slightly more than untreated stock but is well worth the extra cost.

Thorough brush and dip treatments with commonly available preservatives will offer surface protection. However, weather and seasoning cracks and physical abrasions expose inner wood cells to decay and insect attack.

11

WHICH CUT?

Lumber is commonly cut from a log in two distinct ways: It is either plain-sawed or quarter-sawed. These terms refer to the relationship of the saw to the log's growth rings.

In plain-sawing the cut is made tangent to the annual rings. This method yields the maximum number of cuttings from the log with minimal waste. It also brings out more conspicuously the grain patterns resulting from the annual rings. Knots that occur in plain-sawed boards affect the surface appearance less than long spike knots that may appear in quarter-sawed boards. However, wood cut in this manner is more prone to warp.

In quarter-sawing, the cut is made radially to the annual rings. The log is first cut into quarters, then into boards, the cuts being made from the outside towards the center. This method is more wasteful of the log than plain-sawing, but there are advantages which are reflected in the price; you pay more for quarter-sawed lumber. Quarter-sawed lumber shrinks and swells less in width, thus is less distorted by warping. It is less prone to checking and spliting.

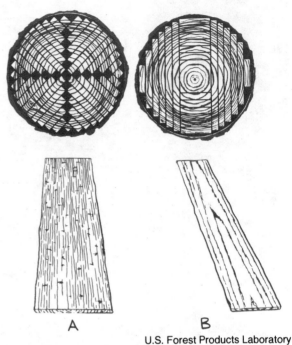

A   B

U.S. Forest Products Laboratory

Quarter-sawed (A) and plain-sawed (B) boards cut from a log. Note the difference in the grain pattern in both cuts.

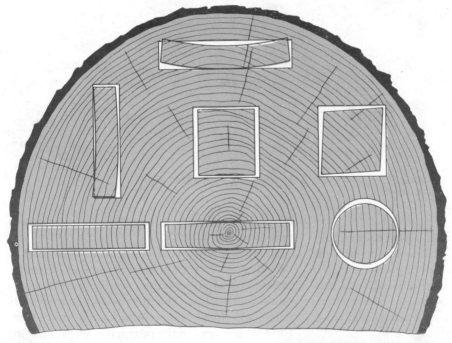

Shrinkage and distortion of lumber is affected by the direction of the annual rings. Tangential shrinkage is about twice as great as radial. Lumber is planed after it is seasoned in order to true the surfaces but distortion will nevertheless continue to some extent.

U.S. Forest Products Laboratory

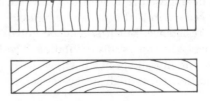

Appearance of the annual rings in the end of a board reveals how it was cut. The edge-grained, quarter-sawed board, top, is less apt to warp.

Also, raised grain caused by separation in the annual rings does not become so pronounced, and it wears more evenly.

Warped lumber can be painfully frustrating when you are faced with the problem of machining it to produce precise, close-fitting joints. If you manage to get by the cutting and joinery phase there's apt to be more trouble in store when you reach the assembly stage.

Wood warps as a result of uneven shrinking during the drying or seasoning process. Wood from freshly cut logs is green or wet; it contains moisture within the cavities and walls of the myriad cells of which it is composed. Its shrinking characteristics are predictable: it shrinks most in the direction of the annual rings (tangentially), about half as much across the rings (radially), and only negligibly along the grain (longitudinally). The combined effects of radial and tangential shrinkage can distort the shape of wood pieces because of the difference in shrinkage and the curvature of annual rings. The diagram illustrates the major types of distortion due to these effects. Be observant of the grain patterns on the edges and faces of boards during selection in order to obtain material that will have minimal tendency to warp.

SEASONING

Lumber is not serviceable until its moisture content is evaporated. This is accomplished by either of two methods: air and kiln drying.

Air drying, as the term implies, is done by stacking the lumber outdoors in uniform piles with spacers between each piece to permit air to circulate freely on all four sides. Air drying will result in lumber with a moisture content of about 12 to 15 percent, which is suitable for general use.

In kiln drying the lumber is similarly stacked but the moisture content is reduced artificially in a moisture- and temperature-controlled oven called a kiln. This method reduces moisture content to about 6 to 8 percent.

While kiln-dried lumber is more expensive, it is the only satisfactory kind to use for quality indoor construction, particularly furniture and cabinetry. When used indoors, air-dried lumber will continue to dry and consequently shrink and possibly warp, whereas kiln-dried lumber is stabilized to a point where further drying is unlikely.

SHOPPING FOR LUMBER

When you shop for lumber your goal should be to buy the material best suited for the project while spending as little money as possible. You can accomplish this by buying the least expensive wood that will do the job in the smallest quantity possible. This requires familiarity with lumber grades and dimensions.

Lumber grades. All lumber is inspected and each piece is assigned to a grade category on the basis of the amount of clear cuttings it contains. This is determined by the number of defects present.

Softwoods and hardwoods are graded separately according to standards established by associations of lumber producers. Since the grading rules for softwood are set up by a number of different associations, the standards may vary somewhat. Hardwood standards are set by one association, however, so they are uniform.

In general, softwoods are divided into three grade categories: Select, Common, and Structural. Select grade is subdivided by the letter designations A, B, C, and D, indicating decreasing quality in that order. Select lumber is graded mostly on the basis of appearance. A and B Select are suitable for clear finishing; the others have defects that can be concealed by painting.

Common grade is subdivided by the number designations 1, 2, 3, and 4; also in decreasing order of quality. Common lumber is of lesser quality than Select due to the presence of more and larger defects such as knots, pitch, splits, and warp.

Structural grades apply to dimension lumber over 2 inches thick which is used essentially for framing. Grading is based on strength rather than appearance. The grades in this category are Construction, Standard, Utility, and Economy.

Grade stamps are required on all framing lumber. Boards usually are not grade stamped as the stamp ink leaves a mark that is difficult to remove. However, boards definitely are graded, and the dealer orders them by grade and keeps different grades in separate bins.

Hardwood is graded in a stricter sense on the basis of the percentage of clear, usable cuttings obtainable from the piece. Starting with the top grade, they are termed Firsts, Seconds, Firsts and Seconds (FAS), Select, Common No. 1, and Common No. 2. While Firsts are the best grade, First and Seconds are usually combined to constitute the top grade.

The most common defects that determine the grade of lumber are as follows:

Knot. A dense mass of fibers in a board that was cut through a section of a limb or branch. The number, size, and soundness are important considerations.

Defects in lumber determine its grade and cost. The board at the top is select; the one below is common. The price difference is usually substantial.

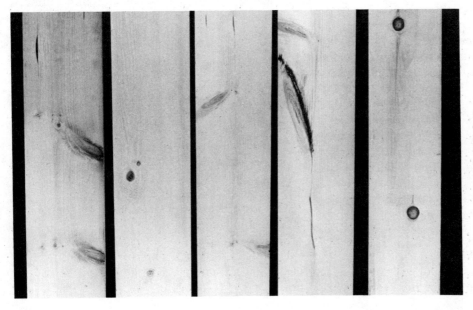

Large knots weaken a board considerably but small, tight knots have little effect on overall strength. A number of small, clear cuttings can be obtained from these common boards.

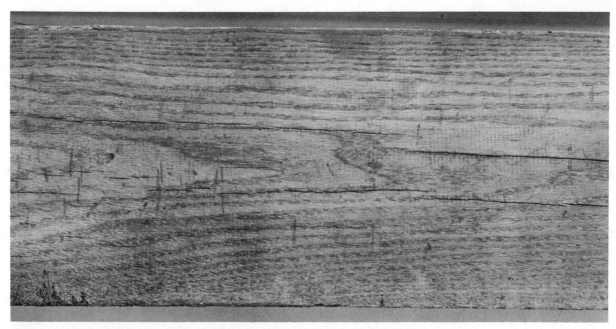

Always check carefully for splits when selecting lumber. Hairline splits running through the length of a board render it useless for some purposes; it may eventually split apart.

Check. A split across the annual growth rings running lengthwise.

Shake. A split along the grain between the annual growth rings.

Warp. A deviation from the true plane surface in the form of a bow, crook, cup or twist.

Decay. Same as rot; a disintegration of wood fibers caused by fungi. Advanced decay renders the wood soft and crumbly.

Pitch. An accumulation of sticky resinous material frequently found in softwoods.

Worm holes. Damage in the form of holes caused by various insects.

Stain. A discoloration that penetrates below the surface.

A pitch pocket is a defect that cannot be corrected by painting. Discard the board.

U. S. Forest Products Laboratory

Advanced decay in untreated wood caused by constant wetting and the action of wood destroying fungi.

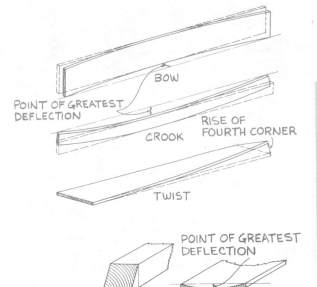

DIAMOND   CUP

U. S. Forest Products Laboratory

Common types of warp.

Manufacturing faults. Defects that develop during the processing of lumber. These include burn marks, torn grain, and skipped planing.

The accompanying grading charts and an awareness of typical defects will help you to understand what you can expect to find and what to look for when you shop for lumber.

While the telephone offers a convenient way to shop for some things, it is not especially recommended when it comes to buying wood. The wise way to buy wood is to select it yourself, to be assured you'll get exactly what you want and need. If you don't abuse the privilege by messing up the lumberyard, most dealers will permit you to hand pick lumber. If not, then be sure to examine the wood before you accept it. If the wood you order must be cut to size, ask to see it beforehand. Be prepared with a shopping list, with dimensions clearly indicated, and take along a steel tape measure.

Hardwood is sold in random widths and lengths. On-the-spot measurements will help you to avoid buying excessive waste. And when buying softwood in particular, bear in mind that you can cull perfectly clear stock by cutting between huge loose knots that frequently occur in the lower common grades. Furthermore, when your project calls for odd-shaped pieces of lumber, it could be advantageous to bring along to the lumberyard full-size paper patterns of those pieces. Use them to work out cutting possibili-

ties around defects. Also, buy air-dried rather than kiln-dried lumber for outdoor constructions; the latter is more expensive.

WOOD GRADING CHARTS

The various lumber associations have developed their own official grading marks which are imprinted on each piece of lumber by the participating member mills.

SOFTWOOD LUMBER GRADES

Selected
Grade A. Suitable for stains and natural finishes and practically flawless
Grade B. Also suitable for natural finishes, but contains a few small defects
Grade C. Contains defects that can be concealed with paint
Grade D. Slightly more defects than "C", but of a type that can be hidden with paint

Common
No. 1. Good, sound utility lumber with tight knots and limited blemishes, free of warp, splits, checks or decay
No. 2. Fairly sound, but with defects such as checks at ends, loose knots, blemishes and discolorations; no warp or splits
No. 3. Construction lumber of medium quality with defects of all types necessitating some waste removal in use
No. 4. Low quality construction lumber with numerous defects, including open knot holes
No. 5. Lowest quality; good only for use as a filler, including considerable waste

Structural
Construction. Best quality structural material
Standard. Similar quality to construction lumber with slight defects
Utility. Poor structural quality; requires added members for strength (closer stud spacing, for instance)
Economy. Lowest quality structural material

HARDWOOD LUMBER GRADES

Firsts. Lumber that is $91\frac{2}{3}$ percent clear on both sides; the best material available for cabinetwork
Seconds. Lumber that is $83\frac{1}{3}$ percent clear on both sides and quite suitable for most cabinetwork
Firsts & Seconds. A selection of lumber containing not less than 20 percent Firsts
Selects. Lumber that is 90 percent clear on one side only (other side is not graded); good for cabinetwork but with some waste
No. 1 Common. Lumber that is $66\frac{2}{3}$ percent clear on one side only; suitable for interior and less demanding cabinetwork
No. 2 Common. Lumber which is 50 percent clear on one side only; useable for painting, some paneling, and flooring

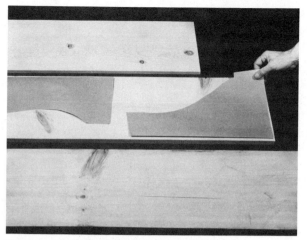

When shopping for lumber, use paper patterns to help select usable stock between defects.

A few saw cuts and patches will convert this board from common to select grade. Fast-setting epoxy adhesive speeds the job.

Lumber sizes.

When lumber is cut from a log, its surfaces are very rough and must be dressed smooth before it goes to market. Lumber sizes are based on the rough (nominal) dimensions before dressing. This operation removes an appreciable amount of material from the lumber. In softwoods what starts out as 2 by 4 inches (nominal) becomes 1½ by 3½ inches (actual). A 1-inch-thick piece becomes ¾-inch thick.

Softwoods are cut to standard thickness, width, and length, but the same is not true with hardwoods. Since they are more costly, hardwoods are cut to standard thickness only. Widths and lengths are cut to sizes that are most economical in order to minimize waste; thus they are termed random widths and lengths (RWL).

Softwoods are surfaced on both sides and edges (S4S). Hardwoods can be purchased rough (RGF), surfaced one side (S1S), surfaced two sides (S2S), surfaced one edge (S1E), or a combination of surfaced sides and edges up to surfaced four sides (S4S). The abbreviated symbol is standard for identifying the surface condition.

Softwood lumber is classified with respect to the cross section dimensions of thickness and width as follows:

Strip. Less than 2 inches thick and less than 8 inches wide.

Board. Less than 2 inches thick and over 8 inches wide.

Dimension. Between 2 and 5 inches thick and from 4 to 12 inches wide.

Timber. Smallest dimension is 6 inches.

Unit of measurement. The board foot is the standard unit of measurement for solid lumber. It represents a piece of wood 1 inch thick by 1 foot square or its equivalent. Lumber quantities and prices are quoted by the board foot; therefore you should know how to compute it in order to estimate costs accurately when planning a project.

The formula for determining the number of board feet in a piece of lumber is quite simple: Multiply the actual length in feet by the nominal thickness and width in inches and divide by 12. For example, to find the board feet in a piece of 2×3 that is 10 feet long:

$$\frac{10' \times 2'' \times 3''}{12} = \frac{60}{12} = 5 \text{ board feet}$$

Hardwood lumber that is 1 inch thick or more is usually referred to in quarter-inch designations, such as ⁴⁄₄, ⁵⁄₄, ⁶⁄₄, etc. (nominal). This applies as well to softwood other than framing stock.

STANDARD HARDWOOD THICKNESS	
Nominal (Rough)	**Surfaced 2 Sides**
⅜"	³⁄₁₆"
½"	⁵⁄₁₆"
⅝"	⁷⁄₁₆"
¾"	⁹⁄₁₆"
1"	¹³⁄₁₆"
1¼"	1¹⁄₁₆"–1⅛"*
1½"	1⁵⁄₁₆"–1⅜"*
2"	1¾"
3"	2¾"
4"	3¾"
*Varies	

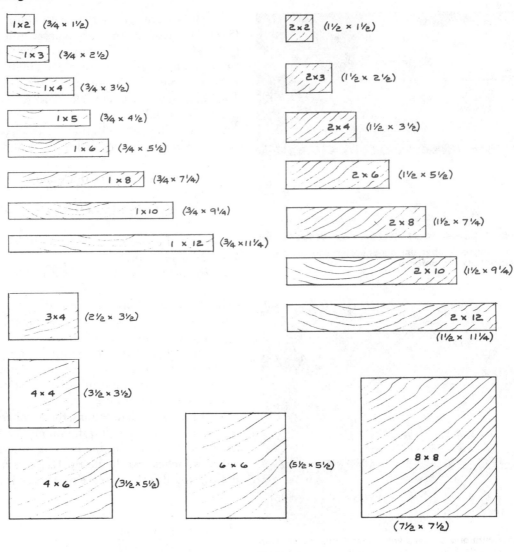

1x2 (3/4 × 1 1/2)

1x3 (3/4 × 2 1/2)

1x4 (3/4 × 3 1/2)

1x5 (3/4 × 4 1/2)

1 × 6 (3/4 × 5 1/2)

1 × 8 (3/4 × 7 1/4)

1x10 (3/4 × 9 1/4)

1 × 12 (3/4 × 11 1/4)

3x4 (2 1/2 × 3 1/2)

4 × 4 (3 1/2 × 3 1/2)

4 × 6 (3 1/2 × 5 1/2)

2x2 (1 1/2 × 1 1/2)

2x3 (1 1/2 × 2 1/2)

2×4 (1 1/2 × 3 1/2)

2 × 6 (1 1/2 × 5 1/2)

2 × 8 (1 1/2 × 7 1/4)

2 × 10 (1 1/2 × 9 1/4)

2 × 12 (1 1/2 × 11 1/4)

6 × 6 (5 1/2 × 5 1/2)

8 × 8 (7 1/2 × 7 1/2)

DRESSED SOFTWOOD DIMENSIONS

Some lumber items are sized and priced by the linear foot rather than the board foot. This means that length alone is the factor. Included in this category are furring strips, molding, dowels, and timbers.

When you have determined your lumber needs for a project write up an order in the proper sequence following standard practice. This will avoid confusion when you ask the lumber dealer for a price quote or when you place an order. The sequence is as follows: quantity, nominal thickness, grade, species, surfacing, seasoning, width and length.

A typical order for hardwood would be written: 50 feet 5/4 FAS White Oak, S2S, KD, RWL. This would indicate that you want 50 board feet of 1 1/4-inch thick white oak lumber of firsts and seconds grade, surfaced two sides, kiln dried, in random widths and lengths. Note that in softwoods the specific widths and lengths would be indicated.

PLYWOOD

When a project contains component parts that are greater than 11 1/4 inches in width, more often than not the plans will specify the use of plywood rather than solid wood. It is usually elected primarily on the basis of size. Solid lumber is generally available up to the nominal 12-inch width (11 1/4 inches ac-

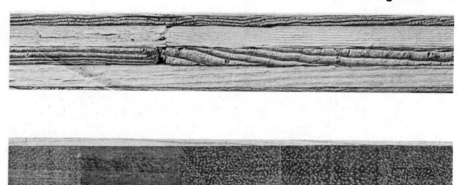

Lumber-core and veneer-core plywood. Lumber-core stock is frequently used with edges exposed; veneer core normally requires concealment.

tual). Plywood, which is available in panels measuring 48 by 96 inches (and even larger on special order), eliminates the painstaking task of edge-gluing boards to make a wide panel. This simplifies construction. But convenience is not the only factor in its favor. In most cases plywood is cheaper than solid lumber. It is virtually splitproof and is highly resistant to warping. Also, cabinet-type plywood utilizes fine hardwood species for the face veneers only. This makes the use of otherwise too expensive woods affordable for large projects.

There are two principal kinds of plywood: softwood and hardwood. The distinction is based on the kind of wood used for the face veneers. Fir softwood plywood is widely used for general construction, furniture making, built-ins and utility purposes both indoors and outdoors. This species is characterized by the familiar contrasting grain pattern. Where better appearance is desired for natural finishing, other softwood face veneers are available such as pine and redwood. Hardwood plywood is the choice for fine cabinetry, paneling, and furniture making.

Aside from the face veneers, there are differences in the core constructions. Softwood plywood is most commonly made with a veneer core wherein the inner plies are about the same thickness as the face veneers or only slightly thicker. It is also made with a particleboard core, but this type is not as versatile as the veneer core because it has poor nail- or screw-holding power.

Hardwood plywood is also available with a veneer core, and in addition, with a lumber core. The latter consists of a thick center composed of low-density, solid-wood strips edge-glued together. Lumber-core plywood is easier to work than veneer core and is especially advantageous for use in cabinetry because the edges can be shaped and tooled with finer results. Screws and nails can be more easily centered

and will hold better in the thick core. Whereas the lumber-core edge is frequently suitable to serve as a finished edge, exposed veneer-core edges usually need to be concealed by one of several methods.

Buying plywood. Softwood plywood is available in two basic types, interior and exterior. They differ mainly in the type of glue used to laminate the plies and in the quality of the wood used in the inner plies. Exterior type is made with waterproof glue and should be used for any application that will expose the wood to the weather or to moisture in general.

Both types of softwood plywood are graded with respect to the quality of the veneer used on the face and back of the panel. The letters A, B, C, and D are used to designate the respective qualities of the face, back, and the inner plies as well. Note in the grading chart that you have a choice of face and back veneer combinations within each group; the veneer grade for the face is given first. The letter is the key to the type and size of the imperfections you could expect to find in each panel as indicated in the veneer grade descriptions.

It is general practice to select interior-type plywood for indoor projects in view of the fact that exterior plywood is more expensive. But note in the chart that all interior panels have D grade inner plies while exterior panels have slightly better rated C grade inner plies. Although the imperfections in the inner plies are not apparent when the panel is whole, the relatively large ones permitted in the D grade plies could cause problems when the panel is cut for fabricating project component parts. Large voids appearing in critical areas can prove more than frustrating during machining and assembly operations and frequently result in poor constructions. Therefore, keep this in mind and opt for the exterior type

PLYWOOD GRADES FOR EXTERIOR USES

Grade (Exterior)	Face	Back	Inner Plies	Uses
A-A	A	A	C	Outdoor, where appearance of both sides is important.
A-B	A	B	C	Alternate for A-A, where appearance of one side is less important. Face is finish grade.
A-C	A	C	C	Soffits, fences, base for coatings.
B-C	B	C	C	For utility uses such as farm buildings, some kinds of fences, etc., base for coatings.
303® Siding	C (or better)	C	C	Panels with variety of surface texture and grooving patterns. For siding, fences, paneling, screens, etc.
T1-11®	C	C	C	Special 303 panel with grooves ¼" deep, ⅜" wide. Available unsanded, textured, or MDO surface.
C-C (Plugged)	C (Plugged)	C	C	Excellent base for tile and linoleum, backing for wall coverings, high performance coatings.
C-C	C	C	C	Unsanded, for backing and rough construction exposed to weather.
B-B Plyform	B	B	C	Concrete forms. Re-use until wood literally wears out.
MDO	B	B or C	C	Medium Density Overlay. Ideal base for paint; for siding, built-ins, signs, displays.
HDO	A or B	A or B	C-Plugged or C	High Density Overlay. Hard surface; no paint needed. For concrete forms, cabinets, counter tops, tanks.

PLYWOOD GRADES FOR INTERIOR USES

Grade (Interior)	Face	Back	Inner Plies	Uses
A-A	A	A	D	Cabinet doors, built-ins, furniture where both sides will show.
A-B	A	B	D	Alternate of A-A. Face is finish grade, back is solid and smooth.
A-D	A	D	D	Finish grade face for paneling, built-ins, backing.
B-D	B	D	D	Utility grade. For backing, cabinet sides, etc.
C-D	C	D	D	Sheathing and structural uses such as temporary enclosures, subfloor. Unsanded.
Underlayment	C-Plugged	D	C and D	For underlayment or combination subfloor-underlayment under tile, carpeting.

VENEER GRADES

A
Smooth, paintable. Not more than 18 neatly made repairs, parallel to grain, permitted. May be used for natural finish in less demanding applications.

B
Solid surface. Shims, circular repair plugs and tight knots to 1 inch across grain permitted. Some minor splits permitted.

C plugged
Improved C veneer with splits limited to ⅛ inch width and knotholes and borer holes limited to ¼ x ½ inch. Permits some broken grain. Synthetic repairs permitted.

C
Tight knots to 1½ inch. Knotholes to 1 inch across grain and some to 1½ inch if total width of knots and knotholes is within specified limits.

Synthetic or wood repairs. Discoloration and sanding defects that do not impair strength permitted. Limited splits allowed. Stitching permitted.

D
Knots and knotholes to 2½ inch width across grain and ½ inch larger within specified limits. Limited splits allowed. Stitching permitted. Limited to Interior grades of plywood.

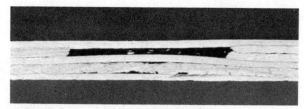

Large voids frequently found in D-grade inner plies can cause problems in making sound joints.

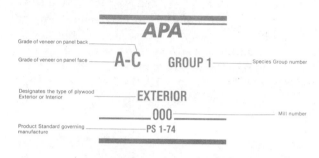

American Plywood Association grade stamps. At top is the typical back mark. Below is the edge mark which is used to avoid marring the backs of A and B grade veneers.

which has better inner plies regardless of the indoor-/outdoor aspect of the project when it involves more than simple joinery and assembly.

Almost all plywood produced in the United States is inspected and certified by the American Plywood Association or other certifying agencies and bears the agency grade stamp. Look for it for the assurance of quality when you buy plywood. It is stamped on the back of *C* or *D* grade panels and on the panel's edge of *A* and *B* grades.

Many dealers stock imported as well as domestically manufactured plywood. Sometimes the imported plywood is the less expensive and sometimes it is not. Usually, however, the quality of the interior plies is very inferior, thus it may be well to avoid it.

The MDO plywood you see listed in the grading chart is a specialty product. It has a resin fiber overlay which is very smooth and is especially well suited for painting. The inner plies are generally of good quality and it cuts nicely without splintering along the kerf. It is essentially an exterior material but is ideal for interior cabinetry and the like. Be sure to buy surfaced two sides (S2S) panels only; those surfaced on one side only tend to warp severely and are used primarily in industry for special purposes. The initials MDO stand for Medium Density Overlaid.

Hardwood plywood is available with face veneers of a number of common species as well as the exotics. It is generally graded by a number and descriptive term as follows:

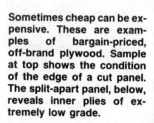

Sometimes cheap can be expensive. These are examples of bargain-priced, off-brand plywood. Sample at top shows the condition of the edge of a cut panel. The split-apart panel, below, reveals inner plies of extremely low grade.

MDO (medium density overlay) plywood has an excellent surface for painting and has good quality inner plies.

plus other defects that do not affect the strength of the panel.

Hardwood plywood is also available in domestic and imported varieties and the same precaution applies here as with softwood plywood. It is not uncommon to find delaminated veneers and lumber-core interiors that exhibit large knots and loose or missing sections of the core material.

Hardwood plywood comes in 4-by-8-foot panels, in thicknesses of ¼, ½, and ¾ inch. Prefinished hardwood veneer wall paneling is available in ⅛ and ³⁄₁₆-inch thickness. While these are too thin to permit freestanding constructions, they can be used for surfacing framed constructions where attractiveness at relatively low cost is desired. Matching solid wood can be used at exposed corners or edges. Or

1. *Custom.* Clear with no visible defects. Veneers may be made with more than one piece but must be carefully color and grain matched.

2. *Good.* Similar to custom but veneer matching not as critical.

3. *Sound.* Suitable for painting but not for clear finishing due to stain and streaks which are allowable.

4. *Utility.* Allows small knotholes, discoloration, and minor spaces between veneer joints.

5. *Backing.* Serious defects including knotholes up to 2 inches in diameter and splits up to 1 inch wide

The set-back strips permit butt joints at corners with adequate nailing surfaces.

Low-cost, ¼-inch, prefinished hardwood plywood paneling can be used to make attractive cube constructions for use as pedestals or end tables. A nail gun and glue are used to build up edge thickness to permit solid assembly. To make a cube, attach ¾" × 1⅛" strips around the edges of two panels. On adjacent panels a strip is added to the tops and bottoms only, with the ends set back 1⅛".

A light bead of glue and several nails are used along each edge to join the sections. A top and bottom panel without cleats are added to complete the cube.

The edges can be rounded and finished or they may be concealed with narrow strips of hardwood molding.

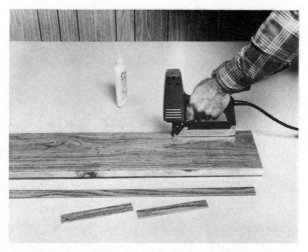

Cut the top and bottom pieces to the exact size of the core board. Add the ends next, then the front strip. This will locate the raw edges of the paneling on the top, bottom, and ends where they'll be least conspicuous. If desired, the edges can be stained and varnished.

You can beat the high cost of fine hardwood shelves by making your own with low-cost materials. Sandwich a piece of # 3 common-grade pine between scraps of hardwood paneling.

the corners can simply be butted; the resultant thin edge line will be inconspicuous.

HARDBOARD

Hardboard is another material that is useful around the home and shop. It is made with refined wood fibers obtained from wood chips. Formed into sheets under heat and pressure in a complex process, the end result is a dense, durable, and grainless panel that can be easily handled with woodworking tools.

Hardboard is available in three types: Standard, Tempered, and Service. Standard is used for general utility, and because of its relatively low cost, it is favored for use as drawer bottoms and case and cabinet backs. Tempered hardboard is highly water resistant and useful for outdoor projects. Service hardboard is a low-density, low-cost panel used where light weight rather than strength is desired.

The most widely used form of hardboard is wall paneling. This is produced in many woodgrain and variously embossed surface patterns. The better quality material that is available is very attractive and durable. You can also buy hardboard that is precut in attractive filigree patterns. Several out of the ordinary applications of these materials are featured in the projects section of this book.

Standard panel size is 4 by 8 feet, in thicknesses of $\frac{1}{8}$, $\frac{3}{16}$, and $\frac{1}{4}$ inch. A special wall-paneling plank called Marlite has tongue-and-groove interlocking edges and measures $\frac{1}{4}$ inch by 16 inches by 8 feet.

3
Measuring and Marking

Careful measuring and marking are important steps in starting any woodworking project. Accuracy in these operations is essential if you are to turn out work of professional quality while avoiding the waste of time and materials. Although extreme accuracy may not be necessary in all phases of woodworking, improved accuracy can frequently be achieved with little or no extra effort. All that is required in accurately marking stock for cutting is the proper use of a few simple tools and correct procedures.

Sighting a rule. Striking off measurements from a rule requires care. Most rules have thickness; therefore the graduations are not sufficiently close to the work surface to permit precise transfer of the mark due to parallax (shift your head and so will the apparent position of the pencil in relation to the graduation). The problem is easily solved by holding the rule on edge in order to put the graduations directly on the work surface.

Pencil point. Accuracy in cutting depends to a great degree upon the neatness and fineness of the layout line; mistakes frequently are caused by markings that are too thick. Start off right by using a sharply

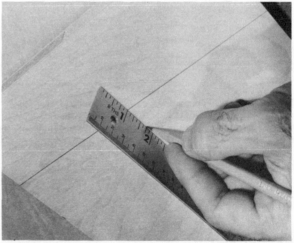

Rule should be held on edge to bring the graduations close to the work. Note that the end of the rule is avoided because it is easier to align a graduation rather than the rule's end on a mark.

pointed pencil of sufficient hardness, such as a 2H. It will hold a sharp point longer than the common No. 2 writing pencil. This is particularly important when drawing many lines or continuous long lines, because as the point wears down the line will

24

A soft lead pencil wears rapidly when used on wood. This sample shows how the line has thickened in the course of drawing along 8 feet of stock.

become increasingly thicker. Here you see the difference in thickness between the start and finish of a line drawn on an 8-foot length of wood using a soft lead pencil.

Ruling a line. The angle at which you hold the pencil is very important when marking a line against the rule's edge. Always hold it at an angle of about 60 degrees so the point is in close contact with the edge. Note how the pencil angle affects the line location.

When marking a line against a square, don't put the pencil to the blade of the square. Instead, put the pencil point on the measured mark; then slide the square until it meets the pencil point. This will insure that the line will coincide precisely with the original mark.

For real precision use a knife instead of a pencil;

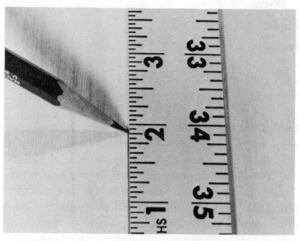

A sharp, hard lead pencil holds it point longer and gets close to the rule's edge when held at an angle of about 60 degrees.

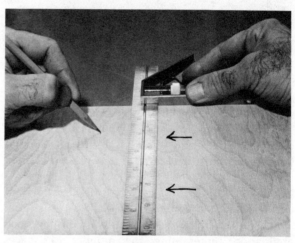

Correct way to draw a line with a square: Place the pencil on the mark, then slide the square up to the pencil point. The line will coincide with the mark.

A blunt pencil point held straight results in two faults: The line is too thick, and it is too far from the rule's edge.

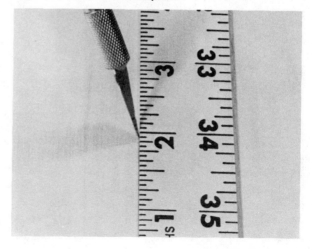

A sharp knife gets closest to a rule's edge. It should be used when great accuracy is required. The knife is held at a slight angle to offset the beveled point.

Use the superimposure method when marking duplicate parts or the mating components of a joint. The knife will assure greatest accuracy.

it gets closest to the rule's edge and produces a finer line of constant width. The knife must be held at a slight angle to offset the beveled point.

When marking for duplicate parts or the mating components of a joint, it is advisable to trace around the actual part with a knife for maximum precision.

Equal spacing. The easiest way to divide a board of odd width into any number of equal spaces is to set a rule on the board diagonally, with the last inch graduation representing the number of spaces desired. For example, if the board is to be divided into six parts, align the 1-inch and the 7-inch

graduations with the edges. Make a mark at each inch graduation, thus dividing the board into 6 parts.

Kerf allowance. Always allow for the saw-kerf waste when laying out boards or panels for multiple cuttings. If the pieces are being cut to exact finished size, it is wise to draw double lines to account for the blade's thickness. Sometimes you can use a blunt pencil that draws a thick line which equals the kerf width. In either case, check the blade to be used; kerf widths vary with different blades. Another point: Be sure to mark the proper side of the stock according to the kind of saw to be used for cutting. Mark the

The diagonal-rule method for dividing a board of odd dimension into equal parts.

The centering rule has identical graduations on both sides of a centered zero—an excellent tool for quick, accurate center finding.

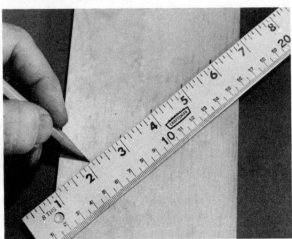

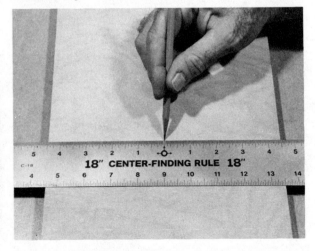

Always allow for the saw-kerf waste factor when laying out cutting lines for multiple cuttings if precise dimensions are required.

better, or finish, face of the work unless you plan to use a sabre or portable circular saw. When using either of these saws, mark the cutting lines on the back. These portable saws cut from the bottom up and cause the wood to splinter along the cutting line on the face-up side.

Guide-mark jig. When the cutting layout has been drawn, particularly on large plywood panels which are to be cut with a portable saw, a straightedge is normally used to guide the saw. It is therefore necessary to mark the work for placement of the guide so the saw will enter the wood and cut precisely on the line. Measuring from the edge of the saw base to the blade is not precise. Instead, make a jig for marking the placement of the straightedge. Use a piece of wood about 12 inches long and about as wide as

This simple jig is used to mark the location for positioning a straightedge guide for sawing. The width of the base represents the distance from the blade to the edge of the saw base.

There's always chance for error in a second-generation drawing. You can avoid error by rubber-cementing the original drawing to the work. Coat only one surface for easy removal.

This procedure also permits a better view of the cutting line, particularly when working with dark wood.

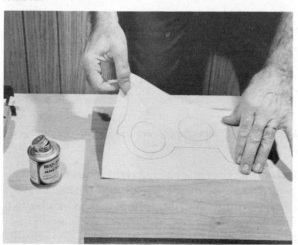

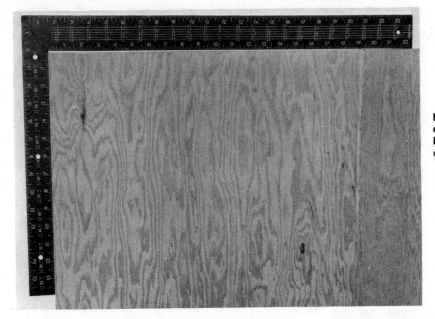

Be on the alert for laxity in quality control when you purchase off-brand plywood panels. This one is off about ¼ inch across the width.

your saw's base. Cut two quarter-round notches at both corners of one side. Nail and glue a strip of hardwood to this edge, of a size to project about ½ inch above the saw base. Carefully ride the saw base against this fence to make a rip cut through the board. The distance from this cut edge to the inside of the fence will represent precisely the offset factor for the saw.

To use the jig you merely place the cut edge on the line which is to be cut on the workpiece, then make a small mark along the inside edge of the fence. Move the jig to the far end of the cutting line and repeat the step. Now you will have the marks for precisely lining up the straightedge.

Plywood size. An important rule: Never take the size and shape of a standard 4 × 8 plywood panel for granted. To do so could result in errors in layout and cutting. This is because quality control does slip up on occasion, particularly on off-brand panels, and the dimensions in width and length are sometimes inexact. And probably more important, panels are sometimes out of square. The sample shown exhibits an error of ⅛ inch in a 2-foot span. Always check carefully and make necessary corrections before marking and cutting. It is also advisable to check thickness, as it can vary as much as ⅟₁₆ inch within the same panel.

DRAWING GEOMETRIC SHAPES

Various geometric shapes other than squares and rectangles are frequently required in layouts. Some of the common ones you're likely to encounter are easily made if you use the following methods.

Hexagon. The hexagon is a six-sided form. To lay it out, use a compass to draw a circle of the desired diameter; the length of the sides of the hexagon will be equal to the radius of the circle. With the compass still set for the radius used to draw the circle, strike off six equal arcs on the circle, starting with the point set on any part of the circle. Connect these points with a marked line to form the six equal sides.

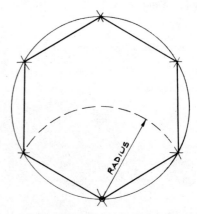

A compass and straightedge are used to draw a hexagon.

Octagon. The octagon is an eight-sided form which is also made with the aid of a compass. Draw a square of the desired dimension; then mark diagonal lines from the corners. Adjust the compass to one-half the diagonal distance. Strike arcs from each cor-

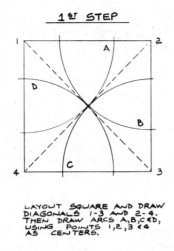

1ˢᵀ STEP

LAYOUT SQUARE AND DRAW
DIAGONALS 1-3 AND 2-4.
THEN DRAW ARCS A,B,C &D,
USING POINTS 1,2,3 &4
AS CENTERS.

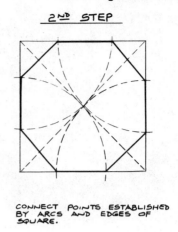

2ⁿᴰ STEP

CONNECT POINTS ESTABLISHED
BY ARCS AND EDGES OF
SQUARE.

The eight-sided octagon figure is easily constructed.

ner and connect the points where the arcs intersect the square.

Ellipse. The ellipse, or flattened circle, is often used for tabletops, frames, and plaques. The pin-and-string method is the simplest for drawing this shape to perfection. Determine the two diameters desired and draw the major and minor axes at right angles to each other. Mark them *A–B* and *C–D*. Adjust the compass to one-half the length of the major axis. Pivot the compass point at *C,* strike an arc intersecting the major axis at *X* and *Y.* Place pins at *C, X,* and *Y.* Tie a nonelastic string taut around the three pins; then remove the pin at *C* and substitute a pencil. Hold the pencil vertical and tight against the string to draw the ellipse.

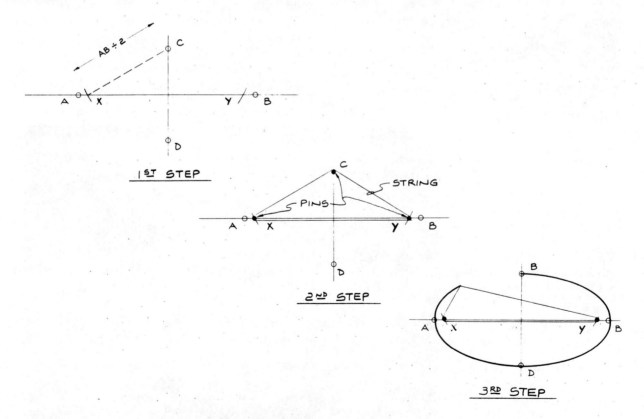

The steps in drawing an ellipse, using pin and string.

The protractor is used to set angles from 1 through 180 and 360 degrees.

Using a flexible aluminum rule to draw curves. Standing nails hold it in position.

Setting angles. The protractor is the instrument to use for laying out angles. It is a semicircular form indexed from 0 through 180 with each graduation representing one degree. It has a hole (or sometimes a cross/hair mark) in the true center which is in alignment with the 0- and 180-degree index marks. To set off an angle, you draw a base line and place the protractor with its base line in alignment. Make a mark in the center of the hole and strike a mark at the desired angle along the edge. Remove the protractor and draw a line through the two points.

Drawing curves. A flexible aluminum rule may be used to draw plain or irregular curves. Partly driven nails are used to hold the rule in position. For a plain curve three nails are used—two near the ends on one side, and one in the center on the other side. The center nail sets the degree of curvature. To make a return curve four nails are used, two on each side, alternately.

Circle guide. A plastic circle template is useful for drawing small circles and for finding the center for drilling holes or cutting them with a hole saw. Each circular cutout has four equally spaced marks at the edge. To find the center you make pencil marks on the work directly opposite these marks. Then you draw two lines to connect the points. True center will be at the intersection of the lines. The templates are available in varying sizes at art-supply stores.

Here's another method for drawing a large curve: A thin wood strip is clamped to two blocks, which are in turn clamped to the work. The blocks are set at angles that will produce the desired degree of bow in the stick. The part being laid out here is a roof section for a small structure.

Using a circle-guide template to set center marks for boring holes. The rule is aligned to index marks which are at four points on the perimeter of the circle.

Irregular curves. The French curve is a template guide used for drawing noncircular curves. It is available in a wide variety of sizes and shapes. A few will generally serve most purposes in the home shop. To use a French curve, lightly sketch the desired curve freehand, then apply the template to the line, selecting a part that will fit a portion of the line most closely. Trace that portion of the line, stopping short of the distance where the guide and the line appear to coincide. Shift the template to find another portion that will closely coincide with the continuation of the curve. Avoid breaks or humps by always checking to see that as the template is moved to the successive position, a small portion of it will coincide with the part of the line already drawn.

How a French curve is used

4

Woodworking Joints

There are a number of joints that can be used in woodworking, ranging from the simple butt to the more complex dovetail. Between these classifications are the lap, rabbet, dado, dowel, miter, and mortise and tenon. As you can see in the illustrations, there are numerous variations among each of these basic types.

The choice of a joint for a particular project should be based upon the requirements in terms of strength, appearance, and workability with the tools available. It makes sense to select the least complicated joint that will do the job satisfactorily.

Regardless of the method used to secure the joining members—nails, screws, or glue in combination—the strength and appearance of the joint will depend upon how well the parts fit together. Accuracy is essential. Therefore great care must be exercised in layout and marking as well as in cutting. To obtain accurate markings use the mating pieces as marking templates.

BUTT JOINT

The butt joint is formed by fitting the square end of one piece of stock against the surface or edge of another. It is the easiest to make and the weakest of

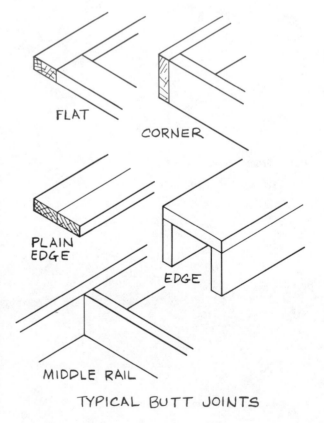

FLAT

CORNER

PLAIN EDGE

EDGE

MIDDLE RAIL

TYPICAL BUTT JOINTS

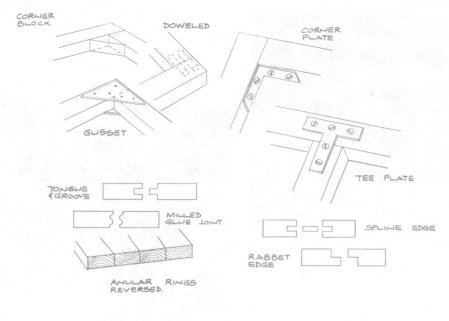

CORNER BLOCK

DOWELED

CORNER PLATE

GUSSET

TEE PLATE

TONGUE & GROOVE

MILLED GLUE JOINT

SPLINE EDGE

RABBET EDGE

ANULAR RINGS REVERSED.

BUTT JOINT REINFORCEMENTS

all joints. However, there are several ways to reinforce the glued joint. These include the use of nails, screws, dowels, cleats, corner blocks, gussets, and various forms of metal brackets.

Edge joints are frequently used to join narrow stock edge-to-edge to form larger surfaces. Dowels, splines, and tongue-and-groove cuts are commonly used to reinforce the edge joint. A special molding head can be used on a table saw to produce what is commonly called a glue or milled joint. Both the tongue-and-groove and the glue joint effectively increase the glue contact area. All the above treatments, however, will simplify alignment and will prevent movement during clamping.

A doweled butt joint is fine for joining an end to a long slab, but this necessitates the use of sufficiently long bar clamps. If you don't have the necessary clamps, an assembly such as this one is best handled with screws. The screw holes can be counterbored and plugged if the surface will be exposed.

Butted framing takes on considerable stability with the addition of plywood gussets. Always use glue and some form of mechanical fasteners such as nails, screws, or long staples. The nail gun is suitable for a light framing such as this.

CONTINUED NEXT PAGE

Corner blocks add strength and rigidity to any joint, particularly the butt. Large contact surfaces hold best.

Corrugated nails have some use in joining strips or boards flat-on. They are quite unattractive and result in marred surfaces where the hammer face strikes the wood in order to drive them flush with the surface. For maximum holding power, they should be driven into both sides of the joint.

When edge-gluing to make up a slab, be sure to alternate the direction of the annual rings to offset warping tendency.

Clamp paired boards face to face when drilling dowel holes for edge-to-edge joints. Draw a common line across both boards and use a doweling jig to bore the holes true. Alternately clamp the jig on both sides for each set.

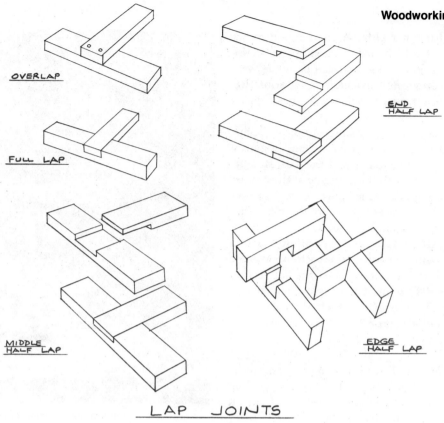

OVERLAP

END
HALF LAP

FULL LAP

MIDDLE
HALF LAP

EDGE
HALF LAP

LAP JOINTS

LAP JOINT

One piece of stock lapped over another consti-
tutes the lap joint. There are many styles of this joint
incorporated in the overlap or surface lap, full lap,
half lap, and full and half edge-laps.

With the exception of the surface lap, the joint is
made by cutting dadoes or rabbets in one or both
pieces so the surfaces will be flush when assembled.
In edge laps the cuts are usually referred to as notches. Lap joints can be cut by hand with a backsaw
and trimmed with a chisel but are most readily and
effectively formed with any of the power saws.

**Marking a half lap. For accuracy, mark half-lap joints in two
stages. Use the overlapped members as templates and make
the cutting lines only along the accessible edges. The second set of marks are made after the first marked parts have
been cut.**

**Lay the cut pieces over the uncut ones and make the second
set of cutting lines. Also in the interest of accuracy, all jointing of the inside edges should be done before marking the
work for cutting. Stock removal from edges after the joints
have been cut will affect the fit.**

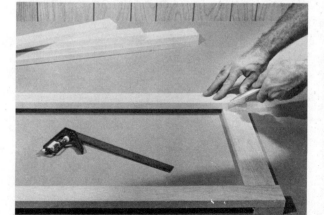

End half-lap for chair side. A chair side member which is somewhat L shaped is a good place to use the end half-lap joint. The joint can be made with minimal waste and results in a grain orientation that is strong because it runs parallel to the basic shape of the piece.

The procedure is relatively simple and can be applied to constructions other than a chair. Begin by making a full-size paper pattern of the part. Rough-cut two pieces of stock so they overlap at the corner. Make sure to leave a flat, trued portion on the lower front edges of both pieces. These are the parts that will form the shoulders of the joint.

Using the pattern as a guide, position the two pieces so they will conform to the pattern. Remove the pattern and strike a line against the flat section that is accessible. Determine the angle of this line in relation to the flat edge of the stock, then set either the table-saw miter gage or the radial-arm saw to the corresponding angle.

Using a dado head, remove half the thickness of the stock at the joint. Place the rabbeted part on the second piece to mark it for cutting. Before making the cut on the second member, make a test cut on scrap stock of the same thickness. If the test piece laps flush proceed with the cutting. Otherwise make the necessary blade adjustment.

The end half-lap joint permits construction of a chair side member with a strong and harmonious grain orientation.

The two members are rough cut, then overlapped and positioned with the aid of a full-size pattern. The inside flats must be jointed true before marking.

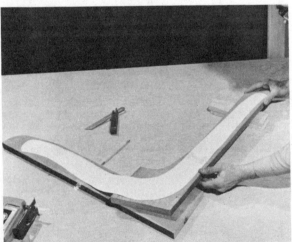

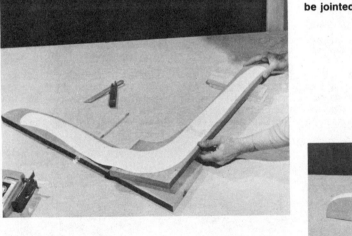

The dado head is used on a radial-arm or table saw to reduce the thickness of each joint section 50 percent. Band-sawing to final shape is done after the parts have been glued.

Half-lap cabinet framing. When the front edge of a cabinet is to be face framed, a combination of end and middle half-lap joints will provide the soundest assembly.

To obtain vertical joint lines, which are usually preferred, the stiles (verticals) are made the outside members and are lapped over the rails (horizontals). To make the layout, tack-nail the rails into place on the cabinet; then tack-nail the stiles in place over them. Check the arrangement carefully with a large square and make adjustments if necessary. It is easier to install the frame accurately than to make crooked doors fit a crooked frame.

The rule of marking the joints in two stages must be disregarded in a situation such as this because access to the marking edges will be lessened after the first parts are cut. Mark all the horizontal and vertical cut lines; then identify each piece before removal. Make the cuts using a dado head on the table or radial-arm saw. Or you can make repeated kerf cuts with a regular blade.

Glue and nail or screw the rails into place first. Use the nail holes previously made in tack-nailing to locate the rails in their original positions. Add the stiles to complete the installation.

Tack-nail all the members into position on the cabinet. Use a large square to check for accuracy before marking.

In a situation such as this, the marks on all pieces are made at the onset.

Check the depth of cut on scrap stock before making the cuts on the work. The marks are aligned with the groove cut in a new section of fence.

Use the original nail holes to reinstate the rails in exact alignment. Glue and nail them first, then the stiles.

Here's another application of the lap joint. This one is called the angled edge half-lap.

RABBET JOINT

The rabbet joint is formed by cutting an L-shaped recess along the edge or end of one of the mating members. The width of the rabbet is usually made equal to the thickness of the mating piece; however, it is generally advisable to cut the width slightly oversize to permit sanding flush after gluing. The depth of the cut can be one-half to two-thirds the thickness of the stock in which it is cut.

The rabbet joint is widely used on cabinet sides to allow the back panel to be inset. When the cabinet is to be backed to a wall it is usually cut about ¼ inch deeper than the thickness of the back panel. This permits trimming the back edge of the cabinet to fit any irregularities in the wall. Other applications for the rabbet include box, case, and drawer construction as well as lipped cabinet doors.

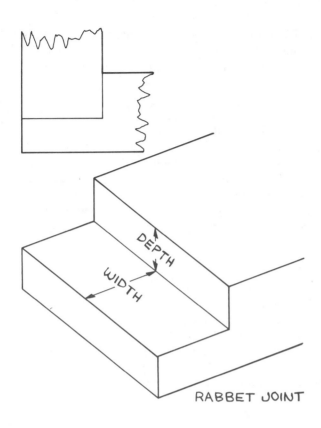

RABBET JOINT

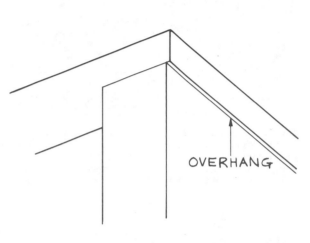

Slight overhang permits flush sanding after assembly.

Typical rabbet applications.

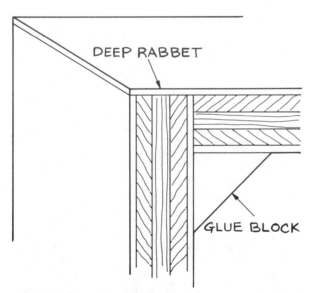

DEEP RABBET

GLUE BLOCK

A deep rabbet effectively conceals most of the unattractive plywood edge but renders the joint quite weak at the shoulder. Glue blocks add strangth.

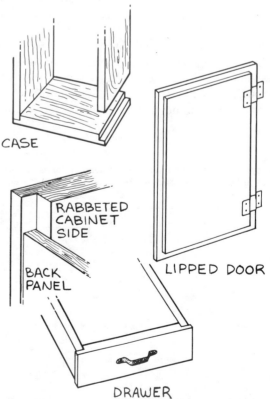

CASE

RABBETED CABINET SIDE

BACK PANEL

LIPPED DOOR

DRAWER

Making an inboard rabbet cut against an auxiliary wood fence. This method is safe and promotes accuracy. A hold-down block clamped to the fence keeps the work in constant contact with the blade. This piece, requiring a very wide rabbet, could not be cut with a normal router rabbeting bit.

Rabbeting fence. If you plan to do rabbeting on the table saw, you should attach a wood facing to the rip fence. This permits inboard rabbeting, that is, with the cutter between the fence and the work. This is a necessity for rabbeting large workpieces that extend beyond the edge of the saw table, but the procedure is advantageous for small work as well because the work cannot go astray since the fence limits the side movement.

Most saw fences have through holes to receive screws for securing a wood facing. If yours does not you can make them. Just be careful you don't bore through the locking mechanism, which usually consists of a bar running through the center. You can

pre-saw a recess to house the dado head or you can form it by positioning the fence over the depressed cutter, then elevating it under power, being careful to avoid making contact between the blade and the metal fence.

Stopped rabbet. A stopped rabbet is made by stopping the cut short of the end of the stock. When this rabbet is cut with a dado head, the bottom of the cut will be rounded at the end. In order to obtain a square corner, hand work with a chisel is necessary. The same cut made with a router will also leave a rounded corner, though of much smaller radius.

DADO JOINT

The dado is a groove cut across the grain to provide a supporting ledge for the butt end of the second member. When the same type of cut is made parallel to the grain it is called a groove. It is a strong joint frequently used in the construction of cabinets, shelves, bookcases, chests, and drawers.

Common dado joints.

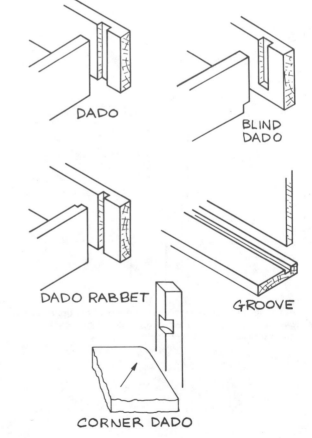

Stopped rabbets made with a dado head or router will leave rounded corners which must be squared with a chisel.

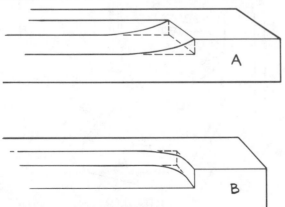

The joint is visible on the edge of the work. If this is objectionable, the stopped or blind dado is used; the dado is cut short of the end of the first member and a corner is notched out of the second piece. As with the blind rabbet, the rounded cut at the end must be squared by hand with a chisel. An alternative is to cut a notch with a matching curve in the mating member.

The router is commonly used to cut dadoes and grooves, particularly on large workpieces that are beyond the capacity of the table or radial saws. If the length of the dado permits, a backsaw and chisel can be used to cut it. Whatever method is used, the width of the cut should permit a sliding fit of the inserting member.

Positioning a router guide. A straightedge is usually clamped to the work surface to guide a router in making a dado joint. To position the guide accurately, mark the outlines of the dado width on the work, then adjust the router bit so it is flush with the base. Place the router on the work near an outer edge, aligning the bit edge with the marked line. Trace a partial circle around the router base. Repeat the step near the other edge of the work. If the router bit is of smaller diameter than the width of the dado groove, a second parallel guide position will be required on the other side for repositioning the guide for the second pass of the router. Position the straightedge so it touches both arcs, then clamp it in place.

The use of two guide strips is advantageous even if only one pass of the router is required to make the dado because the setup protects against the danger of the router base accidentally veering away from the guide and damaging the work.

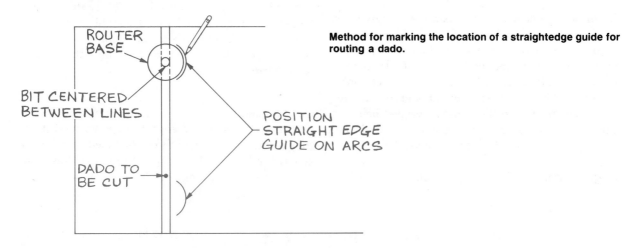

Method for marking the location of a straightedge guide for routing a dado.

A single guide can be used when the router bit is of sufficient diameter to cut the required groove in one pass.

Using double guides to form a dado groove that is wider than the bit. The router base is alternately guided against each edge.

A hold-down block is clamped to the fence to help hold a slightly warped panel flat while making a dado cut.

Dadoing a warped panel. Although plywood is theoretically a warp-free product, warped panels do occur. When it is necessary to cut a dado in a panel with a belly in contact with the saw table, clamp a hold-down block on the fence in a position opposite the blade. This will help to obtain a groove of consistent depth. When the panel is warped belly-up, the best solution is to use the router to make the cut. Its small base will ride with the irregularity.

Aligning dadoes. One of the side benefits of the dado joint is easy alignment of the parts. However, on large assemblies such as the one shown, the alignment of the cross members into the grooves requires special care. An attempt to place the panel into position square-on could result in a miss, thus causing the glue on the ends of the cross members to be smeared onto the surface of the panel. Success is more likely if the panel is tilted and the insertion started at the outer edge.

Stopped dado shortcut. When many stopped dadoes are required you may find it easier to run the dado completely through, then use filler blocks to flush the gap, rather than to square each curved groove bottom with a chisel.

If the work is to be given a clear finish, cut the blocks from the same species of wood and with the grain running parallel to that in the work. The blocks should be of exacting width but slightly thicker and longer than the finished size. This will permit flush sanding after gluing. To position the blocks accurately, insert the mating member into the groove temporarily.

Dadoed cleats. Cabinet doors are sometimes made with boards assembled edge-to-edge without glue; they're held together with cleats nailed or screwed across the back. A better quality door of this type can be made by gluing the cleats in dadoes.

Always start the assembly of dado joints from an edge to assure accurate meshing.

Making a blind dado the easy way; the cut is made completely through the board.

Filler blocks are cut with the grain running in the same direction as the workpiece. A cross member is temporarily inserted in the groove in order to locate the block accurately. It is removed after the block is glued in place.

After sanding flush the plugged ends are barely noticeable.

The dadoes can be cut through all the members at once by using masking tape to hold them in alignment. Cut the boards to length, then butt the edges and run strips of tape over the joint lines.

To simplify cutting a number of wide dadoes to uniform width on the radial-arm saw, you can employ this novel method: Put a fresh section of fence in place and make two saw cuts in it spaced equal to the width of the dado. Mark the work and cut to the desired depth. Shift the work to align the kerf with the second kerf in the fence, and make a second cut. Repeat the step at all the locations. When all the cuts have been completed, make repeated passes to remove the waste between the double kerfs.

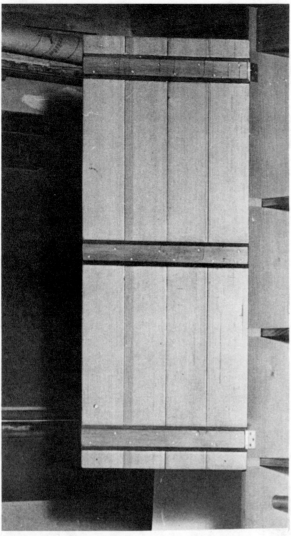

A cabinet door assembled with let-in cleats.

The butted boards are joined with masking tape.

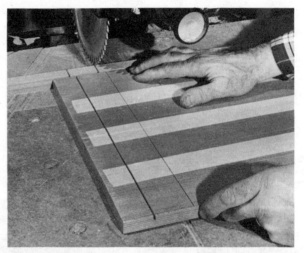

Two kerf cuts made in the backup fence are used to guide the initial cuts.

After the first cut is made, the work is shifted so the kerfs line up. The second cut is then made. When all the kerf cuts are completed, repeated passes are made to clear out the waste in between.

MITER JOINT

The miter is an angled joint usually used to conceal end-grain or to join segments for geometric assemblies. It can be made on-edge for case or boxed constructions, or it can be made flat for framing members. In either application the miter is a weak joint unless it is reinforced with nails, dowels, or with a spline. The spline is usually made of ⅛-inch

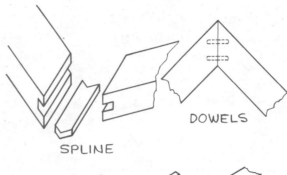

SPLINE   DOWELS

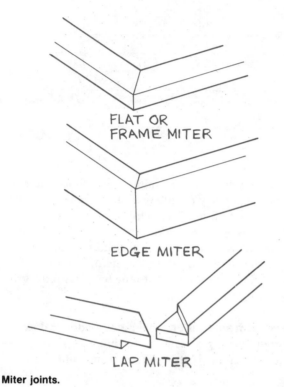

FLAT OR
FRAME MITER

EDGE MITER

LAP MITER

Miter joints.

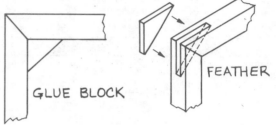

GLUE BLOCK   FEATHER

Reinforcements for miters.

plywood set into grooves cut into the faces of the mating edges. Partial splines are sometimes used to reinforce frames. These are inserted into the outside corner and are called feathers.

Miters are cut at 45-degree angles to form right-angle corners. Those cut at angles other than 45 degrees are called polygon miters and are used to make segments to form constructions of three or more sides.

Mitered segments are cut with the use of the miter gage. Beveled segments are cut by tilting the saw blade. The table shows the settings for working with

TABLE OF COMPOUND ANGLES FOR TABLE SAW

Tilt of Work	4-SIDE BUTT		4-SIDE MITER		6-SIDE MITER		8-SIDE MITER	
	Tilt	Miter Gage	Tilt	Miter Gage	Tilt	Miter Gage	Tilt	Miter Gage
5°	½	85	44¾	85	29¾	87½	22¼	88
10°	1½	80¼	44¼	80¼	29½	84½	22	86
15°	3¾	75½	43¼	75½	29	81¾	21½	84
20°	6¼	71¼	41¾	71¼	28¼	79	21	82
25°	10	67	40	67	27¼	76½	20¼	80
30°	14½	63½	37¾	63½	26	74	19½	78¼
35°	19½	60¼	35¼	60¼	24½	71¾	18¼	76¾
40°	24½	57¼	32½	57¼	22¾	69¾	17	75
45°	30	54¾	30	54¾	21	67¾	15¾	73¾
50°	36	52½	27	52½	19	66¼	14¼	72½
55°	42	50¾	24	50¾	16¾	64¾	12½	71¼
60°	48	49	21	49	14½	63½	11	70¼

Tilt of Work	4-SIDE BUTT		4-SIDE MITER		6-SIDE MITER		8-SIDE MITER	
	Blade Tilt	Track-Arm	Blade Tilt	Track-Arm	Blade Tilt	Track-Arm	Blade Tilt	Track-Arm
5°	½	5°	44¾	5°	29¾	2½	22¼	2
10°	1½	9¾	44¼	9¾	29½	5½	22	4
15°	3¾	14½	43¼	14½	29	8¼	21½	6
20°	6¼	18¾	41¾	18¾	28¼	11	21	8
25°	10	23	40	23	27¼	13½	20¼	10
30°	14½	26½	37¾	26½	26	16	19½	11¾
35°	19½	29¾	35¼	29¾	24½	18¼	18¼	13¼
40°	24½	32¾	32½	32¾	22¾	20¼	17	15
45°	30	35¼	30	35¼	21	22¼	15¾	16¼
50°	36	37½	27	37½	19	23¾	14¼	17½
55°	42	39¼	24	39¼	16¾	25¼	12½	18¾
60°	48	41	21	41	14½	26½	11	19¾

TABLE OF COMPOUND ANGLES FOR RADIAL-ARM SAW

the table saw, assuming the miter gage reads 90 degrees and the tilt scale 0 degrees in the normal positions.

Since the miter scale on a radial-arm saw reads 0 degrees in the normal right-angle position, the table below applies when working with this saw.

Setup for drilling dowel holes in a frame miter with a tiltable drill-press table.

Accuracy is critical in miter work. Since there is always a tendency for the work to creep when making this kind of cut, it is helpful to insert two nails in the miter gage auxiliary fence or the radial-arm-saw fence, with the points protruding slightly towards the work. An alternate method is to tape a strip of fine abrasive paper to the fence with the grit side facing the work.

Doweled frame miter. The holes made for dowels in strengthening a frame miter must be made perfectly perpendicular to the face of the joint. Dowel-

A simple jig to make for drilling dowel holes in frame miters on a drill-press table.

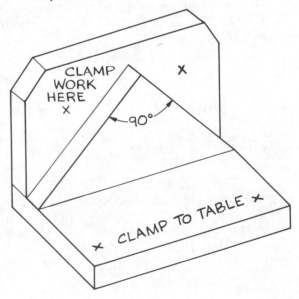

This is the only way a doweled miter can be assembled.

drill-press table can be tilted, the method illustrated is perhaps the simplest. Lacking a press with a tilting table you can make the jig shown.

Assembling a doweled miter. A doweled miter frame can be assembled only if you join two diagonal corners together first to form two right-angled sections as shown. The L's are then brought together to fit the dowels into the holes.

Mitering jig. Cutting 45-degree miters on the table or radial-arm saw is a relatively simple matter of adjusting the miter gage or swinging the arm to cut the angle. However, the use of a homemade jig like the one shown will result in consistent accuracy and faster work. Here's why: If the workpiece does not have parallel plane surfaces on both sides, such as molding, the miter gage or saw arm must be swung alternately to cut the left and right miters. This is an extra step which takes some time. In addition, the readjustment could lead to error. A mismatch of angles, no matter how small, will prevent a perfect assembly. When the stock is the same on both sides

ing jigs can sometimes be used successfully with hand-held drills, but the drill press is by far the best tool to use for the purpose. There are several ways to support the work at the proper angle. If your

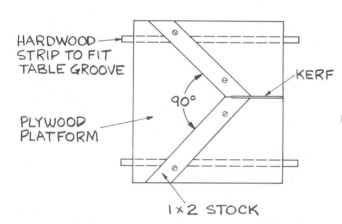

HARDWOOD STRIP TO FIT TABLE GROOVE

90°

KERF

PLYWOOD PLATFORM

1 x 2 STOCK

Design for a simple frame mitering jig.

Cutting accurate, 45-degree miters is easy and quick with this homemade jig.

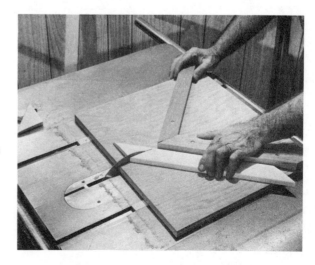

An accessory mitering jig for the radial-arm saw.

Thus the advantage of the mitering jig; it permits cutting the left and right miters with the good side of the work facing up and without making angle adjustments. The jig for the table saw consists of a flat plywood board with two runners attached to the bottom. The runners are sized to fit the miter-gage grooves in the table. Cut a slot into the front of the platform, then carefully attach two cleats to the top so they form a perfect 90-degree angle that will be bisected by the saw blade. Do not attach the cleats permanently until you make test cuts; then glue and nail them into place. A small brad inserted into the front edge of each cleat with the points projecting slightly will prevent the work from creeping.

The same jig, without the runners, can be used on the radial-arm saw. Or you can use a ready-made which is designed for use with this saw. Clamps hold the work in position and prevent creeping.

you could use only one setting of the gage or arm and simply flip the work over, end for end, to obtain both the left and right miters. While this method is fast and accurate, it has a disadvantage; the face of the work is up for one cut and down for the other. Some splintering will always occur on the down face.

MORTISE-AND-TENON JOINT

The strong mortise-and-tenon joint is used for chair and table assemblies, doors, cabinets, and many other applications. There are many forms of this joint; some of the common ones are illustrated.

The open mortise and tenon is the easiest to make

Common mortise-and-tenon joints. As a general rule, the thickness of the tenon should be about one-half the thickness of the mortised members.

Both cheeks of a tenon can be cut at the same time by using two blades of a dado set spaced apart equal to the thickness of the tenon. This technique is useful when numerous identical pieces are required. The shoulder cuts are made with a single blade and miter gage.

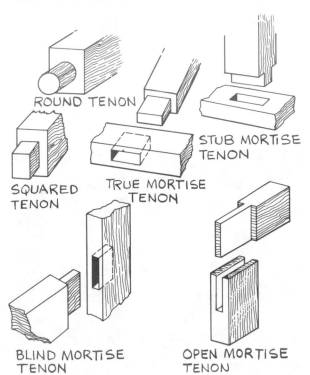

because it can be cut without hand work on the table or radial-arm saws. Round tenons are frequently made as integral parts of lathe turnings so the mortise is easily made by drilling a matching hole in the mating piece. It is important to turn the tenon to a diameter compatible with standard drill bits. The backsaw and chisel are used to make the joint by hand. Since it is somewhat more difficult to form the

The blind mortise is made by boring a series of overlapping holes. The chisel is used to dress the edges and to square the corners.

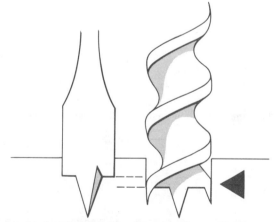

The brad-point bit permits boring a deep hole without penetrating the second surface.

mortise than the tenon, it is a good idea to work on the mortise first. If it does not shape up to perfection, it will be easier to cut the tenon to fit. The sabre saw excels for cutting large through mortises.

Cutting a blind mortise. The usual method of cutting a blind mortise is by drilling a series of overlapping holes to remove the bulk of the stock. The chisel is used to trim the side walls to remove the pips between the holes and to square the corners. The selection of a drill bit for making the holes will be dictated by the depth of the cavity and the thickness of the stock. The flat or spade bit which is capable of boring clean holes frequently cannot be used because its relatively long point will restrict the depth of the hole that can be bored. Depending upon its diameter, the point of the spade bit projects between ⅜ to ¾ inch on the average. The point of the brad bit, on the other hand, usually projects only ³⁄₁₆ inch. Therefore it permits deeper drilling without cutting through the second surface of the stock. When sizing the thickness of the tenon, round it out to a size that will match the nearest drill-bit diameter available. It wouldn't make sense to make a tenon 1 ¹⁄₁₆ inch thick, for example, if the largest size bit in your collection is 1 inch in diameter.

Mortising shortcut. Cutting numerous mortises for a chair project such as this one could be a very time-consuming and painstaking job. Normally, making the rectangular recesses for the slats would entail drilling holes in series followed by much chisel trimming. The method illustrated here makes the task quite easy and results in perfectly sized and aligned mortises. You can apply the technique to any job.

The first step is to cut grooves of the appropriate width and depth into the edges of the upper and lower rails using a dado head. After this, strips of the same stock are ripped to a dimension that will allow them to slide-fit into the grooves.

The filler strips are cut into little blocks equal in length to the spaces between the slats and thick enough so they project slightly above the edge of the rail. A scrap of wood cut from a slat is used as a spacer for gluing in the blocks. Glue is applied sparingly, only on the bottom of the block and on the sides and bottom of the groove. The spacer is carefully lifted out and set into the new position after each block is inserted.

The filler blocks are trimmed flush with a rip cut on the table saw. When sanded and finished, the blocks will blend nicely into the background.

The slats in this chair back are firmly seated in individual, custom-made mortises.

The first step is to cut grooves a touch wider than the thickness of the slats.

Blocks equal in length to the space between slats are glued into place. A sample slat is used as a spacer.

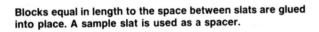

The edge is trimmed flush after the glue has dried.

Slats are aligned and glued into place in this manner. The unit is kept in the horizontal position while the glue sets in order to avoid drippings on the slats.

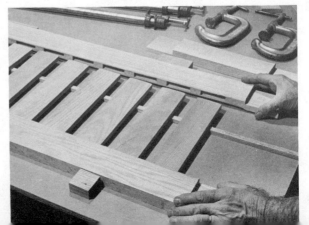

Mortising a turned section. Furniture designs that involve the mortising of round legs to receive rectangular rails normally present a problem. Cutting the mortises safely and accurately can be quite difficult with the equipment available in the typical home shop. Frequently the job is done by hand with a chisel, and this can lead to some frustrating moments. But there is an easy way—by cutting the mortises in advance, while the turning blanks are square.

Simply cutting the grooves won't do, however, because the edges could splinter in turning, so temporary filler blocks are used. The technique is easy and effective.

A dado head is used to cut the mortises in the ends of each turning square. The ends of the cuts are then squared out with a chisel. The filler blocks are cut to size for a snug fit but must nevertheless be temporarily glued in place. They are not glued in wood-to-wood contact, however; otherwise, removing them later would be difficult, if not impossible. Instead, a strip of paper is inserted to facilitate removal. Only a small amount of glue should be applied in the center of the groove. The strip of paper is inserted, dabbed with a touch of glue, then the block is pressed into place. When the turnings are completed, a chisel is used to wedge the blocks out.

The curved groove ends are squared with a chisel. Keep the bevel up.

Snug-fitting wood blocks are glued into the grooves with a slip of paper in between.

Cutting mortises in rounded sections like these could be difficult, but the job is easy if you cut them beforehand.

Start by making stopped grooves on the table saw using a dado head. A block clamped to the rip fence limits the length of cut.

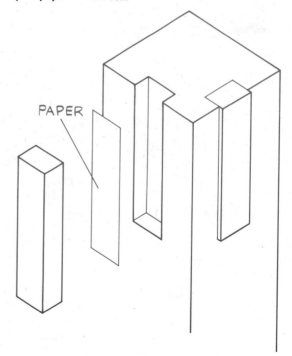

PAPER

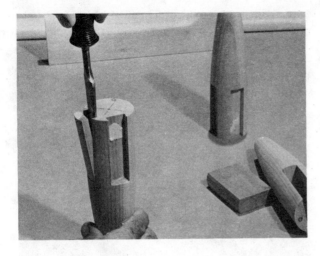

The blocks are easily removed with a chisel after the turning has been completed.

DOVETAIL JOINT

The dovetail is a very strong interlocked joint. The most common forms are the through dovetail and the half-blind dovetail. Handmade dovetails require very careful layout and patient work with a backsaw and chisel. A half-blind dovetail can easily be made with a router and a special dovetail accessory fixture which is commonly available.

Dovetail layout. While there are no hard and fast rules in sizing the joint, the following will serve as a guideline: The widest portion of the pin face should be about three-quarters of the stock thickness. The slope angle of the dovetail and pin should be within a proportion of 1 to 5 and 1 to 8. The center-to-center dimension between pins should be about 2½ times the pin width. The end pins, which are called half pins, are usually about ⅛ inch greater than half width for increased strength.

To obtain the slope angle for a 1 to 5 proportion, set the T-bevel as shown in the diagram. Other proportions are set in the same manner. Use a sharp pencil or knife and the T-bevel to lay out the cutting lines. It is common practice to draw the dovetail portion of the joint at the onset, leaving the pin section to be outlined later by tracing directly from the cut-out dovetails. The basic steps involved in making several types of dovetail joints with hand and power tools follow.

Dovetail joints

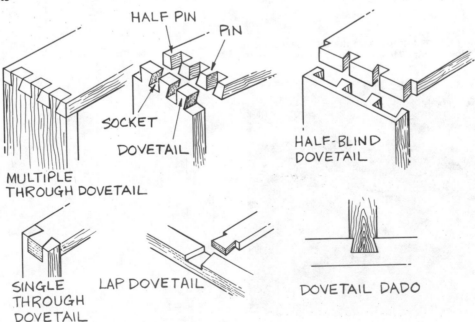

HALF PIN
PIN
SOCKET
DOVETAIL
MULTIPLE THROUGH DOVETAIL

HALF-BLIND DOVETAIL

SINGLE THROUGH DOVETAIL

LAP DOVETAIL

DOVETAIL DADO

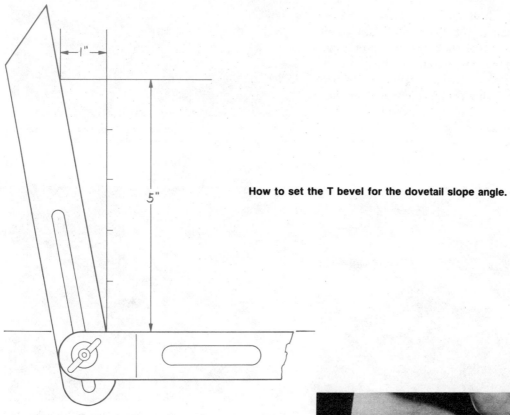

How to set the T bevel for the dovetail slope angle.

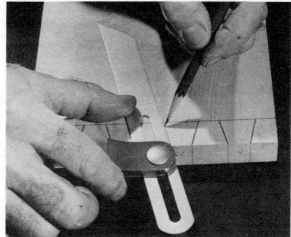

Use the T bevel to lay out the angled cutting lines.

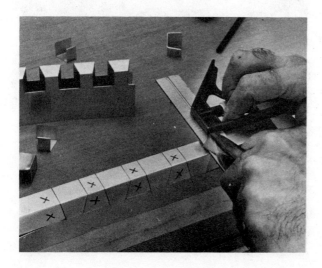

The square is used to mark the right-angle lines. A knife will make finer cutting lines than a pencil.

Multiple through dovetail. Use a fine-tooth back-saw or dovetail saw to cut the tapers. Make sure to cut on the waste side of the lines. A coping saw is used to cut across the grain to remove the waste. Use the largest chisel that will fit the openings to trim the tails to exact size. Using the cut piece as a template, trace the outline with a knife to lay out the pins. Cut them to shape with the saw and chisel. Alternate between the pins and check the fit frequently.

Use the completed tail section as a template to outline the pins. Use a narrow knife to reach into the corners.

Cut on the waste side of the lines using a smooth-cutting dovetail or backsaw.

Pins are cut in the same manner as the tails, with the dovetail saw and coping saw.

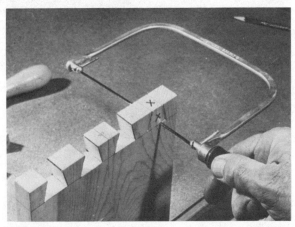

The coping saw is used to cut across the grain to remove the waste between the dovetails.

Check the fit constantly while trimming with the chisel. Note that the joint can be made with a half pin at the ends.

Trim the tail sides and sockets with a sharp chisel.

The completed multiple through dovetail.

Multiple half-blind dovetail. The half-blind dovetail is used when it is desired to conceal the joint from one direction. The procedure is similar to that used for the through dovetail with some minor differences. The tails are shorter by an amount equal to the thickness of the lap in the mating piece. Also, the saw can be used only for a partial angled cut on the pins because they do not go through. Consequently, most of the waste clean-out must be done with the chisel. Secure the work firmly to the bench and work with a sharp chisel.

For the half-blind dovetail, the saw is held at an angle; only a partial cut is made.

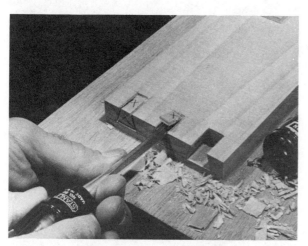

Much of the cleanout is done with the chisel.

Partially fitted half-blind multiple dovetail.

Single through dovetail. This joint is easily cut by hand or with the table or radial-arm saw. A tenoning jig is advantageous for cutting the cheeks of the tail but it is not essential. The miter gage can be used for all the cuts on the table saw.

To make the joint on the table saw, set the blade for the desired bevel angle (15 degrees is used here), projecting an amount equal to the thickness of the mating stock. Clamp the work vertically in the jig, or hold it firmly against the miter gage, and make a pass. Rotate the stock 180 degrees and make the second cheek cut. Remove the tenoning jig from the saw table. Adjust the blade to zero bevel and lower it to make the shoulder cuts to drop off the waste.

Trace the outline for the pins using the cut dovetail as a template. Elevate the blade as required and adjust the miter gage for the required angle (it should match the previous bevel setting). Clamp a stop block to the miter gage to help in holding the piece perfectly perpendicular. Make the cut. Set the miter gage to the equal but opposite angle and make the second cut. Remove the stop block and make repeated close kerf cuts to clean out the waste. The joint is as easily made on the radial-arm saw.

Tenoning jig is used to feed the wood endwise on the table and to make the cheek cuts. Blade is tilted.

Shoulder cuts are made with the miter gage. A clamped stop block assures uniformity.

To make a half-lap dovetail with the radial saw, two straight cuts are made into each end of stock. The blade is then set at an angle to cut off the waste.

Miter gage is set at the required angle to make the beveled cheek cuts. It is readjusted to the opposite angle for the second cut. High stop block keeps piece vertical.

The face is reduced by making repeated passes.

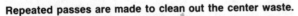

Repeated passes are made to clean out the center waste.

The tail is superimposed on the mating member and the cutting lines are traced with a knife.

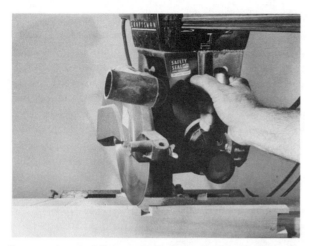

Saw arm is set at the required angle, and the blade is elevated. Repeated passes clean out the waste.

This piece is assembled with both the single through dovetail and the half-lap dovetail.

cut. This serves to condition the work edge to prevent splintering. The router is then moved from left to right, pressed to follow the fingers in the template to complete the shaped cut.

A guide collar insert and dovetail bit are used with the router dovetail guide.

A side and end member are clamped together in the template guide with ends butted.

The router is fed against the template fingers to cut both parts of the joint in one operation.

Dovetails with router. A multiple half-blind dovetail joint can be made in minutes with the router and a special guide. A guide collar insert for the router base and a mortising bit are the only other requirements. Both members are clamped to the fixture, butted at right angle and cut at the same time. Two passes are made; the first, from right to left, is a light

The result is a precise-fitting joint.

Joints for drawers. A drawer is basically a box without a top. It can be made simply by nailing and gluing together four pieces of stock with butt joints and adding a bottom, also butted. But a drawer is constantly subjected to abuse. If it is to hold together it must be constructed with lasting joints.

The kinds of joints used for drawers are quite varied. All are superior to the plain butt because they provide increased glue area on two or more surfaces. Some have interlocking features, such as the dovetail and lock joint. While some of the drawer joints shown are somewhat sophisticated, you needn't use the most complex type to produce a sound drawer.

The procedure for the construction and assembly of a simple but sound flush drawer with a rabbeted front and back and let-in bottom follows, assuming the use of ¾-inch stock for the front, ½-inch for the sides and back, and ¼-inch hardboard for the bottom.

Rip the stock for the front, back, and two sides to width. Cut the pieces to length; then cut a ¼″ × ¼″ groove on all the inside surfaces, ½-inch from the bottom. Adjust the dado head to cut ½-inch-wide rabbets ⅜-inch deep on the ends of the back, then readjust it to cut ½-inch wide by ½-inch deep rabbets on the ends of the front.

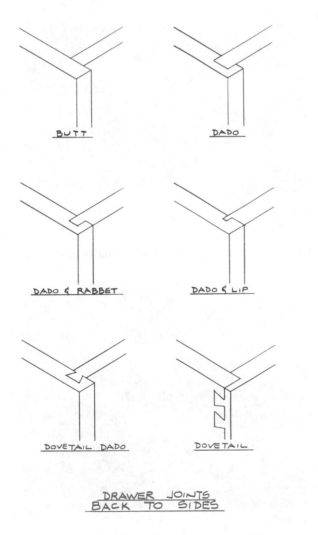

DRAWER JOINTS
BACK TO SIDES

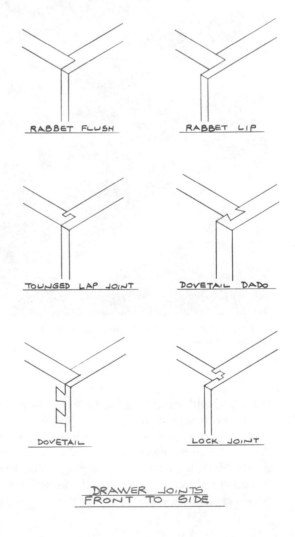

DRAWER JOINTS
FRONT TO SIDE

Set up a molding cutterhead with a corner-rounding shape to ease the top edges of the drawer sides. A stopped quarter-round is cut along each edge to form a full half-round. To make the stopped cuts attach a piece of wood of sufficient length to the rip fence. Clamp stop blocks to the auxiliary fence, located so the work will make contact with the blade to within 1 inch from each end. To make the cuts, elevate the work, pivoting at the back stop. Slowly lower the work until it makes contact with the table (and blade); then advance it to the rear stop. Repeat the step on the other side member.

Cut the bottom so it is $\frac{7}{16}$ inch larger than the inside dimensions of the drawer. Attach one side to the front and back using glue and 1½-inch finishing nails. Apply glue to the grooves, insert the bottom panel, and add the side. Set the nails and fill the holes. Apply a coat of sealer to all surfaces.

The dado head is used to cut the rabbets and grooves in the front, back and side members.

All the parts ready for assembly.

A strip of wood with stop blocks clamped near each end is used to control the length of the cut in forming the stopped rounds for easing the top edges of the side members. A molding cutter head is used to make the quarter-rounds.

Assembly begins by attaching a side to the rabbeted front and back. The bottom goes in next, then the fourth side.

5
Gluing

Regardless of how well you do in cutting and shaping the parts of any woodworking project, unless they're assembled neatly with a lasting permanent bond, your efforts could turn out to be a labor in vain. The strength and appearance of the construction depend on proper gluing techniques. This entails selecting the right glue for the job and following correct application and clamping procedures.

There are several kinds of glue at your disposal for woodworking. The kind of glue you select depends on the project and such factors as assembly time, working temperature, water resistance and gap-filling capability. Strength is assumed because modern glues are all adequate in this respect.

Some glues set more quickly than others. Allowable assembly time is generally of little concern if the job is small, but it is an important factor in large or complex assemblies. If the glue sets on one part while it is still being applied on another, the result could be ruinous.

Some glues can be used at lower temperatures than others. Since you may not be able to control the temperature of the workshop, and surely you cannot control the climate when working outdoors, the choice of a glue that will set in low temperature will enable you to obtain good results when working in a cool environment.

All outdoor projects that are exposed directly to the weather will require a waterproof glue. But water resistance may also be a factor to be considered in some indoor projects. If subjected to moderate moisture conditions, a water-resistant glue will be suitable, but constant wetting of the joint will necessitate the use of a completely waterproof glue. You should evaluate the need carefully because waterproof glue is expensive.

The fit of a joint will have a direct bearing on how well the glue will hold it together. A glue with good gap-filling quality should be selected for joints that are ill-fitted. It will effectively fill the voids (within reason) and produce a solid joint. Such a glue is advantageous for use with joints which must necessarily be made loose fitting in order to permit assembly at all.

Following are general descriptions of the most commonly used glues. The individual package labels should be consulted for specific data because some differences do occur between brands.

Quality woodwork requires well-fitted joints and the application of correct gluing techniques.

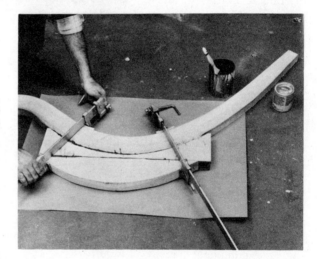

Waterproof glue must be used on outdoor constructions. The resorcinol glue used on this subassembly for a patio lounger will never fail due to water saturation. This glue has great strength and is widely used in boat building.

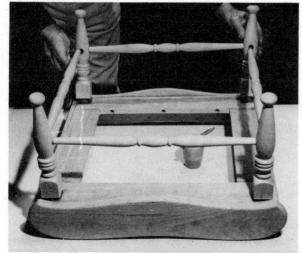

A glue with good gap-filling quality is used when joints are not tight fitting. Angular assemblies such as this one with flared legs dictate some looseness in the joints to permit the parts to fit into place.

Polyvinyl glue. This is the popular white glue widely used for general woodworking and repairs. It comes in a squeeze bottle ready for use. This is a quick-setting glue with a short assembly time, on the order of about 10 minutes. Works best at temperatures above 60 degrees, is low in moisture resistance, dries clear and will not stain.

Aliphatic resin. This is similar to white glue. It is available in convenient squeeze bottles, ready for use, is equally quick-setting, lacks moisture resistance and dries clear without staining. It has the edge over white glue in that it is somewhat stronger, can be used at temperatures above 50 degrees and sands better because it has slightly better heat resistance, which reduces gumming of abrasives. It has very good tack, thus permitting small parts to be joined without clamps.

Liquid hide glue. This is a very strong glue made from animal hooves, bones, and hides. It is available in squeeze bottles, ready for use. Lacks moisture resistance, dries to an amber color and does not stain. It is a good gap filler and is reasonably slow setting; a definite advantage on large assemblies. Working temperature should be 70 degrees or higher. Assembly time at 70 degrees is about 60 minutes.

Casein glue. Casein glue comes in powder form and is mixed with water to a creamlike consistency before use. It is strong and useful for all kinds of woodworking jobs but will stain some species of wood. This glue is highly water resistant but not waterproof. It is a fair gap filler and is particularly suitable for gluing oily woods such as lemon, teak, and yew. Excels for working in cold climate, as it can be used at any temperature above freezing. Assembly time is moderate, about 30 minutes.

Plastic resin. This glue also comes in powder form and is mixed with water for use. It makes a very strong, highly water-resistant bond but is not a good gap filler. It is nonstaining, must be used at 70 degrees or higher temperature. Assembly time is 20 minutes at 70 degrees; 10 minutes at 90 degrees.

Resorcinol resin. This is a completely waterproof glue that comes in two parts: a liquid resin and a powdered catalyst which are mixed together before use. It is a good gap filler and exceptionally strong. Minimum working temperature is 70 degrees; assembly time is about 25 minutes at 70 degrees and 10 minutes at 90 degrees.

Contact cement. Contact cement is a rubber-based liquid ideally suited for bonding veneers and plastic laminates or a variety of dissimilar materials to wood. Both surfaces to be bonded are coated and allowed to air dry before being joined. A permanent bond is made immediately upon contact of both surfaces so clamping is not required. Available in both a highly volatile variety and a nonflammable latex-based type that can be cleaned up with water. The latter is obviously the better choice for safety and convenience. Contact cement is not used where structural strength is required.

Epoxy cement. Epoxy is a two-part liquid preparation that produces a very strong waterproof bond. It is a good gap filler and is especially useful for joining numerous dissimilar materials to wood. It is not a general-purpose wood glue but is most advantageous in joining certain assemblies which are difficult to clamp. Epoxy can be used at any temperature. Assembly time varies with the product and ambient temperature. Quick-setting types allow only a few minutes.

Hot-melt glue. This is not a general woodworking glue. Small cartridges of glue are inserted into a special glue gun which melts and releases the material in liquid form. The glue begins to set almost immediately. The bond is very strong and waterproof. Due to the extremely short assembly time, about 15 seconds, hot-melt cannot be used successfully on assemblies of any size, but it is excellent for spot-gluing small parts. It is a very good gap filler.

GLUING PROCEDURE

To obtain strong, lasting joints the mating parts must be well fitted and the surfaces should be smooth, but not finish-sanded smooth. The surfaces obtained by hand chiseling and planing and machine jointing or sawing with a smooth cutting blade are well suited for glue joints. Hand and portable power sanding generally should be avoided in preparing stock for gluing because of the difficulty in obtaining perfectly true surfaces. A stationary belt or disc sander with a medium grit abrasive (80 or 100) will produce a good glue surface. Extra-fine sanding doesn't afford the glue sufficient grip.

When wetted with glue and brought into contact, two pieces of wood will readily slide out of alignment during clamping or nailing. This is true with open-type joints such as the butt, miter, open-ended rabbets, and some of the laps. The problem doesn't occur with enclosed joints, in which the mating

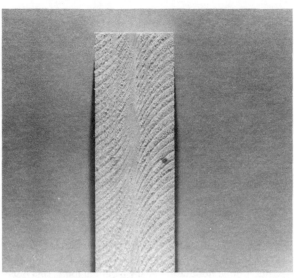

A rough-cutting saw produces a surface that will make a poor glue joint. A surface such as this one should be planed or jointed before gluing.

pieces are interlocked: mortise/tenon, dado, cross and edge laps, and dovetails, nor with any joint that utilizes dowels. A quick glance at the joint diagrams in the section on joints will readily indicate which joints are prone to sliding during assembly.

If the glue joint is being assembled with nails, you should start two nails so they penetrate slightly into the second member to form alignment holes before applying glue. The predrilled pilot holes in a screw-reinforced joint will automatically prevent sliding and ensure alignment.

On those assemblies whose appearance would be marred by using nails, two thin, partly driven nails can be used to hold the parts in alignment until the clamps are applied to the work. The resulting tiny holes can easily be concealed with wood-filling compound. If this procedure is not suitable, concealed nail "pins" are effective for aligning parts. Nail "pins" are used in several projects in this book, including the Butcher Block Table and Curved Back

Always start two nails in a glue/nail assembly to obtain registration holes before applying glue. This will keep the parts from sliding and will assure alignment.

Glue joints that are assembled with screws present no problem in alignment nor sliding of the glue-wetted parts. Note how clamps are used to hold uprights in place.

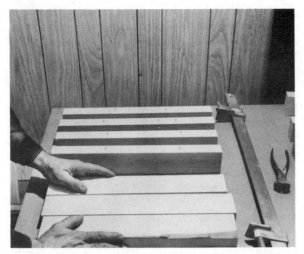

Nail "pins" assure alignment and prevent sliding of multiple butted parts. Members are positioned, then temporarily clamped together to form registration holes. Be sure to locate the nails where they won't subsequently be struck by a saw blade or other tool.

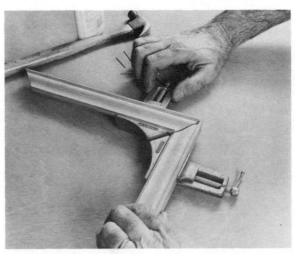

This clamp holds mitered corners in position while the glue sets, but it does not automatically align the joint. This must be done by hand.

Chair. Due to the foolproof results and simplicity of this technique, it merits reviewing here:

The heads are clipped off some nails so you have straight-shanked nails, about ½ inch long, with a blunt and pointed end. One of the headless nails is chucked in a drill with the point exposed and is used to bore two pilot holes in one member of two mating pieces. If multiple pieces are to be joined, such as in assembling a slab, the holes are bored in the same face of each successive member. The depth of the holes should be about ¼ inch. Note that the nail length, depth of insertion and amount of projection as well as the nail diameter are variables. When join-

ing large parts you can increase all the factors, and reduce them for small assemblies.

To form the registration holes, simply insert nails into the holes, blunt end first. Arrange the parts with the appropriate faces in alignment, spaced so the points barely touch the adjoining edge or face. Apply two clamps to bring the parts into contact, causing the nail points to penetrate. Mark the parts so they will be rejoined in the same order, then pull them apart. Apply glue and reassemble with clamps.

Miter joints would ordinarily be troublesome to assemble, but there are several devices and jigs that can be used to simplify the task. A miter clamp,

This miter clamp bears pressure directly behind the joint faces to effectively close the joint. It is used only when holes are permissible on the back of the work.

Using a pinch dog to clamp a glued miter joint.

This wedge arrangement is quite handy for assembling mitered frames. The corner blocks are temporarily secured with nails. Wax-paper barriers prevent the work from sticking to the table.

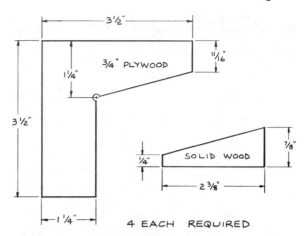

Use plywood for the corner blocks and solid wood for the wedges.

which consists of two adjustable jaws set at a right angle, firmly holds two 45-degree mitered parts together for gluing and nailing. While in appearance it may seem that this clamp forces the faces of the miter joint together, this is a misconception. The face contact is made manually; the clamp then holds the joint in position.

For large frame and case assemblies, a unique miter clamp that actually bears pressure directly on the faces of the joint is available. This is used only if ⅝-inch blind holes can be drilled in the back of the frame members. Another device that can be used to draw the faces of a miter joint together is the pinch dog. This also must be used on the back of a frame. The wedge-shaped points are hammered partly into the wood to force the pieces together. The dog is removed after the glue has set.

You can make two jigs—miter wedges and clamping corners—for gluing miter joints. The former requires no clamps, the latter requires the use of three clamps for each mitered corner. Make these jigs as shown, altering the dimensions as desired to suit your needs.

Clamping corners provide an alternate method for gluing the tricky miter joint.

Dimensions of clamping corners for average-sized work.

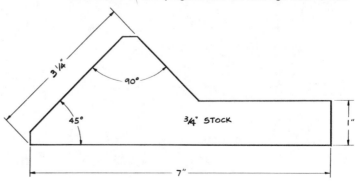

Feather the glue along the edge of the joint that will form an exposed inside corner to minimize squeeze-out. The thinned-out area of the coating dries quickly, so you must make a rapid assembly.

This amount of squeeze-out is not too serious. More is permissible in an area that is easily accessible for scraping or sanding after the glue has set.

APPLYING GLUE

Inside areas of constructions must be finish-sanded prior to final assembly with glue because it is virtually impossible to do a perfect job of sanding in confined areas after assembly. Excessive glue squeeze-out during assembly is also very difficult to remove in confined areas and can readily mess up the work done up to this point. Therefore, you should exercise great care in the gluing operation to minimize, or better, to avoid the problem.

Do this by applying only a reasonable amount of glue. If the joint is well fitted, a thin layer of glue on both surfaces is all that is needed. When the glue has been applied and spread evenly with a stiff brush, run your index finger firmly along the outer edge of the glue coating to feather it. This will help to minimize or prevent altogether glue squeeze-out in critical areas.

After a glue joint has been assembled and nailed, screwed, or clamped, allow any squeeze-out to become slightly set before removing it. Use a very sharp chisel held at a low angle, or flat on the surface if possible, and gently slice between the wood and glue. If you try to wipe off the glue while it is still

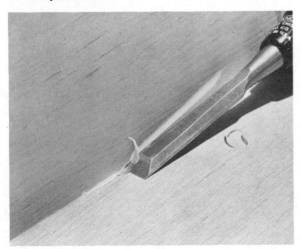

If the excess glue is allowed to set slightly, it can be sliced off neatly with a chisel.

Glue that was scraped while still gooey and not thoroughly removed may go unnoticed until a finish is applied. Here the microscopic film of residual glue prevented stain from being evenly absorbed into the wood.

Always support large assemblies on a level work surface during the gluing operation to avoid permanent twists from developing. Check with a spirit level beforehand and shim the support surface if necessary.

wet, it invariably will be smeared over the surface and worked into the wood. Timing is important. If you allow the excess glue to set hard, you will have a most difficult and tedious job on your hands. Bear in mind that you need not be too fussy about glue removal on outside surfaces which allow easy access with a scraper, power sander, or other means after assembly.

When assembling slip-fit joints such as dadoes, mortise/tenons, cross half-laps and rabbets, don't apply too much glue on the sides of the inserting member. The excess will be scraped off and collect on the outside of the joint. Apply an adequate amount of glue in the receiving member and a thin, well-brushed-out coating on the walls of the inserting member. This also applies when working with dowels.

Note that if excessive squeeze-out does occur, it may indeed be necessary to scrape it off quickly so it doesn't get out of hand. When this happens, follow up immediately with a sponge or cloth dampened with warm water to remove all traces of the glue film. This will raise the grain and necessitate additional sanding. Any glue remaining on the surface will act as a sealer, preventing even absorption of stain when finishing the work.

ASSEMBLY

Some projects can be assembled all at one time while others require gluing up subassemblies. The nature of the construction will dictate this. In either case, unless the piece is exceptionally simple, make

a trial assembly by clamping the parts together without glue. Check to see that all joints fit properly. Mark the parts for rematching. This dry-run assembly will indicate whether you have a sufficient number of clamps to do the job and will also result in setting the clamps to the correct adjustment.

Wood hand screws, or parallel clamps, as they are also called, do not require wood pads (cauls) to prevent marring the surface of the work; metal-faced jaws of bar and C clamps do require protective pads. In addition to protecting the work, wood pads or cleats serve to distribute the clamping pressure over a greater area.

In using pads or cleats, always be certain that they won't become glued to the work. If the pad or cleat will be positioned over a glue line, insert a piece of kitchen wax paper or aluminum foil under it to avoid the problem.

When edge-gluing pieces of stock to make a wide slab, use cleats on both sides near each end, and at several locations in between if the slab is a long one, to prevent buckling. Apply glue to the joint edges and bring them into light contact. Clamp the cleats into place with moderate pressure; then proceed to apply full pressure to the main joint clamps. Be sure not to overtighten the cleat clamps as this could prevent the edge joints from closing fully.

When assembling tables, chairs, or cabinets, it is important to work on a true, level surface. A piece assembled on an uneven surface is prone to receive

Temporary nailed diagonals will true an out-of-square assembly if they're applied before the glue sets.

Glues that come in powder form need to be mixed with water (or liquid resin) to make up a working batch. The label instructions usually tell you the mixing proportions according to both volume and weight. You'll get greater accuracy if you measure by weight. A postal scale is handy for this.

Assemblies with irregular shapes such as this usually present a problem in gluing because of the difficulty in applying clamps. The problem is easily solved with the use of a fast-setting epoxy adhesive. Since clamping is not necessary nor desirable with this adhesive, you can hold the parts together manually. Apply the epoxy to both surfaces and bring them together with moderate pressure. Allow the parts to rest undisturbed for about five minutes. Wax paper is used under each glue line to prevent sticking

Caution. Using smooth dowels for glue joints can split the wood during assembly. The dowel traps excess glue in the bottom of the hole, which exerts internal pressure. Avoid the problem by using spiral-grooved dowels which allow excess glue to flow out. You can use ordinary dowels, but always sand or plane two slight flats on the surface to allow excess glue to escape.

a built-in twist which may be virtually impossible to undo after the glue has set.

When assembling leg-and-rail and framed case constructions with clamps, it is frequently possible to make alignment corrections by shifting the position of clamp jaws. Actually, the problem of an out-of-square assembly may in fact be due to the improper position of one or more clamps in the first place. In glued assemblies which are secured with nails or screws alone, temporarily nailed diagonal cleats can be used to bring the piece into square alignment provided the action is taken before the glue sets.

GLUING POINTERS

• Squeeze bottles are handy for dispensing glue quickly but for most work the bead should be brushed out. A small paintbrush with the bristles cut back about halfway makes a good spreader.

• On extra-large surfaces, consider using a paint roller to spread the glue quickly and with minimal waste.

• All glues set faster at high temperatures. Be especially careful about working in direct sunlight, particularly when using waterproof resorcinol glue. Its very dark color absorbs heat intensely and will cause it to set prematurely.

• End-grain is much more absorbent than face-grain. When an assembly involves both kinds of grain exposure, apply glue to the end-grain first; then go back and apply a second coat to the end-grain only before assembly.

The spiral dowel allows glue to flow freely and its beveled ends make insertion easier.

When edge-gluing more than a few pieces of stock, it is essential to clamp support cleats to prevent the stack from bowing. Use wax paper between the work and cleats to prevent them from sticking together. Or the contact surfaces of the cleats can be waxed as was done here. Take up only moderate pressure on the cleat clamps to keep the slab in alignment. If too much pressure is applied, the glue joints may not close properly.

Clamps are normally applied to the work, but you'll find that you can work more efficiently if you reverse the order and put the work to the clamps. Make clamp stands like these to hold your bar clamps at the ready.

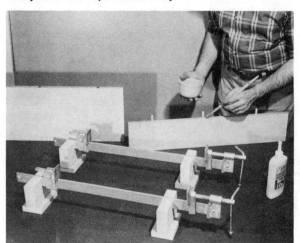

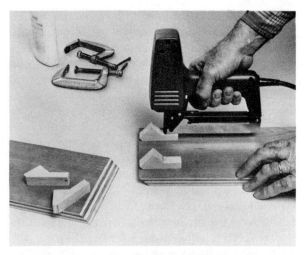

Wide miters are usually difficult to clamp, but this simple trick will enable you to apply pressure exactly where it is needed, at the corners. Cut a series of blocks like these and nail in a pair to the ends of each board.

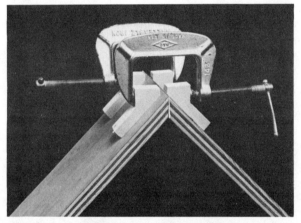

This is how the joint is clamped. When the glue has set, the blocks are removed and the tiny nail holes are filled.

Whenever feasible, a dadoed shelf construction should be assembled on its back. Working in this manner makes it easy to align and fit the shelf ends into the dadoes without accidentally smearing glue from the shelf ends onto the face of the side member. Tilt the side into position to engage the tips of the shelves, then straighten it into final position.

MASKING TAPE ASSEMBLY

Masking tape is indispensable for certain gluing jobs. A good example is in gluing a number of strips side by side to a plywood panel to construct a simulated butcher block tabletop. The problem of getting the edges in close glue contact is easily solved with the use of tape. Here's what you do:

Joint all the edges smooth and straight, then lay them side by side and run several strips of tape crosswise to hold the pieces tightly butted together. Follow up by applying strips of tape lengthwise, centered over each joint line.

For a good job, glue must be applied to the edges as well as to the broad surface. The flexibility of the pack makes it possible to do this. Place the pack with the taped side down over the edge of a 2×4. This will open up several joint lines. Apply glue to both edges of the opened joints, shifting the pack after each course until all edges have received glue. Coat the surfaces and apply clamps. Allow extra time for the glue to set because the tape will slow the setting on the glue lines. When the tape is removed the surface will be quite messy, but a belt sander will do wonders with it.

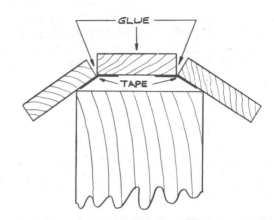

Open the joint lines by placing the taped pack over the edge of a length of 2×4; then apply glue to the edges of the strips as well as to the back surfaces. This takes time, so use a slow-setting glue such as liquid hide.

Place the pack onto a piece of plywood coated with glue. Use a sufficient number of clamps with heavy cross cleats to obtain good overall pressure. Several more clamps will be used in this setup. Wax paper keeps the cleats from being glued to the work.

Remove all masking tape before sanding. The belt sander works well for truing the surface.

To make a simulated butcher-block tabletop, begin by ripping a series of hardwood strips of equal thickness from a 4/4 board.

Run several strips of tape crosswise to hold the pieces in close contact, then apply tape over each joint line.

NAILS

Nails are the simplest fasteners to use for joining wood to wood or to other materials. They differ in size, of course, but they also differ in shape, material, and finish. Nail length sizes are designated in both inches and "penny." The latter is indicated by a number followed by the letter "d." Somewhat confusing, penny sizing is a carry over from earlier days when nails were sold on the basis of so many pennies per one hundred nails of that respective size. The letter "d" was derived from the ancient Roman word for coin, *denarius.* The penny is still used to designate the length of nails from 1 to 6 inches.

There are four kinds of nails widely used in woodworking: *common, box, finishing,* and *casing* nails.

Common nails have a large, flat head, smooth shank, and a diamond point. They are used for general construction and framing where appearance is unimportant.

Box nails are similar to common nails in appearance but differ in one respect: they have a more slender shank. The large heads of both nails serve to hold the nailed member securely by spreading the grip over a relatively wide area. The box nail is chosen when the thicker common nail tends to cause splitting.

Finishing nails are of smaller diameter than common and box nails and have small heads which can easily be driven below the surface and concealed with wood-filling compound. Brads are small finishing nails sized from ⅜ to ⅞ inch.

Casing nails are similar to finishing nails but have fuller tapered heads and are slightly thicker. They are used mainly for molding, window, and door-trim applications.

Nails from 1 to 6 inches are designated in both penny and inch sizes. Those under and over these dimensions are measured in inches or fractions only.

Finishing and casing nails are available with cupped and flush heads. The slight depression in the cupped head makes setting below the surface easier because the nail set is held captive in its center. The nail set tends to slip off the smooth surface of a flush-headed nail and damage the wood.

Generally, the proper nail length is dictated by the thickness of the stock being nailed—the nail should penetrate the second piece by at least two times the thickness of the first. This factor should be increased when nailing into end-grain of softwood in particular because end-grain doesn't hold nails well.

Sharp-pointed nails drive easily because the point slices through the fibers, causing them to separate. This action can cause splitting. You can avoid splitting problems by blunting the point slightly with a

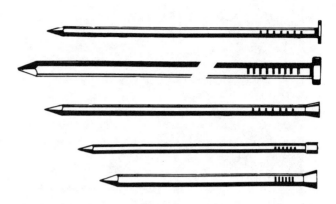

Nail types, from top: box, common, casing, finishing, brad. Note that casing and common nails are heavier than finishing and box nails of equal length.

hammer blow. This will reduce the possibility of splitting because the blunt point shears through the fibers rather than slicing through. When nailing hardwood, however, it is advisable to drill a pilot hole first.

Many nails are available with cement-coated shanks for better holding power. A resin coating on the surface of the shank provides "tooth" which grips firmly against the wood fibers. Better holding power is also obtained with nails that have fluted and ringed shanks.

Outdoor constructions should be assembled only with aluminum or hot-dipped galvanized nails. The latter are heavily coated with zinc and will resist rust much better than the ordinary electrogalvanized type.

For fastening wood to masonry walls and floors, round, square, and fluted nails are available. The latter two shapes provide maximum holding power. All masonry nails are specially hardened and are extremely brittle; thus the heads are prone to chipping when struck with a hammer. For this reason, always wear safety goggles when working with these nails.

Nailing tips

• When nailing on fine work, drive the nail only to within about ⅛ inch of the surface. This will avoid the possibility of denting the surface with the hammer face. The final driving should be done with a nail set.

• Stagger nails when driving them along a grain line to reduce the chance of splitting.

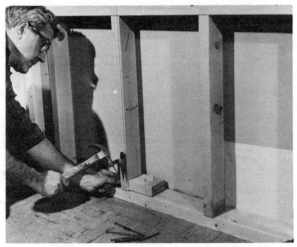

A partly nailed backup block keeps stock from sliding when toenailing.

• Drive nails slightly off perpendicular to gain better holding power.
• When toenailing drive a temporary backup block behind the piece being nailed to keep it from sliding.

SCREWS

Screws require more time to install, but they hold far better than nails. When gluing large assemblies, screws can frequently substitute for clamps which may not be available. Another advantage in using screws is that parts can be disassembled without being damaged.

Wood screws are threaded for approximately two-thirds of the length from the point. Sizes range from ¼ inch to 6 inches in length. Screws up to 1 inch in length increase in size by ⅛-inch increments; those from 1 to 3 inches increase by ¼ inch and screws from 3 to 6 inches increase by ½-inch increments. Lengths are measured from the point to the widest part of the head. The head shapes most commonly used for wood are the flat head, oval head, and round head.

The diameter of a screw is given in gauge size ranging from 0, the smallest, through 24, the largest. The gauge indicates the outside diameter of the shank. Screws from 2 to 18 gauge are the ones most commonly available and used.

As with the nail, improved holding power is obtained when at least two-thirds of the screw length penetrates the second piece of stock. Also, in end-grain, a deeper-penetrating screw will hold better.

The diameter of the shank hole for a screw should be equal to, or slightly larger than, the diameter of the screw; never smaller. The diameter of the pilot hole for a screw in hardwood should be about 10 percent less than the root diameter (solid portion excluding threads) of the screw. For softwood, the pilot-hole diameter should be about 30 percent less than the root diameter.

LENGTH INCHES	SCREW GAUGE NUMBERS																
¼	0	1	2	3													
⅜			2	3	4	5	6	7									
½			2	3	4	5	6	7	8								
⅝				3	4	5	6	7	8	9	10						
¾					4	5	6	7	8	9	10	11					
⅞							6	7	8	9	10	11	12				
1							6	7	8	9	10	11	12	14			
1¼								7	8	9	10	11	12	14	16		
1½							6	7	8	9	10	11	12	14	16	18	
1¾									8	9	10	11	12	14	16	18	20
2									8	9	10	11	12	14	16	18	20
2¼										9	10	11	12	14	16	18	20
2½													12	14	16	18	20
2¾														14	16	18	20
3															16	18	20
3½																18	20	24
4																18	20	24

| No. of Screw | PILOT HOLES | | | | SHANK CLEARANCE HOLES | |
| | HARD WOODS | | SOFT WOODS | | | |
	TWIST BIT (Nearest size in fractions of an inch)	DRILL Gauge No. To be used for maximum holding power	TWIST BIT (Nearest size in fractions of an inch)	DRILL Gauge No. To be used for maximum holding power	TWIST BIT (Nearest size in fractions of an inch)	DRILL Gauge No. or Letter To be used for maximum holding power
0	1/32	66	1/64	75	1/16	52
1	—	57	1/32	71	5/64	47
2	—	54	1/32	65	3/32	42
3	1/16	53	3/64	58	7/64	37
4	1/16	51	3/64	55	7/64	32
5	5/64	47	1/16	53	1/8	30
6	—	44	1/16	52	9/64	27
7	—	39	1/16	51	5/32	22
8	7/64	35	5/64	48	11/64	18
9	7/64	33	5/64	45	3/16	14
10	1/8	31	3/32	43	3/16	10
11	—	29	3/32	40	13/64	4
12	—	25	7/64	38	7/32	2
14	3/16	14	7/64	32	1/4	D
16	—	10	9/64	29	17/64	I
18	13/64	6	9/64	26	19/64	N
20	7/32	3	11/64	19	21/64	P
24	1/4	D	3/16	15	3/8	V

Concealing screws. To conceal a screw, counterbore a hole about 1/8-inch deep, slightly larger in diameter than the head diameter of the screw. For projects that are to be painted, spackle or wood-filling compound is used to fill the void. If the piece is to be given a clear finish, screw holes should be concealed with wood plugs, which can be made with a plug-cutting bit on the drill press. These bits are commonly available in two sizes to make 3/8 and 1/2-inch plugs.

To make the plugs less conspicuous, cut them from wood of the same species and orient them with the grain running in the same direction as the grain in the work. To make the plugs purposely conspicuous for a special effect, use wood of a contrasting color.

Screws may also be concealed with ornamental wood buttons which are essentially wood plugs with oval-shaped heads. They can be purchased at lumberyards or through mail-order supply houses.

Cut plugs about 1/4 inch in length from stock of the same species. Apply glue, then tap in the plugs. Sand flush with the surface after the glue has set.

Wood buttons add a nice touch to Early American style furniture. Counterbore the screw hole just deep enough so the shoulder of the button rests on the surface. Final sanding should be done prior to installing the buttons.

6
Finishing

Once the construction of your woodwork project has been completed, it will be necessary to apply a finish to improve or to alter the appearance of the wood and to protect it against moisture, soiling, and scuffing.

The beauty of wood lies in its grain and color, but in its natural state these qualities are somewhat subdued. The application of a clear finish will make the wood "come to life" by enhancing the color and accentuating the grain. All wood is not finished clear, of course. Paint also produces an attractive finish, and since it is opaque, it permits the use of less expensive ordinary wood for construction. Also, through the use of woodgraining materials, stock of lesser quality can be made to simulate finely figured wood to some extent.

The general procedure in finishing wood involves several steps: bleaching, staining, washcoating, filling, sealing, antiquing, and topcoating. Your work may not necessarily require all these operations—it will depend upon the kind of wood and the appearance desired.

BLEACHING

A bleach is used to lighten the color of wood. Since all woods do not bleach evenly, the results

A clear finish accentuates the color and grain of wood.

could be less than satisfactory, so you should be prepared for this eventuality before deciding on taking this step. A test on a scrap of wood of the same stock may not be conclusive because different parts of the same stock could react differently.

Several kinds of bleach are available. Some are two-solution types which are applied separately while others are mixed together before use and ap-

Bleaches are caustic and must be handled with care. The solution is allowed to react for about a half hour. If necessary, a second application may be made.

Apply stain with a brush or cloth in the direction of the grain, allow to penetrate, then wipe down to obtain uniform color.

plied as a single solution. The solutions are caustic, so it is necessary to wear rubber gloves and protective eye-goggles when applying the bleach. The solution is simply swabbed over the surface with a sponge and allowed to remain on the wood for the period of time specified by the manufacturer. With some formulations a neutralizing solution must be applied after the desired degree of bleaching has been obtained. A plain water rinse usually follows. The treatment raises the grain; therefore a thorough sanding is required before proceeding with further finishing.

STAINING

Many woods do not require staining. The application of a clear finish will suffice to render them at-

Always test a stain on scrap before applying it to a finished project. This sample shows how a blotchy absorption, left, can be avoided by applying a wash coat before staining, as was done on the section at right.

tractive. Stain is used to help bring out the beauty of pale and mildly figured wood or to change the tone or color of wood in general.

Oil stains. These are the conventional types and are the easiest to use. They are available ready-mixed in a wide variety of wood tones and regular colors. You can expand the color range by intermixing stains of the same type of a particular manufacture. It is not advisable to intermix between brands, however, because certain ingredients may not be compatible.

Test the stain by first applying it to a scrap of the workpiece stock. If the workpiece includes end-grain, make sure to include end-grain in the test. For a true idea of what the final effect will be, also coat the sample with the finish that will follow the stain. In addition to the color, the test will also reveal whether the stain will be absorbed evenly. If it appears blotchy, a common occurrence with softwoods, the problem can be avoided by applying a wash coat to the wood before staining. This will result in a lighter but more uniform distribution of color. You can make a wash coat by diluting 1 part of 4-pound-cut shellac with 4 parts of alcohol. End-grain absorbs stain more readily than side-grain. You can prevent this grain exposure from getting too dark by applying a wash coat of a richer mixture; that is, more shellac, less alcohol. Note that if a lacquer-based sealer is to be used subsequently, a compatible wash coat should be used.

Apply the stain with a brush or lint-free cloth, working in the direction of the grain. Don't overextend; apply it to one section or panel at a time so you can control the wiping. Allow the stain to stand for a few minutes; then wipe with a soft cloth until you get a uniform color.

The grain raising caused by water stain can be minimized by lightly sponging the surface in advance with water. When dry, the wood is sanded, then stained.

Water stains. Water stains are nonfading, penetrate evenly, and produce clear, sharp coloring. They raise the grain, thus necessitating additional sanding, and they sometimes weaken glue joints that are not water resistant. These factors tend to offset their advantages in the view of some woodworkers.

Water stains are available ready-mixed, or they may be purchased in powder form and mixed with hot water. The usual procedure is to raise the grain by wetting it with a slightly dampened sponge. After the wood has dried thoroughly, the surface is sanded with 180-grit paper.

Before applying the stain, end-grain is dampened with water to prevent it from becoming too dark. The stain is applied liberally with a brush, but it should not be overbrushed. Work on individual sections and take care not to let the stain slop over or trickle onto other surfaces before they are ready to be coated, otherwise darker streaking will result. Lightly sand with 280-grit paper after the surface has dried for twelve hours or so.

Note that nongrain-raising (NGR) stains are available, but are rather tricky to handle and results could be poor when used by other than a professional wood finisher. They have the same nonfading and brilliant color characteristics as water stains.

WASHCOATING

A washcoat is applied after staining and before filling. It serves several functions. It prevents the stain from bleeding; prevents the stain in the filler from darkening areas adjacent to the pores; allows the filler to be wiped off more readily. The washcoat is prepared by diluting the sealer, which is to be used in a proportion of about 10 parts thinner to 1 part sealer. The thinner would be the type that is compatible with the particular sealer. If it is intended to use shellac as the sealer, a wash coat can be made with a 7 to 1 dilution of 4-pound-cut shellac—that is, 7 parts alcohol to 1 part shellac. The washcoat is applied with a brush. A light sanding with 220-grit paper follows.

FILLING

Some woods such as oak, walnut, and mahogany are open grained; they have large, open pores. If a smooth finish is desired these pores must be filled with a paste-wood filler. This is a special material and should not be confused with wood-patching fillers.

Fillers are available in natural light gray or in colors to match different woods. A common practice is to buy the natural filler which can then be mixed with pigmented oil colors to achieve special effects,

Open-grain wood such as oak is filled to level the pores. Apply the paste first with the grain, then across. Work one section at a time.

A coarse cloth is used to wipe off the excess filler while packing the pores. Wipe across the grain, then rub lightly with a clean cloth in the direction of the grain.

such as lighter or darker pores. Or it can be mixed with the stain so that the staining and filling operations can be carried out at the same time.

Wood filler comes in paste form and must be diluted with turpentine to brushing consistency. Apply the filler with a stiff brush, working it into the pores. Brush first with the grain, then across. Work small areas—if the filler gets too dry before the residue is removed you will have a very difficult time of it. Allow the filler to set until it loses its glossy appearance, then wipe off the excess by rubbing across the grain with a pad of burlap or other coarse cloth. When the excess has been cleaned flush to the surface, use a clean soft cloth and wipe with the grain.

SEALING

After filling and before the application of a top-coat, the surface of the wood is given a coat of sealer to "lock" the fibers and to provide good adhesion for the topcoat material. If the work does not require staining or filling, the sealer will then be the first step in the finishing operation. This should be applied to all surfaces of the work including those out-of-view parts that will not receive a topcoat. The purpose is to seal all the wood from moisture.

The type of sealer to be used is dictated by the type of topcoat that will be applied; they must be compatible, so be sure to read the label instructions carefully. If the use of shellac is permissible, a suitable sealer can be made by diluting equal parts of 4-pound-cut shellac and alcohol. Lacquer-based sanding sealers are available ready-mixed for use under lacquer-based topcoats, or other topcoat material that is compatible. Some manufacturers recommend the use of a diluted topcoat for sealing. When applying alcohol or thinner-based sealers with a brush, work quickly and avoid overbrushing. Follow sealing with a light sanding with 220-grit paper.

Fir plywood. Due to the characteristic wide bands of both soft and dense areas in fir plywood face veneers, stains do not absorb equally when applied to the raw wood. The soft areas absorb the stain readily, but the dense areas do not, producing a garish effect. When the plywood is painted, there is a contrast in surface texture. Special penetrating sealers such as Firzite and Rez effectively minimize the problem by reducing the ability of the soft areas to absorb stain or paint. These sealers are available in both clear and white and should always be used as the first step when applying stain or paint to fir plywood unless a special effect is desired.

Fir plywood does not stain evenly unless a special penetrating sealer is applied first. Note how the "wild" grain is accentuated on wood which has not been sealed.

ANTIQUING

Antiquing is a popular form of wood finish which gives the wood an aged appearance. This is usually done in one of three ways or the three procedures may be combined. These are glazing, spattering, and distressing.

Glaze. Glaze is available in a variety of colors and wood tones as a separate item or as part of a wood-graining or antiquing kit which includes a base-coat material and sometimes a brush. The glaze is applied over the sealer coat to produce highlights and shading. It can also be applied over painted work.

Apply the glaze with a brush or cloth. Allow it to set until it loses its wet look, then wipe off the excess with a soft cloth. High spots such as moldings and carvings, and edges and central areas where an aged piece might normally have worn, are wiped fully; depressions and corners are wiped lightly to allow the buildup of a heavier deposit for the shaded appearance. This is followed with a light brushing with a soft, dry brush to blend the tones.

A realistic woodgrain effect can be achieved with the use of antiquing finish materials. The procedure is quite simple and foolproof; if you don't obtain the desired effect you simply wipe and start over.

Woodgraining starts with the application of an opaque base coat. Quick-drying latex type is the most popular.

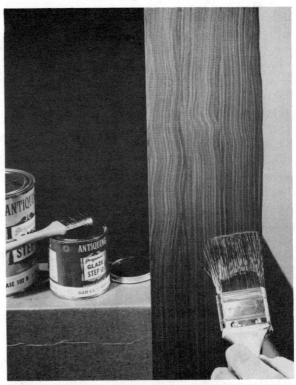

Grain pattern is produced by passing a dry brush lightly over a glaze coat, which is applied after the base has dried. An unsteady hand usually works fine.

The opaque base coat is applied and allowed to dry. If you use the latex type it will dry within an hour. This is followed with the application of the glaze. It is applied fully, then stroked lightly with a dry brush in a slightly waving motion. The result will be a grainlike effect which will very likely be quite good on the first attempt.

Spattering. This is done to simulate fly specks. A variety of materials may be used to get the random patterns of small, dark spots. Black or brown lacquer is frequently used. To obtain the specks, dip a toothbrush into the material and shake off the excess; then flick the bristles with a stick, allowing the little drops to strike the work. It is advisable to test the procedure on a piece of paper beforehand.

Distressing. A piece of furniture ages suddenly when the surfaces are purposely dented in any number of ways—striking them with a chain, nail heads,

Spattering results in a random pattern of specks.

Distressing can be done in many ways. Here a piece of chain is struck lightly to produce small dents.

a small rock, or even a bunch of keys. This can be done on the raw wood or after sealing. When the glaze is applied it is allowed to remain in the depressions. When the glaze has dried, a topcoat is applied overall.

TOPCOAT

The protective and wood-enhancing clear topcoat finish material is applied after the surface of the work has been stained, filled, and sealed. If the wood is to be left natural it is sealed, then topcoated. The wood may be finished with varnish, shellac, or lacquer, or it may be given a penetrating resin finish which eliminates the need for all the previously described steps.

Varnish should be applied with a good-quality bristle brush. It is brushed with the grain, then across it, and finally with the grain again.

VARNISH

Varnish is a relatively slow-drying finish as compared to lacquer and shellac. While all finishing demands a dust-free environment during application and drying, the slower-drying varnish is especially vulnerable to collecting dust because it remains wet longer. Therefore, whenever possible, apply varnish in a room away from the typically dusty shop. If this is not feasible, do sweep the shop well in advance to allow the dust to settle. Ideally, of course, all finishing steps should be done in a dust-free area.

There are many fine varnishes designed to enable you to achieve the exact finish and durability desired. You need only to examine the product labels to determine which is best suited to your needs. While application procedures may vary slightly between specific products, the basic method applies.

Varnish is available in high-gloss, medium-gloss and in satin finish as well as completely flat. The urethanes are the most durable of the present-day varnishes and are probably the most widely used. They are relatively fast drying and are not affected by humidity during application. They are applied in much the same way as regular varnishes with one notable exception: scuff sanding is not required between coats if they are applied within a period of about twenty-four hours.

If the wood has not been sealed, the first coat of varnish, thinned according to the manufacturer's instructions, serves as the sealer. Use a good quality brush and avoid dipping it into the varnish deeper than one-third its bristle length. Brush on a liberal coat with the grain. Before recharging the brush, stroke it lightly across the grain to remove any bubbles, then finish with very light brush-tip strokes, again with the grain.

To remove excess varnish from the brush, do not drag the bristles against the rim of the can. This causes tiny bubbles to form in the varnish and will make it almost impossible to achieve a smooth finish. Instead, tap the bristle tips lightly against the inside of the container above the surface of the liquid.

When sanding is required between coats, use a 220-grit aluminum-oxide paper after the first coat and 400-grit silicon-carbide waterproof paper after the second and subsequent coats. Lubricate the latter with soapy water. Always remove sanding dust completely before applying the next coat.

RUBBING

No matter how carefully it is applied, the final coat of varnish will very likely have dust specks or pimples which mar its finished appearance. If a tough high-gloss type was used it may have too much gloss. These conditions can be corrected by a final rubbing and polishing with special abrasives. Rubbing should not be attempted until the final coat has been allowed to harden for about one week.

Specially prepared compounds are available for rubbing the topcoat, or you can make your own using pumice powder and oil.

SHELLAC CUT DILUTIONS

Stock Cut	Desired Cut	Shellac Volume	Alcohol Volume
4-pound	1-pound	1 quart	2 quart
4-pound	2-pound	1 quart	1½ pint
4-pound	3-pound	1 quart	½ pint

When ready, mix a paste of powdered pumice stone and motor oil or machine oil, then rub with a padded soft cloth. Rub with the grain using moderate pressure. This operation will leave the surface smooth to the touch but cloudy or dull in appearance.

To restore a high luster (not a high gloss), a second rubbing is required using a still finer abrasive. Mix a second paste of powdered rottenstone and oil and rub again. After the surface has been polished to the desired luster wipe off all paste and oil using clean, soft cloths.

SHELLAC

While it is not waterproof and is affected by alcohol and strong soaps, shellac is frequently used as a topcoat finish because it is easy to apply and fast drying. It should never be used on tabletops however.

Shellac is available in its natural orange color and in a white bleached form. The orange shellac imparts an amber tone to the wood while the white has very little visible effect. Shellac is usually sold in a 4-pound cut. This means that 4 pounds of shellac flakes were dissolved in a gallon of alcohol to make the solution. This is considered a stock solution and is never applied full strength. For use as a topcoat, dilute a 4-pound cut with an equal amount of alcohol. Brush it on in full coats with long strokes. Work rapidly and avoid overbrushing but be sure to overlap each stroke slightly. Allow the first coat to dry thoroughly. In good weather this may require only thirty minutes or so.

When the shellac has dried hard, sand it lightly with 180-grit paper, then apply a second coat mixed slightly richer, using less alcohol and more shellac. Follow with a light sanding using 320-grit paper, then rub the surface with a ⁵⁄₀ pad of steel wool charged with paste wax. If a third coat of shellac is required, apply it before the wax treatment.

LACQUER

Regular lacquer is a fine, durable topcoat material that is applied by spraying. It should never be applied with a brush because it dries extremely fast; it would begin to dry even before a normal brush stroke were completed. A slower-drying brushing lacquer is available, however, that also produces a very good finish. Make sure to use a lacquer product

Three coats of lacquer will produce a tough, durable finish.

A shellac topcoat is usually finished off by rubbing lightly with fine steel wool charged with paste wax.

that is compatible with the stain, filler, and sealer; otherwise these precoatings may bleed and soften.

When coating a large workpiece, it is generally advisable to thin the lacquer. Brush it on in full wet coats without excessive brushing. Scuff sanding is not usually required between coats because the new coat slightly softens the previous one. But a light sanding may be in order to level high spots or to shave off dust particles. Three coats usually build up a very good surface. Brushing lacquer is available in high gloss, satin, and flat. For a rich luster, lacquer is usually rub-polished; however, there are many satin-finish products that dry to a fine hand-rubbed appearance without the need for rubbing.

PENETRATING RESIN

Penetrating resin is a one-step, clear finishing material. It penetrates deeply into the wood to harden the fibers and provides a protective coat that is resistant to water, alcohol, heat, and abrasion. It brings out the beauty of the grain and color while retaining the natural texture of the wood.

The application is quite easy. The resin is brushed onto the surface generously and allowed to soak in for a half hour or so. Additional resin is added to saturate the wood fully and is then wiped off after a short waiting period as prescribed by the manufacturer's instructions. The treatment hardens the wood not only on the surface but below it as well.

The resin is available in clear and in several wood-tone colors. Penetrating oil finishes are also available, but they do not provide the same hardening and lasting protection as do the resins.

PART II

STEP-BY-STEP PROJECTS

7
Spoon Rack

This is a good project for warming up with some basic hand-tool operations, particularly if you're relatively new at woodworking. The steps involve several elementary but important skills that you should develop.

As you attempt other simple projects that follow you will pick up more hand-tool skills. While all the projects including this one can be done easier and faster with power tools, it nevertheless is advisable to work with hand tools on occasion because every now and then the need will arise.

The rack is made of ½-inch pine stock, an easy-working softwood that takes finish nicely. A board 6 by 48 inches will yield all the pieces needed with minimal waste if you follow the cutting plan shown.

Start by laying out the rectangular pieces on the board, then make a full-size drawing of the side piece on paper. Use the square grid method to duplicate the curves. Cut out the pattern with a knife or scissors, then trace the pattern on the wood. Also draw and transfer the curves for the front and back.

Note that the sides are attached to the back and bottom pieces. It is important that both the back and bottom be cut exactly the same width to insure a good fit of the parts. For this reason the back and bottom pieces adjoin each other in the layout so that

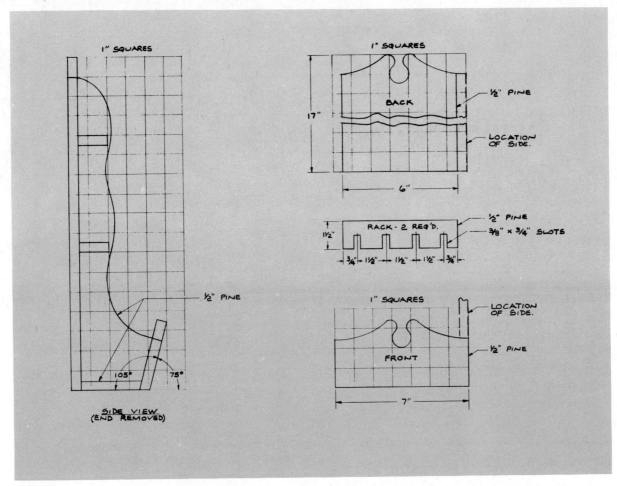

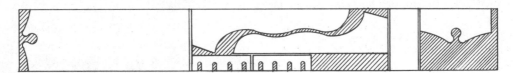

Cutting plan for spoon rack. Double lines allow for saw-kerf waste.

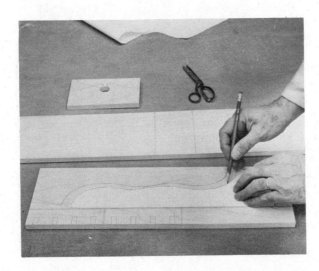

1. Cut out full-size patterns and trace the cutting lines onto the stock. Draw double lines on the straight parts that adjoin to indicate saw kerf.

a single saw cut along the side will eventually produce two pieces with the same dimension. Bear in mind when laying out pieces alongside each other that the saw cut (kerf) removes stock in the form of sawdust equal to the thickness of the blade, so allow for this by drawing double cutting lines.

As the front edge of the bottom piece requires a slight bevel, the first step is to make a beveled crosscut so you come up with a board containing the back and bottom. To make a reasonably accurate bevel cut, try this: Adjust a sliding T bevel to 105 degrees. Clamp the board to the workbench and rest the T bevel close to, but not touching, the cutting line. Use a crosscut saw tilted slightly sideways so it is parallel to the guide. Saw slowly on the line, keeping the saw always parallel to the blade of the T bevel.

Next, cut the board to width with a ripsaw. Smooth and true the sawed edge with a block plane. Adjust the plane for light cuts and check squareness with a try square. When this is done you can make the crosscut to separate the back piece from the bottom. This time you want a perpendicular cut so a try square could be used for a guide if needed. Set it up the same way as the T bevel.

The coping saw is used to make the fancy cuts. For a shortcut you can predrill holes for the small-radius curves on the front and back pieces. To make a clean hole, be sure to back up the work with a piece of scrap wood and clamp both together firmly, otherwise the emerging drill bit will splinter the back surface of the work.

Clamp the work firmly to a table or bench. Insert the coping-saw blade with the teeth pointing downwards toward the handle and make the contoured cuts, approaching the drilled hole from both directions.

Again, use the coping saw to cut the side pieces. When the frame of the saw gets in the way, you simply rotate both blade clamps identically to swing the frame for clearance.

Cut the two strips for the spoon shelves to length, making sure they match the width of the back. Since these pieces are so small, a smooth-cutting backsaw can be used to make the crosscuts. Note that these parts could not originally be cut from the same piece together with the back and bottom because the grain direction differs. The reason for this is that, whenever feasible, end grain should be the smallest dimension of a piece because it is weaker, more difficult to tool, and visually less attractive than edge grain.

The drill is used again to form the backs of the notches for the spoons. After the holes are drilled, use a backsaw to make tangent cuts to drop out the waste.

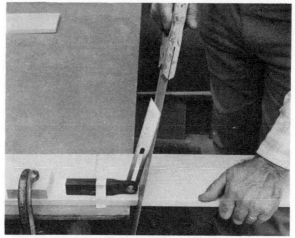

2. Tape a T bevel in place to guide the saw for the bevel cut. Note that the saw seems to be out of alignment—this is due to the camera angle.

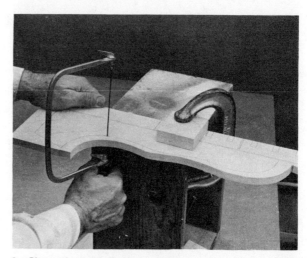

3. Clamp the work firmly to cut the curves with the coping saw. The teeth should point down.

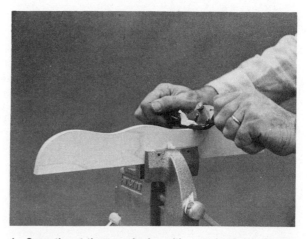

4. Smooth out the saw ripples with a spokeshave. Change direction of stroke as required so the cut is always "with" the grain.

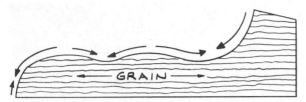

5. Correct spokeshave directions relative to grain are indicated by the arrows.

6. Bore holes to form the backs of the slots, then make tangent saw cuts to drop out the waste.

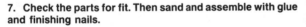

7. Check the parts for fit. Then sand and assemble with glue and finishing nails.

When all parts have been cut to size, there still remains the job of smoothing out the coping-saw ripples and rounding the curved edges. The appropriate tool to use for this is the spokeshave. It functions much like a plane with the exception that it is designed to follow curves. The important thing to remember in using this tool is that you must always draw it *with* the grain, otherwise it will skip and dig into the edge. The accompanying diagram shows how to use the tool.

Smooth out all irregularities by making flat-on cuts. Then make repeated light cuts with alternately changing angles to achieve a nearly rounded edge. Final rounding is obtained by sanding with a felt-padded block. Sand all interior flat surfaces before assembly.

Assemble the parts with glue and 1¼-inch finishing nails in this order: Attach the shelves to the back by nailing through the back. Do the same with the bottom. Attach the sides. The front goes on last. When the glue has set, sand the outside surfaces and ease all sharp corners after setting the nails and filling the holes. Use the block plane to bevel the bottom edge of the front flush with the base.

Apply finish of your choice, such as several coats of white or orange shellac, clear varnish, or paint. If you want to stain the piece, the stain should be applied before the shellac or varnish.

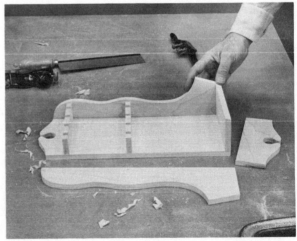

8

Book Cradle

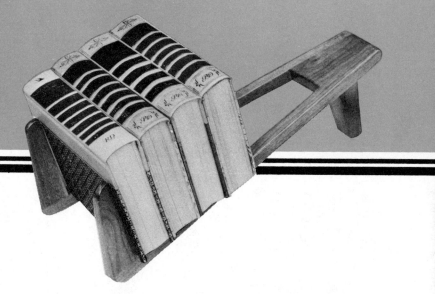

This is a simple hand tool project that you can complete in an hour or two. The square stock for the runners may be obtained readymade or you can rip your own from a ¾-inch-thick board. Make all the saw cuts slightly outside the layout lines, then smooth the surfaces with a block plane. Use white glue and 1¼-inch finishing nails for assembly. Set the nail heads below the surface and fill the depressions with wood-filling compound. Sand all the sharp corners and finish as desired.

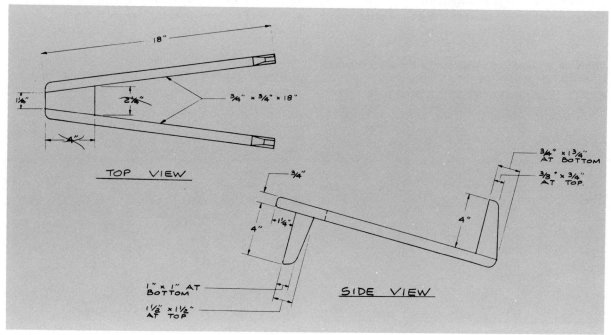

1. Use a fine-tooth backsaw to cut the tapers. Saw slightly outside the line to allow for planing.

3. Grip the parts in a vise and start two nails. Vise jaw must be smooth for this; if not, protect the work with scrap wood.

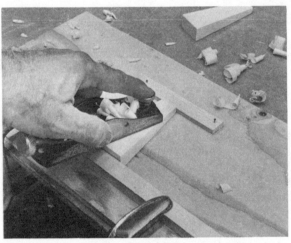

2. Smooth the sawed surfaces with a block plane.

4. Remove the work from the vise for gluing.

Cleats on a board are used to hold the small, irregular-shaped pieces for planing and sanding.

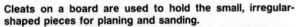

5. Support the far end level while nailing the uprights.

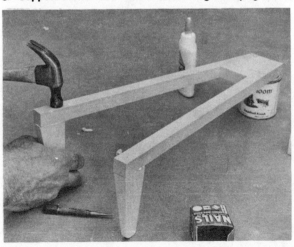

9

Cookbook/Recipe Holder

This handsome shelf will serve nicely to keep cookbooks handy while adding a decorative touch to your kitchen. The roomy drawer can store a sizeable collection of recipes.

Assembly is done with glued and nailed butt joints—the simplest type of construction—so you should be able to complete the project in several hours, particularly if you work with power tools. The steps outlined here require a table saw, jigsaw (or sabre saw) and router. If you're just starting out with these tools, the project is a good one with which to break in.

All the parts except the drawer interior are cut from ½-inch solid pine or poplar stock. The drawer sides and bottom are made of ¼-inch plywood. The front is added-on pine.

The choice of a table-saw blade is the first consideration. If available, select a combination hollow-ground, smooth-cutting blade as this will produce an extremely smooth edge requiring no further tooling. Since it is a combination type, it will be suitable for both crosscutting and ripping operations.

As with the spoon rack project, the sides are attached to the inside pieces; therefore the latter must all be cut the same size. In all woodworking, regardless of the size of a construction, you should always

find a way to make matched multiple cuts. The table saw certainly makes the task relatively easy provided you use it properly.

If all the straight cuts for this project could be made by using the rip fence, repeat sizing would be automatic. However, two types of guided cuts are involved here: ripping against the fence and crosscutting with the miter gage. A mixture of the two types of cuts is common in table-saw operations.

Let's start with the crosscuts for the upper and lower cross members and the apron strip. If your miter gage has an adjustable stop rod, you need only to set it up for the desired dimension. Resting the ends of the boards against the stop will permit cutting a number of pieces to exact length. Lacking this

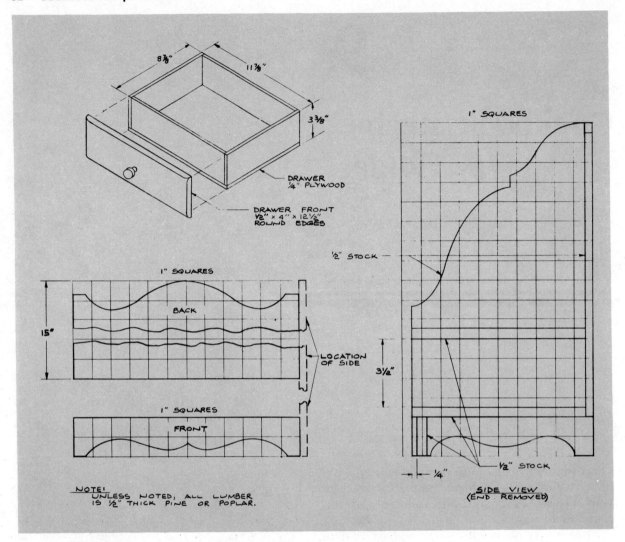

8⅜"   11⅞"

3⅜"

DRAWER
¼" PLYWOOD

DRAWER FRONT
½" × 4" × 12½"
ROUND EDGES

1" SQUARES

BACK

15"

LOCATION
OF SIDE

1" SQUARES

FRONT

NOTE:
UNLESS NOTED, ALL LUMBER
IS ½" THICK PINE OR POPLAR.

1" SQUARES

½" STOCK

3½"

¼"

½" STOCK

SIDE VIEW
(END REMOVED)

useful accessory you can use another method—a stop block clamped to the saw table. The workpiece is held against the miter gage and the end positioned against the stop. This is a simple, effective method, but there is a caution to observe. Always place the stop block well forward of the blade so that the work is clear of the stop before it contacts the blade. Otherwise, the stop can cause dangerous binding and kickback.

Now that you have the cross members cut to length it will be necessary to set up the rip fence to cut the back piece to matching width. Eyeing a pencil mark on the work against the blade can lead to error. There is a more positive method: Place one of the previously crosscut pieces against the saw blade then simply slide the rip fence up to the sample and

lock it in place. Sometimes the fence shifts slightly during the locking action. You can check the final adjustment by sliding the workpiece through (with power off)—it should lightly brush against the teeth. Make the cut to yield the back panel.

The side pieces are ripped to a width equal to that of the cross members plus the thickness of the back, which is ½ inch. Follow the same procedure for setting the rip fence, with the exception that you add a ½-inch strip between the sizing piece and the fence.

The foregoing procedures may seem excessively detailed for sawing a few pieces for a relatively simple project, but the methods can be applied to other projects, regardless of size.

Cutting the curves is next. You can do this with

1.   A stop block assures crosscutting several pieces to exact length when using the miter gage. Locate the stop so the work clears it before contacting the saw blade.

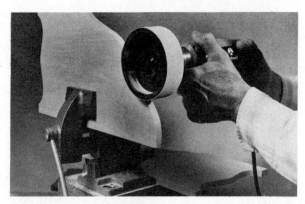

4.   Sand out all irregularities before the next step.

2.   One of the cross members is used as a guide for setting the rip fence to cut the back panel to the same dimension. Butt the sample against the blade, then move the fence up to the other edge.

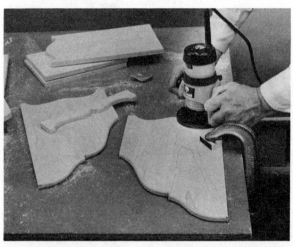

5.   A router with a quarter-round cutter is used to round the edges. Adjust the depth of cut so a small flat remains on the edge. This will provide a surface for the cutter pilot when the second cut is made on the other side of the work.

3.   Cut the curves with a scroll saw or by hand with a coping or sabre saw.

6.   Scraps clamped along the sides of the back panel will prevent splitting the edges. The edges must be kept flat for the butt joint.

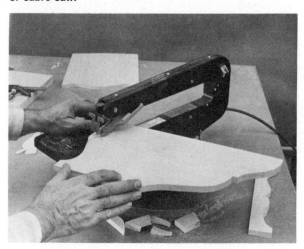

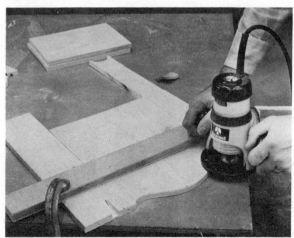

a jigsaw or portable sabre saw. Use a smooth-cutting, fine-tooth blade which will cut pine easily. A large-tooth blade with heavy set will leave a rough edge. Any imperfections in the curved cuts can be smoothed with a drum sander or by hand.

A router with a 3/16-inch quarter-round bit is used to round the edges. The bottom edges of the apron and sides as well as the top of the back are rounded only on the front.

The drawer is made like a box. The four sides are butted together, glued and nailed. The bottom is attached to the four sides. The pine front is made separately and added to the box.

Sand all exposed surfaces then assemble as follows: Attach the apron to the drawer shelf, then the back to both shelves and finally add the sides. Use white glue and 1¼-inch finishing nails. Set the nail heads, fill the voids, and apply finish.

Sometimes warped boards pose a problem. To straighten them, cut kerfs on out-of-sight surfaces with a table or radial-arm saw.

Note how a gentle finger pressure readily straightens the boards. The bottoms of the shelves and the back panel were treated in this manner.

10
Coffee Mill

You can brew a cup of really good coffee with beans freshly ground in this charming mill.

The mechanism is readily available from various mail-order sources and needs only a little box with a drawer to house it.

Construction of the box and drawer differs from the previous project because rabbet joints are used instead of butt joints.

Although this is a rather elementary project, it may be of interest to you to learn how the design evolved. It was simply a matter of appearance rather than utility.

The first consideration was the choice of wood thickness. Since the mill hardware is made to be attached to the top edge of the box with two #8 wood screws, this dictated the use of at least ½-inch stock.

If butt joints were used for the sides of the box and the drawer, with the drawer front added on as in the preceding project, both the drawer front and the end sections of the box would appear much too thick and out of proportion. The end rabbet provided a simple solution.

To make the box rip a 16-inch-long board to 4¼ inches width then crosscut to obtain the two sides and back. Cut another piece 4⅜ inches wide for the front. The extra ⅛ inch will allow for kerf waste when this piece is cut into two parts to obtain both the box and drawer front.

A router could be used to cut the rabbets but, due to the smallness of the pieces and the deep cuts required, a table saw with dado head would be better suited. Make the cuts with the blade set for a ⅜-inch deep rabbet with the fence positioned 4¾ inches from the inside edge of the blade. Use a saw blade and cut the front panel into two pieces for the box and drawer fronts. Set up for a cut again and increase the width of the rabbets on the drawer front. Cut a square piece for the base and round the corners by sanding or sawing. The drawer sides are attached to the rabbet shoulder on the front and butted to the back strip.

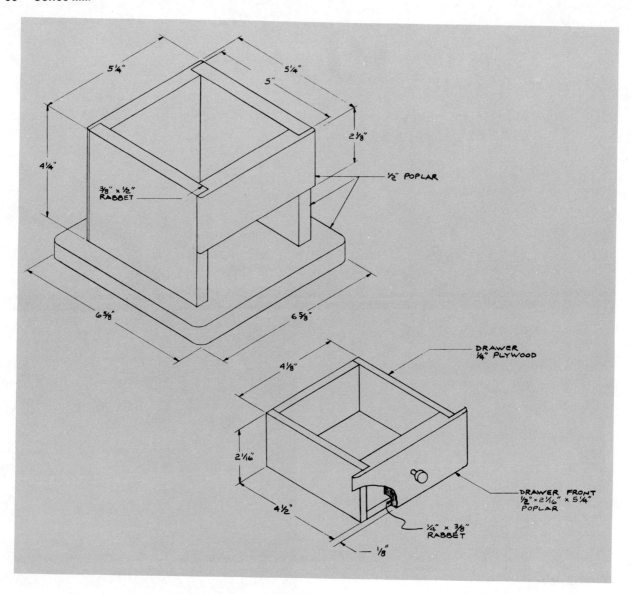

5¼"   5¼"   5"   2⅛"   ½" POPLAR

4¼"   ⅜" x ½" RABBET

6⅜"   6⅜"

DRAWER ¼" PLYWOOD

4⅛"

2¹⁄₁₆"   DRAWER FRONT ½" x 2¹⁄₁₆" x 5¼" POPLAR

4½"   ¼" x ⅜" RABBET

⅛"

1. Crosscut the box sides to length using the miter gage and a clamped stop to assure obtaining similar dimensions.

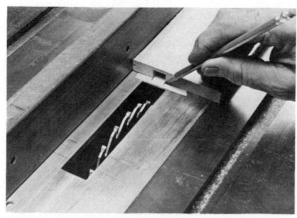

2. An adjustable dado head blade rests at an angle; thus it is not possible to measure precisely where it will make its cut by using a rule against the teeth. The solution is to make a test cut in scrap wood, back off the piece, and mark the location of the cut on a piece of tape affixed to the saw table.

4. *Safety tip:* Use a block of wood to push the work along the fence. This block will help to keep the workpiece squarely against the fence. Also, note how one finger straddles the fence to limit lateral hand movement.

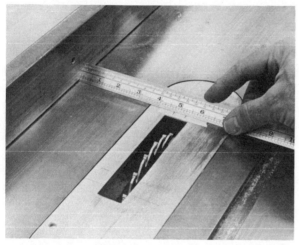

3. To make the rabbet cuts for the front and back members, simply measure from the inside mark and set the rip fence accordingly.

5. The front piece is ripped in two to produce the front for the drawer. This is then rabbeted again, slightly wider, to allow space for the drawer sides.

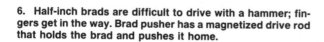

6. Half-inch brads are difficult to drive with a hammer; fingers get in the way. Brad pusher has a magnetized drive rod that holds the brad and pushes it home.

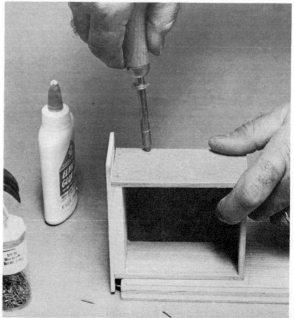

7. The parts ready for assembly.

8. The coffee-grinding mechanism attaches to the top edge with two screws.

11
Wall Cabinet

This is a short-cut project that utilizes a ready-made shutter for the door. While the spindle is an easy one to turn, it too can be purchased ready-made as was the one shown here, if you don't have a lathe.

The sides and cross members are made of ¾-inch pine and assembled with butt joints. The back is ¼-inch fir plywood which is inset in a rabbet.

The rabbet joint is generally used in preference to the ordinary butt joint when greater holding power is desired. In this case, however, it is used simply to permit attaching the back panel with its side edges concealed. The alternative would be to butt the ¼-inch edges against the sides, but this would prove to be a poor substitute for the rabbet due to the difficulty of accurately driving nails into the thin plywood edges.

Begin construction with the sides. Rip the boards to width, then cut the curved shapes at the ends. The rabbet can be cut with a variety of tools: the circular saw, dado head, router, shaper, or jointer. Since the rabbet does not extend the full length of the sides, you have the choice of stopping the cut short of the end or running the cut completely through and filling the void with a filler strip of wood. If you want to make a stopped rabbet, you'll have to square out the radial kerf at the inside corner with a chisel.

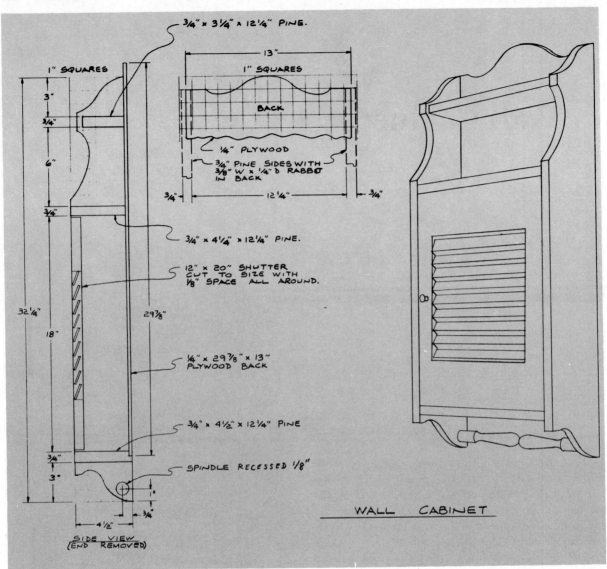

3/4" × 3 1/4" × 12 1/4" PINE.

1" SQUARES

3"

3/4"

6"

3/4"

32 1/4"

18"

3/4"

3"

4 1/2"

3/4"

SIDE VIEW
(END REMOVED)

13"

1" SQUARES

BACK

1/4" PLYWOOD

3/4" PINE SIDES WITH
3/8" W × 1/4" D RABBET
IN BACK

3/4"   12 1/4"   3/4"

3/4" × 4 1/4" × 12 1/4" PINE.

12" × 20" SHUTTER
CUT TO SIZE WITH
1/8" SPACE ALL AROUND.

29 7/8"

1/4" × 29 7/8" × 13"
PLYWOOD BACK

3/4" × 4 1/2" × 12 1/4" PINE

SPINDLE RECESSED 1/8"

WALL   CABINET

With any of the above-mentioned tools except the circular saw, the rabbet cut is made in one pass; two are required with the saw. See the illustrations.

Measure from the front edge of the board to the rabbet edge to determine the width of the cross members; then rip them to size.

To obtain an accurate dimension for the back panel width, take the measurement directly from the work: stand the two sides on their front edges against the upper and lower shelves.

When the back has been cut, sand all the pieces and assemble with glue and 2-inch finishing nails in this order: attach one side to the three cross members and spindle. Turn the work over and add the other side. The back goes on last, held with glue and 1-inch nails.

Trim the shutter door to size so it will fit with a ⅛-inch clearance all around. Attach the hinges to the door, then put the door in place on the cabinet, resting on two cardboard shims, to obtain equal spacing at the top and bottom. Mark the hinge position on the cabinet side with a sharp pencil. Now you can remove one of the hinges from the door for use as a template. Hold it in place on the cabinet side and mark the screw hole locations. Drill pilot holes for the screws and install the door.

The finish is optional, but since three varieties of wood are used, a pigmented woodgrain or solid-color paint may be preferable to a clear finish. The cabinet could be dark stained, of course, but the "wild grain" of the fir-plywood back would nevertheless show through in contrast to the pine.

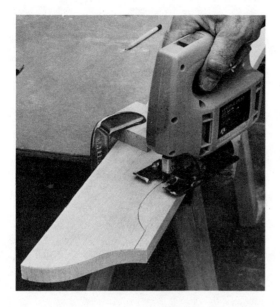

1. Clamp the side firmly to a workbench and use a saber saw with a hollow-ground blade to cut the contours.

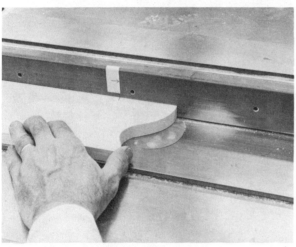

2. Cut a stopped rabbet for the back panel. Mark the rip fence to indicate where the blade cut ends. Also, mark the work to indicate where to stop the cut. Set the blade projection and cut to the point where the two marks meet.

3. Reposition the mark onto the saw table and repeat the step to make the edgewise cut. Note that normally the edge cut is made first when cutting a through rabbet, but in this case it doesn't matter since edge remains intact at rear.

4. Remove waste and square corner with chisel.

5. Bore the holes for the spindle. Glue and nail one side to the shelves. Start the nails on the second side panel, then remove it and apply the glue.

6. Insert the spindle, align the nail points with the started holes, drive in the nails. Check the assembly for squareness. If it is out of true, install the back panel before the glue sets. This will bring it into square.

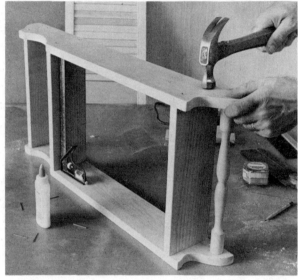

7. To hang the door, attach the hinges to its edge first. Insert shims to obtain equal spacing at the top and bottom. Mark the hinge location on the side panel and mark the screw hole centers. Remove and use a hinge as a marking template.

12
Bentwood Planters

Unlike typical bentwood constructions which require involved procedures such as kerfing, laminating, or steaming, these novel planters utilize flexible plywood to achieve their graceful shapes.

This project entails some straight and curved sawing and simple assembly with glue and nails using a regular hammer and a brad pusher. Aligning and fitting the shelves to the irregular configurations could be tricky, but won't be, if you follow the procedures outlined.

The curvatures in the plywood are produced by the shape of the end block(s), in the case of the tear-drop and boat-profiles. The round planter is made simply by joining the overlapped ends.

The wood used for this project is ⅛-inch poplar plywood (some lumber dealers refer to it as "skin"). Although it is flexible in both directions, this wood bends more readily parallel to the grain of the outer plies. Therefore, correct grain orientation is necessary to make the relatively small bends.

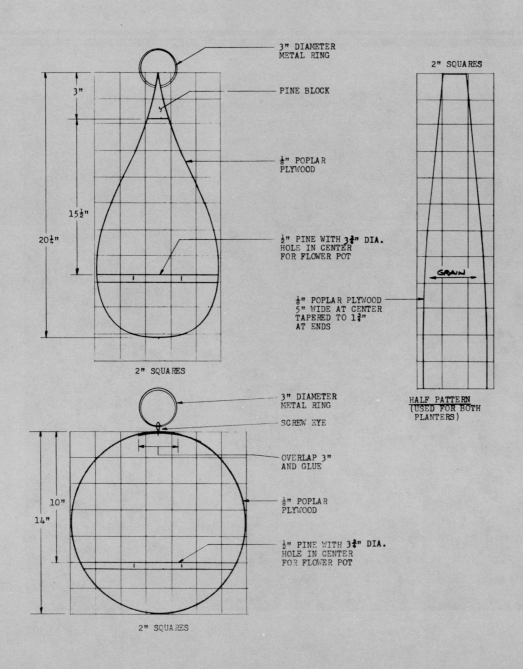

If you plan to make all three of the planters, start by cutting three pieces of plywood to the overall sizes indicated in the plan. Draw the outlines by using a flexible piece of wood as a curved rule. A helper can hold the rule or you can drive three nails into the work table, positioned to hold the bowed stick.

A variety of saws can be used to cut the plywood, including the band saw, jigsaw or sabre saw. Whichever tool you use, select a fine-tooth blade to prevent splintering along the edges. If you elect to use the sabre saw, be sure to work with ample support under and close to the cutting line to prevent the plywood from bouncing.

The sawed edges should be sanded smooth while the wood is flat. Sandwich it between two boards in a vise so the ends don't whip about or deflect. Also sand the surfaces before assembly.

The end blocks are cut from clear pine or other softwood stock. If you have wood of ample size you

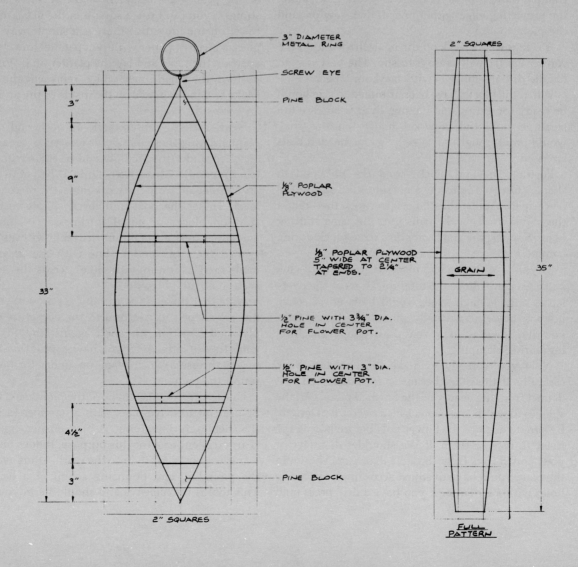

can make the blocks from single pieces. Otherwise glue up several pieces of ¾-inch stock.

The tear-drop end block has two concave (inward) curves and the other blocks have convex curves. These outlines must be cut precisely to the indicated shape otherwise the plywood will not form symmetrically.

The fronts and backs of the blocks require shaping as well, but this is not done until after the side profiles have been cut. Use the band saw or sabre saw to make the cuts. If you use the latter, work with a blade of sufficient length to penetrate the thickness of the block. Also, the blade should have deep-set teeth. A hollow-ground, smooth-cutting blade with no set should be avoided because it will drift when cutting through thick stock, resulting in a lopsided edge.

To determine how much to trim off the fronts and backs of the blocks you'll have to make a dry assembly. Assemble the tear-drop unit by holding the ends of the plywood onto the block with a C clamp. You can use the curved cut-off scraps to cushion the clamp jaws so they don't mar the wood. Trace along the projecting edge with a pencil, then saw or sand the piece to size.

A clamp won't work on the boat-shaped unit; the convex curves will cause it to slip. The best way to handle dry assembly is with masking tape.

When the blocks have been trimmed to size you'll be ready for gluing and nailing. Brad heads are too small to hold the plywood under tension (they would pop through) so ¾ × 17 gauge headed nails are used.

Position the end block, bend the plywood to shape, start two nails on each side then spring the piece apart. Apply glue to both surfaces, then rejoin the parts, inserting the nails into the same starting holes. Support the end firmly on a scrap block during hammering.

The ends of the circular piece are joined with glue and a C clamp. Since the total thickness at the overlap is only ¼ inch, nails would have no effective holding power. Two nails should be driven temporarily, however, to prevent the overlap from shifting during clamping.

Now you're ready to make the shelves. Work carefully at this stage because a lopsided shelf will detract from the beauty of the finished piece. Cut the shelves to width and about 1 inch oversize in length. Be sure to acquire the flower pots before boring the holes to receive them. If the shoulder diameter of your pots differs from the hole diameters shown in the plan, you'll have to adjust accordingly. Bore the holes with a fly cutter if you have a drill press (and

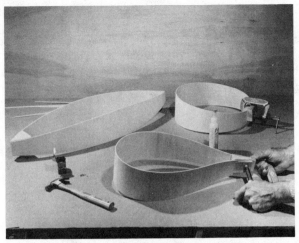

1. **Curved cut-off scraps are used as clamping pads for the concave end block of the tear-drop unit.**

cutter); otherwise use a sabre, jig, or coping saw. Drill a blade-entry hole first to start the saw cut.

Guidelines for positioning the shelves and applying the glue must be marked on the inside surfaces of the plywood. Inasmuch as the surfaces are not straight, you can't use a square in the usual manner to set off the lines. But there is a simple way. First, place a piece of paper with two parallel lines ½ inch apart on the table and lay the planter on it. Visually position the ruled lines, which represent the shelf. Make two index marks on the inside of the plywood, on each side.

Next, make a center mark on each end of the planter. Using these marks for reference, set a block of wood under the shallow end of the circular and tear drop units. Check with a rule. When both marks are equidistant from the work table, the piece will be level. To set the boat unit level, simply rest both ends on blocks of equal thickness. To draw the guidelines, rest a square on the table with its blade against the work and in line with the previously made marks. Continue the lines across the interior surface of the plywood.

Note that the ends of the shelves are not straight but are shaped to conform to the curvature of the plywood. Position the shelf against the edge and mark the cut-offs. After you have sawed the shelves to length, use a block plane or sander (or both) to round the ends.

Due to the irregular shape of the planters, it would be difficult to drive nails with a hammer to secure the shelves during gluing. A brad pusher, however, is an excellent tool for this purpose. It does just that —pushes a brad firmly into the work—thus avoiding the pounding and bouncing action of a hammer. This tool is inexpensive and should be in your tool

Procedure for marking shelf locations: Place planter flat on table. Prop up end with block of wood so planter is held in horizontal position. Place ruled paper under unit at desired shelf location. Make index marks on the inside surface of the plywood at points X. Then rest square on table, aligned with mark, and draw the guidelines.

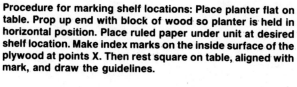

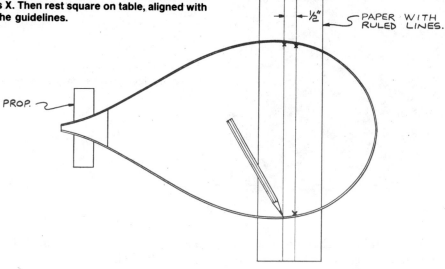

½"

PAPER WITH RULED LINES.

PROP.

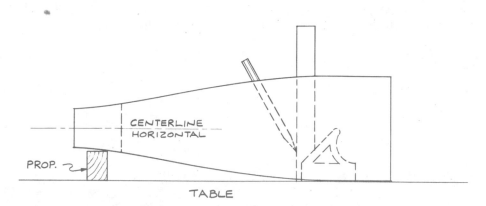

CENTERLINE HORIZONTAL

PROP.

TABLE

2. Planter is propped up level by measuring from end centers to tabletop. Square is then used in this manner to mark the shelf location.

3. Trace curvature of inside edge onto paper.

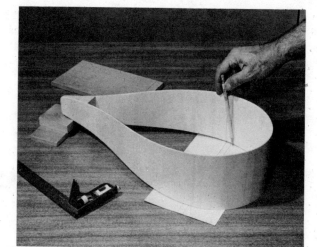

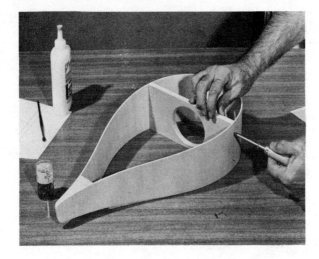

4.   A brad pusher is used to drive the brads smoothly into the curved sides. Headed nails affix the end blocks.

kit, for it will prove useful for delicate nailing jobs. To operate, you simply insert a brad in the end. When you push the handle, a rod smoothly slides the nail into the work.

To set the shelves, apply glue (sparingly) to both surfaces, then press in 1-inch brads. Since there is no tension at these points, the small-headed brads will not pop through.

Hang the planters with strings and apply two coats of paint. Then hang them with lamp-hanging hardware, which is available at most hardware stores and home centers.

13

Foul-Weather Bench

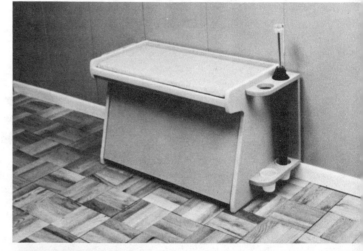

In the typical home, rain shoes or boots are usually stored in a mismatched heap at the bottom of a closet while dripping umbrellas find temporary storage hanging from doorknobs.

This functional bench will solve the problem. Roomy compartments store the footgear neatly in pairs and, when opened, the hinged front forms an inclined foot rest which permits shoeing up in comfort. Umbrellas stand in racks on each side of the seat.

A standard piano bench cushion is used to pad the seat and durable 9-ounce plastic drinking cups serve as pans for the umbrellas. The cups selected should be of the type with a pronounced rim at the top which will prevent them from sliding through the holes.

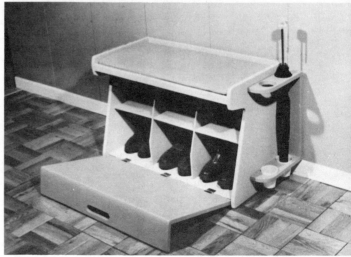

Construction requires clean, straight cuts for the butt joints as well as for the edge half-laps for the nested compartments, similar to the treatment for the swivel book rack. While a variety of power saws can be used, the one least likely to be chosen by most woodworkers, the sabre saw, was used to do all the cutting for the bench shown, with the exception of the holes in the umbrella racks, which were made with a hole saw.

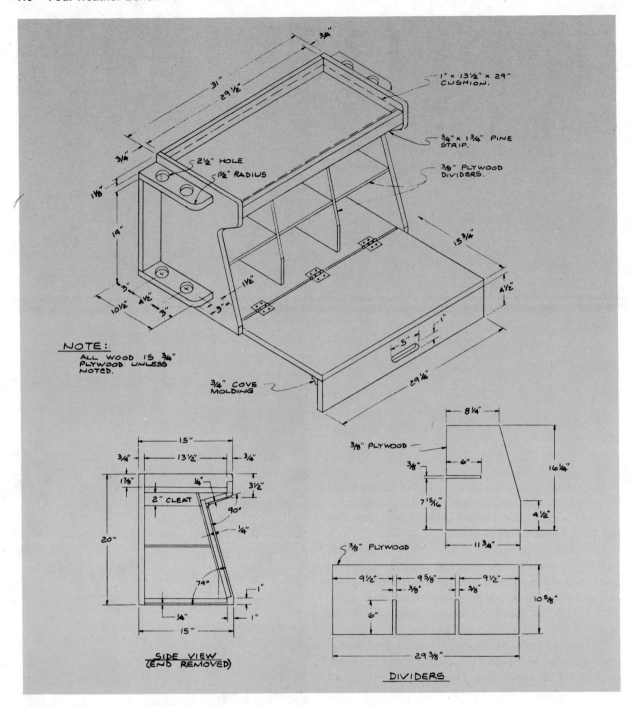

CUTTING THE SIDES

To get started, cut two pieces of wood 15″ × 20″ for the sides; you'll learn shortly how to guide the saw. Note that the slanted portions are indicated in degrees of angle. To lay out the angled lines you use a protractor and a 90-degree triangle as follows: Make two pencil lines about 6 inches long on the 20-inch side; one mark 3½ inches from the top, the other 1 inch from the bottom. Place the protractor base on the latter line, positioned so its center mark is at the edge of the board. Make a pencil mark opposite the 74-degree graduation. Place a rule on this mark and the zero point and draw the slanted line.

1. This shows how a protractor and 90-degree triangle are used to lay out the angled profile of the bench side.

2. A straightedged strip of wood tack-nailed to the work guides the sabre saw for precise cutting. The predrilled hole forms the inside corner radius.

Next, place the triangle on the slanted line, positioned so its second edge intersects the 3½-inch mark at the edge of the board. Draw the line. Complete the layout of the side by drawing in the corner radius. Lay out the cutting lines for the other parts.

The bench is made of ¾-inch plywood and the compartment insert with ⅜-inch stock. Check the actual thickness of the ⅜-inch plywood before you lay out the cutting lines for the slots. The width of the slots should exactly match the thickness of the plywood. Don't assume the thickness to be precisely ⅜ inch because variations do sometimes occur in plywood.

To obtain straight, square cuts for good butt joints the sabre-saw base must be set at a perfect right-angle to the blade. If your saw has a fixed blade, you'll have no problem in this respect. Saws with adjustable tilting bases must be checked and adjusted carefully before use. You can't rely on the angle-setting scale for precise work because the graduations are too coarse, and at best, only approximate. The best way to check for a true 90-degree cut is as follows: Make a cut through a scrap of wood. Turn the cut-off piece upside down and butt the edge against the edge of the original piece. Do this on a flat surface. The edges will match perfectly if the cut is square. A space at the top or bottom indicates the need for an adjustment.

Bore a 1-inch-diameter hole tangent to the two lines to produce the inside corner curve in the side panel. To make the straight cuts you simply attach a straightedged strip of wood parallel to the line to be cut, offset by the distance between the saw base edge and the blade. Although the guide can be secured with clamps, you may find it quicker and easier to hold it in place with partly driven 1½-inch finishing nails. The tiny holes made in the workpiece are later filled with compound. Saw in both directions to the corner hole.

A sabre saw will track properly through ¾-inch stock when guided by a straightedge so long as it isn't forced and provided two other conditions are met: the blade's drive rod must be free of play and the blade used should be of sufficient thickness so it doesn't whip or flex.

The use of a smooth-cutting, hollow-ground blade will substantially reduce the amount of sanding required on the exposed edges. But bear in mind that this type of blade is more vulnerable to distorting and cutting out of square than a blade with set teeth, particularly if the saw is forced or if there is too much play in the blade drive rod.

UMBRELLA RACK

The round holes for the umbrella rack are made with a 2½-inch-diameter hole saw chucked into a portable drill (or a drill press if you have one). Since these pieces are relatively small, it is advisable to lay them out in a group of four on one board measuring 6⅛" × 21⅛". When all the holes have been cut, the four pieces are sawed apart. The extra ⅛" allows for kerf waste.

In order to avoid having the waste disc becoming jammed in the saw when the hole is cut through, it is advisable to cut only about halfway through, then turn the work over and complete the cut from the other side. This will leave part of the waste exposed for easy removal.

The hand slot is made by drilling two 1-inch-

3. Cut two side panels and add a cleat near the top of each to reinforce the butt joint with which the seat is attached.

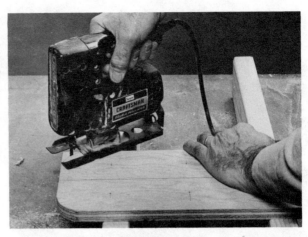

5. Cut outside corner curves freehand with sabre saw.

4. Elaborate joints are not needed on this project; the main parts are assembled with glue, nails, and butt joints.

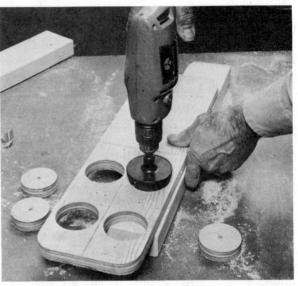

6. Use a hole saw to cut out the round openings for the umbrella rack.

diameter holes 5 inches apart, then sawing two cuts from hole to hole, tangent to the edges.

If you have a router, use it with a ¼-inch corner-rounding bit to round all exposed corners. Otherwise ease the corners by sanding.

ASSEMBLY

To assemble, attach the two cleats first, then glue and nail the sides to the top and bottom. Make up the umbrella racks separately and nail them from the inside, taking care to locate the nails so they don't penetrate through any of the holes.

The nested compartment is assembled without glue and is simply inserted freestanding in the bench enclosure.

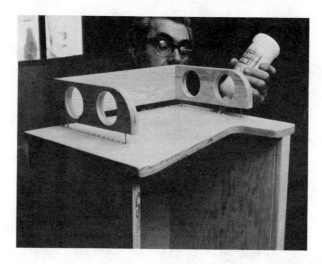

7. Start the nails into the rack, then pull it up and apply a bead of glue. Turn the piece on end with the rack resting on the workbench and drive in the nails.

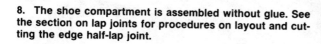

8. The shoe compartment is assembled without glue. See the section on lap joints for procedures on layout and cutting the edge half-lap joint.

9. Set all nail heads, fill and sand. Apply a primer to tame the wild grain of fir plywood, then paint the bench.

14

Molding Chest

Common crown molding is used to form the gracefully contoured sides of this chest. Construction is relatively simple, but you must do a careful job of cutting neat miter joints.

Size is optional. As dimensioned in the plan, the chest will be useful to store a wide variety of small things including coin collections, playing cards with chips, jewelry, chessmen, or stationery supplies.

Crown molding in the 4-inch width required is a stock item available at lumber dealers and is sold and priced by the linear foot. A 4-foot length is needed for this project. In addition to the molding you'll need ½-inch stock for the top and bottom, a length of 1⅛-inch-diameter closet pole, some triangular strips for the lid, four blocks of wood for the feet, and a strip of continuous (piano) hinge.

For the top and bottom you can use fir plywood or clear pine. Since ½-inch solid wood is rarely available wider than 11¼ inches, it will be necessary to add a ¾-inch strip to the board to obtain the full 12-inch width required for the top. With this in mind, you might prefer to use plywood.

Start by cutting the molding to size with 45 degree end miters. Whether you use a backsaw and miter box or a table saw, one thing is important: each pair of moldings must match if the miter joint is to fit

perfectly. To achieve this, cut a miter off each end of the four pieces of molding. Then clamp one of the angled cut-offs to the saw table or miter box. Positioned upside-down, the mitered end of the molding will nest firmly against the miter of the scrap (see drawing).

The inside dimensions of the mitered moldings determine the length and width of the bottom. Disregard the dimensions for the bottom shown in the drawing if your molding lengths should differ slightly. Adjust accordingly and cut the bottom rectangle true and square.

You'll note that crown molding has a bevel at the top and bottom of the back. For this reason the bottom panel is attached slightly offset from the bottom of the molding in order to make contact on the flat surface.

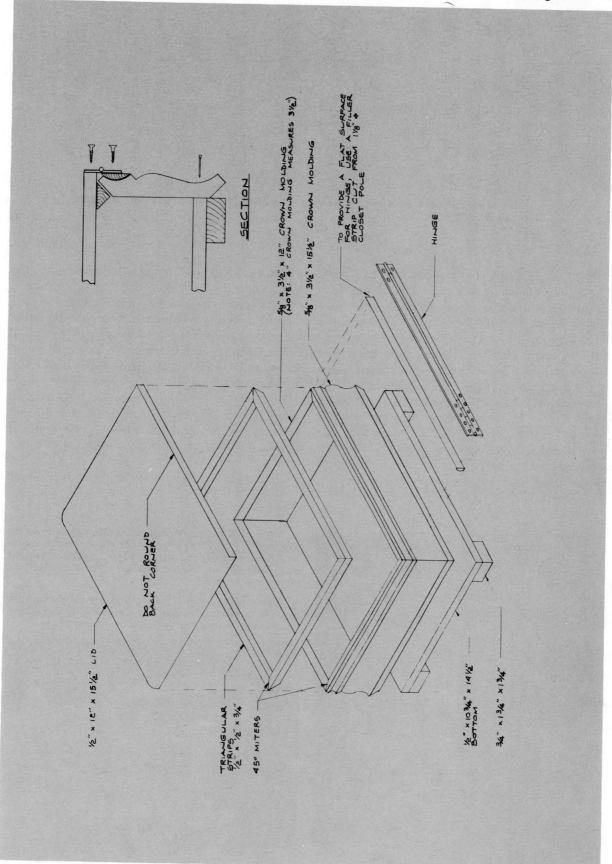

SECTION

5⁄8" x 3½" x 12" CROWN MOLDING
(NOTE: 4" CROWN MOLDING MEASURES 3½")

5⁄8" x 3½" x 15½" CROWN MOLDING

TO PROVIDE A FLAT SURFACE
FOR HINGE, USE A FILLER
STRIP CUT FROM 1⅛" Φ
CLOSET POLE

HINGE

½" x 12" x 15½" LID

DO NOT ROUND
BACK CORNER

TRIANGULAR
STRIPS
½" x ½" x ¾"

45° MITERS

½" x 10¾" x 14½"
BOTTOM

¾" x 1¾" x 1¾"

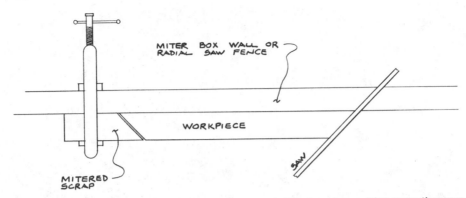

1. How to use mitered scrap as a stop to obtain uniform lengths when cutting more than one piece of molding.

Begin assembly by gluing and nailing two sides. Use 1¼-inch finishing nails to hold the glue joint in contact. The irregular shape of the molding precludes the use of clamps. The best way to hold the piece for nailing is in a bench vise. This is particularly important after the first two sides have been attached because you don't want the exposed points of the miters to rest against the work table. Scraps of wood should be used for stand-offs on both sides of the bottom panel so that the vise jaws do not come in contact with the molding. Apply glue and drive three nails into each miter corner (on alternate faces) to obtain a tight joint. Set all nail heads and fill the voids.

Cut the lid to size, then quarter-round three top edges only; the back edge must remain square in order to accommodate the hinge. A router with a quarter-rounding bit can be used or you can round the corners by planing and sanding.

A ridge made with triangular strips is attached to the inside of the lid to fit against the beveled edges of the side molding. The strips are made by cutting a 45-degree bevel from the corner of a ¾-inch board. The ends of the four strips are then mitered 45 degrees so they fit together like a frame. Glue and nail them with ¾-inch brads to the underside of the lid.

The concave curvature at the upper rear of the

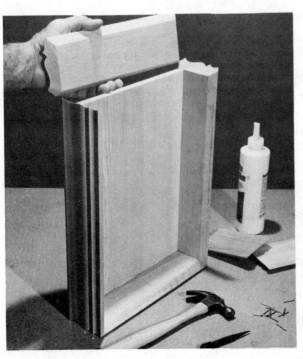

2. It is essential to cut the end miters with a smooth-cutting saw blade so the sharp edges of the molding will not splinter. Check the fit of each piece before gluing and nailing. The inside edge of the miter should line up precisely with the corner of the base.

3. The best way to nail the molding without marring the faces is to secure the unit in a woodworking vise. Scrap blocks keep the jaws away from the molding edges.

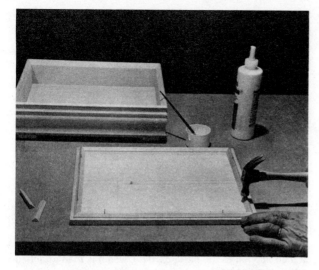

4. Triangular strips are nailed to the underside of the lid to make it dustproof. Corners of the strips are mitered.

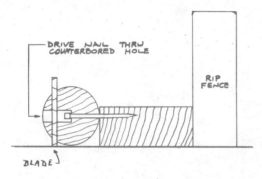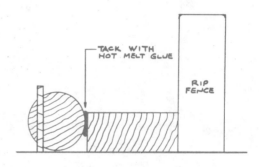

5. Two methods for securing round stock for cutting a longitudinal slice on the table saw.

molding prevents normal attachment of the continuous hinge. A flat surface is readily provided to seat the hinge by gluing in a filler strip sliced from a length of 1⅛-inch-diameter closet pole (round stock up to 1 inch diameter is called a dowel; over 1 inch is called closet pole).

Any attempt to make this cut without a jig on a table, band, or jigsaw is bound to be difficult and dangerous because the round stock will surely twist during the cut. In addition, holding the piece would necessitate having your fingers much too close to the blade. The solution is quite simple: Temporarily attach the pole to a flat board using nails in three counterbored holes or use a few dabs of quick-setting hot-melt glue. Be sure that the bottoms of both pieces are in alignment. Set the saw fence and make the slice cut (see illustration). If a power saw is not available secure the pole in a vise and make the cut by hand using a ripsaw. Cut slightly oversize then attach the slice to the molding and use a block plane to shave off the excess.

Sand all surfaces smooth and ease the sharp cor-

ners of the miters before applying finish. A sheet of 220-grit abrasive paper cushioned with a piece of plastic foam will simplify sanding the contours of the molding.

The chest can be stained and varnished or given a woodgrain finish. Another interesting possibility is to apply several coats of metallic-bronze spray finish. Regardless of the finish desired, the wood should be given a coat of sealer, inside and out.

An optional lining for the interior of the chest is made by cutting pieces of cardboard to fit the bottom, sides, and the inside of the lid and covering them with Contact imitation felt in the desired color.

Cut the Contact about ½-inch larger than the cardboard on all sides and snip off the corners as shown in the photo. Peel off the protective backing and simply wrap the material over the cardboard and press it firmly with a small roller or lay a piece of wrapping paper over the surface and rub briskly with the fingers. Attach the lining boards to the box with rubber cement, coated on both surfaces and allowed to dry.

6. Paint the inside before installing the lining

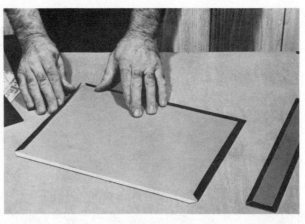

7. Cardboard is cut slightly undersize to fit the inside surfaces of the chest. Felt-like self-adhesive contact sheeting
is then applied to the cardboarding, which is then attached
with rubber cement.

15

Bric-a-Brac Cabinet

This project features a variety of joints including the butt, rabbet, dado, and miter. The drawer is built with ordinary butt joints while the two upper shelves require beveled butts. The latter are not difficult to make if you follow the instructions.

Note in the plan that the sides of the cabinet are angled inwards above the drawer enclosure. Thus, they must be made in two sections, which are joined at the lower shelf. The boxed drawer section could be assembled with butt joints, but then it would be impossible to attach the upper side panels with butt joints also. Instead, dado joints are used.

Both a straight and angled dado are required for this project. Note that the two lower cross members project beyond the sides. Normally this would require a blind or stopped dado: a groove which does not continue completely across the board. Actually, blind dadoes are somewhat of a nuisance to produce, requiring added handwork with a chisel.

There is an easier method of obtaining the same result as a blind dado. This is accomplished with a filler block. You'll find the technique to be a great time saver on this and other projects.

The cabinet is made of ½-by-8-inch common pine. Select boards that will permit obtaining suita-

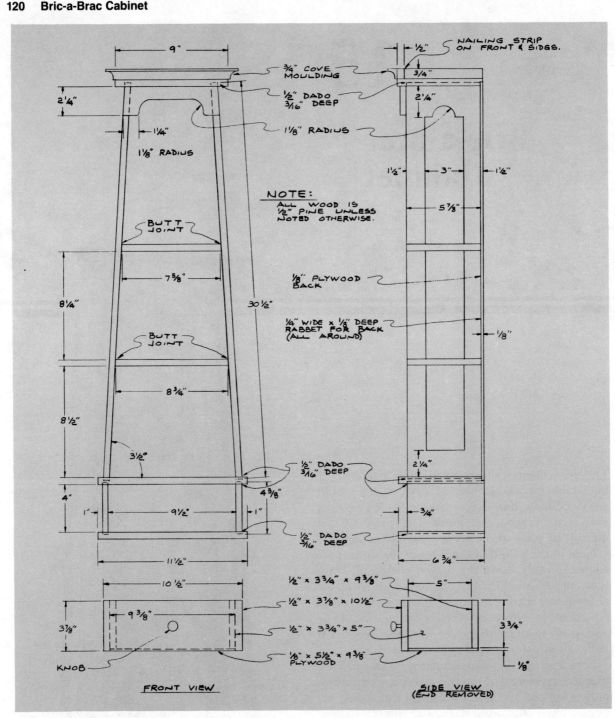

FRONT VIEW

**SIDE VIEW
(END REMOVED)**

ble sized pieces between the knots to minimize material cost.

Start with the side panels. Use the table saw equipped with a smooth-cutting, hollow-ground planer blade. Rip two pieces 6 inches wide; then crosscut to 30½-inch lengths. Lay out the outline for the cutout. Then use a 2¼-inch hole saw to bore a hole near the top, as indicated in the plan.

Next, to make the two long, parallel cuts, you employ a simple table-saw operation called inside sawing. Adjust the rip fence for a 1½-inch wide cut, measuring from the inside of the blade to the fence. Depress the blade until it is below the surface of the table. Position the work over the blade, then turn on the power. Slowly elevate the blade while firmly holding down the work with one hand. When the blade has penetrated the top of the board, slowly feed the work along the fence until the cut has been completed to within an inch or so of the cross line. Stop the saw and wait until the blade has come to a full stop before lifting the work free. Repeat the step along the other side, then use a sabre saw to continue the cuts to the corners and to make cross-cuts to drop out the waste.

Cut three pieces to size for the top and lower cross members. Insert a dado blade into the saw adjusted for a ½-inch-wide cut, ³⁄₁₆ inch deep. Set the fence ½ inch away from the inside of the blade. Run a piece of scrap wood through to check for proper adjustments. Use a push stick to keep the fingers safely away from the blade. Make the dado cuts clear through on the parts which will receive the short side panels.

Now tilt the dado blade to a 3½-degree angle to

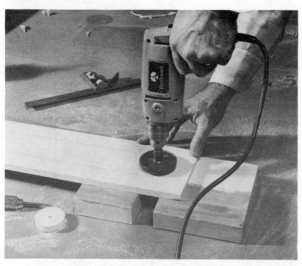

1. A hole saw is used to form the curved part of the cutout at the top of the side panels. Work against a backup block so the edge won't splinter on the underside.

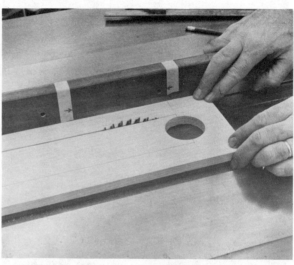

3. When the back mark on the work reaches the rear mark on the fence, stop the work and turn off the power.

2. To make an inside cut, elevate the blade a specific number of turns on the crank; then mark the front and rear limits of the blade on the rip fence. Depress the blade, position the work, then switch on the power and elevate the blade, cranking the same number of turns.

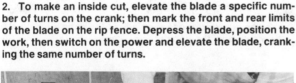

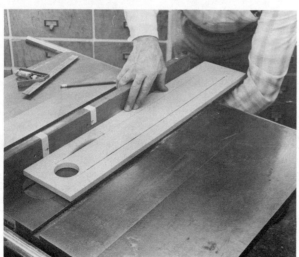

4. Use a sabre saw to drop out the waste.

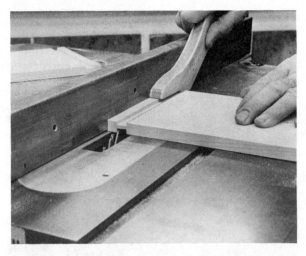

5. Two dado cuts are made on the lower shelf, back to back. The blade is tilted 3½ degrees to make the angled dado required on the top side. Use a push stick for this operation.

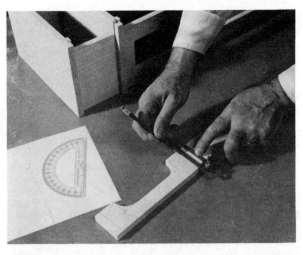

7. The T bevel is set for a 3½-degree miter to mark the cutting lines for the arch.

6. Filler blocks are glued in the gaps to close the dado. The side members are temporarily assembled in order to assure the blocks are properly located.

8. Nailing strips added to the back of the cove molding are in turn nailed to the cabinet top. Glue all joints.

make the angled dadoes. Again, make a test cut to check particularly for proper depth of cut. When the dadoes have been completed, cut the short side panels to size. Then temporarily assemble the pieces, back side down, on a flat work table. This will enable you to glue the filler blocks in place for a perfect fit.

The filler block is merely a small piece of wood dimensioned to fit snugly into the gap. Cut the block to precise width, but slightly oversize in thickness and length. This will permit trimming flush. If the same wood is used and with the same grain direction, the result will be practically invisible. Press the blocks into place so they just touch the adjoining side panels. When the glue has set for about five

minutes, carefully separate the side members without disturbing the blocks. If any glue has seeped onto the edges of the panels, be sure to wipe it off. Also check in the dado grooves behind the filler blocks for glue runoff. If there is any glue there, scrape it off with a chisel; otherwise the joints will be ill fitting. When the glue has set, trim the blocks flush with a saw and block plane.

The ⅛-inch-thick back panel is set into a recess so its edges will not be visible from the sides. A ⅛" × ¼" rabbet (right-angle cut along the edge of a board) is required at the rear of the side panels and the top and lower cross members. The rabbet is cut clear through on all four pieces and, as with the dado, filler blocks are used at the ends of the cross members only to fill the gaps.

The two center shelves are cut to size with the saw blade tilted to a 3½-degree angle, to crosscut the required side bevels. Since the bevels will tend to cause the pieces to slide during gluing and nailing, it is advisable to clamp temporary positioning cleats across the side panels to assure precise alignment.

Cove molding is used to crown the top. Since it cannot be nailed directly to the top, nailing strips are added to build up the back. Join the molding to the strips with brads and glue; then cut 45-degree miters to form return corners. Nail through the top of the strips into the cabinet top.

Sand all parts before final assembly. Assemble the drawer enclosure section with glue and brads, then add the sides and the top. The shelves are added before the back. Set all nails and fill the holes.

The drawer is assembled with butt joints. The front is flush with the top and bottom but is lipped at the sides to extend ½-inch on each side so it fits flush with the side of the cabinet side wall. Assemble the drawer with glue and 1¼-inch finishing nails in this order: Attach the back to the sides, then add the bottom, and finally the front. The front is nailed only to the sides; glue will suffice on the edge of the ⅛-inch bottom.

Finish is optional. Use stain, shellac, clear topcoat varnish, or one of the woodgraining or antiquing finishes. A worthwhile tip: Insert the back panel only temporarily during the final assembly in order to keep the unit true; remove it during the finishing

9. The completed unit ready for finishing. The back panel is added later to permit easier application of the finish.

operation. This will enable you to do a neater, quicker job of it. This is particularly true if you would like to finish the back panel in a neutral or contrasting color to set off the displayed curios. Finally attach the back with glue and brads.

16
Tree-Trunk Lamp

For most homeowners the expiration of a favorite ornamental tree is a great disappointment indeed. If the home has a fireplace, the tree may be cut into logs and burned as fuel. Otherwise, it is unceremoniously carted to the dump. Then follows the tough, backbreaking task of digging out the stump.

If one of your trees has to be cut down and uprooted, there are two things you might consider doing: First, save a piece of the trunk or a section of branch and turn it into an attractive lamp base. It will serve as a lasting memento with sentimental value. Secondly, rather than struggling to remove the stump, you can let it remain as a sturdy post to support a comfortable swiveling chair that you can make for a nominal cost, as shown in the next chapter.

To make the lamp, select a fairly straight log about 16 inches long with a diameter of at least 6 inches.

Don't rush the log to the lathe and begin turning; the wood must be properly seasoned (dried) before it can be worked. The wood in a freshly cut log contains a large amount of moisture (sometimes accounting for more than half its weight). While in this green or wet state the wood is stringy and spongy, very difficult to cut with basic tools and is prone to develop serious defects.

The water in wood is contained in the cell walls and in the cell cavities. When the free water in the cavities evaporates, there is little effect on the properties of the wood. However, when the water *within* the cell walls diminishes, the walls contract. The cells squeeze closer together and become harder and stronger, causing the wood to shrink overall as a result.

If some parts of the wood dry at a faster rate than others, inconsistent shrinkage will occur, causing checks (lengthwise splits) and internal stresses.

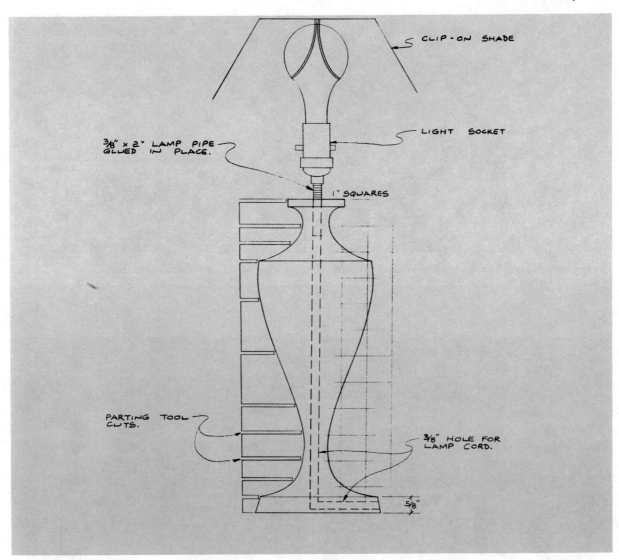

There are two ways you can promote proper drying. First, you can apply a coating of melted paraffin to each cut end and store the log in a cool, dry place where there is ample air circulation. The log will be ready for the lathe in about a year, so you must be patient. The alternative is quicker: Soak the log in a 30% solution of PEG-1000. This is a wood stabilizing agent (polyethylene glycol) developed by the Dow Chemical Company. A six-week soak is usually required at temperatures of about 70 degrees F. This must be followed by about two or three months of air drying. The treatment renders the wood dimensionally stable because the PEG molecules replace all the water molecules in the cell walls, pre-

venting the cell walls from shrinking as the wood dries. It should be noted that the treatment is not effective on wood that has already begun to dry.

If your log is not fully seasoned it may not show any signs of defects at the onset of turning, but it invariably will develop them as you shave away surface wood and progressively expose "new" wood. Or it will develop cracks and warp later, after the project has been finished.

When the log has completely dried, check the ends and, if necessary, trim them as nearly square as you can. Any log is bound to be somewhat lopsided, so it will be necessary to mount it lightly between the points of the live and dead centers, temporarily,

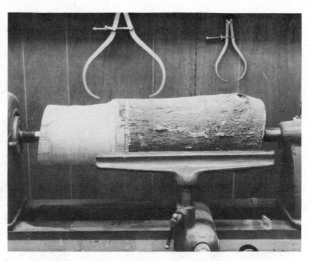

1. Cut a section of log from the trunk or a branch to a length of about 15 inches.

3. A view of the partially rounded log.

2. The log will spin eccentrically until a true cylinder is formed. Hold the gouge firmly and feed it lightly while running the lathe at a slow speed.

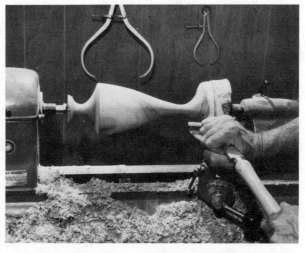

4. The lathe speed is increased after the cylinder is formed. The profile is shaped with the parting chisel, round nose and skew.

in order to find the most promising center axis. You do this by trial and error. Start by setting the points in the center of the annual growth rings. Feed the tailstock just enough so that the log will remain suspended, then spin it by hand and observe the rotation. If it seems to be considerably off balance, reposition it between the centers. Repeat the process until you obtain a reasonable centering. Mark the corrected center locations, remove the log and centers from the lathe and tap the centers into place with a mallet to make the indents. Firmly mount the log on the lathe.

Start shaping to a rough cylinder with a large

gouge gripped very firmly and with the lathe operating at very low speed. Feed the tool slowly so it doesn't get hung up by the eccentric spin of the log. When the cylinder has been formed, the operating speed can be increased. Use the gouge to remove the bulk of the stock; then work with the parting chisel, round nose, and skew, and turn to the profile indicated, or one of your choice.

Use the parting chisel to square off the base end, and then make another parting cut to establish the lamp's actual base. Don't cut all the way through. Complete the turning by sanding and finishing. Apply the finish with the piece running at slow speed. If the wood was treated with PEG, a polyurethane finish should be applied as it will be compatible.

Now you are ready to bore the holes for the wire. Unless you have a very long drill bit, you'll have to bore the hole from both ends. Usually, when drilling a long hole from both ends of stock, even the slightest misalignment of the centerline marks on the ends can be fatal to a perfect match. You won't have this problem because the lathe center-marks are at dead center. Remove the work from the lathe and bore $\frac{1}{16}$-inch pilot holes through the centers of both ends, making sure to penetrate deeper than the waste. These holes will locate the centers for boring the $\frac{3}{8}$-inch holes from both ends for the lamp cord. Cut off the waste and bore the hole. A horizontal hole bored halfway through the base section carries the wire off to the outlet. Don't use an ordinary drill bit, as it will tend to slide off the slanted surface. Use a brad-point bit. Cushion the turning on a piece of cloth and prop it so the base bottom is perfectly perpendicular.

Hardware consists of a 2-inch length of $\frac{3}{8}$-inch O.D. lamp pipe and a slide-switch lamp socket. Use a countersink to ream the insides of the pipe ends to remove any sharp burrs. Secure it in the wood with a few drops of epoxy adhesive.

Thread the lamp cord through the lamp and fish it through the horizontal hole; attach a plug and connect the socket. Glue a piece of felt to the lamp bottom to protect finished surfaces on which it will be placed.

17

Swiveling Lounger

This comfortable body-contoured lounger is ideal for sunbathing because you can rotate it to follow the sun. It spins on a heavy-duty chair swivel mounted on a tree stump that projects about 12 inches above the ground. If you don't have a stump, you may want to build the seat anyhow and install it on a length of fence post sunk into the ground. If so, use a post-hole digger to make a hole about 24 inches deep. Drop a 36-inch length of post, back fill and tamp.

The sides and upper and lower cross members are cut from ordinary 2×4 construction lumber; the central cross member and sub-base are pieces of 2× 8 lumber. Select stock that is fairly straight grained and free of knots and splits. Or you may want to consider using Wolmanized lumber, which will cost only a few pennies more per foot. This is ordinary stock which has been pressure treated with preservative. The treatment renders the wood absolutely immune to decay and insect attack.

The sides are formed with half-lap joints. This joint is especially advantageous for a construction such as this. It is strong, attractive, and economical. Consider the alternative—cutting the contoured side section from a single board. You would have to obtain an expensive 18-inch-wide board, much of

which would be wasted. And, perhaps most important, a side section cut from a single board would be structurally unsound due to the weak end-grain exposure at critical areas.

To lay out the cutting lines for the half-lap joints, as well as the curved profile, make a full-size drawing of the side on a sheet of wrapping paper. Rule a grid of squares on the paper to simplify drawing the pattern. Use a protractor to set the angles on the drawing.

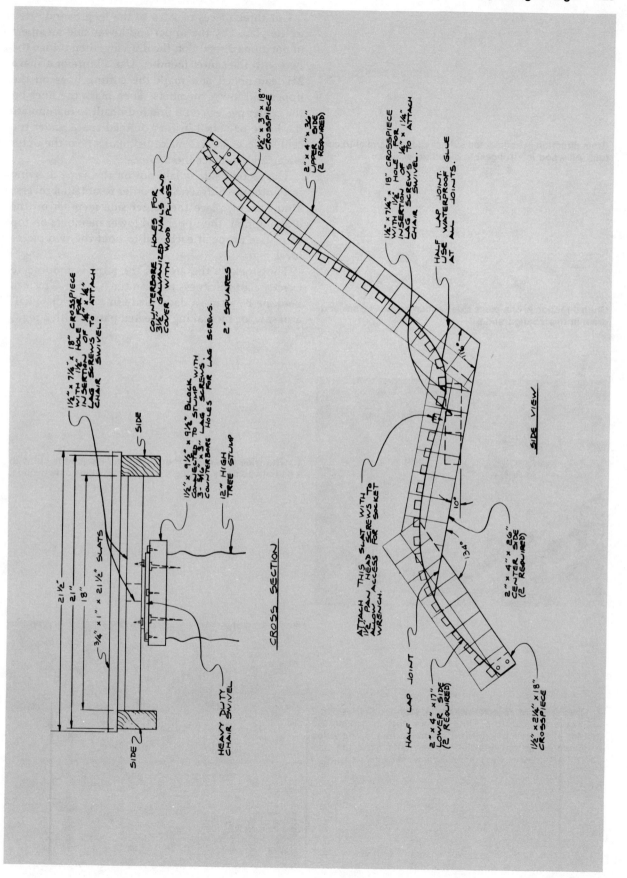

1½" × 7¼" × 18" CROSSPIECE WITH 1½" HOLE FOR INSERTION OF ¼" × ¼" LAG SCREWS TO ATTACH CHAIR SWIVEL.

COUNTERBORE HOLES FOR 3½" GALVANIZED NAILS AND COVER WITH WOOD PLUGS.

2" SQUARES

½" × 3" × 18" CROSSPIECE

2" × 4" × 36" UPPER SIDE (2 REQUIRED)

1½" × 7¼" × 18" CROSSPIECE WITH 1½" HOLE FOR INSERTION OF ¼" × ¼" LAG SCREWS TO ATTACH CHAIR SWIVEL.

HALF LAP JOINT. USE WATERPROOF GLUE AT ALL JOINTS.

SIDE

1½" × 9½" × 9½" BLOCK CONNECTED TO STUMP WITH 3-5/16" × 3" LAG SCREWS. COUNTERBORE HOLES FOR LAG SCREWS.

12" HIGH TREE STUMP

21½"

21"

18"

¾" × 1" × 21½" SLATS

CROSS SECTION

SIDE

HEAVY DUTY CHAIR SWIVEL

ATTACH THIS SLAT WITH 1½" PAN HEAD SCREWS TO ALLOW ACCESS FOR SOCKET WRENCH.

10°

34°

HALF LAP JOINT

2" × 4" × 17" LOWER SIDE (2 REQUIRED)

2" × 4" × 26" CENTER SIDE (2 REQUIRED)

1½" × 2¼" × 18" CROSSPIECE

SIDE VIEW

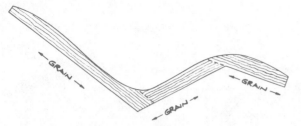

Grain direction in segmented side section is parallel to contour. All wood is strongest in direction of grain.

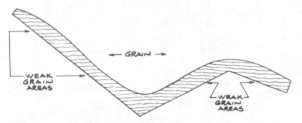

Grain direction in one-piece side section exposes weak endgrain in this configuration.

Cut three pieces of 2×4 to the lengths indicated in the plan. Lay the upper and lower side members in positions directly on the drawing; then bridge the two with the center member. Use a knife or a sharp 2H lead pencil and mark the cutting lines on the upper and lower members. Then mark the lines on the center piece. You'll find it difficult to manipulate the knife or pencil in the confined space under the center piece, so just make tickmarks near the outer edges and connect them later.

The second side is laid out on the same drawing but with one difference: In order to obtain a reverse arrangement, place the center side member on the drawing first, the upper and lower members on top of it. Use props at each end to hold the two pieces level.

The stock in the area of the joint is reduced to exactly half thickness to form the half lap. This can be done by using a dado blade in a table or radial-arm saw, or by making repeated passes with a regu-

1. The wide recess for the angled half-lap joint is cut with a dado head or by making a series of kerf cuts side by side.

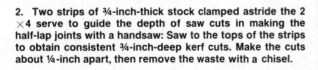

2. Two strips of ¾-inch-thick stock clamped astride the 2 ×4 serve to guide the depth of saw cuts in making the half-lap joints with a handsaw: Saw to the tops of the strips to obtain consistent ¾-inch-deep kerf cuts. Make the cuts about ¼-inch apart, then remove the waste with a chisel.

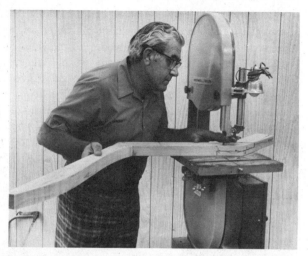

3. The parts for the sides ready for gluing. Use waterproof glue for lasting, strong joints. Drive a few small nails into the joints before clamping to prevent the parts from sliding.

4. Using the band saw to cut the curved portion of the side member. A sabre saw can also be used.

lar blade. Make a test cut on two pieces of scrap to check for correct blade-height adjustment before cutting the work.

The angled half-lap joint can also be made with hand tools, if necessary, in this manner: Nail two strips of ¾-inch stock to the work table astride the 2×4. These strips will hold the work and serve as depth-of-cut guides. Saw a series of kerf cuts about ¼ inch apart, ¾ inch deep (half the thickness of the 2×4). Hold the saw in a horizontal position and saw until the teeth just make contact with the guide strips. Or, for another approach, you can clamp two strips of wood to the saw blade, ¾-inch above the teeth points. This will allow the blade to cut to precisely the correct depth. Use a chisel to clear out the waste.

Waterproof glue such as Resorcinol or highly water-resistant plastic resin type glue is used to join the pieces. After applying the glue, drive a couple of 1¼-inch finishing nails through the joints to keep the parts from slipping. Clamp the joints until dry.

With a scissors or knife, cut out the outline of the side from the full-size drawing. Use this as a template to draw the curvature onto the wood. Cut the curved outlines on the front edges of the glued-up members with a band saw or portable sabre saw.

The sides are joined to the three cross members with glue and 3½-inch galvanized common nails. Before driving the nails, bore ⅜-inch holes ⅜ inch deep so wood plugs can be glued in to conceal the nail heads.

The swivel is attached first to the lounger cross member with ¼-inch hex-head lag screws, 1¼ in-

ches long. An access hole for a socket wrench is predrilled in this cross member to permit reaching through to attach the swivel to the base on the stump. The base on the stump is a block 1½″ × 9¼″ × 9¼″ attached with three ⁵⁄₁₆″ × 3″ hex-head lag screws. Heavier screws are used here because screws don't hold as well in end grain as they do in side grain. Counterbore the holes deep enough to contain the screw heads and washers just below the surface.

5. The sides are attached to the cross members with glue and nails. Counterbored holes permit setting the large nail heads below the surface so they can be concealed with wood plugs.

Drill the counterbore hole before you drill the screw clearance hole otherwise you will be unable to center the second drill bit. The counterbore hole should be wide enough to allow entry of the wrench socket. All lag screws used should be hotdipped galvanized.

Before you attach this block, it is advisable to bore a few ¼-inch holes into the top of the stump, as deep as possible. Fill these holes with a liquid wood preservation, such as Wood Life, to prevent decay.

If untreated lumber is used for construction, apply several liberal coats of wood preservative to all pieces, including the slats and stump top before final assembly.

Use a spot of glue and two 1½-inch galvanized finishing nails at each end of each slat. Note that the one slat over the swivel access hole is not permanently attached, but is fastened with two rustproof pan head screws so you can reach the swivel to remove or install the lounger. You may want to take it inside during winter months.

Brush on two coats of exterior varnish or paint in a color of your choice to complete the project.

6. A heavy-duty swivel is secured to the seat bottom with lag screws. Note the access hole for later driving the lags into the base from the opposite direction.

7. Three lag screws are used to attach the swivel-support block to the stump. Use shims if necessary, to level the piece. Stump is treated with wood preservative before block is attached.

8. Attach the frame temporarily and check it for ground clearance in a full swing. If it touches ground at any point a thicker base block may be required.

9. One slat, located over the swivel-screw access hole, is not glued and nailed; it is attached with stainless-steel, pan-head screws to permit the seat to be removed.

10. A ¾-inch spacer strip is used between each pair of slats to obtain even spacing for gluing and nailing.

18
Compact Hutch

This handsome piece is ideally suited for tight quarters. It is smaller than most hutches, taking up only 2⅓ square feet of floor space. Nevertheless, it is roomy enough to store twelve place settings.

Construction is rather easy. Ordinary butt joints predominate, but rabbets, lap joints, cove cuts, and miters are also employed.

You can economize on lumber cost by using common No. 2 grade pine for the basic construction. Bear in mind that clear lumber cuttings can be obtained by cutting between or around major defects.

Select boards with sound, tight knots in the cuttings that will be used. If you take a rough sketch of the board requirements to the lumberyard, you can readily choose boards which have defects in areas that can be selectively avoided in the subsequent sizing cuts.

The fir plywood doors are enhanced with Waddell hardwood molding, which is generally available at lumberyards. This is a top-quality molding that comes in straight lengths and curved corner sections. The latter have precut end miters which make installation relatively easy—you need to cut miters only on the straight lengths. Similar shaped molding in ¾-inch width is used to trim the edges of the top, center, and base.

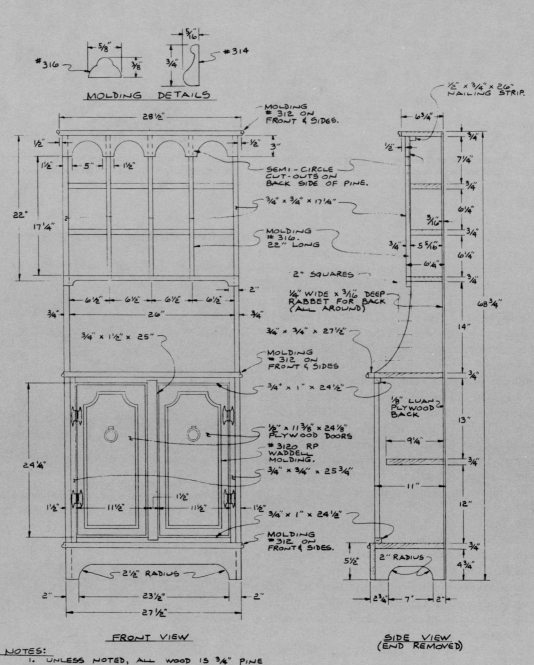

#316

5/8"
3/8"

5/16"
3/4"   #314

MOLDING   DETAILS

28½"

MOLDING #312 ON FRONT & SIDES.

½"   3"
½"
1½"   5"   1½"

SEMI-CIRCLE CUT-OUTS ON BACK SIDE OF PINE.

¾" × ¾" × 17¼"

22"
17¼"

MOLDING #316. 22" LONG

2" SQUARES

6½"   6½"   6½"   6½"
26"
¾"   ¾"   2"

¼" WIDE × 3/16" DEEP RABBET FOR BACK (ALL AROUND)

¾" × 1½" × 25"

¾" × ¾" × 27½"

MOLDING #312 ON FRONT & SIDES

¾" × 1" × 24½"

½" × 11⅜" × 24⅛" PLYWOOD DOORS

#3120 RP WADDELL MOLDING.

24¼"

¾" × ¾" × 25¾"

1½"
11½"   1½"   11½"   ½"

¾" × 1" × 24½"

MOLDING #312 ON FRONT & SIDES.

2½" RADIUS

2"   23½"   2"
27½"

FRONT VIEW

NOTES:
1. UNLESS NOTED, ALL WOOD IS ¾" PINE
2. USE BUTT JOINTS FOR SHELVES.

½" × ¾" × 26" NAILING STRIP.

6¾"
½"

¾"
7¼"
¾"
6¼"
3/16"   ¾"
¾"   5 5/16"   6¼"
¾"

68¾"

14"

¾"

⅛" LUAN PLYWOOD BACK

13"
9¼"
¾"
11"
12"
¾"
5½"   2" RADIUS   4¾"
2¾"   7"   2"

SIDE VIEW (END REMOVED)

1. Use a flexible rule to draw the sweeping curve on the side piece. Note how a large defect in the common-grade lumber is bypassed. This is one way to save on the cost of material.

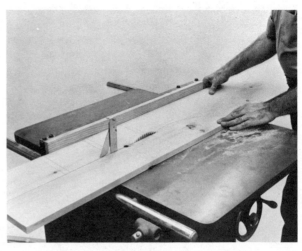

2. A partial rip cut is made to form the straight portion of the side panel. Stop the cut when the blade reaches the section requiring the curve cut.

The back panel is a piece of ⅛-inch luan plywood. Due to the variety of woods used, the hutch is best finished with an opaque woodgrain or paint. If you prefer a stain and/or clear overcoat finish, you'll have to use one kind of wood throughout.

Begin construction with the two sides. Lay out the shelf locations, then draw in the curved midsection. A flexible metal rule can be used to scribe the sweeping curve. Drive two nails to flank the rule as shown, then flex it and trace along the edge. Otherwise you can draw the outline with the square grid method.

The upper, narrower sections of the sides can be ripped to width by making partial cuts on the table saw. Simply stop feeding the work just before the blade reaches the curve. The curve may be cut with a sabre saw or a band saw. In either case, give the edges a few strokes with a spokeshave to remove the saw ripples.

The inside back edges of the sides and top are rabbeted to form a recess for the back panel. You can do this with a router equipped with a rabbeting bit or with a table saw.

The shelves are attached to the sides with butt joints. They can be aligned accurately if you tack-nail temporary cleats at each shelf position on the side members.

To assemble the case, start two 2-inch finishing nails along the center of each joint so the points protrude slightly. Apply glue to both surfaces, start-

3. Prop the board on two blocks to support the work solidly for making the sabre-saw cut. Use a hollow-ground blade for a smooth cut.

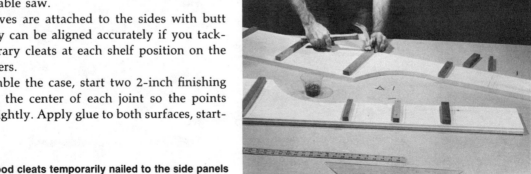

4. Scrap-wood cleats temporarily nailed to the side panels will simplify accurate assembly of the shelves. Leave the nail heads protruding for easy removal.

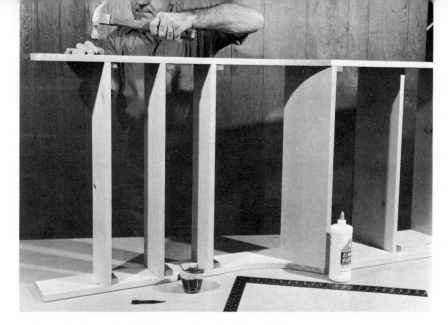

5. Start the nails until the points just enter the shelves, then remove the panel and apply glue. The cleats must be removed before the glue sets so they won't accidentally stick in place.

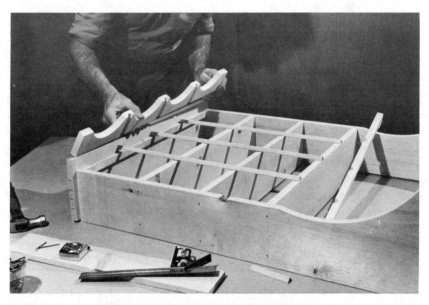

6. The upper and lower facia strips are grooved on the backs to permit them to fit flush over the vertical molding strips. Drilled half-round holes do the trick (see text).

ing with the shelf ends, then the sides. Softwood end-grain soaks up glue like a blotter, so it is advisable to apply a second coat to the shelf ends. When you are through applying the glue to the sides, you can apply the second coat to the shelf ends.

Drive the nails to within ⅛ inch of the surface to avoid the possibility of hammer dents, then sink them slightly below the surface with a nail set. Be sure to remove the cleats immediately after assembly

so that any squeezed-out glue won't bond them to the work.

When both sides have been attached, lay the piece on its back, on a flat work surface, and check for squareness with a large square or triangle. If it is out of square it can be trued (before the glue sets) by nailing two strips of wood diagonally across two corners while springing the piece into square. Two nails should be used at each juncture. The top and

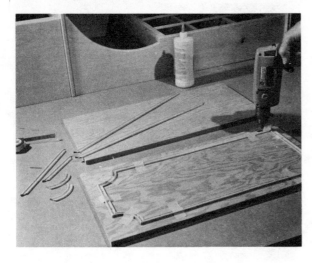

7. Hold the molding strips in place with masking tape while drilling pilot holes for nails. Use glue sparingly for a neat job.

back panel are added after the glue has dried on the assembly. Use glue and 1-inch nails to attach the back.

Three strips of Waddell ⅝-inch half-round/-beaded molding are used for the open shelf dividers. Drill pilot holes into the hardwood moldings to prevent splitting, then nail and glue them to the top, bottom, and shelves. A nailing strip is attached to the underside of the top to serve as a backstop.

The upper (scalloped) and lower facing pieces are cove grooved at the rear to permit flush installation across the vertical moldings. The simplest method to cut the half-round grooves is by clamping two pieces of ¾" × 3" stock, back to back. A hole ¹¹⁄₁₆ inch in diameter is then bored between the strips at each location. When separated, each piece will reveal half-round grooves. The two pieces are then cut to size and shape and attached.

The framing for the doors is made by butting strips to the edges of the sides and to the base and bottom of the main shelf. Middle half-lap joints are used to join the center vertical to the upper and lower cross members. Cut these joints before assembly. The doors are cut ¹⁄₁₆ inch shy of the openings on all sides (a total of ⅛-inch). Use cardboard shims to space the doors evenly while installing the flush-mounted hinges. When the doors are fitted, remove the hinges.

To install the door-trim molding, position the curved corner sections and use masking tape to hold them in place. Measure and cut straight pieces with 45-degree end miters. Tape all the pieces in place and make any corrections or adjustments. Then drill pilot holes for ½-inch brads in the molding only. You'll also have to counterbore a slightly larger hole to allow the brads to be set without splitting the narrow molding. Remove the tape from one piece at a time, apply a thin bead of glue and nail into place. Fill all nail depressions throughout before finishing.

The finish used on the prototype produced an interesting effect. You might try a similar approach. An antiquing kit in Country Yellow tone was used. The kit consists of a latex base coat and a glaze coat which produces the shading and grain effect.

The base coat was applied directly to the raw wood and allowed to dry for about an hour. The glaze coat was then applied to all surfaces except to the back and insides of the open shelf area. These areas, as well as the inside of the base cabinet, were left in the base coat color for contrast. A crumpled pad of facial tissue was used to wipe off the excess glaze to produce a subdued grain effect. A clear, satin topcoat was then applied overall. You can hardly fail with this finish because if the results are not to your liking you can simply wipe off the glaze coat with mineral spirits and try again.

19

Veneered Table

This table was designed to meet three important criteria: beauty, simplicity of construction, and low cost. The use of plywood and veneer readily makes it possible to satisfy these requirements.

The basic parts of the table are made of ordinary ¾-inch fir plywood. Surfaced with richly grained, exotic zebrawood veneer, the result is an eye-catching conversation piece worth many times the cost of materials. But, beyond any monetary value, consider your sense of accomplishment when you complete this project. Additionally, once you gain the experience you can apply the techniques to other projects or to bring new life to old pieces of worn furniture with simple lines.

Follow the cutting plan shown to obtain all the parts needed (with minimal waste) from a 26-by-66-inch plywood panel. The combined leg and apron sections are easily cut out on a table saw by making a series of inside cuts. If you don't have a table saw, all the cutting can be done with a sabre saw or a portable circular saw.

After drawing the cutting lines on the plywood, cut the panel into three sections for easier handling before you start the internal cuts. The inside cuts are made by depressing the saw blade so its teeth are completely below the surface of the table. With the

rip fence adjusted for the desired width of cut, the panel is positioned and held in place with one hand while the power is turned on and the arbor is cranked to elevate the blade until it cuts through the top surface of the wood. Once the blade has penetrated the wood, remove your hand from the elevating crank and use both hands to advance the wood to within about ½-inch of an inside corner. The inside corners are purposely incompletely cut in order to forestall binding problems. If the small web were to be removed during the initial cutting, the panel on the free side of the blade could bind as the subsequent pass is made. It's safer to separate the parts with a band or sabre saw later.

In order to anticipate precisely where the blade will come through the top surface of the panel it is advisable to make a test cut on a scrap of wood.

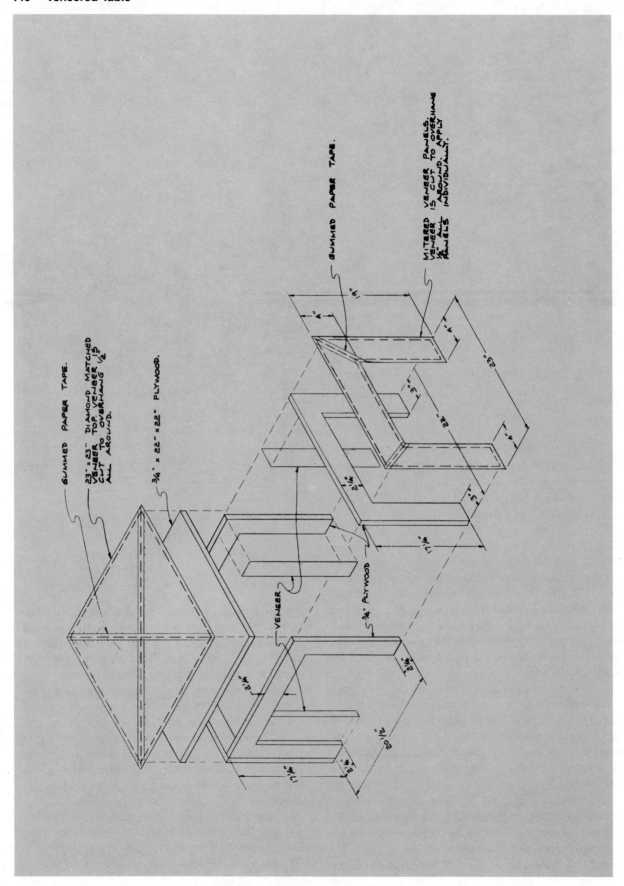

GUMMED PAPER TAPE.

23" × 23" DIAMOND MATCHED VENEER TOP. VENEER IS CUT TO OVERHANG 1/2" ALL AROUND.

3/4" × 22" × 22" PLYWOOD.

VENEER

3/4" PLYWOOD

GUMMED PAPER TAPE.

MITERED VENEER PANELS. VENEER IS CUT TO OVERHANG 1/2" ALL AROUND. APPLY PANELS INDIVIDUALLY.

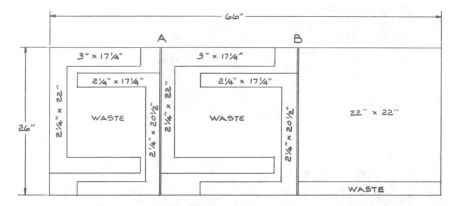

1. All the parts required for the table can be cut from a 26″ × 66″ plywood panel. Make cuts A and B first.

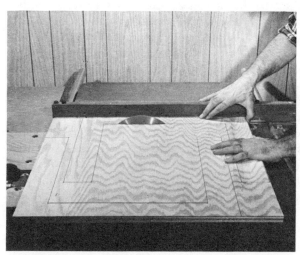

2. Table-saw blade is raised into the work while running to make the inside cuts necessary to produce one-piece leg and apron sections.

3. Clamp the leg sections together, then drill pilot holes for nails to obtain perfectly flush butt joints. Simply holding the parts in place by hand usually won't do because when a nail point strikes a dense section of fir grain it will slide into softer section, thus shifting the alignment.

Depress the saw blade until it bottoms and the crank will turn no further. Turn on the power and elevate the blade. When the blade has surfaced about an inch or so, cut the power. Place a square piece of wood against the fence so it touches the rear of the blade, then make a mark on the rip fence. Use this mark as a guide for positioning the work panel for starting the blind cuts. Note that there are two leg width dimensions, so it is advisable to make all the 2¼-inch-wide cuts for the aprons and legs before readjusting the fence for the 3-inch cuts.

Veneer is very thin and would readily "telegraph" any surface irregularities; therefore, perfectly flush butt joints are essential. To obtain a perfect assembly clamp the parts together and drill pilot holes for the nails. Then use finishing nails and glue. Sink the nails with a nail set and wipe off all squeezed-out glue.

The zebrawood veneer, as well as the glue, saw, and roller, are available from mail-order sources.

4. Nail on the square top, then scrape off all glue.

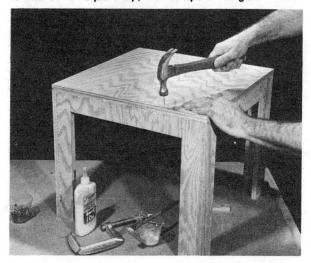

5. Insides of legs are veneered first, then the edges. Tape the narrow strips down while applying veneer cement.

Quite reasonably priced, the $\frac{1}{28}$-inch-thick veneer is usually offered in units of 9 square feet. Each piece measures approximately 12 by 36 inches. To cover this table you should obtain about 18 square feet. This is more than you will need, but this quantity allows for waste and some leeway in grain choice and matching. A pint of veneer glue will suffice. Ordinary contact cement can also be used for veneering.

Most veneers are somewhat bumpy and difficult to handle. You can minimize the bumps by lightly dampening the surface with a sponge, laying the veneer between newspapers, and pressing with a hot iron. Then insert the veneer between dry newspapers and weight with a stack of books. Allow the wood to dry thoroughly before use, otherwise the glue will not adhere properly.

The veneer laminating procedure is really quite simple since most pieces are cut oversize, then trimmed after they are attached. Begin with the inside surfaces of the legs. Cut one edge of veneer perfectly straight. Allow at least ¼-inch to overhang. Apply the glue to both surfaces, being careful to avoid getting it on the adjoining edges. Allow the glue to dry twenty to thirty minutes. Check readiness for bonding by touching the surface with wrapping paper. If the paper does not stick you can begin. Carefully position the straight edge of the veneer into the corner, then lay it down to make contact. The bond will be immediate and permanent. Install the other inside veneers the same way. Tap over the entire surface of the veneer with a block of soft wood and hammer to obtain a good contact.

There won't be sufficient space to manipulate a router in the confined areas on the insides of the legs so you'll have to use a knife for trimming off most of the excess. It is extremely important to cut *with* the grain of the workpiece (see diagram) so that you cut *into* the grain on the waste side where any splitting, which invariably will occur, won't matter. Also, when cutting off the excess at the bottom of the leg, clamp a block of scrap wood against the veneer and overhang the end slightly to serve as a backstop for the knife point. Use a smooth file to complete the trimming flush with the plywood edges. Hold the file level and draw it along the edges, being careful not to round the corners.

Next, cut the narrow edge strips of veneer. Cut them at least 1-inch wide, apply glue, attach, and trim.

Now the outsides can be veneered. The best way to assure well-fitting mitered corners is to laminate an entire side as a single unit. Select pieces of veneer

6. When trimming overhanging veneer, cut with the grain, not against it. Incorrect direction may cause the veneer to split into the good area.

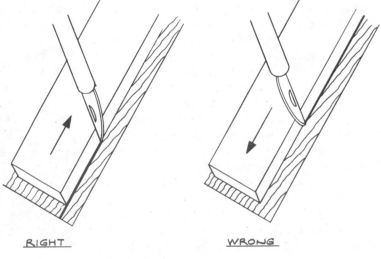

RIGHT   WRONG

for the apron and legs about 1 inch wider than the finish size. If you don't allow ample excess you could run into trouble in positioning the veneer. Cut a 45-degree miter on each end of the apron piece and on the top ends of the leg pieces. If you are working with a veneer saw, use a piece of wood or a rule as a straightedge to guide the saw. Slide the saw along with the side of the blade rubbing against the guide. To make the cuts with a knife use a rule straightedge. Butt the mitered joints of the three pieces together, then apply tape to the joint lines to hold them in place.

Apply glue to both surfaces and allow to set. Paper slipsheets will be necessary to obtain accurate alignment and to prevent accidental adherence. Lay sheets of paper on the apron and legs, overlapping at the top so no glue surface on the plywood is exposed. Carefully position the veneer, paying particular attention to the alignment of the miter joint. A light pencil line drawn on the tape will indicate its location. The joint line should coincide with the inside and outside corner of the leg and apron—it should run diagonally from corner to corner. When satisfied with the alignment, pull out one of the slipsheets to allow wood-to-wood contact. When the first piece has adhered, pull out the second sheet, make contact, then repeat with the third piece. Apply pressure with a roller or hammer and block.

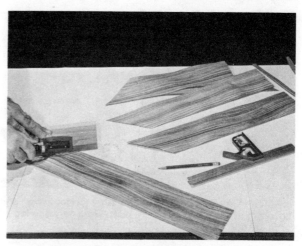

7. A veneer saw or knife is used to cut the 45-degree miters for the leg and apron sections. Miters must be cut exactly to size; other parts are cut oversize.

If you have a router with a piloted straight cutter, the trimming will go rapidly. Otherwise use a knife and file.

The leg sides must be veneered one at a time to avoid laying a glued surface on the table where it could pick up dust or other bits of foreign matter.

The reverse-diamond top is formed by making two 45-degree cuts diagonal to the grain. Allow 1 inch extra at the base. Affix a strip of masking tape

8. Cut veneer from edge to center when using knife, to avoid splitting. Or you can make a nick cut at the opposite edge, then cut into it.

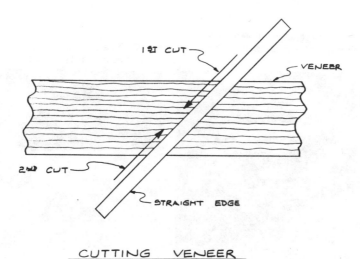

CUTTING   VENEER

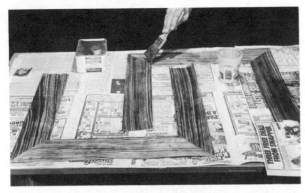

9. After taping mitered corners together (on face side) and checking for fit, apply veneer cement. Work only one leg/apron section at a time.

12. A pair of 45-degree cuts are made diagonal to the grain to form the reverse-diamond pattern. The straightedge is taped in place so it won't slip during cutting.

10. Three kraft-paper slipsheets are used to line up the veneer. They're pulled out to allow contact when the veneer is properly aligned.

to the bottom side of the veneer, under the cutting line, to prevent splitting at the ends. Also, cut from both edges toward the center to minimize splitting. This is especially true if you use a knife instead of a veneer saw.

When the triangles have been cut, test them for fit. If the fit is good, tape them together at the joints. If not, adjustments can be made by clamping the edge to be treated between two pieces of hardwood to facilitate controlled sanding.

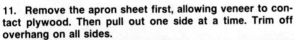

11. Remove the apron sheet first, allowing veneer to contact plywood. Then pull out one side at a time. Trim off overhang on all sides.

13. Gummed-paper veneer tape is used to assemble the mitered sections. This is applied to the face side only.

Use two slipsheets overlapped at the center. Align the diagonal joint lines to coincide with the corners of the table. Pull out a slipsheet, make contact at one edge, then pull out the other slipsheet while holding the unattached edge up. Gradually work the veneer down by rubbing with the fingers in a broad sweeping motion. Gummed paper over the joints can be sanded off; masking tape should be carefully peeled off before sanding.

Sand with 220-grit abrasive paper with a finishing sander or by hand with a block. Lightly hand sand all corners with a felt padded block to form a minute radius. Apply a coat of sanding sealer and two coats of varnish to obtain a warm, grain-enhancing finish.

14. Veneer glue, which is actually a form of contact cement, must be applied in a fairly uniform coat. Charge the brush fully and make long strokes. Avoid overbrushing.

15. A small roller is used over the entire surface to assure good contact. Be careful not to ride beyond the overhanging edges or the veneer may break off.

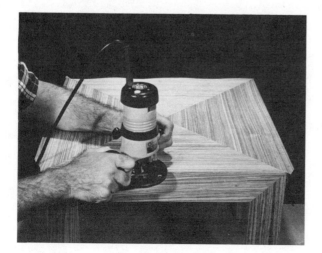
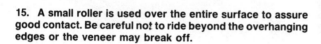

16. A router with a bearing-piloted straight cutter does a fine job of trimming the overhanging edges flush. A knife may be used if a router is not available.

17. Ease all sharp corners by hand sanding with a felt-padded block, then sand overall with a finishing sander using 220-grit paper.

18. Apply several coats of satin clear finish.

20

Marquetry Backgammon Board

The ancient game of backgammon has gained phenomenal popularity in recent years. Playing boards are widely marketed and are available in a broad price range. The finer ones, made with wood veneers of varying tones or colors fitted together to form the face design (marquetry), are extremely costly.

The board illustrated is comparable in workmanship and beauty to the typical higher-priced boards, and you can duplicate it on a very low budget. You'll enjoy the fascinating game even more when you play on a handsome board you made yourself.

A background of ribbon-stripe mahogany sets off the 24 points which alternate between East Indies rosewood and contrasting limba veneers. A final touch of elegance is added with ready-made inlay border trim.

The base is made of ½-inch-thick, smooth-surfaced, choice hardwood plywood. Unlike fir plywood, this material has sound, attractive interior plies which can be left exposed at the edges. Thinner plywood, such as ¼ or ⅜ inch, is not recommended.

Plywood is not prone to warp because the core is surrounded by plies with the grain direction arranged at right angles in each successive layer. This offsets the likelihood of warp since the stress is equalized on both sides of the core. When an additional veneer surface is applied, the plywood becomes unbalanced. If the new layer expands or contracts, a base that is too thin will warp as a result of more stress on one side of the core. This is a condition that occurs with freestanding, unsupported members such as this game board, or with flush doors, table drop-leafs and the like. This does not mean that you can't apply veneer to ¼-inch or even ⅛-inch plywood. You can, provided you add a crossband veneer of equal thickness to the bottom surface. Bear this in mind for future veneering projects with unsupported panels.

The veneers, plywood, inlay decorative border strip, and veneer glue can be obtained from mail-order firms. The tools required include: saw, knife, hammer, pencil, rule, combination square, metal

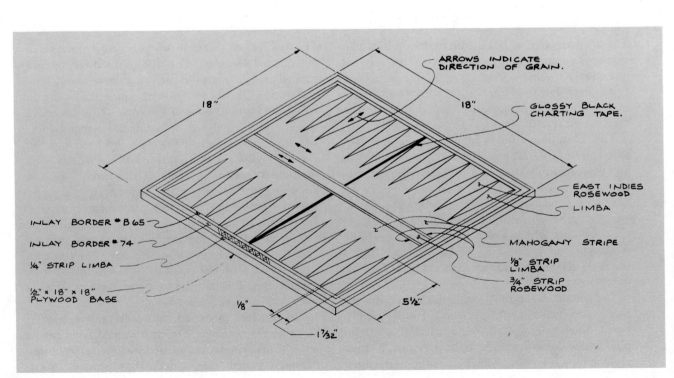

ARROWS INDICATE
DIRECTION OF GRAIN.

18"

18"

GLOSSY BLACK
CHARTING TAPE.

EAST INDIES
ROSEWOOD

LIMBA

INLAY BORDER #B65

INLAY BORDER #74

1/4" STRIP LIMBA

MAHOGANY STRIPE

1/8" STRIP
LIMBA

3/4" STRIP
ROSEWOOD

1/2" x 18" x 18"
PLYWOOD BASE

1/8"

5 1/2"

1 7/32"

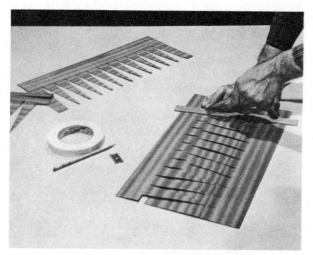

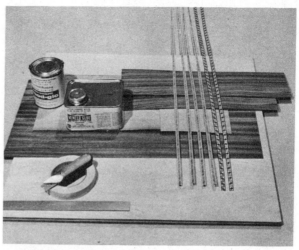

1. Tools and supplies for making the backgammon board.

2. Mahogany veneer background is cut into 12 points for each half of the board.

straightedge, masking tape, charting tape, and sandpaper.

The first thing to do is to check the veneer for bulges. If they are excessive, the veneer will not lie flat and this will make it difficult to mark, cut, and glue. Follow the procedure for flattening as outlined for the veneer table project.

Marquetry is not really difficult, but it is an exacting job; therefore an extremely sharp knife and pencil are essential for accuracy in layout and cutting.

Begin with the mahogany background panels. Lay out the series of V's on two pieces of veneer. All of these diagonals run across the grain, so it is imperative that you start the cuts at the points of the pattern and work into the crotch of the V. If you work in the opposite direction the veneer will split off near the point upon completion of the second cut. Cut against a flat, firm surface of wood or cardboard (not corrugated).

Now you are ready to cut the triangular inserts to exact size. This is accomplished by using the cut background piece as a template guide. Inasmuch as there could possibly be some slight discrepancies in the background points, it won't do to use only one of the V spaces as a form for cutting all the inserts. Each insert must be cut in its own corresponding space.

Place the piece of veneer to be cut under the "template" with its grain running lengthwise. Use a strip of masking tape to hold it in place, bridging several points of the template. Align the straightedge with the guide's edge, tilt the knife handle backwards at an angle of about 45 degrees and make the cut. Use numbered tabs of masking tape to identify each segment so you can match the fitted edges when assembling.

When all the triangular inserts have been cut, slide them into place against the background panel. Remove the number tabs, then run long strips of masking tape over the entire surface. Butt the tape edges; do not overlap. Repeat the procedure for the other half section, then cut the center strips of con-

3. When cutting across the grain start at the point and cut towards the crotch.

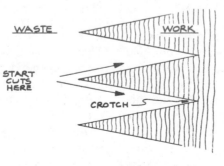

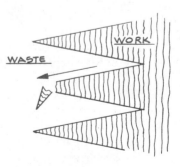

WASTE   WORK

WORK

WASTE

START CUTS HERE

CROTCH

RIGHT   WRONG

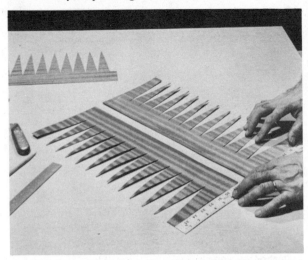

4. Measure the background's center spacing so the board ends up square. Cut the center strips of veneer to fit.

5. Tape the inlay veneer under the background points to make precise cuts. Use a metal straightedge and a razor blade in a holder or a sharp utility knife. Identify each piece with a numbered masking tape tab.

7. When all pieces have been cut, run long strips of tape across the entire surface to make a firm bundle which won't come apart in handling.

6. After checking for fit, tape each wedge into place.

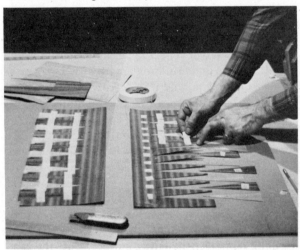

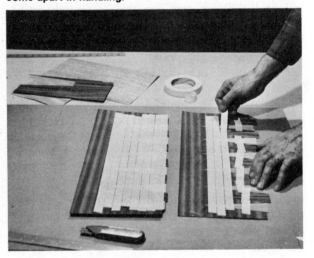

trasting veneers and tape them to join both sides. Turn the pack right side up and trim the edges to form a perfect square.

The inlay borders go on next. Cut 45-degree miters to form the corners using the combination square to guide the knife. Tape the border in place around the perimeter of the pack. Complete the border by adding strips of leftover veneer beyond the inlay strips. Dimension the outer border strips so they overhang the baseboard about ¼ inch. The pack is now ready for gluing to the base.

Cut the plywood base to size with a smooth-cutting saw blade. Dust off all surfaces, then apply a full coat of veneer glue to the veneer pack and the board. Try to brush in one direction only; do not brush back and forth as with paint. Allow the glue to set until it can be touched without sticking to your finger. This may take from twenty to thirty minutes or more, depending upon temperature and humidity.

When the glue-coated surfaces meet, the bond will be immediate and permanent. You'll have no second chance for realignment, so you must get it right the first time. Use the slipsheet method to ensure accuracy. Lay two pieces of wrapping paper on the base panel, lined up evenly with the base edges and overlapped about an inch or two at the center.

8. Cut and tape the inlay borders to the pack. Bottom side is up here. Scrap tapes will be removed when the other side is fully taped to the edges.

9. Brush cement liberally but smoothly on both surfaces; avoid overbrushing.

Lay the veneer pack on the paper. Hold a rule against the base edges to check for an even overhang on all sides. Press gently along one side of the pack to keep it from shifting, then slip out one sheet of paper from the other side. Now run your fingers across the side of the pack that has made contact with the base so it can no longer shift. Lift the veneer pack at the other side, holding it so it forms a slight curve. Pull out the second sheet of paper. Starting at the edge where initial contact was made, sweep over the pack with the fingers. Gradually allow the rest of the pack to make contact.

To complete the bonding, carefully remove the masking tape by pulling it back at an acute angle, as shown in the drawing; then firmly tap the entire surface with a softwood block and hammer.

To trim off the excess overhang at the ends, turn the board face down on a flat surface and run the knife along the base edges.

Sand the veneer and edges of the board with 120-grit paper and slightly round the corners and edges. Finish up with 220-grit.

Apply a paste-wood filler to fill the open grain pores of the mahogany. When this has dried, coat all

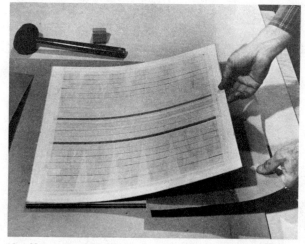

10. Use paper slipsheets to accurately align the veneer pack and backboard.

surfaces with sealer (back and front). Finish with two coats of clear satin varnish.

The division bar that separates each player's twelve points into an inner and outer table of six points is made by applying a strip of ¼-inch glossy

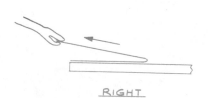

RIGHT   WRONG

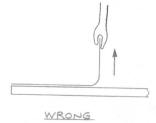

11. Peel masking tape at an acute angle to avoid lifting any veneer that has not yet made full contact.

charting tape. This material is available at art-supply stores in black, white, or in colors. Simply unroll a length and press it into place, then burnish it with your thumbnail. It will become a permanent part of the board. Be sure to apply the tape only after the finish has been applied to the wood.

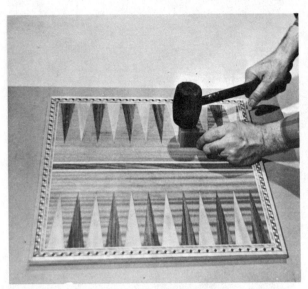

12. Remove the masking tape, then firmly tap the entire surface with a block and mallet to obtain good contact.

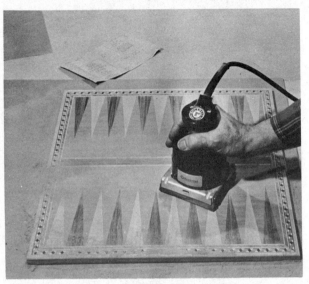

13. Sand the surface carefully. Don't overdo or you may wear through the thin veneer.

21
Multilevel Candlestand

In days gone by when the candlestand served an important purpose, adjustable ones were quite the rage. As the candles burned down, the crossbar was progressively raised to maintain a wide distribution of light over a tabletop.

This unique stand will serve as a charming accent, and if you enjoy an occasional supper by candlelight, so much the better; the elevated flames will definitely improve the illumination.

Shaping the contoured base presents no special problem because it requires routine freehand lathe operations. But turning the center post perfectly straight to a fairly exacting diameter is the type of lathe operation that often leads to frustration. Since this is not too easily done freehand, the problem is readily solved with a jig.

Make a full-size drawing of the base, including the parting-tool depth cuts as shown in the drawing. Use a ½-inch ruled grid to enlarge the pattern. You can save time by drawing only half the pattern carefully to scale; then fold the paper along the centerline. Place it on a sheet of face-up carbon paper and trace over the half-section drawing. When you unfold the paper, you will have a full drawing.

Cherry is a good choice for this project, but you can use any hardwood you prefer. You'll need a

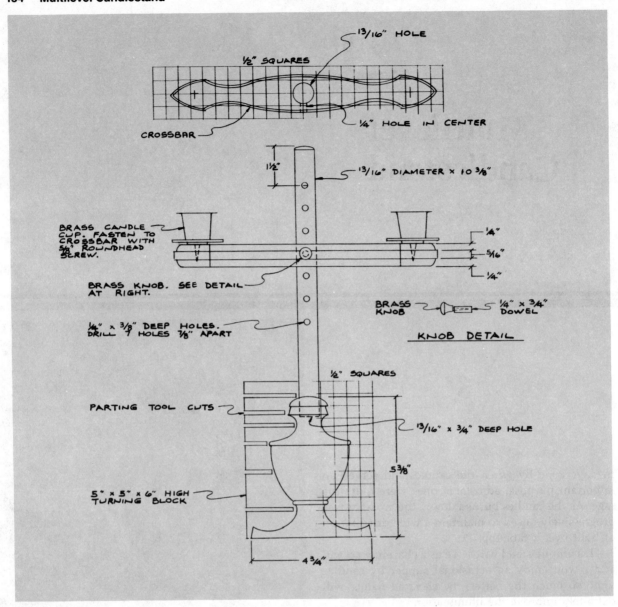

13/16" HOLE

1/2" SQUARES

1/4" HOLE IN CENTER

CROSSBAR

1 1/2"

13/16" DIAMETER x 10 3/8"

BRASS CANDLE CUP. FASTEN TO CROSSBAR WITH 5/8" ROUNDHEAD SCREW.

1/4"

5/16"

1/4"

BRASS KNOB. SEE DETAIL AT RIGHT.

BRASS KNOB

1/4" x 3/4" DOWEL

KNOB DETAIL

1/4" x 3/8" DEEP HOLES. DRILL 7 HOLES 7/8" APART

1/2" SQUARES

PARTING TOOL CUTS

13/16" x 3/4" DEEP HOLE

5 3/8"

5" x 5" x 6" HIGH TURNING BLOCK

4 3/4"

5-inch-square turning block about 8 inches in length. The finished base is only 6 inches high, but the extra length will allow tooling the ends without getting too close to the lathe centers. A 5-inch square of hardwood is not an item you can readily purchase so you'll have to glue up stock for the base.

Trim off the corners of the block with a band saw or table saw to give it an octagonal shape. This will give you a head start on the initial rough shaping.

1. Mark the centers of the turning block. Then make 45-degree bevel cuts to remove some of the waste.

Mount the block on the lathe and rough shape it to cylindrical form with a gouge. Make pencil marks on it spaced to match the grooves on the drawing. Using the drawing as a guide, adjust the calipers for the various diameters, and make those diameter-sizing groove cuts to the required depths using a parting chisel. The radial grooves serve as references for forming the basic shape.

Reduce most of the bulk between the grooves with the gouge, then begin the final shaping. Work with a round-nose chisel to make the concave curvature at the lower section of the base. The spear-point chisel is best for forming the small head immediately

above. The skew is used to shape the broad convex curve at the midsection. Continue to work towards the top of the base. Use the spear point for the second bead and the round-nose chisel again for the convex shoulder. The spear point is used to shape the remainder of the head.

The original parting-tool sizing cuts come to within about $\frac{1}{16}$ inch of the final diameters. Increase the operating speed to make the finish cuts to the final diameters. This will result in a smoother surface, thus reducing the need for excessive sanding.

Sand the base and apply the finish before remov-

2. Work the block into a rough cylinder with the gouge. Cut from the center towards both ends to minimize splintering during the initial stage.

4. Run the lathe to pencil the marks so they're visible.

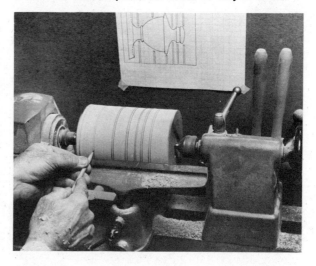

3. Mark the locations for the parting-tool cuts as indicated in the full-size pattern.

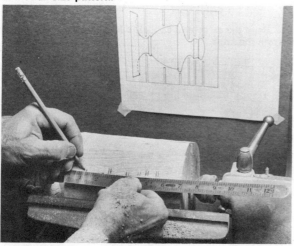

5. Use the parting chisel to make the initial depth-setting cuts. Check the diameter of each groove with the caliper. If you cut too deep you'll alter the design.

6. The gouge can be used again to remove much of the bulk quickly.

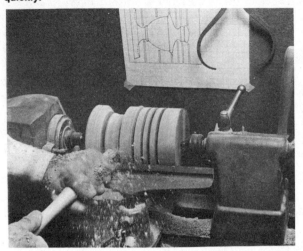

7. Use the skew and spear point to shape the contours. Work from groove to groove, referring to the pattern from time to time.

8. Set the caliper against the pattern to check the progress of each major feature.

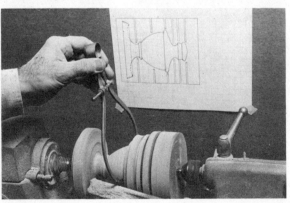

9. Round-nose chisel is used to form the concave section of the base.

10. To form the top of the base, move the tool rest and cut from this angle.

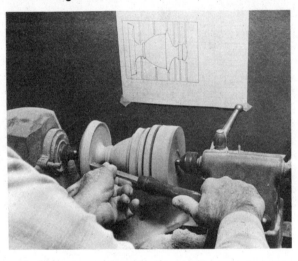

11. Sand the piece and apply the finish before you remove it from the lathe.

12. A length of plywood with an angled dado is used to support the skew chisel for making a controlled parallel cut. The chisel is clamped into the dado with aid of wood block.

ing it from the lathe. This will permit even scuff sanding between coats and even application of the finish. Two coats of clear satin finish will bring out the rich color of the wood and will impart a hand-rubbed effect. Operate the lathe at low speed while applying the finish. When the finish is dry, remove the work from the lathe and bore a $^{13}/_{16}$-inch hole $^{3}/_{4}$ inch deep for the post.

The jig for turning the post to diameter is nothing more than a piece of $^{3}/_{4}$-inch plywood, 2 inches wide and 10 inches long, with an angled notch cut into one side. Its purpose is to hold a skew chisel with its edge parallel to the lathe's axis. It also functions as a stop to limit the depth of cut. The depth of the notch should be equal to the thickness of the chisel. The angle should be such that the lead edge of the chisel will be parallel to the edge of the wood block.

To mark the cutting lines accurately for the notch, place the skew on the plywood, then press the front edges of both against a piece of wood. Draw pencil lines along both edges of the chisel. Cut the notch using a saw and chisel.

To make the post, rough turn a length of stock to the approximate finished diameter. Remove the work from the lathe. Align the tool rest so it is perfectly parallel to the axis of the lathe centers. Do this by measuring from the points of both the live and dead centers to the tool rest's back edge; that is, the edge closest to you. If the tool rest is shorter than the post, hold a straightedge against it. Next, adjust the chisel in its block so it projects to within $^{13}/_{32}$ inch from the lathe center when the block rests firmly against the tool rest.

Replace the work and make a series of jab cuts to

13. The jig helps you to cut a straight-sided post. Make small jabs into the roughly shaped post, then slide the chisel along, the front edge of the block riding against the edge of the tool rest. The tool rest must be aligned in advance.

reduce the diameter of the post close to the limit. Then slide the lead edge of the jig against the tool rest to make the finish scraping cut. The result will be a perfectly formed post exactly $^{13}/_{16}$ inch in diameter.

Remove the work from the lathe but do not cut off the waste ends. Tape the post into a V groove cut into a length of wood to facilitate drilling the peg holes on the drill press. Put the post aside while you work on the crossbar. Cut the shape with a band saw or jigsaw. Sand the edges. Then form the decorative edge with a router equipped with a $^{1}/_{4}$-inch bead-

cutting bit. Bore the ¼-inch hole for the peg and the
¹³⁄₁₆-inch center hole for the post.

Return the post to the lathe and sand until it will
slide freely through the center hole in the crossbar.
Apply the finish to the post and crossbar. Make the
pin assembly by drilling a pilot hole in the end of a
¼-inch dowel. Attach the knob. See the source of
supply listing for the metalware.

**14.   A V-grooved strip is used to cradle the post for drilling
the blind holes. Masking tape holds it in place.**

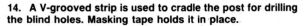

**15.   This arrangement holds the crossbar in place for shap-
ing the edge. The parallel block keeps the router on an even
keel. A bead cutter is used.**

16.   Detail of the crossbar components.

22

Rotating Centerpiece Server

This attractive server, mounted on a lazy-Susan bearing, gently brings the item you want to your side of the table with a flick of a finger.

You can make the piece by turning the parts on a lathe, but this tool is by no means essential. You can achieve the same result using a sabre saw and router, and buying ready-made gallery spindles.

To make the server on the lathe, you would do faceplate turning. The base is screwed directly to the faceplate. The stock for the ring is screwed to a scrap board of the same size, which is in turn secured to the faceplate. Make sure to locate the screws in the back-up board and the work so they will be centered within the confines of the ring to avoid cutting into a screw with the turning chisel. If your lathe can't handle an 18-inch disc, the turning will have to be done outboard. Although your roughing cuts to round the pieces are correctly made from the face side of the work, it is advisable to pre-saw the squares to a rough round form for safety. Accidentally touching spinning square corners could result in serious injury. After sizing the diameter of the base and ring with a parting chisel, most of the shaping is done with a spear-point chisel.

So much for lathe procedures; the rest of the chapter explains how to make the server without a lathe.

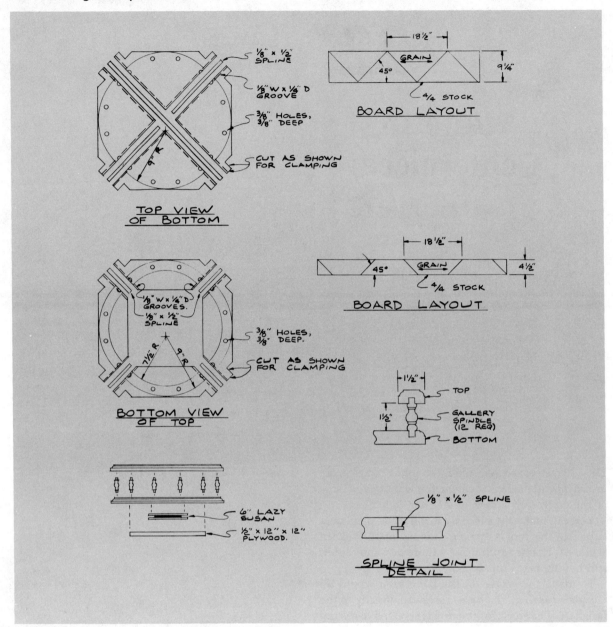

The circular base and the ring are made with ¼ cherry stock or other hardwood of your choice. Both are 17½ inches in diameter, so you'll have to glue up stock to obtain workpieces of sufficient size.

The simplest way to obtain the 18-by-18-inch square required would be to edge-glue two 9-by-18-inch boards together, but this won't work. Such a board would be prone to warp. The ring in particular would be weak and apt to split in the end-grain areas. Also, end-grain is always somewhat difficult to shape to a molded edge and to sand and finish-

coat satisfactorily. Additionally, the end-grain pattern would run off the edges; not particularly attractive for a circular design.

The alternative is to make the board by gluing together four triangular segments. The result will be a warp-resistant piece featuring an interesting symmetrical grain pattern, minimal end-grain throughout, and a structurally sound ring and base.

The square for the base is made by cutting four 45/45/90 triangles from a piece of stock measuring 9¼ by 48 inches. Set the radial-arm or a table-saw

1. The parts for the ring and base are cut from two boards in this format, thus minimizing waste.

2. Here's how to cut uniformly sized segments: Set the saw for a 45-degree miter cut. Make the first cut and use the cut-off as a stop. Clamp it in place so its point just touches the blade. After each succeeding cut, flop the workpiece over so the mitered end butts against the stop.

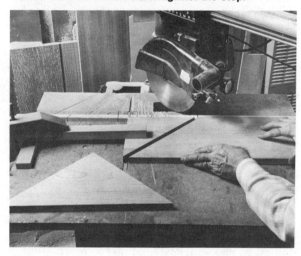

miter gage for a 45-degree miter cut. Flip the board over front to back after each pass, cutting each triangular segment so it has an 18-inch base.

Follow the same procedure in preparing the stock for the ring. However, here you can economize on lumber by making truncated triangles. These pieces, with the same 18-inch base, can be cut from a piece of 4½-by-60-inch stock. When these four segments are joined, a square opening will result in the waste area in the center.

Several kinds of edge joint can be used effectively to join the segments, including tongue-and-groove, dowel, or the spline-reinforced edge joint illustrated. A plain butt joint should be avoided because it would be rather weak, particularly for the ring.

When the pieces have been cut, arrange them with the best side up and mark them for identification. This is important whenever grooves (or tongues) are to be cut, or when holes for dowels are to be drilled for a joint. The same surface of the parts should face the guide fence, be it on the saw or drill press. The same applies when using any one of a variety of

doweling jigs. This approach allows some leeway in centering—if the grooves (or dowels) are slightly off center it won't matter since the error will be consistent. A point to remember if you decide to use dowel joints: Locate the dowels so they won't be in the path of the cutting line.

Cut the grooves centered on the edges of each joint surface, then cut the splines and check them for a good fit; they should be neither too tight nor too loose. Cut them from the same stock so they won't be prominent in the finished work.

Regardless of the kind of joint used, gluing four triangular segments ordinarily could prove quite try-

3. To cut the grooves for the splines, press the work firmly against the fence. Determine which side of each piece is desired for the face and mark accordingly. Be sure to face the same side of each piece against the fence. Thus, if the groove is not precisely centered it will not matter; the grooves will nevertheless match up.

6. Clamping notches are cut at the corners of each segment, and the splines are cut to size and tested for fit prior to gluing.

ing. But the task is readily accomplished in the manner illustrated, using four C clamps and two bar clamps. Two flats are cut at the corners as indicated in the plan to provide positive bearing surfaces for the clamps. The C clamps apply pressure to the outer sections of the joints while the bar clamps exert pressure on the center area. When assembling, apply the C clamps to the corners first, then add the bar clamps.

8. Using the circle guide to cut the upper ring. The center strip has been added to support the pivot. Note that the outer circle must be cut first to retain pivot support.

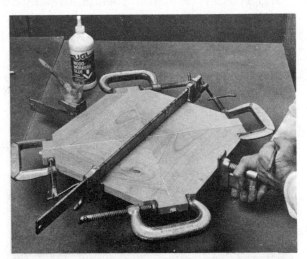

7. Apply glue to all joint surfaces, then assemble by joining two pairs of segments with the short splines. Bring the two pairs together with the longer spline. Apply the C clamps to the corners with moderate pressure and add the two bar clamps. Increase the pressure alternately.

The sabre saw with a circle-cutting pivot guide is used to make the circular cuts. In order to track perfectly true, the pivot point must be in precise lateral alignment with the front edge of the blade. This factor is discussed elsewhere in this book but bears repeating. You can check the alignment by carefully measuring with a rule, then confirm the accuracy by making a test cut in a piece of cardboard.

If your guide does not feature an adjustable pivot, and should your test cut prove erratic (spiral in or out), it may be possible to correct the problem by using a blade with a different width or by boring a new pivot hole in the guide.

Bore a blade entry hole in the waste area, adjacent to the cutting line, and large enough to permit the blade to be positioned tangent to the cutting line. Set the radial distance between blade and pivot, use a smooth-cutting blade, and feed slowly.

When cutting the ring it will be necessary to insert a strip of wood across the center of the opening to provide a base for the circle guide pivot. This can be toenailed with a few brads or held in place with a spot of glue. The outer circle must be cut first in order to preserve the pivot support.

Sanding follows sawing. The pivot-guided cuts will result in fairly smooth edges free of saw-blade ripples, so you won't have to do too much sanding. Use a stationary disc sander for the outside curves and a large-diameter (3-inch) sanding drum for the inside curve. If neither of these tools is available, you can do an adequate job by hand. Use segments of the cut-off waste as shaped sanding blocks.

A router with a ⅜-inch-radius beading bit is used to form the decorative edge. Route *clockwise* on the outer edge and *counterclockwise* on the inside edge. Otherwise the blade will gouge the wood and spoil the work.

A protractor is used to locate the twelve positions for the spindle holes. Turn the base upside down and make a pencil line across the center. Place the protractor's center mark in the dead center of the disc and tick off pencil marks spaced 30 degrees apart. Shift the protractor to the other side of the line to continue the marks. With a rule, draw radial lines from the center point through each tick mark. You can use a marking gage or a compass to make hole marks on the radial lines, ¾ inch from the edge.

To assure perfect alignment of the spindles, tape the ring to the base and drill ¹⁄₁₆-inch pilot holes through the bottom of the base and partly into the

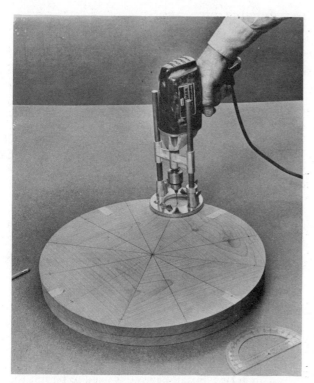

9. Tape the ring to the base, turn the pack bottom-side up, and use a protractor to lay out twelve radial lines 30 degrees apart. Bore small pilot holes through the base and partly into the ring, ¾ inch from the edge, to locate the spindles. Make a match-up mark on both pieces so they can later be assembled in the same position.

10. Bore ⅜-inch holes for the spindles in the top of the base and in the bottom of the ring at the locations of the pilot holes. Next, shape the edges with the router using a bead cutter.

11. Shape both upper edges of the ring.

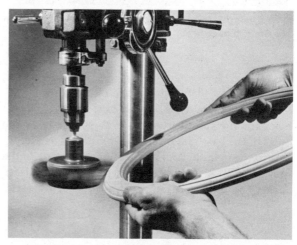

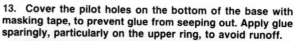

12. A flexible sanding disc is handy for smoothing the irregular molded edge. Light contact is used to avoid eroding the shape.

13. Cover the pilot holes on the bottom of the base with masking tape, to prevent glue from seeping out. Apply glue sparingly, particularly on the upper ring, to avoid runoff.

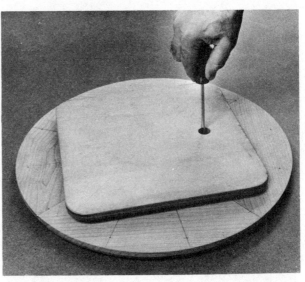

14. A lazy-Susan bearing is used to swivel the piece. Attach it to the sub-base first.

15. Insert screws through the access hole to secure the bearing to the server.

ring. Make an identifying mark on both pieces for later rematching, then take them apart. Drill the holes for the spindles. Apply glue sparingly to the holes in the base and insert the spindles. Then apply glue to the holes in the ring. Do not apply glue to the spindle ends; it would be smeared onto the surface during the fitting operation. Flip the base over and guide the spindles into the holes in the ring.

A 4-inch lazy-Susan bearing is used to permit the server to turn. Attach the bearing to a piece of ½-inch plywood 12 inches square. Drill a 1 inch diameter screw access hole in this sub-base, centered over the screw holes in the bearing plate. Attach the bearing first to the sub-base, then to the server base.

23

Scrap Lumber
Lamp

With the cost of lumber what it is today, it may be worthwhile for you to dig through your scrap-wood pile and use leftovers for useful projects. The lamps shown in this chapter are examples of what can be done with very little.

The turning block for the large ball is made by gluing up seven squares of ordinary 2×12 fir construction lumber. The teardrop version is made of "second generation" scraps left over from the ball. The dropout discs are simply glued together to produce another turning block!

If you don't have the necessary 2×12 stock on hand you can possibly obtain scraps at your local lumberyard. Dealers usually have cut-offs which they'll be happy to unload free or for a nominal fee. Or you can purchase an 8-foot length and cut it up.

Select pieces which are free of large knots, splits, or serious warps. The actual dimensions of 2×12 lumber are 1½ by 11¼ inches, so you'll need seven pieces cut into squares in order to come up with a block which will make a ball approximately 10½ inches in diameter.

Rarely do you find lumber of this type which is perfectly flat and completely free of any warp. Ordinarily, it would be impossible to apply sufficient clamping pressure to squeeze seven blocks of such size together to obtain the contact for good glue joints. But here's a novel trick: Bore large holes in all but the two outer blocks. By removing most of the bulk from the centers of the five pieces they become lighter and more flexible, permitting tight joints to be made using regular bar clamps.

A circle fly cutter mounted in a drill press is used to bore the openings. *Never* use this tool with a hand-held portable electric drill—a serious accident would surely result. Drill a pilot hole through the centers of all the blocks before starting with the fly cutter. This will serve as a centering guide, which is necessary because fly cutters do not have the capacity to penetrate thick stock. Therefore, a pass from each side will be required. Clamp the wood firmly to the press table and bore the holes to the diameters shown. Run the press at low speed and use protective goggles or a plastic face mask.

The blocks are cut into rings with the band saw prior to gluing. Before you take them to the saw, drill two small holes close to the inner rim of each block, the same diameter of some 1-inch nails. Clip the heads from the nails and insert them, blunt end first, into each pair of holes. They will serve to keep

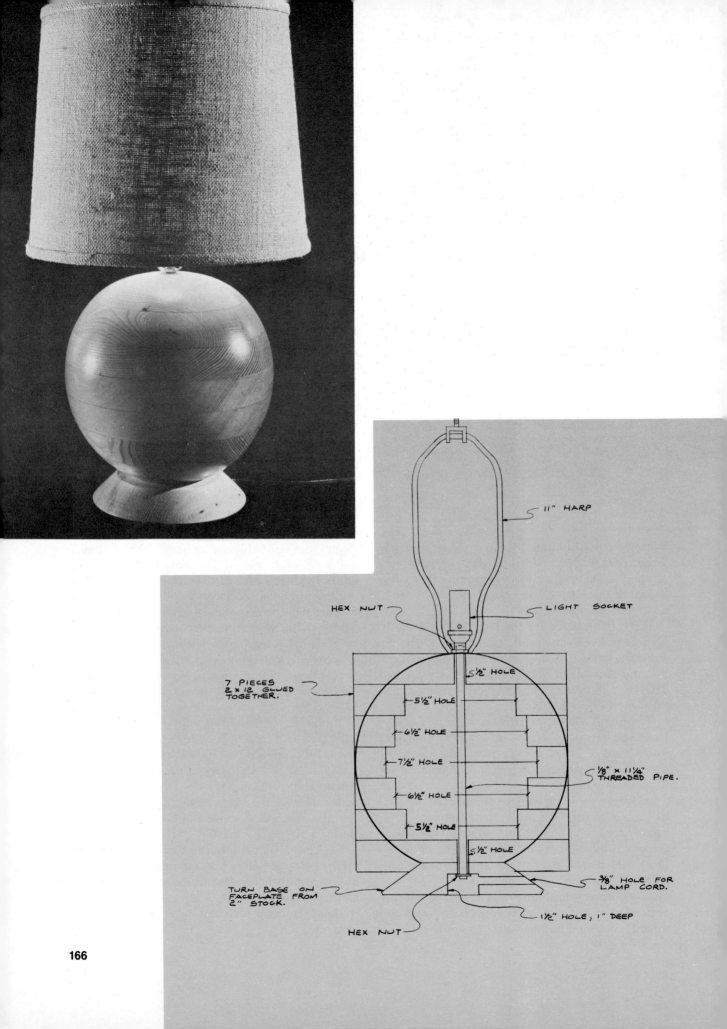

11" HARP

LIGHT SOCKET

HEX NUT

7 PIECES
2 x 12 GLUED
TOGETHER.

5½" HOLE

5½" HOLE

6½" HOLE

7½" HOLE

⅛" x 11¼"
THREADED PIPE.

6½" HOLE

5½" HOLE

5½" HOLE

3/8" HOLE FOR
LAMP CORD.

TURN BASE ON
FACEPLATE FROM
2" STOCK.

1½" HOLE, 1" DEEP

HEX NUT

166

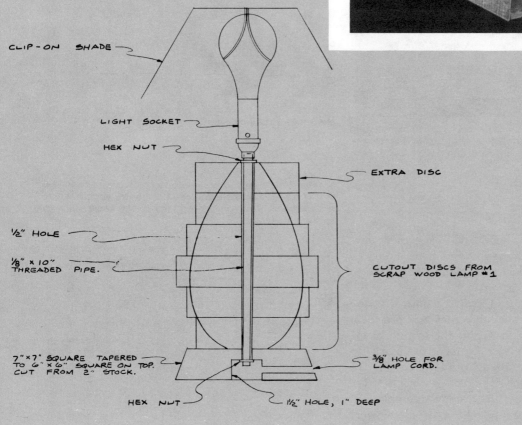

CLIP-ON SHADE

LIGHT SOCKET

HEX NUT

EXTRA DISC

½" HOLE

⅛" X 10"
THREADED PIPE.

CUTOUT DISCS FROM
SCRAP WOOD LAMP #1

7"X7" SQUARE TAPERED
TO 6"X6" SQUARE ON TOP.
CUT FROM 2" STOCK.

⅜" HOLE FOR
LAMP CORD.

HEX NUT

1½" HOLE, 1" DEEP

167

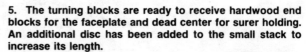

1. A fly cutter is used to make the large holes. The cuts are made from both sides to get through thick stock.

3. Apply glue to both surfaces; then work the nail points into their original holes.

2. Alignment between blocks is accomplished by inserting two headless nails with points protruding. Pieces are pressed together, then band-sawed into rings. Number each piece in sequence.

4. A half-dozen bar clamps, equally spaced, will press the stack into a solid cylinder.

5. The turning blocks are ready to receive hardwood end blocks for the faceplate and dead center for surer holding. An additional disc has been added to the small stack to increase its length.

the pieces from sliding about and in alignment during gluing. The pilot holes for these nails should be drilled to a depth which will permit the points to project about ¼ inch.

Stand the blocks on end, two at a time, with the grain running in the same direction. Squeeze them together so the points penetrate the mating block. Use C clamps for pressure. Number the blocks in sequence, then take them apart and band-saw the outer edges to form the rings that will be glued up.

Quick-setting white glues are not recommended for a glue-up of this type. Use a strong, slower-setting glue such as plastic resin or hide glue. Apply the glue to both surfaces, line up the holes with the nail points, stacking each ring flat on the table, one atop the other as you go along. When all the pieces have been assembled apply plenty of pressure, using a minimum of six bar or pipe clamps.

The cylindrical turning block is mounted on the lathe with a small faceplate. But this alone would never do for such a massive turning; therefore the dead center is also utilized. Glue a scrap of hardwood to both ends so that the faceplate and dead center will be clear of the working area.

Start the initial rough shaping with the lathe running at low speed. Use a large gouge but not in the usual manner. The normal procedure with most turnings is to work the gouge into the face. But for this piece you approach directly on the flat end, gradually shaving the stock from the end towards center. A perpendicular approach with the gouge will jam into the work (since at this stage a true

round will not yet have been formed), possibly tearing into the surface and causing damage. Work this way with the gouge from both ends towards the center.

When the ball is roughly formed you can increase the speed to about 1000 rpm and switch to a spear-point and skew chisel to dress it down to final shape. A quarter-section cardboard template will aid in checking the curvature as the turning progresses.

Sanding is best done with a 3-inch-wide cloth belt cut apart and handled shoeshine fashion. When the bulk of the sanding has been completed, the turning can be severed at the tailstock end. At this stage the weight will be sufficiently reduced to permit this. Now you can proceed to sand the free end. Apply a clear finish of your choice while the work is still on the lathe.

The base is turned separately. Before turning, it is advisable to bore the horizontal lamp-cord hole, as this will be easier to do at this stage.

6. Start shaping the ball with the gouge, working from the flat end towards the center. Do the same from the opposite end. Use a sharp tool and feed it slowly. Do not feed the tool broadside during the initial stage.

8. The bulk of the sanding is done with a sanding belt. Note that the work is still connected to the dead center.

7. Shaping the ball to perfection with the skew. Make light scraping cuts for best results.

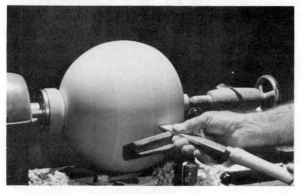

9. The dead-center end is severed after the main sanding is done. Although it seems precarious, the faceplate alone will support the work to permit sanding the end.

10. Clear finish is applied while the work is still on the lathe, turning at slow speed.

Hardware for the lamp, obtainable at lamp-supply stores and home centers, consists of standard threaded pipe (⅜-inch O.D.), two hex nuts, a socket, a harp, and a shade-securing finial.

When the threaded pipe has been cut to size, smooth the ends by reaming the inside with a countersink and the outside by grinding or filing to prevent damage to the lamp cord.

Gouge is used to rough-shape the teardrop, followed by the spear point and skew. A simple contour such as this can be shaped by eye, but if you prefer, use a caliper to measure progress against a full-size pattern.

Turnings are secured to the bases with glue. The threaded pipe and hex nuts provide the clamping pressure. The harp is optional on the smaller lamp; it is not needed if the lampshade has a snap-on clip.

If you want to try a different method, use a Surform tool for some of the basic shaping. Be sure to grasp the tool firmly with both hands.

24
Hexagonal
Tree Bench

Enjoy a shady resting place beneath rustling leaves by wrapping an attractive bench like this one around your favorite tree.

Construction involves angular cutting almost exclusively; normally a task ideally accomplished with a table or radial-arm saw. However, as illustrated here, you can achieve excellent results with a portable circular saw using several simple jigs.

Wolmanized 2×4 lumber is used for this project. Pressure-preservative treated, this wood is totally resistant to fungus, damp rot, bacteria, and all insects including the notorious termite. Although the photos show the bench resting on a gravel base, the treated lumber could just as well be placed directly on the ground.

The dimensions given are for a bench to fit a tree trunk about 12 inches in diameter—allowing for an additional 4 inches of tree growth. If your tree trunk differs in size appreciably, you'll have to alter the dimension accordingly. Also consider the tree's growth habit; if it is a rapid grower you might want to expand the inside diameter of the bench to forestall a tight squeeze in the near future.

The procedure for altering the size of the hexagon is relatively simple. Work with a piece of paper large enough to lay out a half section. With a beam com-

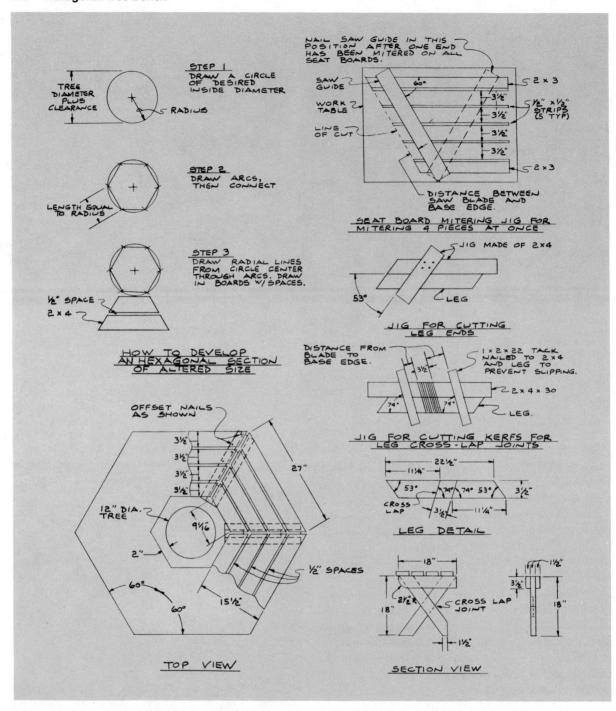

pass, draw a circle of the desired inside diameter (tree diameter plus clearance). Without changing the adjustment of the compass, place the point on any part of the circle and strike an arc on the circle. Move the point of the compass to the arc and strike another arc on the circle. Repeat this until you have three arcs (if you want to draw the full pattern you would use a large sheet of paper and strike six arcs).

Draw a straight line to connect these points. Next, draw straight lines from the center point of the circle through each arc; this will establish the sectional wedge. Now draw in the individual boards, ½-inch apart. This need be done for one segment only. The result will be a layout showing the exact length of each mitered board. Use this layout to set up the cutting jig.

THE BENCH

The bench is constructed in two half-sections, each composed of three-seat segments, which are then joined at the tree site. This procedure allows you to work in your shop or on level ground outside where you will have a firm work surface for solid and accurate nailing.

Each segment of the hexagon is made up of four seat boards, two seat supports, and a pair of cross half-lapped legs. This adds up to 72 miter cuts and a dozen angled dadoes—thus the need for jigs which will enable you to make the cuts with speed and accuracy.

Start by making straight crosscuts to get the 2× 4 stock down to working size for the seat tops. Cut six each of the following lengths: 14", 19", 24", and 29". Set up an old work board on saw horses and nail five lengths of ½-by-½-inch spacer strips, parallel to each other, spaced apart the width of a 2×4. Nail a scrap of 2×3 (or 2×4) outside the first and last spacer strip to serve as supports for an angled saw-guide strip.

Place one set of four seat boards to be mitered into the jig and draw a line at a 60-degree angle across one end of the four boards. Measure the distance between the saw blade and the edge of the saw base. Nail a guide strip into the front and rear 2×3 supports parallel to the angled pencil line but offset by the blade-to-base-edge dimension. This guide strip should extend about 8 inches beyond each end so the saw base is in contact with the guide as it enters and leaves the work. Adjust the saw-blade depth so it cuts through the 2×4 and about ¹⁄₁₆-inch into the

work table. Cut only one end of the four seat boards Then miter one end of the other five sets.

Leaving the bridged guide strip in place, nail a stop strip to the table at the other end of the jig, also set at an (opposing) 60-degree angle. Position it so the second cuts will produce mitered seat boards of the correct length, as shown in the plan. Slide the 2×4s into the jig so the previously mitered ends butt against the stop.

As you can see, the jig is basically quite simple and can readily be adapted to make other equal-sided geometric forms such as the pentagon, octagon, and

2.   Nail a 2×4 flush with the first and last guide strip.

3.   Measure the distance between the blade and base edge to determine the amount to offset the saw guide from the cutting line.

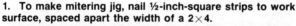

1.   To make mitering jig, nail ½-inch-square strips to work surface, spaced apart the width of a 2×4.

4.   Attach a guide strip, angled 60 degrees from the baseline, to the two outer 2×4s. The guide bridges the workpieces. Miter cut only one end of all the seat boards.

5. Attach a stop strip at the far end, then insert the boards so the mitered ends rest against the stop.

6. After making the second miter cut, remove the seat boards from the jig.

7. The six sets of seat boards required. Only one miter has been cut on all the pieces except those in the foreground

the like, by merely changing the miter angle. The procedure can be used for making interesting patio decks or laying interior floors.

Use a block plane to ease the sharp front and rear top corners of each seat board, then mark the nail locations. The paired nails should be slightly staggered to avoid splitting the seat supports. Put the seat boards aside while you work on the legs.

8. A block plane is used to ease the top corners of the seat members. A light sanding does the trick on the end corners.

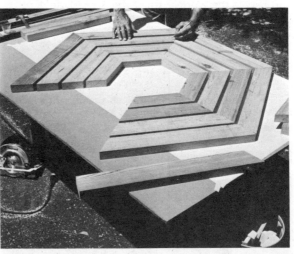

9. Mark the nail locations on each board for uniformity. Each pair of nails should be slightly offset to lessen the chance of splitting the seat supports.

THE LEGS

Cut 12 pieces of stock for the legs with parallel 53-degree miters on each end, to obtain an edge measurement of 22½ inches. These can be cut from 26-inch lengths of 2×4 using a jig made by nailing two scraps of 2×4 together as shown in the plan. If your tree flares out at ground level (as most do), it will be necessary to cut back slightly at the bottom rear of each leg to allow for necessary clearance.

The final jig required is the one used to form the cross half-lap joints. The dadoes for the joints are made by cutting a series of saw kerfs through half the thickness of the legs.

To make the jig, nail two strips of wood to a scrap of 2×4, angled at 74-degrees and parallel to each

12. A broad chisel is used to knock out the waste between kerfs. Also use the chisel to shave off any high spots that may remain.

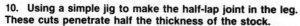

10. Using a simple jig to make the half-lap joint in the leg. These cuts penetrate half the thickness of the stock.

other. The spacing between these strips is the sum of the width of a 2×4 leg plus the dimensions from each side of the blade to the edge of the saw base. The blade projection is adjusted for a depth of cut equal to half the thickness of the 2×4. Make a series of about eight kerf cuts on the jig, then clear out the waste with a chisel.

Next, center a leg section against the notch in the jig. Partly drive two nails through the guide strips and into the work to prevent slipping. Make the kerf cuts by running the saw against both guides as was done to make the jig. Note that all twelve legs are identical, so you needn't be concerned about left or right miters or dadoes.

Use a sabre saw to cut the radius on the fronts of the seat-support members.

11. Unobstructed view of the jig. Partly driven nails keep the work from sliding. The guide strips, which are positioned to control the overall width of the notch, are angled 74 degrees. The inner cuts need not be guided; they are simply made freehand.

13. Round off the ends of the seat supports with a sabre saw. Use a coarse, set-tooth blade.

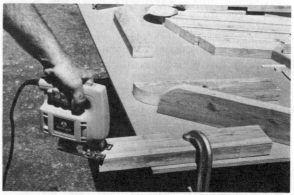

ASSEMBLY

This completes the sawing operations; the parts are now ready for assembly. You'll need 1¼-inch and 3-inch hot-dipped galvanized nails to assemble the bench.

Join the crossed leg members by driving four 1¼-inch nails, two on each side, diametrically opposed. Then attach a seat-support member to each side of the crossed legs using the 3-inch nails. If the wood has a tendency to split, blunt the points of the nails with a hammer blow. The blunt point reduces the

15. Use hot-dipped galvanized nails to assemble the bench. They hold firmly due to their rough surface and will not rust or stain.

14. All the parts necessary to make up one complete seat segment.

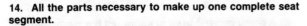

16. Nailing in the seat boards. The tack-nailed strip on the left end centers the leg section.

chance of splitting because it shears through the wood fibers; a sharp point wedges them apart.

Nail a set of four seat members to a pair of legs spaced ½ inch apart and overhanging the seat supports so the ends will center over the legs. A temporary cleat tacked to the seat support along the centerline will assure precise end alignment.

Assemble three seat segments on four leg sections. The second unit will be temporarily assembled on only two legs. However, in order to facilitate nailing and accurate alignment of the miters, you can temporarily tack-nail the free ends of the second half-unit to the seat boards of the completed first unit. Partly drive smooth finishing nails for this—rough-surfaced galvanized nails are very difficult to withdraw. When the two half-sections have been completed, pull out the temporary nails to separate them for final assembly around the tree.

Place the bench around the tree and check the seats with a spirit level. Lawn surfaces are rarely

17. Nearing the final stage of assembly. Note that the two segments in the foreground are only tack-nailed to the triple section at the rear.

18. The completed, but separated, half-hex sections. The sharp points at the corners will be sanded smooth.

A pointed mason's trowel and an ice chopper can be used to cut the 1½-inch-wide trench. To do an accurate job of it, drive two 3-inch finishing nails partly into the bottoms of the border strips, one near each end. Push these "spikes" into the soil to hold the strips in alignment. Press the trowel in a sawing motion against the strips to slice the turf. Deepen the cuts, if necessary, with the ice chopper; then lift out the strips of sod.

Lay the plastic sheeting around the tree, allowing the edges to rest in the trench. Push in the border strips, then set up the bench. Pour and spread the gravel.

Wolmanized lumber weathers to an attractive natural gray that blends well with most surroundings. It can be painted, however, as was the bench illustrated.

perfectly level, particularly around a tree, so it may be necessary to dig out soil under some legs to obtain solid footing and a level bench. When all is level, nail the last two sets of seat boards to the seat supports to permanently fit the bench around the tree.

If you prefer a weed-free stone base, it should be installed before final assembly of the bench.

To make the base you'll need six pieces of 2×4, black plastic sheeting, and gravel. The 2×4s are mitered 60 degrees at each end. The overall length of each strip is 40 inches. Make the cut by tilting the blade to 30 degrees and saw from the face of the work. These strips are set into a 2¾-inch-deep hexagonal trench dug in the soil. Projecting about ¾-inch above the surface, they will contain the stones and permit you to mow the lawn neatly up to the edge.

19. Use a level to check for even placement and dig out high spots if necessary. Note how the bottom back corners have been cut back to clear the tree trunk at ground level. As this was done belatedly, the cuts do not show in previous photos.

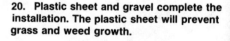

20. Plastic sheet and gravel complete the installation. The plastic sheet will prevent grass and weed growth.

25
Filigree
Window Panels

The window is generally the most prominent feature of a room and therefore warrants special attention in a decorating scheme. With the right treatment you can transform an ordinary window into the focal point of a room.

One interesting approach is this filigree open paneling which you can construct to surround a recessed window. The window doesn't have to be recessed either. You can adapt the paneling to box one or several flush windows or you can build it to span an entire wall.

Filigree paneling is made of durable ⅛-inch hardboard that is smooth on both sides. It is generally available in a variety of patterns and sizes—2′ × 4′, 16″ × 72″, 2′ × 6′ or 4′ × 8′.

The frame is constructed of ¾-inch by 1½-inch stock; oak was used here but practically any species will do. Several kinds of joints are employed, including the tongue-and-groove, lap, and dowel. The arched center framing that bridges the upright panels is done by kerf bending in a manner that is somewhat different from the usual procedure.

Obviously, dimensions are of little value in a project such as this because you will have to lay out the unit to suit your own space requirements.

Begin construction by cutting ¾-inch stock to

Before filigree panels were installed, window was rather ordinary and lacked interest.

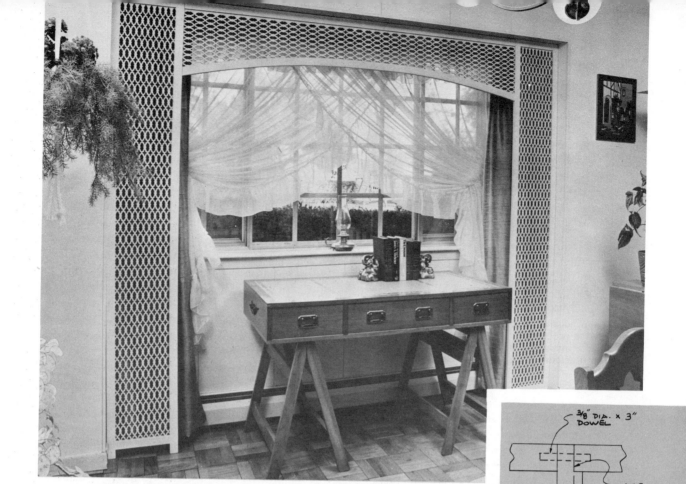

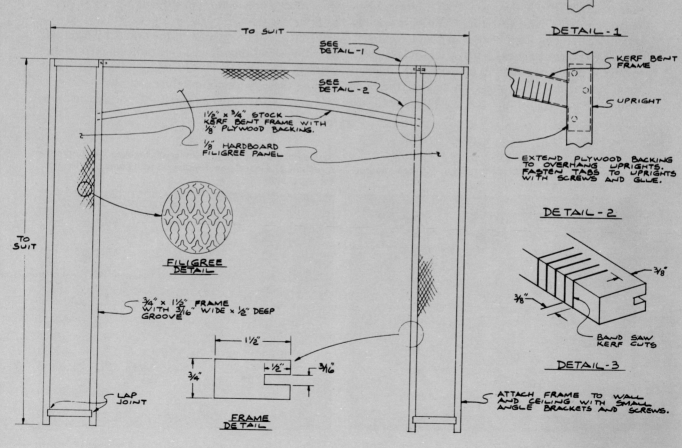

DETAIL-1

3/8" DIA. x 3" DOWEL

1/2"

LAP JOINT

DETAIL-2

KERF BENT FRAME

UPRIGHT

EXTEND PLYWOOD BACKING TO OVERHANG UPRIGHTS. FASTEN TABS TO UPRIGHTS WITH SCREWS AND GLUE.

DETAIL-3

3/8"

3/8"

BAND SAW KERF CUTS

TO SUIT

SEE DETAIL-1

SEE DETAIL-2

1½" x ¾" STOCK KERF BENT FRAME WITH 1/8" PLYWOOD BACKING.

1/8" HARDBOARD FILIGREE PANEL

FILIGREE DETAIL

¾" x 1½" FRAME WITH 3/16" WIDE x ½" DEEP GROOVE

TO SUIT

LAP JOINT

1½"

½"

3/4"

3/16"

FRAME DETAIL

ATTACH FRAME TO WALL AND CEILING WITH SMALL ANGLE BRACKETS AND SCREWS.

179

1. A dado head or regular blade can be used to cut the tongues and grooves. If the latter is used, make repeated passes after making sizing cuts. Note the clamped stop, which assures consistent sizing.

touching, wrap some masking tape around the center, then measure the stick.

When you have the four uprights made, set up a dado head in your table saw to cut a ³/₁₆-inch-wide groove ½-inch deep in one edge of each piece. The crosspieces are cut next. Note that the upper ones are slightly longer than the lower because they're joined differently. The upper crosspieces are butted in laps or notches cut into the verticals and reinforced with dowels. The lower crosspieces are tongued at the ends to fit into mating grooves in the verticals. The upper joints are more substantial to withstand stress at these points when moving the unit. Cut the notches in the uprights, then cut an upper crosspiece to length. Fit it in the notches and measure the inside dimension between the vertical members to determine the length of the lower crosspiece. Add 1-inch to the length of this crosspiece to allow for the tongues. Use the table saw to cut the shoulders to depth to produce ³/₁₆-inch-thick tongues. You can make repeated saw cuts to remove the waste or one pass with a dado head. Temporarily assemble the frame with clamps while you bore dowel holes in the upper corners. Use a doweling jig for this.

When the parts for the two frames have been cut, dry assemble them and set them in place. Measure the distance between them and cut a piece of stock to fit across the top between the two inside edges. This piece will be secured to the others by fitting it over the extra-long dowels left projecting from the edges of the frames. The doweling jig is used again to bore these holes accurately.

Note that the upper edges of the uprights require

1½-inch width. Make enough strips for the entire job and include a few feet extra for testing various cuts. Cut the four lengths for the uprights, dimensioned so they fit the space without forcing. Floors are seldom truly level, so measure both ends of the area before cutting. Flexible steel rules are fine for many purposes, but they can lead to error when measuring from floor to ceiling. The best way to obtain a perfect measurement from floor to ceiling is the easiest: Use two sticks, each of which is slightly greater than half the span to be measured. Overlap them at the center and press one against the floor and the other against the ceiling. When both are

2. A fine-tooth plywood blade is used to cut the tempered-hardboard filigree panel.

3. Combined half-lap and dowel joint makes a strong construction. The insert panel should fit with some play to allow for expansion.

4. Always use spiraled dowels so excess glue can escape.

5. Partial kerf cuts at close intervals render the oak framing sufficiently flexible to bend on edge. When the band-saw column gets in the way, simply make slightly angled cuts. Work from both ends towards the middle.

a partial groove to receive the center filigree section. These can be cut in advance if you know the dimension of the arched section. Otherwise it could wait until you've made the arched frame. This will give you an opportunity to vary the position of the arch for a balanced effect.

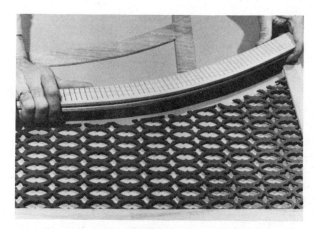

6. The kerfed strip bends with ease. The cuts are made up to the bottom of the groove. Note plywood backing in background. It will be added after the bent strip has been glued to shape.

KERFING THE ARCH

Now you're ready to make the curved lower crosspiece. This is done by kerfing on edge—making a series of saw cuts partially through the wood, at close intervals, to render it flexible. This operation is not particularly difficult, but it does require great care in handling the piece during cutting. Until it is finally formed and glued the flexible strip is rather fragile.

The kerf cuts are made from the solid edge towards the grooved edge of the strip. This way, the kerfs will close on themselves when the bend is made. Kerfing is usually done with a circular saw, but the relatively wide kerf it cuts is not necessary nor particularly desirable for this job. Deep cuts are necessary to allow the stock to bend on edge. Wide cuts would weaken the strip considerably. If possible, use a band saw or jigsaw. The band-saw column will not interfere if you feed the strip at a slight angle. Start at one end and work toward the center, then flip the piece over and work the other end towards the center so the cuts will slant symmetrically from each end. Make a series of cuts spaced ⅜ inch apart, to within ⅜ inch of the grooved edge.

Determine the amount of curvature desired with

7. Partly driven nails serve as fulcrum points for bend.

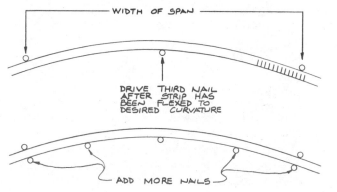

a long, flexible stick or by making a full size drawing of the section on paper. The piece is bent by gluing the kerfs while it is tensioned against standing nails.

Drive three nails partly into a table or workboard. Two nails should be positioned to correspond to the length of the span. Place the kerfed strip against these two nails and flex it to get the correct curve. The third nail is centered on the opposite edge and partly driven into the table. Additional nails are used but are not driven until the glue has been applied.

Remove the strip and tape down pieces of kitchen wax paper in its place. This will prevent the workpiece from gluing itself to the table.

Make up a pasty glue mixture by stirring in some fine sawdust. With the piece in the straight position and the kerfs open, apply regular glue to both surfaces, brushing briskly to work the glue well into the crevices. Then apply the sawdust-thickened glue and work it in with a putty knife. Do this on both sides. Carefully scrape the excess from one surface and place that side down, on the wax paper, between the nails to form the curve. Add extra nails as required, then use the putty knife to remove excess glue from the top surface. Check the groove and clean out any glue that may be present by running a stick through it.

When the glue has set, sand the surfaces. Clamp the strip in place on the uprights to mark the ends for angled cutoffs. A ⅛-inch plywood backing with ends overhanging is glued to the back of the bent strip. This serves to reinforce the piece. The overhanging tabs permit gluing and screwing onto the back of the uprights. Use a spokeshave or a router with a corner-rounding cutter to trim the plywood skin to size.

9. Flex the strip to shape by bridging with nails set in predetermined positions. Layer of wax paper keeps the work from sticking to the table. Scrape off excess glue before it sets.

10. Clamp the bent strip to mark the ends for cutoff.

8. White glue and fine sawdust are mixed together to make a paste. Brush it onto both sides before bending and work it into the open kerfs with a putty knife.

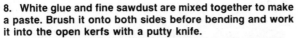

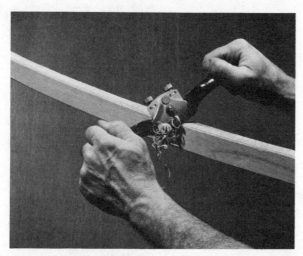

11. Add the plywood backing and trim the edges with a spokeshave, then sand.

12. Curved piece goes on last. It is secured with screws driven through plywood tabs on back.

When all the framing members have been completed, cut the filigree panels to size and assemble the two end frames. Small angle brackets are used to secure the unit to the walls, ceiling, and floor.

Join the end frames to the top-center crosspiece with glue and one dowel in each end; then move the unit into place and secure the brackets. The shaped filigree panel will have to be bowed slightly to spring it into the grooves. The curved strip is added last.

Paint the unit with a few cans of good quality spray enamel. This should be done outdoors or in the garage near opened doors. Be sure to apply a primer coat first, then two or three light applications of the enamel.

26
Layered
Veneer Turning

Generally, a solid block of wood is preferred for lathe turning. Glued-up stock is usually used when the material available isn't thick enough or when you want an inlayed effect.

An extreme example of the latter is the veneered turning shown here, which is composed of fifty different kinds of wood. The unique turning block is made by laminating veneers of exotic woods.

The saltshaker and peppermill set is one application of the idea, but the attractive turnings can be used as pencil/pen holders when drilled with the appropriate holes or simply left as is to serve as paperweights. However they're used, the turnings are sure to provoke conversation.

The project is economically feasible because you use two low-cost sample packets of veneer specimens which are available from one of the leading cabinet-wood supply houses—Constantine (address listed in back of book). These veneers, measuring approximately $\frac{1}{28}$" $\times$ 4" $\times$ 9", are labeled with the common and botanical names of the species and country of origin. With these samples you can quickly learn to recognize the color, grain, and figure of some of the woods used on furniture. They will also be helpful for making a selection for shop projects before buying stock in large quantities.

One hundred pieces of veneer must be glued together in order to build up a turning block approximately 4 inches square by 7 inches long. Two pieces of each specimen are used so the veneers are clearly visible in cross section.

The gluing task will be somewhat of a challenge. You will have to apply glue to ninety-eight surfaces! It would be virtually impossible to attempt this in one operation. So much time would elapse during the application that the glue would begin to set, or perhaps even dry, on the early pieces before the clamps could be applied. Also, some of the burl veneers are so wavy that it would require more pressure than can be exerted with ordinary clamps to squeeze all 100 pieces into perfect contact. It can, however, be done in two or perhaps three stages.

The choice of glue is very important. Most modern glues, particularly the white glues, have very short setting times. Old-fashioned liquid hide glue, on the other hand, has a long setup time, so this is what you should use.

As mentioned before, glue-wetted surfaces are

slippery and will shift when clamp pressure is applied. The problem is normally solved by driving two nails in a waste area. Obviously, this method cannot be used here. A simple but effective gluing jig is used instead.

The jig is made with two blocks of ¾-inch-thick stock measuring about 6 by 9 inches.

Draw an outline 4⅛ by 7⅛ inches centered on one block. Drill eight holes around the outline, two on each side as indicated in the drawing. This will be the upper block. The diameter of the holes should be large enough to allow free passage over the heads of 3-inch finishing nails. Lay a piece of wax paper on the surface of the other (lower) block, allowing it to overhang the edges slightly. Place the upper block onto the lower and drive nails through the predrilled holes partly into the lower block. The wax paper serves as a barrier to prevent the work from sticking to the jig.

The veneers are quite varied in color. For the most striking effect they should be arranged so that contrasting colors will be next to each other. Lay them out in pairs on a large table, arranged in order of assembly. Trim off the portions with the labels with a knife and straightedge, then stack the veneers in a pile ready for gluing. Have five sturdy C clamps of sufficient jaw capacity handy.

Apply the glue to both surfaces of the veneers with a brush, but coat the first and last pieces on one side only. Work on a piece of scrap board or cardboard. Place each veneer into the jig, one atop the other, as they are coated. Although the jig will hold about fifty pieces of veneer, it is advisable to stack about thirty pieces for each gluing session. If you exceed this number it will be difficult to apply adequate clamp pressure to achieve good contact throughout the pack. When the last veneer of the group has been placed, lay a sheet of wax paper over it and add the upper block. Apply the clamps, one in the center and four near the corners. Squeeze the pack very tightly. Repeat the operation for the second or third pack.

Before final glue-up of the partial packs, check the mating surfaces for absolute flatness. Press them together and observe whether there is any rocking, which indicates a high spot. If there is, it must be sanded perfectly flat in order to obtain a good final glue joint. If you see a hollow (not likely), sanding also will be necessary.

Square off the ends of the completed block and glue solid, hardwood, lathe-center blocks onto each end. This permits utilizing most of the veneer block without waste. Allow the block to dry thoroughly, about a week, before turning.

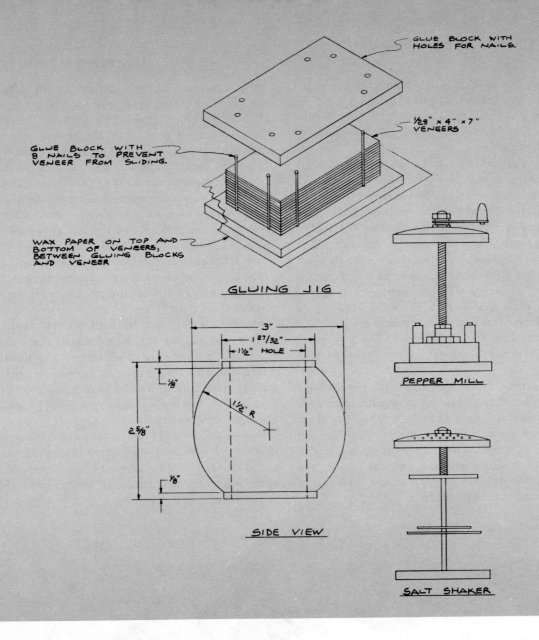

GLUE BLOCK WITH
HOLES FOR NAILS.

1/28" x 4" x 7"
VENEERS

GLUE BLOCK WITH
8 NAILS TO PREVENT
VENEER FROM SLIDING.

WAX PAPER ON TOP AND
BOTTOM OF VENEERS,
BETWEEN GLUING BLOCKS
AND VENEER

GLUING JIG

3"

1 27/32"

1 1/2" HOLE

1/8"

2 5/8"

1 1/2" R

1/8"

SIDE VIEW

PEPPER MILL

SALT SHAKER

1. Arrange the veneers in an order which will create interesting color contrasts. Two of each species should be combined to provide sufficient thickness.

2. Use a wide brush and, working quickly, apply glue to both sides. Glued veneers are stacked on the jig, which consists of a "fence" of eight nails. This keeps them from sliding during clamping.

186

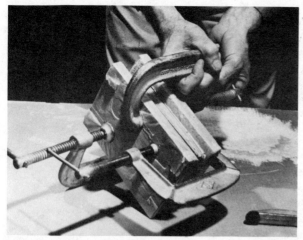

3. Apply heavy clamp pressure to offset wavy surfaces of some veneers. Holes in upper block allows projecting nails to pass through freely.

4. Parting-chisel cuts are made to set the diameters.

The plan shows dimensions for typical 3-inch saltshaker and peppermill mechanism. It is advisable to obtain the hardware beforehand so you can check the actual size requirements because variations occur. They're available through several of the woodcraft supply houses (see listing at back of book).

Insert the block between the lathe centers and, with a caliper, check against a full-size drawing to turn the two balls. Most of the shaping can be done by eye after preliminary depth-gauging cuts are made with the parting chisel. Start with a gouge to rough-turn a cylinder; then set the caliper for approximate diameters and make the appropriate depth cuts. Round the balls with a spear point and skew. Pay particular attention to the end shoulder diameter, which must conform to the dimensions of the hardware.

When the shaping has been completed, sand and apply several coats of clear finish of your choice while the piece is still between centers. Next, turn down the waste ends to a size which will fit a three-jaw chuck or a screw center (either can be used). Separate the balls with a parting chisel. Then secure the waste end of one into the chuck.

To bore the hole through the center for the hardware, insert a wood drill bit of the appropriate diameter into an accessory geared chuck installed in the tailstock. Operate the lathe at moderate speed and slowly feed the drill bit into the work by turning the tailstock feed handle. A pencil mark or a piece of masking tape on the drill is used to gauge the depth of the hole. This is a practical and safe way to bore such a large hole in a relatively small turning.

5. You can approximate the midsections, but you must make careful checks of the end diameters with a caliper so the hardware will fit properly.

6. The best way to bore the large holes for the hardware is to feed the drill bit into the work slowly with the lathe running at moderately high speed.

27

Dry Sink Bar

The dry sink was an important piece of furniture in households of yesteryear when it was used for storing water and utensils, and for taking sponge baths and washing dishes.

With the advent of indoor plumbing the original function fortunately became obsolete, but the charming design has endured.

This slightly modified version, with open shelves and a colorful ceramic tile-lined basin in lieu of the traditional copper lining, serves ideally as a bar. But it can also be used to contain plants, books, or a TV set and audio components.

Relatively simple construction details have been incorporated into the design of the unit, so you should be able to duplicate it with ease.

The basic cabinet is made of ½-inch plywood and features a one-piece face frame. This is a shortcut that eliminates the need for cutting, jointing, and gluing individual stiles and rails. Ordinary rabbet and butt joints with cleats predominate for the main assemblies, thus simplifying fabrication and assembly. The use of cleats assures accurate alignment of the plywood cabinet components during nailing and gluing and results in strong joints.

Start by cutting the top, bottom, back, two sides, and front. The one-piece frame is made by dropping

out the two door openings with a series of inside, or pocket, cuts on the table saw. The procedure is basically the same as was described earlier for the veneer table project—you raise the rotating blade into the work, essentially a plunge cut in reverse.

Since the blade is concealed by the work at the start of the cut, it is important to make a guide mark on the fence before starting. Then you'll know where to position the work so the blade will emerge in the right place. To make the mark, move the rip fence close to the blade and put a pencil mark on the fence at the point where the rear edge of the blade just protrudes above the surface of the saw table. Continue this mark on the fence so it will be clearly visible. Also make a mark opposite the front edge of the blade, to indicate where to avoid putting your hand during the operation.

Draw the outline for the cutouts on the face of the panel. Adjust the fence for the desired width of cut, measuring from the fence to the side of the blade facing the fence. Depress the blade below the table surface, then position the work so the rear limit of the cutting line is about ¼-inch beyond the guide mark on the fence. Hold the panel in place firmly with one hand, safely away from the blade area. With the other hand turn on the power, then grasp

Closeup of the waterproof ceramic-tile top.

the elevating crank and elevate the blade slowly. When the blade has cut through, use both hands to advance the panel to continue the cut to the near limit. Hold the work in place, stop the saw, depress the blade and reposition the work for the next cut. Make all cuts of the same width before readjusting the fence.

It is advisable to leave a small, uncut web at the corners to prevent the waste from shifting and possibly binding against the blade as the final cut is made. The webs can be cut out by hand to free the waste. One of the dropout pieces will yield the two open shelves. The other can be used for another project.

The four corner posts are made by cutting 1⅝-inch-square pine baluster stock to length. The two that attach to the back panel require a wide rabbet. This is best done by making two saw cuts at right angles. The back posts receive a straight dado across the face, but the front posts require a corner dado. This can be done by making two shoulder cuts into the corner using a handsaw. The waste is then cleaned out with a chisel.

Next, the cabinet is partially assembled. Mark positions for the cleats on the front, back, and bottom panels, and attach them with glue and nails. Attach the corner posts to the back panel, making sure the

top edges are flush, and put it aside. Using 1½-inch finishing nails, glue/nail the front to the sides, then add the bottom panel. The back panel is attached last. The top panel is not attached at this time because it must first be fitted with the sink walls.

The inside shelf rests on cleats and is nailed from the outside, through the sides and back. Note that this shelf is made of ¾-inch stock. The outside shelves cannot be nailed since they do not back up to any solid support; therefore they are attached with glue and screws.

SINK SECTION

While the glue dries on the cabinet you can begin work on the sink section. Rabbets are required on the bottom of each of the four wall members as well as on the ends of the front and back pieces. Note that the rabbet on the bottom of the front wall is angled 12 degrees so it fits properly against the plywood base. Use a dado cutter to cut the rabbets, before sawing the contours.

Use a band or sabre saw to cut the contours, then smooth the edges with a spokeshave and sand. A router with a ¼-inch corner-rounding bit is used to ease the top edges of the sink sides. The outside

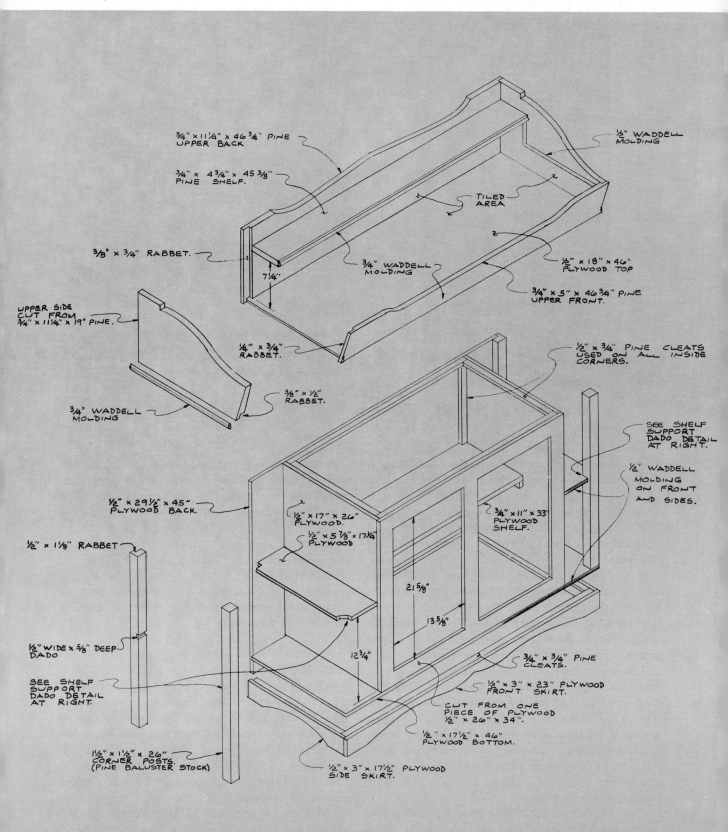

3/4" x 11 1/4" x 46 3/4" PINE
UPPER BACK

3/4" x 4 3/4" x 45 3/8"
PINE SHELF.

3/8" x 3/4" RABBET.

7 1/4"

UPPER SIDE
CUT FROM
3/4" x 11 1/4" x 19" PINE.

1/4" x 3/4"
RABBET.

3/4" WADDELL
MOLDING

3/8" x 1/2"
RABBET.

1/2" WADDELL
MOLDING

TILED
AREA

3/4" WADDELL
MOLDING

1/2" x 18" x 46"
PLYWOOD TOP

3/4" x 5" x 46 3/4" PINE
UPPER FRONT.

1/2" x 3/4" PINE CLEATS
USED ON ALL INSIDE
CORNERS.

SEE SHELF
SUPPORT
DADO DETAIL
AT RIGHT.

1/2" WADDELL
MOLDING
ON FRONT
AND SIDES.

1/2" x 29 1/2" x 45"
PLYWOOD BACK.

1/2" x 17" x 26"
PLYWOOD.

1/2" x 5 7/8" x 17 1/4"
PLYWOOD

3/4" x 11" x 33"
PLYWOOD
SHELF.

1/2" x 1 1/8" RABBET

2 1 5/8"

13 5/8"

3/4" x 3/4" PINE
CLEATS.

1/2" WIDE x 5/8" DEEP
DADO

12 3/4"

1/2" x 3" x 23" PLYWOOD
FRONT SKIRT.

SEE SHELF
SUPPORT
DADO DETAIL
AT RIGHT.

CUT FROM ONE
PIECE OF PLYWOOD
1/2" x 26" x 34".

1/2" x 17 1/2" x 46"
PLYWOOD BOTTOM.

1 1/2" x 1 1/2" x 26"
CORNER POSTS.
(PINE BALUSTER STOCK)

1/2" x 3" x 17 1/2" PLYWOOD
SIDE SKIRT.

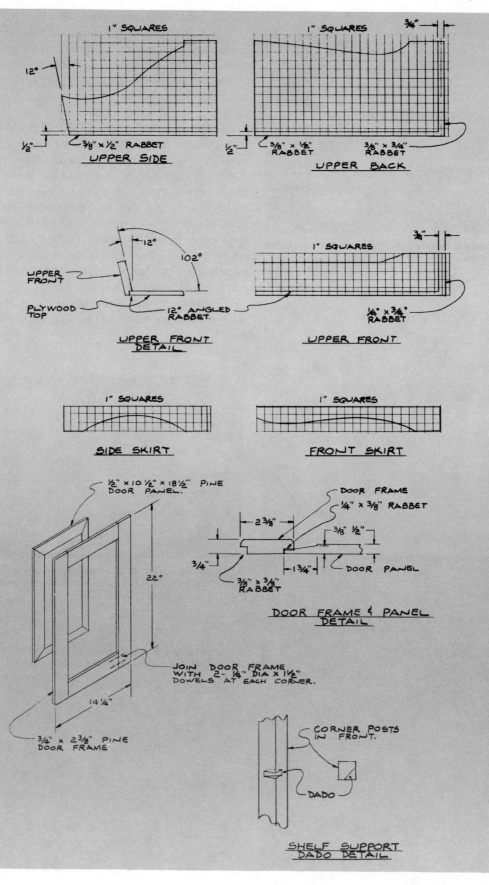

1" SQUARES

12°

½"   ⌐ 3/8" x ½" RABBET
UPPER SIDE

1" SQUARES   3/4"

½"   ⌐ 3/8" x ½"   3/8" x 3/4"
RABBET   RABBET
UPPER BACK

12°

102°

UPPER FRONT

PLYWOOD TOP   12° ANGLED RABBET.

UPPER FRONT DETAIL

1" SQUARES   3/4"

¼" x 3/4" RABBET
UPPER FRONT

1" SQUARES
SIDE SKIRT

1" SQUARES
FRONT SKIRT

½" x 10 ½" x 18 ½" PINE DOOR PANEL.

22"

14 ¼"

3/4" x 2 3/8" PINE DOOR FRAME

JOIN DOOR FRAME WITH 2 - ¼" DIA X 1½" DOWELS AT EACH CORNER.

DOOR FRAME
¼" x 3/8" RABBET

2 3/8"

3/8" ½"

3/4"
1 3/4"   DOOR PANEL

3/8" x 3/8" RABBET

DOOR FRAME & PANEL DETAIL

CORNER POSTS IN FRONT.

DADO

SHELF SUPPORT DADO DETAIL

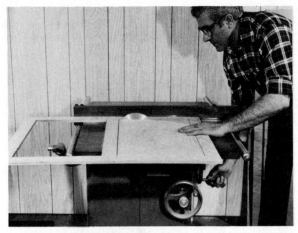

1. The saw blade is elevated into the work to drop out the openings for the doors in the front panel.

2. Cleats reinforce the butt joints and help to keep the parts in precise alignment.

3. Outside shelves are attached with glue and screws. Shelves and posts are notched to form dado joints.

edges can be rounded after assembly. You can run the router completely off the edges of the front and back walls, but you must stop short near the ends of the side walls; otherwise there will be a depression at the top edges of the rabbet joints. Put a pencil mark ¼-inch in from each end of the side walls and start and stop the router at these points.

Attach cleats to the bottom side of the base panel, then proceed to attach the sidewalls using glue and nails. Nail in the ends first, then the front and back. Attach the front posts, then add the sink assembly to the cabinet. Apply glue and make sure to drive the nails into the cabinet, not into the cleats. If you predrill a few pilot holes into the panel bottom, ¼-inch away from the cleats, the holes will indicate where to nail. The bottom skirts are attached by nailing into the edge of the plywood base. The cleats provide added strength.

Now you can make the raised panel doors. The door frames are made of ¾-inch solid-pine stock

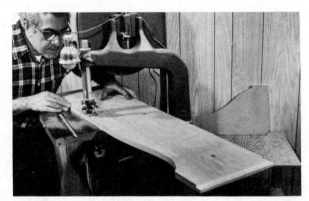

4. Contours are cut with a band, jig or sabre saw. This is done after rabbets have been cut at bottom and ends.

5. Spokeshave is most effective tool for removing saw-blade ripples. Be sure to stroke with the grain.

6. Sink walls are glued and nailed; the back first, then sides and front. Inside edges have been rounded with router in advance.

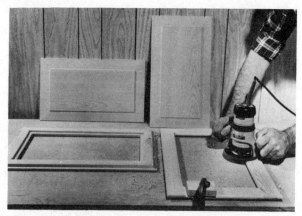

8. Inner, rear edges of door frames are rabbeted with the router to form a recess for raised panels. Corner-rounding bit is used to ease the front edges. Rabbet is also cut on rear, outside edges to form lip.

7. The outside edges are rounded with router after assembly. Use a quarter-round bit with a pilot end.

assembled with doweled edge joints. Cut the rails and stiles to size and mark the edges for the dowel holes. Use a drill press or a portable drill with a doweling jig for accuracy. Apply pressure to the joints with two bar clamps.

Round the front edges of the door frames with the router and a ¼-inch corner-rounding bit. Do this before cutting the rabbets on the back so there will be an edge for the piloted bit to ride against. This is particularly so for the outside rabbet, which is made to form the lip. This rabbet is cut on the table saw using a dado head. The inside rabbet for the raised panel is shallow and can be made with the router as there will be sufficient wall to support the pilot end of the bit.

The raised panel for the door is easy to make using a rotary planing accessory attached to the arbor of a

radial-arm saw, or by tilting the blade on a table saw and running the piece through on edge.

To make the cut with the planer, set it up as shown in the photograph, with the arbor tilted 5 degrees off vertical. Clamp a piece of wood about 4 by 30 inches to the saw table, butted against the fence. This auxiliary fence should have a round cutout at center to allow clearance for the cutter. Position the planer so it will cut 1¾ inches from the edge of the work. Lock the carriage in place. Turn on the power and run the work from right to left past the rotating cutter, shaving off stock to form the wide bevel. This accessory, available from Sears Roebuck, causes no kickback and you'll find it easy and safe to use.

After the bevels have been cut, you will have to perform two more operations to complete the panels. The second step is to make a minute cut at the top of the bevel to square the angled shoulder resulting from the original angled approach of the cutter. Zero the arbor, adjust the carriage position and the cutter height and make the passes. Finally, cut a small flat into the beveled edge so the panel will fit flush into the door-frame recess. This is done by setting the arbor of the radial-arm saw at vertical, and repositioning the carriage to obtain a ⅜-inch-wide cut.

To cut the raised panel with the table saw, tilt the blade 5 degrees and elevate it to make a 1¾-inch-high cut. Do not attempt this cut without a safety jig. The combination of a high blade setting and the relatively low fence would bring the hands too close to the blade. The clamped arrangement shown will enable you to make this cut safely.

When the four bevels have been cut, zero the

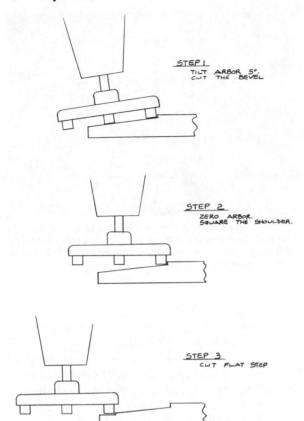

STEP 1
TILT ARBOR 5°.
CUT THE BEVEL

STEP 2
ZERO ARBOR.
SQUARE THE SHOULDER.

STEP 3
CUT FLAT STEP

How to form the raised panel with a radial-arm saw using a planer attachment. The tool is safe and effective.

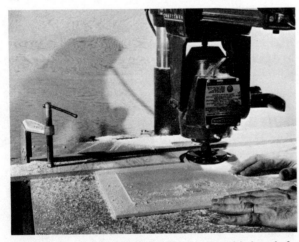

9. The planer attachment quickly cuts the wide bevels for the raised panel inserts.

blade and repeat the steps described previously. Make the shallow shoulder cuts with the work face flat on the saw table and the edge up against the fence.

Note that the raised panel is made of ½-inch solid-pine stock. Plywood is not recommended because the plies would be exposed and show up vividly on the beveled surface. They would be difficult to conceal even with a heavy finish.

The doors are hung with ⅜-inch offset hinges. Attach them first to the door, then to the frame.

Glazed ceramic tiles are used to line the sink. A pattern with straight-edged pieces is easier to fit. The tiles come in 12″ × 12″ squares, held together by a mesh backing. Cut through the mesh as required to fit the tiles in place. Do not apply adhesive until all the tile sections have been fitted. In some areas it will be necessary to cut through individual tiles to obtain the fit. A tile nipper, which can be borrowed from the tile dealer, will enable you to cut the tiles. Some cutting can be avoided by rearranging individual small tiles.

When all the tiles have been fitted, mark them in sequential order with tabs of masking tape before removing them. Apply a layer of tile adhesive to the wood using a notched spreader. Lay the base tiles first, then the sides.

When the tile adhesive has set, the tile joints are filled with grout cement. Available in a variety of colors, it comes in powder form and is mixed with

10. Safe and accurate method for cutting a raised panel on the table saw.

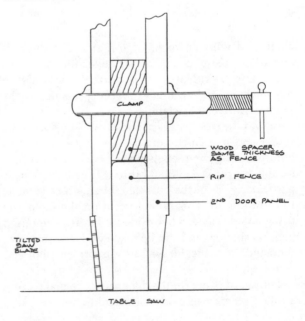

CLAMP

WOOD SPACER
SAME THICKNESS
AS FENCE

RIP FENCE

2ND DOOR PANEL

TILTED
SAW
BLADE

TABLE SAW

11. Prefitted sections of ceramic tile are bedded into a serrated layer of tile adhesive.

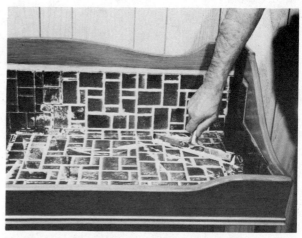

12. Window squeegee is used to work tile grout into the grooves. Excess is wiped off before it hardens.

water. Mix the grout according to the manufacturer's instructions and apply with a window-washing squeegee. Work the material well into the joints and wipe off the excess. When the grout has set for the length of time specified in the instructions, wipe clean with a damp cloth and polish with a dry cloth. The shelf is installed after the tiling has been completed.

Hardwood molding in ½-inch and ¾-inch widths is used to cap the tiles and to trim the cabinet. Drill pilot holes in the molding to prevent splitting and attach with brads and a small bead of glue.

Due to the variety of wood species used, a transparent stain finish is not suitable. Use a solid-color paint or an opaque woodgraining finish. The latter was used on the prototype, followed with two coats of clear satin varnish.

The grained finish is accomplished in two steps. A solid-color base coat is applied overall. This may be a latex or oil-based flat paint, depending on the type of kit you purchase. The latex base material is usually preferred because it dries quickly. The glaze coat is applied fully to one area at a time. A dry brush is then stroked over the wet glaze to produce the grain.

28

Bunk Bed Group

You'll get plenty of use in limited space from this three-piece module. Measuring 32 inches wide by 11 feet in length, it features lots of shelving for books, ample table surface, and five storage drawers. The bunk section is dimensioned to accommodate a 30-by-75-inch spring mattress, which provides maximum comfort for sitting, lounging, and sleeping.

You can arrange the pieces in-line if space permits or you can set them up separately.

Furniture of this kind has traditionally been over-built, with ¾-inch plywood serving as the basic structural material. This grouping has been designed with a consideration for economy: ½-inch plywood is used for all but the center bookshelves and the L-shaped tops of the end sections, which are made of ¾-inch ply.

Fir plywood is the logical choice for this project if you want to keep cost as low as possible. This dictates an opaque, pigmented finish of paint or simulated woodgraining due to the characteristic wild grain of this wood. You can subdue the contrasty grain to permit a stained clear finish by precoating with a penetrating sealer as described in Chapter 6. The alternative would be to use an attractive hardwood veneer plywood which could be clear-finished either natural or stained. But this approach would be considerably more costly and more involved as well. Involved because the large number of exposed veneer-core edges would require concealment by edge-banding with matching solid-wood strips. If you prefer this course, it will be necessary to reduce the dimensions shown by ⅛-inch in anticipation of a ⅛-inch buildup with solid edge strips. A ¼-inch overall reduction would be required where two opposite edges are involved. Now to get on with the construction of this project.

The unit is assembled with cleat-reinforced butt joints, nailed and glued. While the butt is looked upon as the weakest of the joints, bear in mind that when it is bolstered with a cleat, it becomes, in effect, a rabbet. If two cleats surround a butted member, the joint is basically not much different than a dado. Nails do strengthen a joint to some extent, but in a construction such as this their primary function is to aid in assembly. They keep the parts in alignment and serve to provide the contact pressure needed to achieve a good glue joint without the need for a large number of bar clamps.

You can use *A-C* grade plywood for this project. As described earlier, the *A-C* designation refers to the quality of the face veneer: *A* denotes a smooth, paintable surface with some neatly made repairs; *C*

The bunk bed group can be set up in-line against one wall . . .

. . . or it can be arranged in this manner. Another alternative is to put the three pieces in the center of the room with the cabinets backed up against the back of the bunk bed.

Three of the five roomy drawers. Decorative hardware is not yet installed.

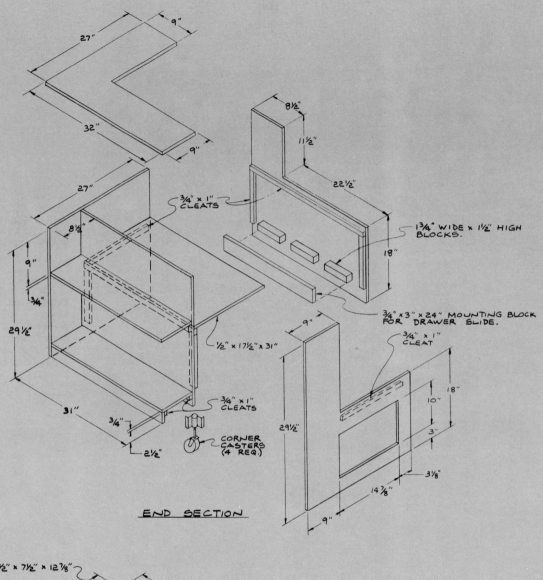

27"
9"
32"
9"
27"
8½"
11½"
22½"
8½"
3/4" x 1" CLEATS
1 3/4" WIDE x 1½" HIGH BLOCKS.
9"
18"
9"
3/4"
29½"
½" x 17½" x 31"
3/4" x 3" x 24" MOUNTING BLOCK FOR DRAWER SLIDE.
9"
3/4" x 1" CLEAT
18"
10"
3"
29½"
14 7/8"
3 1/8"
31"
3/4"
3/4" x 1" CLEATS
2½"
CORNER CASTERS (4 REQ.)
9"

END SECTION

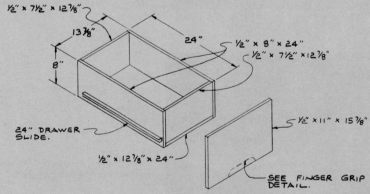

½" x 7½" x 12 7/8"
13 7/8"
24"
½" x 8" x 24"
½" x 7½" x 12 7/8"
8"
½" x 11" x 15 7/8"
24" DRAWER SLIDE.
½" x 12 7/8" x 24"
SEE FINGER GRIP DETAIL.

END SECTION DRAWER

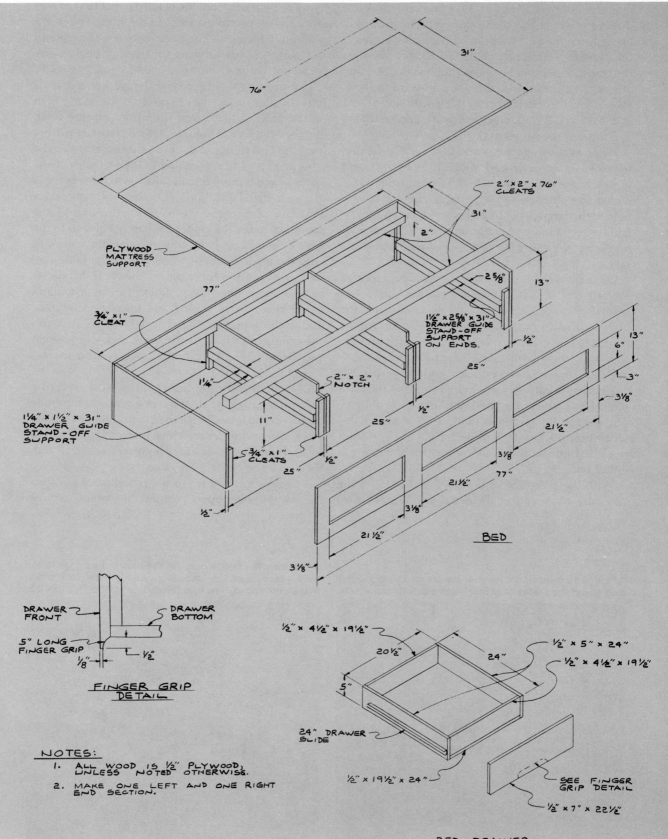

76"

31"

2" x 2" x 76"
CLEATS

31"

2"

PLYWOOD
MATTRESS
SUPPORT

77"

2 5/8"

13"

¾" x 1"
CLEAT

1½" x 2 5/8" x 31"
DRAWER GUIDE
STAND-OFF
SUPPORT
ON ENDS.

½"

13"

6"

25"

3"

3⅛"

1¼"

2" x 2"
NOTCH

½"

21½"

1¼" x 1½" x 31"
DRAWER GUIDE
STAND-OFF
SUPPORT

11"

25"

3⅛"

77"

¾" x 1"
CLEATS

25"

½"

21½"

3⅛"

BED

½"

21½"

3⅛"

3⅛"

DRAWER
FRONT

DRAWER
BOTTOM

5" LONG
FINGER GRIP

½"

⅛"

FINGER GRIP
DETAIL

½" x 4½" x 19½"

20½"

24"

½" x 5" x 24"

½" x 4½" x 19½"

5"

24" DRAWER
SLIDE

½" x 19½" x 24"

SEE FINGER
GRIP DETAIL

½" x 7" x 22½"

NOTES:
1. ALL WOOD IS ½" PLYWOOD,
   UNLESS NOTED OTHERWISE.
2. MAKE ONE LEFT AND ONE RIGHT
   END SECTION.

BED DRAWER

indicates a veneer which may contain defects. With the exception of the bookcase compartments, only one side of the panels will be exposed. If you select the panels carefully, checking the backs as well as the fronts, you should have no problem in obtaining one or more with reasonably good areas on the back face to use for the bookcases. You will also need 1 ×2, 2×2 and 2×4 lumber for cleats, and bedboard and drawer-slide supports.

When measuring the plywood for cutting, be sure to allow for the saw-kerf width between adjacent pieces. Make the initial cuts with a clamped or tack-nailed straightedge and a portable circular saw to reduce the large panel to pieces small enough to be handled on a table or radial-arm saw. Of course, if necessary, the entire job can be done with a portable saw.

Large plywood panels must be firmly supported for safe and accurate cutting. Two sawhorses and several pieces of 2×3 or 2×4 set up as shown in the photo will serve as a temporary work surface. Adjust the blade projection so it cuts about ⅛-inch into the support. When sawing an 8-foot panel lengthwise, use four supports, two on each side of the cut.

Five inside cutouts are required to make the one-piece front panels for the bunk and end cabinets. The pocket-cut procedure with a table saw is described for the Dry Sink project. Here the operation is carried out with a radial-arm saw. You can use either one.

With the exception of the small end-cuts for the bunk drawer openings, the radial-arm saw is set up in the out-rip position: the blade parallel to the table fence and closest to the front of the table. The in-rip position, which puts the blade between the column and motor, is not advised for making pocket cuts because it limits visibility of the blade on the work.

The procedure for making the pocket cut is as follows: Elevate the blade; position the work; turn on the power; then lower the blade into the work and feed the work through. Before you start cutting there are two things to do: First, make a mark on the table and fence to correspond to the rear edge of the blade where it intersects the stock when the blade is in the lowered position. This line will serve as a guide for positioning the work for the start of the cut. Next, lower the blade so it barely bottoms in the table's rip trough. Now turn the elevating crank to raise the blade to about 1 inch above the table surface, counting the full turns of the crank handle as you go. Remember the number of turns made and repeat them when raising and lowering the blade during the actual cutting. This will insure that you cut completely through the work and will prevent you from accidentally cutting deeply into the tabletop.

Lay out the cutting lines on the work, carrying them to the edges so they can be aligned to the guide marks on the table. Raise the blade and position the work against the fence. Move the carriage in or out to position the blade for the correct width of cut; then lock the carriage in place.

You may know this but it bears emphasis: When the saw is in the ripping position the workpiece must

1. Large 4×8 panels are tough to handle on a table saw. It's best to cut the pieces to manageable size with a portable.

2. Making the inside cuts for the drawer openings in the bunk's face panel. The blade is lowered into the work, which is then advanced. Saw is in the out-rip position for this job.

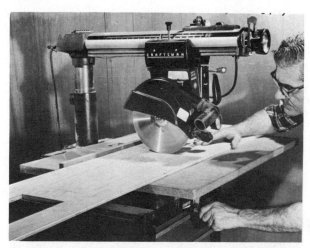

3. Carriage is locked in the crosscut position and blade is cranked down to make the smaller, inside end-cuts.

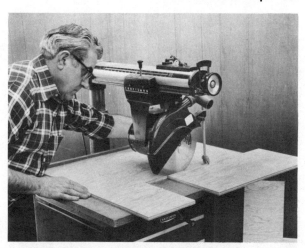

4. Inside corners are easily managed with the radial-arm saw. Be sure blade comes to a full stop before withdrawing the piece. Slight kerfs at the intersection can be patched with wood-filling compound.

always be fed in the direction *against* the rotation of the blade. This means the work is moved from left to right when *out-ripping.* Also, always use the anti-kickback fingers when ripping.

To make the cut, turn on the power, crank the blade down the required number of turns, then slowly feed the work forward until the blade reaches the inside corner. When all four cuts have been made, the corners will still be connected since the radial kerf will not have cornered at the bottom of the work. Sever the corners with a hand or sabre saw.

The saw is repositioned in the normal crosscutting mode for making the small inside end-cuts on the bunk-face panel. Center the blade over the cutting line, then lock the carriage and make the cut. You'll find that with a 10-inch-diameter blade the cut will fall short of the full 6 inches of cut required when the blade bottoms. The rest of the cut is made with a hand or sabre saw.

The L-shaped members of the cabinets are also cut with the saw in the out-rip position. In this case, the right-angle cuts are made completely into the corner so that the second cut will sever the waste. The resulting intersecting radial kerfs at the corners are easily patched with wood-filler compound.

If your workshop is not equipped with a radial-arm or table saw, you can make the pocket cuts with a portable circular saw. A simple guide fence—a 30-inch length of 2×4—will enable you to make the cuts with ease and accuracy. This high-walled rip guide is necessary to insure that the saw base is held true and square to the workpiece at the onset of the plunge cut. Clamp or tack-nail the guide to the work, offset from the cutting line an amount equal to the blade-to-base-edge distance. Tape the blade guard up and out of the way and exercise great care during this operation. See page 000 for photos of this procedure.

Rest the toe of the saw base on the work, with the rear raised so the blade is not in contact with the wood. Put slight sideways pressure on the saw so the edge of the base is in contact with the high fence. Switch on the power; then, with a pivoting motion, lower the saw into the work. When the saw base is fully down and in contact with the work, push the saw forward and continue the cut up to the inside corner. Make sure the blade has come to a full stop before withdrawing it from the kerf. Reposition the guide and repeat the step.

When all the parts have been cut, sand all surfaces that will be exposed, particularly those that would be in confined areas after assembly.

ASSEMBLING THE UNIT

The correct order of assembly is important. Start with one of the end units. Cut ¾-inch by 1-inch cleats to length and nail and glue them into place as indicated in the plan. Position the cleats on the front and side L-shaped members exactly ½-inch from the outside edges to assure flush-fitting butt joints. Through-nail the shelves to the backup panel.

Begin the final assembly by attaching the tabletop to the left and right sides. A couple of temporary nails started into the corners of the top and into the

5. Sanding is much easier if you do it before assembly. Sand only those parts that will be exposed to view. Be careful not to round butting edges.

7. Set all nail heads as you progress with the assembly. This gives them a better grip.

cleats on the sides will help to keep it from sliding while through-nailing from the sides. The back goes on next, then the front. The upper L-shaped top member goes on last.

Glue can be applied to both surfaces of the joints (as well as the cleats) with a squeeze bottle, but a brush should be used to spread it evenly and quickly.

To assemble the bunk, nail the back onto the four crossmembers, then flip the assembly onto its back, on the floor, to nail in the front. When all nailing is

8. L-shaped top goes on last. Start the nails, then remove the piece and apply glue.

6. Bookshelves are attached first; then the left and right sides are glued to the tabletop panel. Nails are driven into the cleats as well as the butted edges.

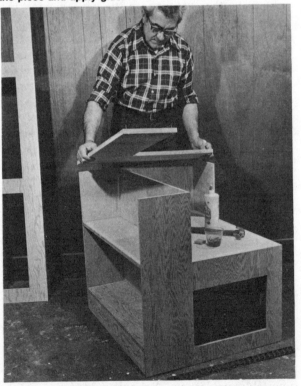

Exploded view shows cleat arrangement of end section.

10. Bottom view of end cabinet. Special corner-mounted swivel casters are required for this project. Note how blocks are used to support the drawer slide in line with the drawer opening.

9. Assembled bunk section is checked for trueness with a large square. Temporary braces are used to square the piece, if necessary, before the glue dries.

11. Best way to align the add-on drawer fronts: Let nail points protrude from the front of the drawer, then press together to make nail-point indents. The strip across the bottom assures alignment of three drawers.

done, lay the bunk right-side up and check it for square with a large square. If necessary, tack-nail two diagonal braces as shown to keep it true while the glue dries.

When all the units have been assembled, set all nail heads and fill; then give them a final sanding, making sure to ease all sharp corners.

12. Finger grips can be cut into the bottom of the drawer fronts if you want to avoid using drawer pulls. Router with a cove-cutting bit is used for this.

DRAWERS

The drawer slides are next. Use a 24-inch heavy-duty slide for lasting service. Install stand-off blocks as shown, in order to support the slides in line with the drawer opening. The standard space allowance for slides is ½ inch on each side, so the drawers should be 1 inch narrower than the drawer opening.

To play it safe, the drawers could be made 1¹⁄₁₆ inches narrower.

The drawers are made up with four sides and a bottom plus a separate front, all of ½-inch plywood. Assemble the drawers and attach the sliding hardware. Then slide the drawers into place. The following procedure will enable you to attach the drawer fronts in perfect alignment, even if the drawers are misaligned:

Drive four small nails through the inside of the drawer front so the points just emerge on the outside. Back off the drawer, position the separate front against the frame precisely where you want it, then push the drawer into it. The nails will mark the exact position for gluing.

When attaching the bunk drawers, tack a strip of wood across the bottom to make sure the three fronts are aligned.

If you prefer a plain, unadorned appearance, you can shape out finger-grip recesses along the bottom inside edges of the drawers using a router with a cove-cutting bit. Adjust the depth of cut so the tool cuts to within ⅛ inch of the front. This operation must be done before the fronts are attached to the drawers.

Optionally, you can use a special surface-mounted, low-profile drawer pull which won't in-

13. Completed units ready for finishing

terfere with your legs when seated. Matching brass corners may be used to complement the pulls.

If you plan to use casters like the ones shown, you'll find it necessary to bore a clearance hole into the front left and right drawer-slide supports on the bunk. These casters, designed for mounting onto a vertical inside corner, are not regular hardware store items but are available through mail order, together with the pulls and decorative corners (see Sources of Supply at back of book).

29
Jumbo
Director's Chair

You'll never find a chair like this in a furniture store. The only way you can have one is to build it yourself. It is styled much like a traditional director's chair with one obvious difference—all the components have been more than doubled in cross-sectional dimensions in order to achieve the distinctive husky look. Even the canvas seat and back have been padded to maximize the effect. The result is a very comfortable chair.

Ordinary construction lumber is used instead of expensive cabinet hardwoods in the interest of economy. Lengths of 2×4, 2×6, and 4×4 in any of the readily available species will do. Closet pole is used for the front arm-rest supports and leg spacers. One-inch hardwood doweling is used for the joints.

MAKING THE COMPONENTS

Begin construction of the chair at the bottom and work your way up. Cut the four legs to length from a piece of 2×4 stock; then cut cross-lap joints ½ inch deep at an angle of 12 degrees. This can be done with either a radial-arm or table saw. All four pieces are cut identically. When lined up with the cross-lap joints facing up, all the legs should look alike.

The next step is to bore the holes in the ends to

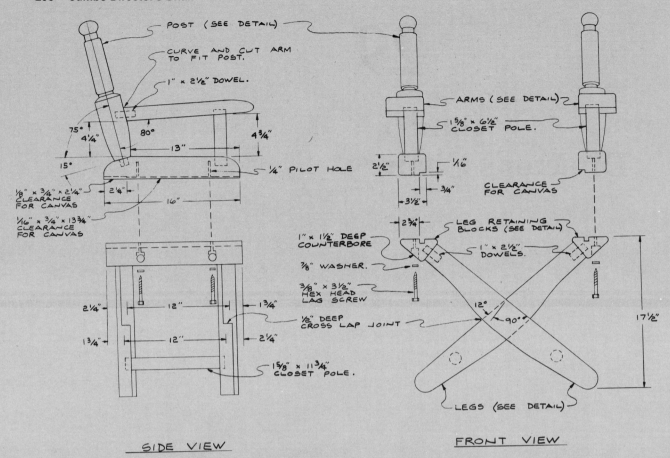

POST (SEE DETAIL)

CURVE AND CUT ARM TO FIT POST.

1" x 2½" DOWEL.

75°
4¼"
80°
13"
4¾"

15°
¼" PILOT HOLE

⅛" x ¾" x 2¼" CLEARANCE FOR CANVAS
2¼"
16"

1/16" x ¾" x 13¾" CLEARANCE FOR CANVAS

2¼"
12"
1¾"

13¾"
12"
2¼"

15⁄8" x 11¾" CLOSET POLE.

SIDE VIEW

ARMS (SEE DETAIL)

15⁄8" x 6½" CLOSET POLE.

2½"
1/16"

3½"
¾"
CLEARANCE FOR CANVAS

2¾"
LEG RETAINING BLOCKS (SEE DETAIL)

1" x 1½" DEEP COUNTERBORE
1" x 2½" DOWELS.

⅜" WASHER.

⅜" x 3½" HEX HEAD LAG SCREW

12°
90°

½" DEEP CROSS LAP JOINT

17½"

15⁄8" x 11¾" CLOSET POLE.

LEGS (SEE DETAIL)

FRONT VIEW

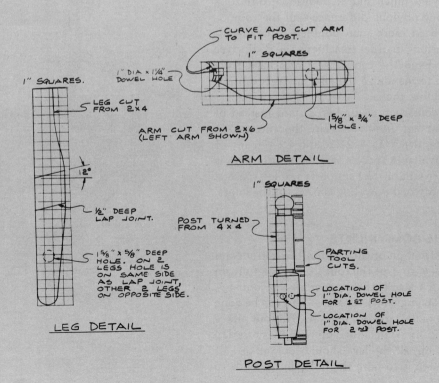

CURVE AND CUT ARM TO FIT POST.

1" SQUARES

1" DIA x 1¼" DOWEL HOLE

1" SQUARES.

LEG CUT FROM 2x4

ARM CUT FROM 2x6 (LEFT ARM SHOWN)

15⁄8" x ¾" DEEP HOLE.

ARM DETAIL

12°

½" DEEP LAP JOINT.

POST TURNED FROM 4x4

1" SQUARES

PARTING TOOL CUTS.

15⁄8" x 5⁄8" DEEP HOLE. ON 2 LEGS HOLE IS ON SAME SIDE AS LAP JOINT, OTHER 2 LEGS ON OPPOSITE SIDE.

LOCATION OF 1" DIA. DOWEL HOLE FOR 1ST POST.

LOCATION OF 1" DIA. DOWEL HOLE FOR 2ND POST.

LEG DETAIL

POST DETAIL

LEG RETAINING BLOCK

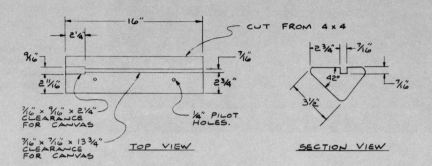

16"

2'4"

9/16"

2 11/16"

CUT FROM 4 x 4

7/16"

2 3/4"

7/16" × 9/16" × 2 1/4"
CLEARANCE
FOR CANVAS

7/16" × 7/16" × 13 3/4"
CLEARANCE
FOR CANVAS

1/4" PILOT
HOLES.

TOP VIEW

2 3/4"   7/16"

42°

7/16"

3 1/2"

SECTION VIEW

SEWING DETAILS - LIGHT CANVAS OR DUCK CLOTH

SEAT

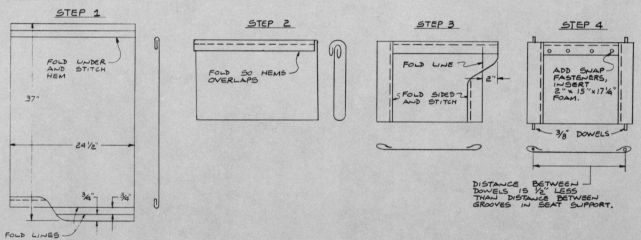

STEP 1

FOLD UNDER
AND STITCH
HEM

37"

24 1/2"

3/4"   3/4"

FOLD LINES

STEP 2

FOLD SO HEMS
OVERLAPS

STEP 3

FOLD LINE

FOLD SIDES
AND STITCH

2"

STEP 4

ADD SNAP
FASTENERS,
INSERT
2" × 15" × 17 1/4"
FOAM.

3/8" DOWELS

DISTANCE BETWEEN
DOWELS IS 1/2" LESS
THAN DISTANCE BETWEEN
GROOVES IN SEAT SUPPORT.

BACKREST

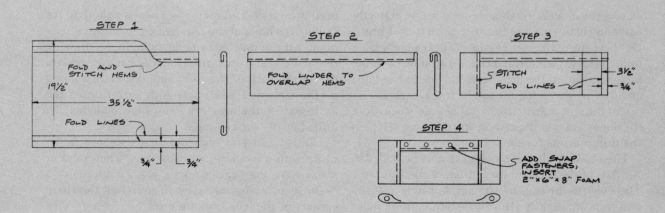

STEP 1

FOLD AND
STITCH HEMS

19 1/2"

35 1/2"

FOLD LINES

3/4"   3/4"

STEP 2

FOLD UNDER TO
OVERLAP HEMS

STEP 3

STITCH

FOLD LINES

3 1/2"

3/4"

STEP 4

ADD SNAP
FASTENERS,
INSERT
2" × 6" × 8" FOAM

You can save money by using ordinary construction lumber for this project. Select kiln-dried pieces that have small, tight knots.

1. A series of passes with a regular crosscut blade will serve in lieu of a dado head to clear out stock for the cross-lap joint. The saw is set for a 12-degree miter.

2. To bore dowel holes accurately and safely, tilt the drill-press table to the vertical position. Clamped guide block must also be perfectly plumb.

receive the dowels. As these holes must be perfectly perpendicular, they are best bored on a drill press. Do this before shaping the edges. Tilt the press table to the vertical position and clamp a stop block to the table to position the leg. Clamp the leg to the table and against the guide for safety and accuracy.

Cut the arm rests to length out of 2×6 stock. Bore the dowel holes in the ends, using the same setup on the drill press as for the legs.

The 1⅝-inch-diameter holes can now be drilled in the flats of the legs and the bottom of the arm rests. The holes in the legs are straight, but note that the arm rests are slightly slanted; therefore, those holes

need to be angled accordingly. There is a shortcut for drilling the holes at the required angle without fussing to tilt the drill-press table. Note in the drawing that there is a ½-inch rise from the back of the arm rest to the back of the front support. Place a board on the table and insert a ½-inch spacer under the back end of the arm rest. The hole will then be drilled at the correct angle.

The leg and arm-rest contour cuts can now be made with a band, jig, or sabre saw. Then sand or spokeshave the edges smooth. Use a router with a ½-inch corner-rounding bit to round all the sharp corners of the legs and arm rests.

3. **Band saw makes quick work of cutting contours for the legs and arm rests. Make these cuts only after the end holes and joints have been made.**

4. **All corners are rounded with a router. Use a ½-inch corner-rounding bit.**

Cut the closet pole to length for the legs and arm rests. Insert the poles into the respective holes, draw a pencil line around the circumference, withdraw them and shave a few slight flats from the line to the end of the pole. This is to allow excess glue to escape. Sand all the parts and put them aside for a while.

The back posts are turned from 4×4 stock 20-inches long. Use a large gouge to rough out a cylinder about 3⅛ inches in diameter; then make a series of diameter sizing cuts with a parting chisel at several locations, as indicated in the drawing, to within ⅛ inch of the final contour diameters. Use the skew and spear-point chisels to work down to the level of the parting cuts, then trim to final diameters.

It would be difficult to bore a perpendicular dowel hole accurately into the bottom of the turning; therefore a round tenon is formed on the lathe. This is, in effect, a built-in dowel. Although this tenon will subsequently mate with a 1-inch diameter hole, it should be turned slightly undersize to allow some play, which will be necessary for assembly. Set your calipers to $^{15}/_{16}$ inch and turn the tenon to that diameter.

The hole in the post that receives the arm-rest dowel must be drilled accurately. While the plan does indicate the location of the hole, drilling it could be troublesome. The curvature of the post prevents pinpointing the hole center with any degree of accuracy with a rule. The problem is easily solved, however, if you hold off drilling this hole until the post-support block is made.

Cut the post-support blocks from 4×4 stock. Tilt the drill-press table 15 degrees to bore the angled hole for the tenon at the rear. Use the band saw to cut the profile. Be sure to maintain a flat on the rear

5. **Sand all the parts before assembly. Go easy on the edges at the joints to avoid reducing the width.**

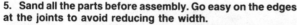

6. **Turn a cylinder to 3-inch diameter; then make a series of parting-tool grooves to set the depths for the shaping cuts. Work carefully when turning the tenon to size.**

7. The drill-press table is tilted 15 degrees to bore the rear hole for the turned post tenon in the arm-rest support block.

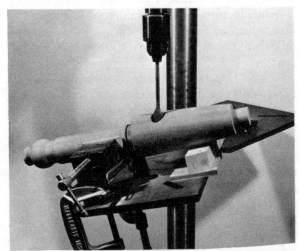

8. A drill-press vise is especially handy to hold the work for boring dowel hole in arm rest. End is propped up for extra support.

angled surface so the post bottom will seat properly.

Insert the turned post into the support block. Then, with a half-round rasp, form a curved bevel at the back end of the arm rest so it conforms to the angled curve of the post. This is strictly a trial and error operation so you must work slowly and check the fit frequently. When a good fit is obtained, you can proceed to mark the location for the dowel hole in the post.

Make four hole-center index marks on the end of the arm rest and continue these marks to the surface. Temporarily join the pieces of the arm-rest assembly; then transfer the hole-center marks on the arm rest to the rear post. Disassemble the parts and con-

tinue the center marks on the post to obtain the center mark for drilling the dowel hole.

Tilt the drill-press table 10 degrees off horizontal. Secure the straight portion of the turning in a drill-press vise, bottomed so it will be perfectly horizontal in relation to the table. Clamp the vise in place; then insert a support block under the extended portion of the post and drill the hole.

The triangular leg-retaining blocks are cut from 4 ×4 stock. You cannot slice diagonally through the center in order to yield the two pieces because they would be slightly undersize. Tilt the saw blade to rip a 42 degree bevel. Unless yours is a huge saw, you will have to make this cut in two passes, shifting the fence for the second cut.

Tilt the drill-press table to drill the holes for the leg dowels perpendicular to the surface. Note that although the center-to-center distance between holes is the same on both triangular blocks, there is an offset factor resulting from the partial cross-lap joint of the legs.

This chair is designed to permit the padded seat and back to be easily removed for laundering. This is accomplished by removing the arm-rest assembly to free the dowel-ended seat cushion. The dowels, encased in the looped ends, rest in a pair of $7/16''$ ×

9. Masking tape is used to hold both blocks in alignment while drilling the holes for the lag screws. Bore the large hole first. The V block was used as a pad for clamping the work to the table. A flat bit is good choice for boring a hole on a slanted surface.

7/16" grooves which are cut into the tops of the triangular blocks. Two 3/8-inch hex-head lag screws, 3½ inches long, are used to attach the arm-rest assembly.

Note that the arm-rest support blocks have shallow rabbets in their bottom surface, on the inside, to allow clearance for the thickness of the seat cloth. Be sure to cut these before assembly. Due to the design of the seat cushion, there is extra thickness at the rear flap. Therefore, when the cushion is made, you'll find that a bit of hand chiseling will be necessary at the rear ends of the grooves, as well as at the rabbets of the arm-support blocks, to enlarge the clearance for the bulkier ends of the cushion.

Use masking tape to hold the upper and lower blocks together in alignment to drill the holes for the lag screws. Start the holes in the angled surface with a 1-inch flat bit to counterbore sufficiently to conceal the bolt head and washer. Follow with a ¼-inch body hole and 3/8-inch shank hole. If you drill the latter holes first the large bit will not center. A standard socket wrench will fit the 1-inch counterbore hole.

ASSEMBLING THE CHAIR

Assembly is not particularly difficult. Use a plastic-resin glue in powder form that you mix with water. Use a bit less water than is recommended in the instructions so that the mixture won't be too runny. This is particularly advantageous for the arm-rest assembly where the angled parts must have a slight play in order to be coaxed into place. Also, the thicker glue is less subject to runoff.

Apply glue and join the crossed leg sections using C clamps at the centers. Insert the two lengths of closet pole between the leg sections and secure with a pair of bar clamps. The triangular blocks go on

11. Begin the assembly by gluing leg sections together. Then insert closet-pole "dowels" and join the sections. Position the bar clamps as shown. If leg-retaining blocks (one being installed here) fit snugly, clamping's unnecessary.

12. Due to the angles involved, it is necessary to insert the arm rest into the post first. Then ease the two sections together as shown.

13. The arm-rest block is secured with heavy lag screws.

10. All the components for the chair prior to assembly.

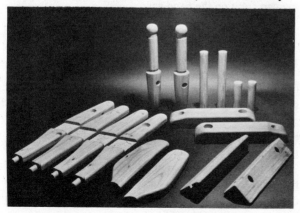

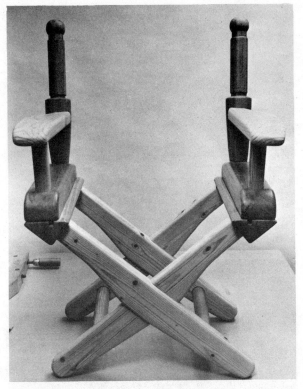

Front view

Side view

14. Sew the canvas seat and insert the foam padding before installing the fasteners. Special setting tool is available at sewing-supply stores.

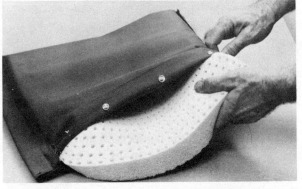

15. Two-inch-thick foam should be cut a bit oversize so it fits the pouch with no play. If the foam has sufficient body you can cut it on the band saw.

next, fitted over the dowel-ended legs. If the fit is good, you may not have to apply pressure. However, should pressure be required to close the joints, use rope tied crisscross around the block and the pole diagonally opposite.

To assemble the arm rest, insert a dowel into the end of the arm rest and connect it to the post. Slide these parts onto the base, which has a pole inserted

in the front hole. Apply a clamp to bear downward pressure on the arm rest.

The seat cushion and back rest are next. Use duck cloth or lightweight canvas so that folded seams do not build up too thickly.

The dimensions shown in the plan will work out fine, but bear in mind that your finished chair may come out with slight differences in various dimen-

16. This shows how the cushion is installed. You should have to force the second dowel into place. The back pad slides over the posts.

sions. If so, you'll have to make necessary changes accordingly. The important thing is to size the cushion and back rest so they are stretched into place. This tension will prevent wrinkles and sags.

The seat cushion is installed by inserting a length of dowel into the end loops. Place the dowels into the grooves, then secure the arm rests by taking up on the lag screws. The back rest slides over the post ends.

Finish is optional. For a natural look apply clear varnish. Or you can stain, then varnish. Or you can apply a woodgraining finish, as was done here.

30
Cupola/
Weathervane

Architecturally, a cupola is the icing on the cake. Perched on the hip of the roof, it will add an interesting ornamental feature to your house. With an opening cut in the roof and in its base, it functions as a very effective ventilator to exhaust heat and water vapor from the attic.

The plan is for a moderate-size unit suitable for a garage, breezeway, or small house. Construction is simplified to some extent by the use of ready-made shutter doors for the louvered midsection.

Shutter doors are available in a variety of sizes with either fixed or movable louvers. You'll need a pair of 3' × 3'1" fixed louver doors for this project; "three by three-one" in the lumber dealer's parlance. This is the overall dimension of the pair. Each door measures 18 inches wide by 37 inches long. Start the project by acquiring the doors.

The standard stock shutter door of this size normally has a top and middle rail of equal width, and a bottom rail which is extra wide. The four panels required are obtained by cutting through the center of the middle rails. The lower halves are trimmed at the bottom so the four panels are of equal length. The lower panels are turned front to back and upside-down in order to locate the wider rails at the top, with the louvers angled down and outwards.

There will be a discrepancy of ¾ inch between the original and the new top rails, but this is of no consequence.

Cut 1½-inch square stock to length and glue and nail two pieces to the edges of two panels. Use 3-inch hot-dipped, galvanized finishing nails and waterproof glue to make the butt joints. Nail again through the posts at right angles to join the other two panels to form the boxed walls. Check the assembly for squareness. If it is not true, bring it into shape by tack nailing wood strips diagonally across two posts on both ends.

The ornamental cornice is made with 2⅝-inch crown molding attached to a support built up on the top edge of the shutter section. Plywood strips, ½″ × 1⅞″, are nailed and glued to ½″ × ⅝″ ledge strips, which are in turn nailed and glued to the posts and shutter tops. The corners are butted to form the shallow wall. Four pieces of ½″ × 3″ plywood with mitered corners are attached horizontally to the wall.

Crown molding is designed to be installed in a sloped position. Thus, in order to achieve a 45-degree mitered corner joint, a compound angle must be cut. Many workers experience great difficulty in making the compound-angle cut properly, but there is a simple way. Regardless of whether you use a table or radial-arm saw or even a handsaw and miter box, the molding must be held and cut in the same position as it is installed. Note that the saw blade is not tilted as for other normal compound-angle cuts. The tilt of the molding automatically produces a beveled edge.

A high fence on the radial-arm saw will support the molding at the required angle if the flats are

2. Waterproof glue and hot-dipped galvanized nails are used to attach the corner posts to two of the four panels.

3. Box in the unit by nailing through posts again. For a neat job, nail heads should be set and filled.

1. Cut through center of middle rail to obtain two louvered sections from each shutter.

4. Upper members of the cornice frame are mitered and attached with nails and glue.

CONTINUED

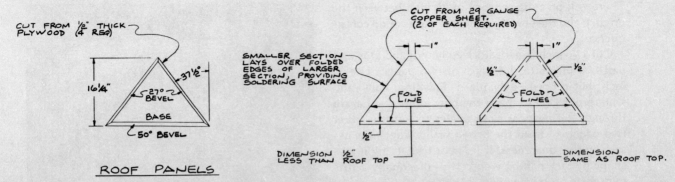

CUT FROM ½" THICK
PLYWOOD (4 REQ)

16¼"

37½°

27°
BEVEL

BASE

50° BEVEL

ROOF PANELS

CUT FROM 29 GAUGE
COPPER SHEET.
(2 OF EACH REQUIRED)

1"

SMALLER SECTION
LAYS OVER FOLDED
EDGES OF LARGER
SECTION, PROVIDING
SOLDERING SURFACE

FOLD
LINE

½"

DIMENSION ½"
LESS THAN ROOF TOP

1"

½"   ½"

FOLD
LINES

DIMENSION
SAME AS ROOF TOP.

COPPER ROOF

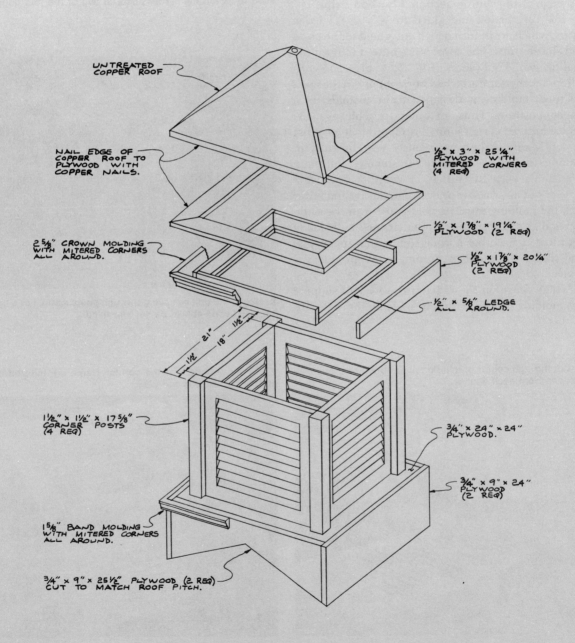

UNTREATED
COPPER ROOF

NAIL EDGE OF
COPPER ROOF TO
PLYWOOD WITH
COPPER NAILS.

½" x 3" x 25¼"
PLYWOOD WITH
MITERED CORNERS
(4 REQ)

2⅝" CROWN MOLDING
WITH MITERED CORNERS
ALL AROUND.

½" x 1⅞" x 19¼"
PLYWOOD (2 REQ)

½" x 1⅞" x 20¼"
PLYWOOD
(2 REQ)

½" x ⅝" LEDGE
ALL AROUND.

21"

18"   1½"

½"

1½" x 1½" x 17⅝"
CORNER POSTS
(4 REQ)

3/4" x 24" x 24"
PLYWOOD.

3/4" x 9" x 24"
PLYWOOD
(2 REQ)

1⅝" BAND MOLDING
WITH MITERED CORNERS
ALL AROUND.

3/4" x 9" x 25½" PLYWOOD (2 REQ)
CUT TO MATCH ROOF PITCH.

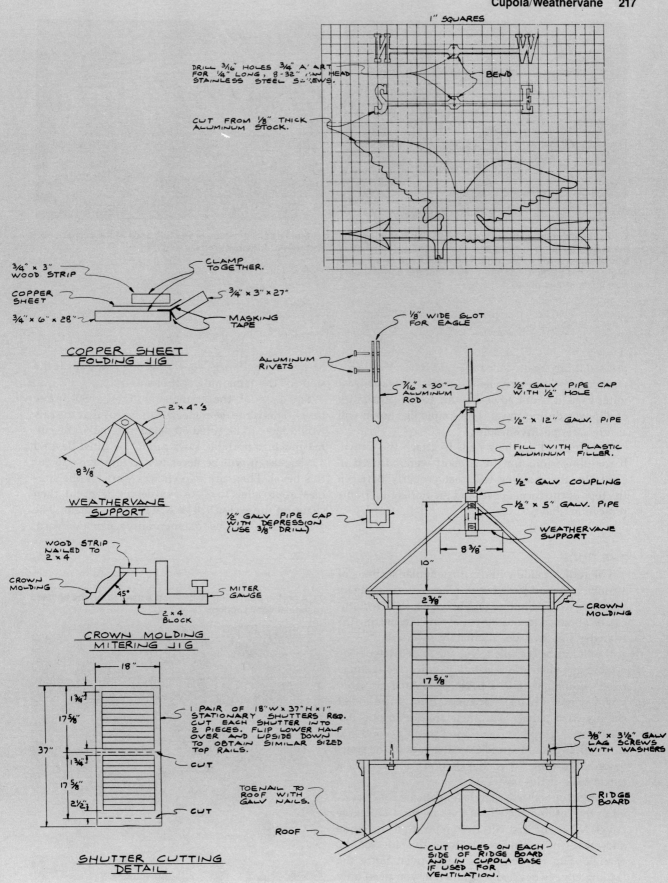

1" SQUARES

DRILL 3/16" HOLES 3/4" A'ART FOR 1/4" LONG, 8-32" 'AN HEAD STAINLESS STEEL SCREWS.

BEND

CUT FROM 1/8" THICK ALUMINUM STOCK.

3/4" x 3" WOOD STRIP

CLAMP TOGETHER.

COPPER SHEET

3/4" x 3" x 27"

3/4" x 6" x 28"

MASKING TAPE

COPPER SHEET FOLDING JIG

2" x 4" 's

8 3/8"

WEATHERVANE SUPPORT

WOOD STRIP NAILED TO 2 x 4

CROWN MOLDING

45°

MITER GAUGE

2 x 4 BLOCK

CROWN MOLDING MITERING JIG

18"

1 3/4"

17 5/8"

37"

1 3/4"

17 5/8"

2 1/2"

1 PAIR OF 18"W x 37"H x 1" STATIONARY SHUTTERS REQ. CUT EACH SHUTTER INTO 2 PIECES. FLIP LOWER HALF OVER AND UPSIDE DOWN TO OBTAIN SIMILAR SIZED TOP RAILS.

CUT

CUT

SHUTTER CUTTING DETAIL

1/8" WIDE SLOT FOR EAGLE

ALUMINUM RIVETS

7/16" x 30" ALUMINUM ROD

1/2" GALV PIPE CAP WITH DEPRESSION (USE 3/8" DRILL)

1/2" GALV PIPE CAP WITH 1/2" HOLE

1/2" x 12" GALV. PIPE

FILL WITH PLASTIC ALUMINUM FILLER.

1/2" GALV COUPLING

1/2" x 5" GALV. PIPE

WEATHERVANE SUPPORT

8 3/8"

10"

2 3/8"

CROWN MOLDING

17 5/8"

3/8" x 3 1/2" GALV LAG SCREWS WITH WASHERS

TOENAIL TO ROOF WITH GALV NAILS.

RIDGE BOARD

ROOF

CUT HOLES ON EACH SIDE OF RIDGE BOARD AND IN CUPOLA BASE IF USED FOR VENTILATION.

CROSS SECTION

5. To obtain compound miter cut, a block beveled to hold the crown molding in the same slope as when installed is placed against the miter gage. The miter gage is set at 45 degrees; the blade is not tilted. Note that the cut-off is the workpiece in this photo.

6. Molding fits between projecting ends of the corner posts and frame. Attach with nails and glue.

pressed firmly against the table and fence. While the work can be similarly held against the table-saw miter gage, it is not advisable due to the possibility of slippage during travel. The simple jig shown will assure safe, positive results.

Use glue and finishing nails to attach the crown. If the dimensions for the support were adhered to carefully, the molding will seat properly between the tops of the corner posts and the horizontal frame projection above.

THE ROOF

The roof is made with four triangular sections of ½-inch plywood joined with mitered corners, again requiring compound angle cuts. The four sections can be obtained from a 1½' × 6' panel by cutting the triangles side by side, alternately reversed.

It will not be feasible to cut the large triangles on a table or radial-arm saw unless you have factory-sized equipment. Use a portable circular or sabre saw. Lay out only one triangle, starting at the end of the plywood panel. The others are drawn one at a time after each piece is cut because the second and fourth triangles are sawed from the back of the panel in order to obtain two bevels and miters from a single pass of the saw.

Clamp a straightedge guide for the saw base parallel to the cut line and adjust the saw for a 27 degree bevel. Make the first cut; then reposition the guide and make the second cut to form the sides of the triangle. Flip the remaining panel over. Since the leading edge is beveled and mitered, you need only

to measure and mark for the second cut. Repeat the step for the remaining sections.

The base of the triangle requires a 50-degree bevel. This is the *cut* angle, which means that the saw would have to be tilted 50 degrees to make the cut. Inasmuch as portable saws cannot be tilted beyond 45 degrees, it will be necessary to improvise to cut this bevel. There are two choices. Perhaps the simplest approach is to make a 45-degree bevel cut, then shave off the excess 5 degrees with a hand plane. The alternative would be to temporarily nail a flat board,

7. A portable saw with blade tilted is used to cut the beveled triangular roof sections.

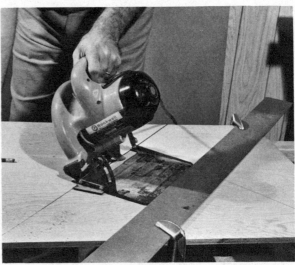

large enough to support the saw base and guide, butted at right angle to the surface of the work. With this setup, an edgewise cut with the saw tilted 40 degrees will result in a 50-degree bevel.

The four roof sections are glued together but are not attached to the cornice until later, during final assembly on the roof. To facilitate gluing, temporarily tack-nail two opposing sides to the cornice with the top points touching so they will support each other. Insert a piece of wax paper under each corner to prevent the roof panels from sticking to the cornice. Apply glue to the beveled edges and fit in

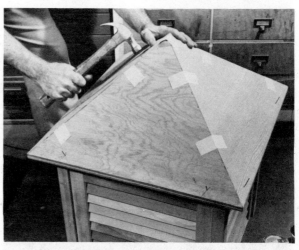

9. Glue is applied to the edges, and third and fourth panels are nailed in. Masking tape helps to keep the panels in alignment. The roof is not permanently attached to the cornice until later.

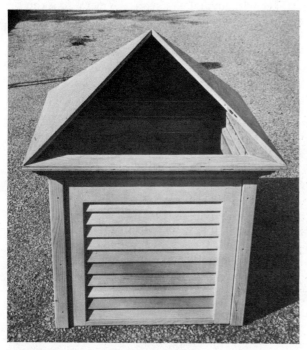

8. Two opposing roof panels are tack-nailed into place to begin assembly.

10. How weathervane post is attached. Pipe cap serves as a nut against the block.

the third and fourth sides. Use a wide masking tape over the corners to close the joints. A few 1¼-inch finishing nails alternatively driven into the corners from both faces will help to strengthen the joints.

When the glue has set, withdraw the nails from the cornice, turn the piece over and glue in the weathervane pipe-support blocks, which can be cut from 2×4 stock. Be sure, however, to bore the pipe hole into the block in advance. Use a drill press or portable drill with a guide to get this hole perfectly true. After the block is glued in you can continue the hole up through the roof.

THE BASE

The main base of the three-part cupola is made of ¾-inch plywood with butt joints. The best way to determine the roof pitch accurately for matching the base is to make a template. Place two sticks of wood so they cross at the peak of the roof and clamp them together firmly at this point. This gives you the correct pitch. Trace the angle onto the work. Note that the height of the base can be increased if warranted by an extra-steep roof pitch.

After the angled cuts have been made in two sides of the base, they should be taken to the roof and

11. Unit is turned bottom side up to attach the base. Holes for lag screws are bored into center of posts.

checked for fit. Make adjustments if necessary because a good fit is important. Assemble the base with nails and glue, then trim the top edge with mitered band molding.

Four lag screws are used to attach the louvered section to the base. Turn the midsection bottom side up, place the base, also bottom side up, onto it. Bore pilot holes for the lags so they locate directly in the center of the corner posts.

If your cupola is to serve only as an ornament, the platform of the base is left solid. If you want the cupola to provide ventilation for the attic you will have to cut an opening about 16 inches square in the platform. An opening must be cut into the roof as well.

Rather than cut through the house roof's ridge board, which would weaken the structure, two holes of about 8-inches diameter can be cut on each side of the ridge. To do this, drill a blade entry hole, then use the sabre saw to make the cutouts.

SURFACING THE ROOF

The roof of the cupola is surfaced with copper sheet, which is available at roofing and building supply dealers and sheet-metal shops. Thin, 29-gauge

stock is recommended for the lining because it is easy to solder with typical home-shop soldering equipment. Another factor is cost. Copper is relatively expensive and cost increases with weight.

Note that two copper sheets are cut ½ inch undersize and two are 1 inch oversize in width. This allows for soldering an overlap joint. The smaller sheet lays over the folded sides of the larger sheet to provide a joint line ¼ inch from the edge. It is best to cut the copper with a utility knife or a sharp-pointed awl rather than with a tin snip. The latter tends to curl the edge of the metal, which would cause difficulty in soldering. Use a metal straightedge to guide the tool. With a knife you can cut clear through; a few strokes with an awl will score the metal so it can be folded over a table edge to make a clean break.

You won't need a special bending brake to make the required bends along the edges of the copper sheets. You can form the bends to perfection with a simple jig made with a few pieces of wood and masking tape. To make the jig, butt two pieces of wood together and run a strip of tape along the joint line. Hinge the flap over and add a strip of tape to the joint line on the edges. Now you'll have a base and a flap that pivots on the joint line.

Mark the fold lines on the copper with a pencil. Position the sheet on the jig so the fold line is directly over the joint. Clamp a strip of wood with its edge on the fold line, then lift up on the flap to make the bend. Make the side bends first, then the bottom. Note that the hold-down wood strip is mitered at the ends so it fits within the folded-up sides without interference.

12. Scoring is the best way to get a smooth cut in thin copper sheet. Make several passes with an awl or sharp knife, then fold the sheet over a sharp corner of the workbench to separate.

13. Jig for bending copper consists of two boards hinged with masking tape. Note how clamped hold-down block has been mitered to fit within the bent-up sides.

14. Copper sheet is clamped in place in this manner. A wood block is rubbed against edge to conform bend to roof.

The copper is soldered in place on the wood roof section. Position the two sheets with the folded sides on the roof. Apply flux to clean the copper surfaces where they'll be soldered, then tin the contact surfaces: heat the metal with the soldering iron and apply a thin coating of solder to the bent-over flaps and to the back of the adjoining piece. Tape the sheet in position. Heat the metal to the point where it will melt the solder and apply solder to make the overlap joint. Work with a fair-sized soldering iron, or at least a 275-watt soldering gun.

The cupola is now completed with the exception of the weathervane. You can make your own weathervane or you can buy a ready-made. If you decide to use a ready-made you should disregard drilling the hole through the support block as described earlier. The ready-made is attached from the outside with a special bracket.

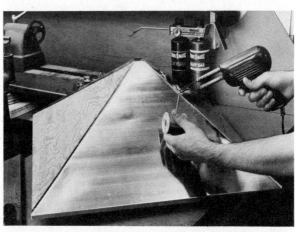

15. Large copper sheets such as these can be soldered only with a heavy-duty soldering gun or a large soldering iron. Clean the surfaces with flux, tin the contact surfaces, then solder. A torch cannot be used successfully for this operation because the intense heat would deform the thin sheet.

16. Inside view of the soldered copper roof lining.

WEATHERVANE

The weathervane figure and the cardinal (compass points) are cut from ⅛-inch aluminum sheet. Draw the outline on paper, using 1-inch squares to enlarge the pattern. Cut out the pattern and mount it on the aluminum with rubber cement. This will provide an easy-to-see sawing guideline. Cut out the figures on a jigsaw equipped with a fine-tooth blade. Use a narrow-belt sander or a file to smooth the saw ripples.

The cardinal is made in two sections. Each section is bent into a right angle from a center radius which wraps around the pipe-mounting post. Bending is accurately controlled with two blocks of wood and

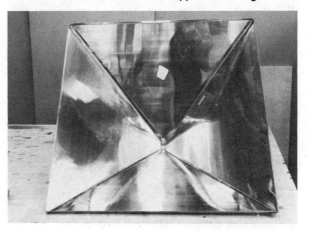

17. Paper patterns of the weathervane parts are rubber cemented to the aluminum sheet to provide an easy-to-see cutting guideline.

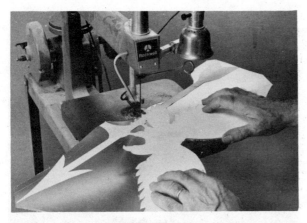

18. Use a fine-tooth metal-cutting blade in a jigsaw to cut the one-piece arrow and eagle figure.

the pipe. Make the bending jig by cutting a half circle in a block of 2″ × 2″ × 8″ stock as shown. Sandwich the block, cardinal bar, the pipe and a 2″ × 2″ × 6″ block of wood between the jaws of a vise. Take up on the vise to force the bar to bend around the pipe to form a 90-degree angle. Next, place the straight portion of the bar in the vise and use the pipe for a lever, as shown, to make the return bends. Note that it is very important to make the bends in the proper direction, otherwise the compass points will be erratic.

Two pieces of ½-inch galvanized pipe, a coupling, and two caps are used to make the post. Bore four holes in the cardinal bar and into the pipe. Tap threads in the pipe holes to receive ¼-inch-long 8–32 round-head screws. Bore a ½-inch-diameter hole in the center of the upper pipe cap. Drill a shallow, centered dimple on the inside of the lower cap. Use a ⅜-inch bit for this and simply start the hole, do not drill through. The purpose of the depression is to seat the pointed bottom of the vane rod.

Attach the top cap and the coupling to the longer piece of pipe.

The exposed threads are concealed with a plastic aluminum fillet to give the post a finished appearance, thus avoiding the "plumbing" look. Use a product such as Devcon Aluminum, which comes in a tube, and make sure to clean all traces of oil from the pipe, otherwise this material won't stick. Grind or file the end of the vane rod to a blunt point; cut a slot in the top and install the figure with aluminum rivets.

19. Sander/grinder makes quick work of removing burrs and smoothing the edges. This can also be done by hand with a file.

20. Making the first bend with the work sandwiched between a pipe and the forming block. Be sure to start out with the piece held perfectly horizontal.

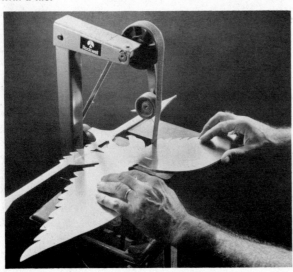

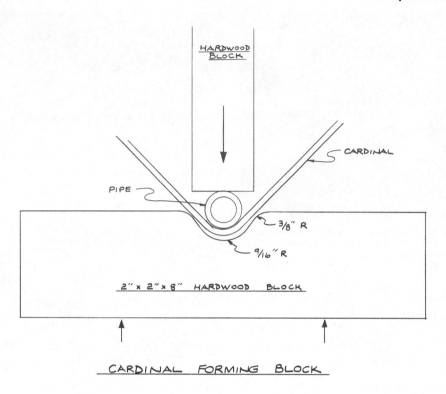

HARDWOOD
BLOCK

PIPE

CARDINAL

3/8" R

9/16" R

2" x 2" x 8" HARDWOOD BLOCK

CARDINAL FORMING BLOCK

21. Second phase of bending is done with flat portion held firmly between vise jaws. Pipe is used as a lever.

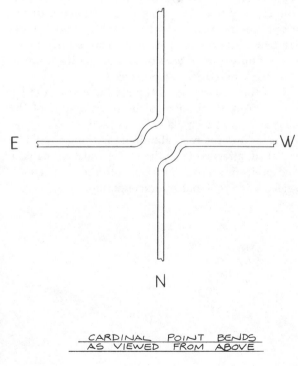

S

E

W

N

CARDINAL POINT BENDS
AS VIEWED FROM ABOVE

22. Fillets are formed with plastic aluminum compound to conceal the exposed pipe threads. When hardened, the material is filed to finished shape.

23. The finished parts, ready for assembly.

Apply an aluminum primer and paint all the parts with a good-quality, flat black paint.

INSTALLING THE CUPOLA

Apply wood preservative to the cupola, and paint all woodwork white. Do not paint the copper—it will weather to the characteristic green patina.

Move the components to the roof for final assembly. Start by placing the copper shell over the roof section. Insert the vane-support post through the top and secure it by drawing up tightly on the bottom cap. Fill this cap with grease before you thread it onto the pipe end. Make sure the compass points are correctly oriented before the cap is fully tightened. Apply a small bead of caulking at the point of the roof where the pipe emerges.

Join the midsection to the platform with the lag screws. Apply caulking to the bottom edge of the base and set it into place. If ventilation holes have been cut into the roof, aluminum flashing should be installed, attached from the inside walls of the base and projecting about 3 inches onto the roof. This is sealed with roof-patching compound.

24. Closeup of the cardinal. Holes in pipe are threaded to receive aluminum or stainless-steel screws.

Secure the base to the roof with 3-inch hot-dipped galvanized common nails driven in at a slight angle. Apply additional caulking around the perimeter of the base.

Position the roof section and attach it by driving copper nails through the top and into the cornice frame. The bottom ends of the copper lining are secured by driving copper tacks into the edge of the cornice frame.

31
Cheval Glass

That's what the dictionary calls a full-length swinging mirror. You'll call it great, once you get it made and put it to use.

This one's made of cherry, but you can use any of the fine hardwoods. Since a relatively small amount of wood is involved, you can duplicate the piece at reasonably low cost—provided you shop around for a good buy on the mirror. Prices for mirrors vary considerably, but you can purchase one of suitable quality at low cost in the housewares section of a department store.

Obtain the mirror before you begin construction of the frame so you can alter the dimensions shown if the size differs. These low-cost mirrors usually come with a lightweight metal frame and a cardboard backing. Plan to use yours as is, with the frame and backing intact.

The frame and base are cut from ⁵⁄₄ stock; the turning squares for the posts are made by gluing up two thicknesses. Start with the frame, ripping three lengths to equal width for the sides and bottom. The top is slightly wider. If you use a smooth-cutting planer saw blade you can cut exactly to size. With a coarse-cutting rip blade, allow a bit extra for smoothing by jointing or hand planing.

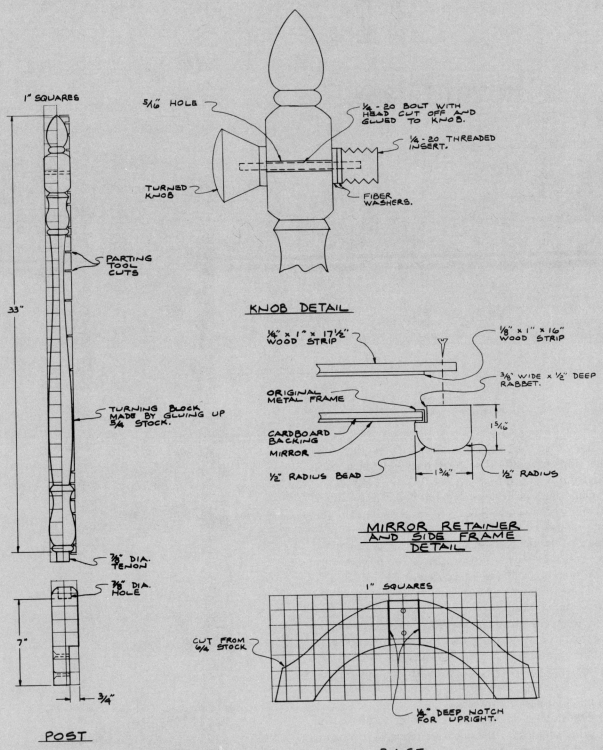

1" SQUARES

5/16" HOLE

1/4 - 20 BOLT WITH HEAD CUT OFF AND GLUED TO KNOB.

1/4 - 20 THREADED INSERT.

TURNED KNOB

FIBER WASHERS.

KNOB DETAIL

PARTING TOOL CUTS

33"

TURNING BLOCK MADE BY GLUING UP 3/4 STOCK.

1/4" × 1" × 17 1/2" WOOD STRIP

1/8" × 1" × 16" WOOD STRIP

3/8" WIDE × 1/2" DEEP RABBET.

ORIGINAL METAL FRAME

CARDBOARD BACKING

MIRROR

1/2" RADIUS BEAD

1 5/16"

1 3/4"

1/2" RADIUS

MIRROR RETAINER AND SIDE FRAME DETAIL

3/8" DIA. TENON

3/8" DIA. HOLE

7"

3/4"

POST

1" SQUARES

CUT FROM 6/4 STOCK

1/4" DEEP NOTCH FOR UPRIGHT.

BASE

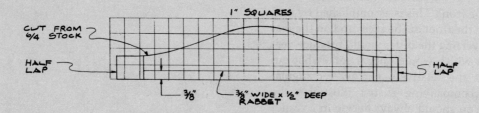

CUT FROM
6/4 STOCK

1" SQUARES

HALF
LAP

HALF
LAP

3/8"

3/8" WIDE x 1/2" DEEP
RABBET

TOP FRAME

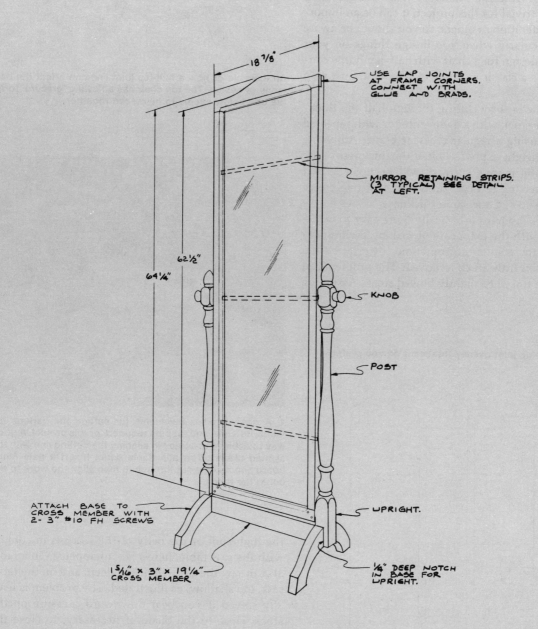

18 7/8"

USE LAP JOINTS
AT FRAME CORNERS.
CONNECT WITH
GLUE AND BRADS.

MIRROR RETAINING STRIPS.
(3 TYPICAL) SEE DETAIL
AT LEFT.

62 1/2"

64 1/4"

KNOB

POST

ATTACH BASE TO
CROSS MEMBER WITH
2- 3" #10 FH SCREWS

UPRIGHT.

1 5/16" x 3" x 19 1/4"
CROSS MEMBER

1/8" DEEP NOTCH
IN BASE FOR
UPRIGHT.

The frame is assembled with end half-lap joints. Note that the joint lines run horizontally when viewed from the front. This is accomplished by cutting the laps on the front of the stiles and on the rear of the rails. Reversing the order would produce vertical joint lines which would appear somewhat out of balance for the relatively narrow rectangular frame. The accompanying sketch illustrates the point clearly. You should always decide in advance which way you want the joint lines to run because it is important to face the better side of the wood to the front. While the matter of joint-line direction may seem trivial for this project, it can be an important consideration in others, so you should be aware of it particularly when you design things on your own. The design for a chair with half-lap frame construction is a classic example of why you must plan carefully.

Make the laps by cutting through half the thickness of the stock with a dado cutter or with repeated kerf cuts using a regular crosscut blade. Adjusting the blade height to precisely half the thickness of the stock so the mating surfaces will be flush is best done by making test cuts on the ends of two pieces of scrap wood of the same thickness.

The half-lap joint is basically quite easy to make, yet even with the extra care of making preliminary test cuts, the results can sometimes be erratic—too much or too little stock removed. The problem can usually be traced to slightly bowed stock. Assuming

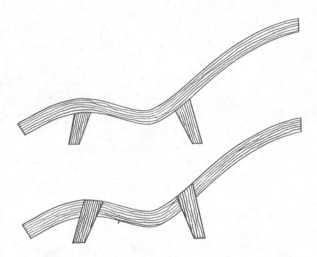

An example of how a half-lap joint line can affect the harmony of design. The top chair has a flowing, graceful form; the one below seems to be pieced together.

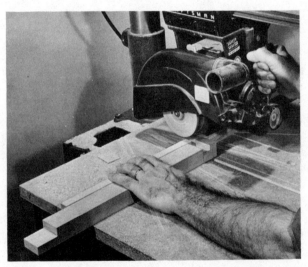

1. A dado head is invaluable for cutting the various lap joints, notches, and rabbets required for this project. A good way to achieve accuracy in aligning the cutting line with the slanted blade of an adjustable dado: Insert a new fence board and make a cut through it; then align the work to the cut in the fence.

Which half-lap-joint overlay treatment do you prefer?

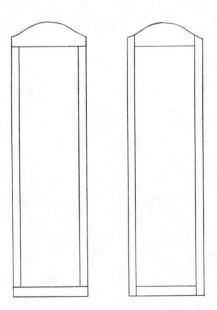

the high spot or the belly of the work is in contact with the saw table, here's what happens: On a radial-arm saw the cut will be too deep, and on the table saw, too shallow, as illustrated. The problem is usually solved if you bear downward pressure on the stock, close to the blade, if necessary, to close the gap. This can be done by hand or with clamped pressure.

After the laps have been made, you can cut the

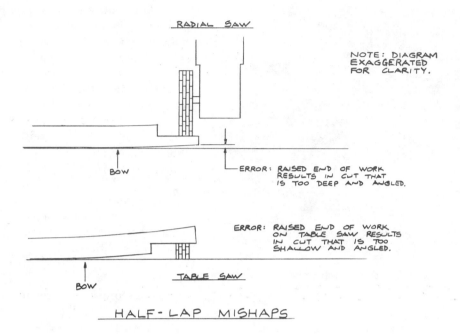

RADIAL SAW

NOTE: DIAGRAM
EXAGGERATED
FOR CLARITY.

BOW

ERROR: RAISED END OF WORK
RESULTS IN CUT THAT
IS TOO DEEP AND ANGLED.

ERROR: RAISED END OF WORK
ON TABLE SAW RESULTS
IN CUT THAT IS TOO
SHALLOW AND ANGLED.

BOW

TABLE SAW

HALF-LAP MISHAPS

curvature on the top frame member. Then decide how you want to handle the next step, which is cutting the rabbets on the rear of the frame to receive the mirror. You have two choices—you can cut them on the individual pieces before assembly by running them through on the saw, or you can assemble the frame and then cut the rabbets with a router.

If you cut the rabbets with the saw, the through

2. You can cut through-rabbets at the rear of the side frame members, then fill the gaps with snug-fitting blocks. The end laps can be assembled with glue and 1-inch flathead screws, or with brads and clamps as described in the text.

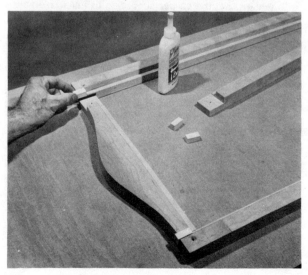

cuts on the vertical members will result in spaces at the tops and bottoms at the back between the stiles and rails. The gaps are easily filled by inserting small glued-in wood blocks. If you make the rabbets after assembly with the router, the inside corners will have a radius which can be squared with a chisel.

To assemble the frame without difficulty, bore two pilot holes for 1-inch brads into the back of each corner joint. Apply glue, drive the nails to keep the pieces in alignment, and clamp. Use wood blocks to distribute the clamp pressure evenly and to prevent the clamp jaws from marring the wood. Since some glue will necessarily squeeze out of the surface joint lines, be careful in the placement of the blocks so they don't rest over the joint lines and become glued to the work.

Two router cutters are needed to shape the inside and outside edges of the frame. Use a ½-inch corner-rounding bit to shape the outside corners, a ½-inch bead-cutting bit to cut the decorative inside edge.

Work on the base next. Note that the curved members are notched to receive the square base of the posts. These notches are cut with a dado head or repeated kerf cuts on the radial-arm or table saw. This should be done while the blank of wood has a straight edge across the top, before the contour is cut. This will permit placement against the fence of the radial saw or the miter gage of the table saw.

To determine how wide to cut the notches, it will be necessary to make up the square blanks for the

3. Shape the inside and outside corners of the front of the frame with a router.

turned posts so the actual width can be measured. It should be 2 inches, but this could vary. Square the posts and smooth the square end sections before measuring.

The typical home-workship lathe does not have the capacity for turning work greater than 36 inches in length. It is therefore necessary to make up the posts in two sections. Unless you have full, 2-inch-square turning stock available, you'll have to glue up two pieces of 5/4 or 6/4 material. Glue up two squares at least 50 inches in length if you like, then cut off a piece from the end of each square to use for the base section of the post. Joint or plane the squares to size so the square sections of the post will need no further machining except light sanding.

The square base section of the post makes a good dividing point for the two-part turning. But the rounded shoulder must be shaped. Draw diagonal lines across the ends, from corner to corner, to find the center of the block. Drill a small pilot hole 1/16 inch in diameter, about 2 inches deep, in the top end to provide a center mark for boring the round mortise after the waste has been cut off. Mount the piece on the lathe and make a pencil mark at the point where the shoulder begins. Use a skew chisel held vertically to nick the corners to prevent splintering. Use a spear-point chisel to make the curved shoulder cut. Sand the surface; then use a parting tool to cut the block almost completely through. Remove the work from the lathe and complete removal of the waste with a hand or band saw. Bore a hole 7/8 inch in diameter in the end, 1 inch deep. This can be done by returning the work to the lathe and chucking a

flat spade bit into the live center. Or you can bore the hole on the drill press.

Draw a full-size pattern of the main turning with depth-sizing cuts clearly indicated. Start the turning at the square section. Again make nicks at the shoulders to prevent splintering at the corners. Then, working with the spear point, shape the shoulders on both sides of the square. Next, rough-round the remainder of the blank using the gouge. Use the parting chisel and make a series of concentric grooves at the locations, and to the depths indicated in your working pattern. These grooves are very shallow so you must work slowly and check constantly with an outside caliper. When the grooves have been made, the basic shape of the turning will be set. Work with the spear point, round nose, and skew to remove the stock between the grooves to form the shape.

Carefully form a round tenon, 7/8 inch in diameter, at the bottom. A small portion of the pointed top of the post is left connected until the piece has been sanded. The final shaping of the point is best done by hand after removing the turning from the lathe. You could easily ruin the work in trying to shape and make the cutoff on the lathe.

Now you can proceed to cut the notches in the lower square section of the turning. Fit the piece into the notch in the stand member to outline where to start the cut. Set the dado head to make a 3/4-inch-deep cut. The piece is relatively small, so you'll have to work carefully, making sure to keep your fingers away from the blade.

The edges of the stand are rounded with the

4. Form the shoulders on the square portion of the turning with a skew. Set the caliper according to full-size drawing when checking cuts on initial turning.

router, but leave square corners where the crosspiece butts.

The two stand pieces are attached to the crosspiece with glue and two screws. It is important to join the three pieces so the four feet will be in a level plane. To get it right, use two bar clamps to hold the three parts together with the feet resting firmly on a flat surface. Attach the clamps on both sides of the notches, allowing clearance for a portable drill. Bore the holes and countersink for 3-inch #10 flathead screws. Remove the clamps; glue and screw the parts together.

The mirror pivots on two bolts, which connect to $\frac{1}{4}$–20 steel threaded-inserts that are recessed on both sides of the frame edge. These are fittings that have a machine thread on the inside which will accept a $\frac{1}{4}$-inch bolt. The outside has a thread that will form its own threads in a slightly undersize hole bored in wood. One end is slotted to permit driving with a screwdriver. They're available through woodcraft supply houses and at some hardware stores.

Before gluing the posts to the stand, the holes for the connecting bolts must be bored. Do this on the drill press or with a drill guide because these holes must be true. Bore $\frac{5}{16}$-inch-diameter through-holes centered on the upper flats of the posts. After this has been done, the upper posts can be glued to the lower posts and in turn to the stand.

The next step is to mark the hole locations in the edges of the frame for the threaded inserts. Place the frame in the stand with a $\frac{3}{8}$-inch spacer at the bottom to allow clearance for swinging. Insert a pencil

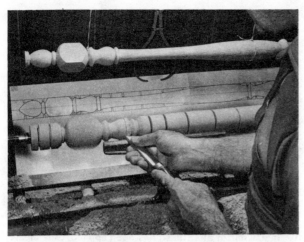

5. Use the first turning as a model for caliper measurements when turning the second. Thus if minor deviations occur in the first, they will be duplicated in the second.

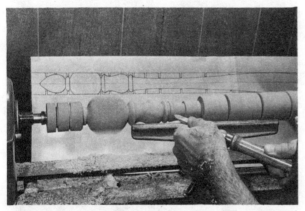

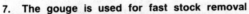
6. Work each section from groove to groove. The measured diameters at these points indicate how deep to cut.

7. The gouge is used for fast stock removal

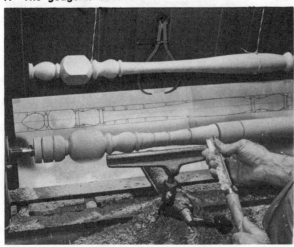

8. Attach the stand members to the crosspiece with glue and screws; then glue and clamp the separately turned post bottoms in place. All edges are rounded and sanded.

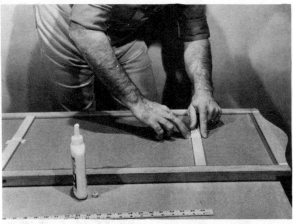

10. Install mirror after finish has been applied. Glue cleats to the mirror backing, then screw cleats to the frame.

9.   Closeup of knob that locks mirror in position. The bolt screws into the threaded insert. Fiber washers, not shown, go in between.

into the holes in the posts to mark the centers. The ¼–20 inserts require a ³¹⁄₆₄-inch hole for seating. Bore these holes into each side of the frame, then screw in the inserts.

Turn two wooden knobs on the lathe. Bore ³⁄₁₆ -inch-diameter holes into the ends. Use a ¼–20 tap to form threads in the holes. Saw off the heads from two ¼–20 × 3″ bolts or use threaded rod and insert them into the knobs. Use a drop of epoxy to lock the bolts into the knobs. Several fiber washers take up the space between the posts and frame.

The simplest way to secure the mirror in the frame is with three ¼″ × 1″ cleats glued to the mirror's cardboard backing. The ends of the cleats are made to overhang the mirror about 1 inch on each side and are secured to the frame with roundhead screws.

Cherry wood exhibits a rich, warm tone with a natural finish. Apply a coat of sealer, then two coats of clear satin varnish.

11. Several coats of clear satin finish enhance the rich tone of cherry wood.

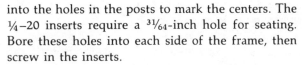

32
Mobile Greenhouse

This interesting greenhouse consists of a three-segment frame which forms an attractive hexagonal structure when closed. Swing it open and it presents a broadside display of the plants on its nine shelves.

The compact unit is castered so it can be rolled about from shade to sun or vice versa, as conditions warrant. In the dreary winter months it can be moved indoors for continued growing and enjoyment.

Construction involves numerous miters and bevels as well as a few compound-angle cuts, so you must have either a radial-arm or table saw at your disposal to tackle this project.

The choice of wood is optional, provided it is given a coat of good paint. This one is made of pine with exterior-grade plywood for the bases and shelves.

The design calls for the use of $\frac{1}{10}$-inch (.100) thick Plexiglas sheets which are set into Reynolds aluminum storm-sash sections. Since the almost unbreakable Plexiglas is permanently installed in the wood frame and cannot be replaced, it is logical to

This compact greenhouse on wheels can be moved about, indoors or out.

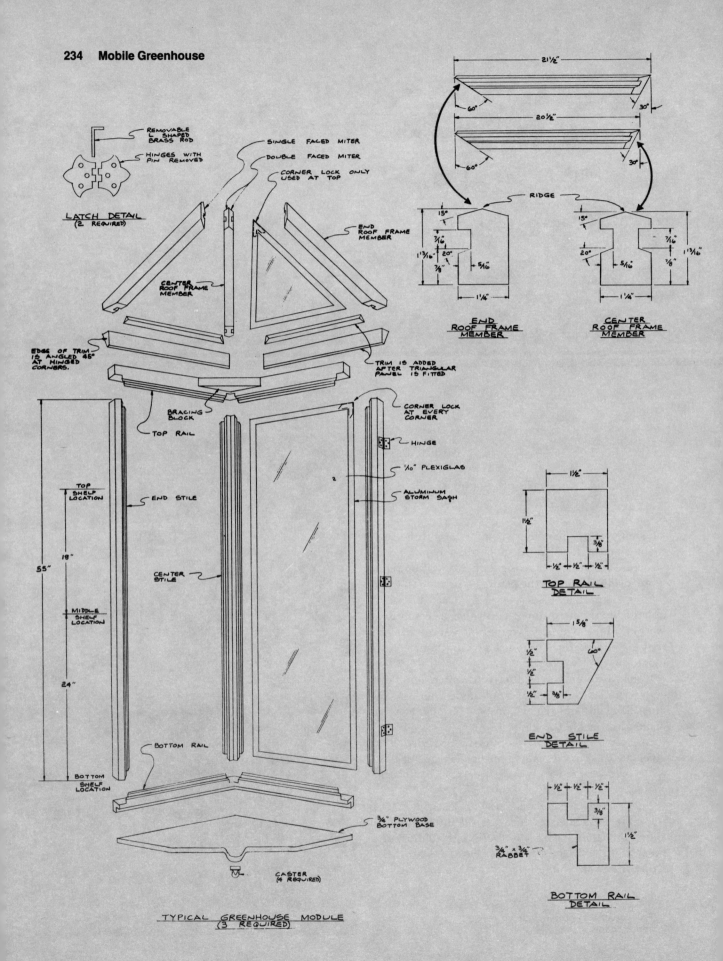

REMOVABLE L SHAPED BRASS ROD

HINGES WITH PIN REMOVED

LATCH DETAIL
(2 REQUIRED)

SINGLE FACED MITER

DOUBLE FACED MITER

CORNER LOCK ONLY USED AT TOP

END ROOF FRAME MEMBER

CENTER ROOF FRAME MEMBER

EDGE OF TRIM IS ANGLED 45° AT HINGED CORNERS.

TRIM IS ADDED AFTER TRIANGULAR PANEL IS FITTED

BRACING BLOCK

TOP RAIL

CORNER LOCK AT EVERY CORNER

HINGE

¹⁄₁₀" PLEXIGLAS

ALUMINUM STORM SASH

END STILE

TOP SHELF LOCATION

CENTER STILE

MIDDLE SHELF LOCATION

BOTTOM RAIL

BOTTOM SHELF LOCATION

¾" PLYWOOD BOTTOM BASE

CASTER (4 REQUIRED)

TYPICAL GREENHOUSE MODULE
(3 REQUIRED)

55"

18"

24"

21½"

20½"

60°

30°

60°

30°

RIDGE

15°

⁷⁄₁₆

1¹³⁄₁₆

20°

⅞

5⁄₁₆

1¼"

END ROOF FRAME MEMBER

15°

⁷⁄₁₆

20°

5⁄₁₆

1¹³⁄₁₆

⅞

1¼"

CENTER ROOF FRAME MEMBER

1½"

1½"

⅜

½" ½" ½"

TOP RAIL DETAIL

1 ⅝"

½"

½"

½"

60°

⅜

END STILE DETAIL

½" ½" ½"

⅜

1½"

¾" x ¾" RABBET

BOTTOM RAIL DETAIL

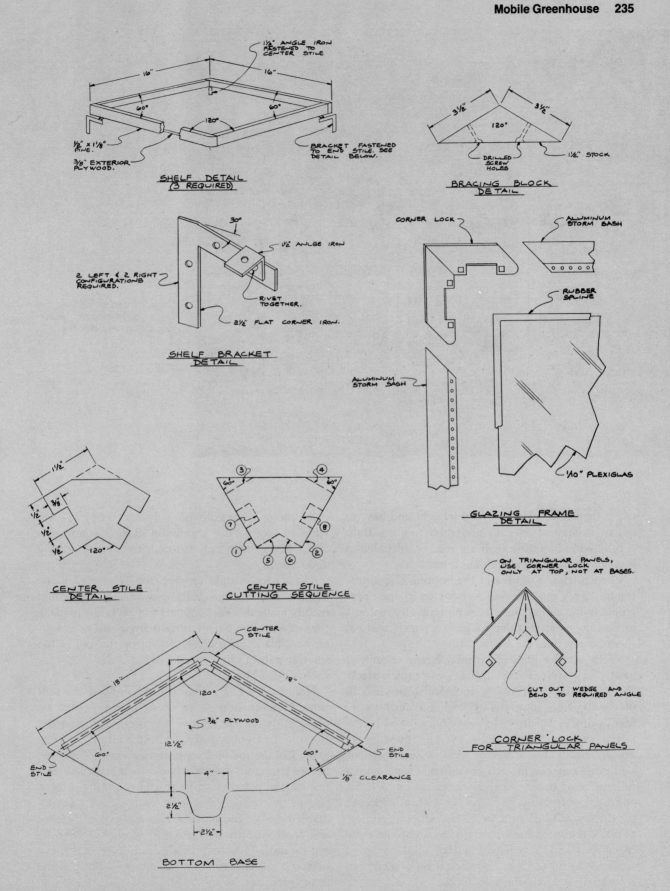

1½" ANGLE IRON FASTENED TO CENTER STILE

16"   16"

60°   120°   60°

½" X 1⅛" PINE.

3/8" EXTERIOR PLYWOOD.

BRACKET FASTENED TO END STILE. SEE DETAIL BELOW.

SHELF DETAIL
(3 REQUIRED)

3½"   120°   3½"

DRILLED SCREW HOLES   1½" STOCK

BRACING BLOCK
DETAIL

30°

½" ANGLE IRON

2 LEFT & 2 RIGHT CONFIGURATIONS REQUIRED.

RIVET TOGETHER.

2½" FLAT CORNER IRON.

SHELF BRACKET
DETAIL

CORNER LOCK

ALUMINUM STORM SASH

RUBBER SPLINE

ALUMINUM STORM SASH

1/10" PLEXIGLAS

GLAZING FRAME
DETAIL

1½"

3/8"

½"

½"

½"

120°

CENTER STILE
DETAIL

③   60°   ④   60°

⑦   ⑧

①   ②

⑤   ⑥

CENTER STILE
CUTTING SEQUENCE

ON TRIANGULAR PANELS, USE CORNER LOCK ONLY AT TOP, NOT AT BASES.

CUT OUT WEDGE AND BEND TO REQUIRED ANGLE

CORNER LOCK
FOR TRIANGULAR PANELS

CENTER STILE

18"   18"

120°

¾" PLYWOOD

12½"

60°   60°

END STILE   END STILE

1/8" CLEARANCE

4"

2½"

2½"

BOTTOM BASE

Sections can be opened for plant maintenance, watering, airing, and display.

use it instead of glass. It is lightweight and easy to cut—two reasons why it's preferable to glass. Both acrylic and aluminum sash are readily available at local hardware stores or home centers.

Construction is started at the bottom. Use a protractor to lay out the base sections on ¾-inch plywood. You can cut the pieces individually, using a sabre saw, or stack three rough-cut panels and cut them at one time on a band saw.

Work on the rails (horizontal frame members) next. They are cut from full 1½-inch-thick stock. Rip enough material to 1½-inch width to yield 12 pieces 20 inches long; the upper and lower rails are identical. Cut 30-degree miters on each end of the rails so they measure 18 inches overall. You will save much time and be assured of lengthwise accuracy if you miter one end of each piece first. Then clamp a mitered scrap to the radial-saw crosscut fence at the appropriate location, to serve as a stop. Butt the previously mitered ends up to this stop, as shown, to make the second miter cuts. You can do the same thing on a table saw if you add an auxiliary wood fence to the miter gage. This should be long enough to permit clamping the stop block.

All the rails are grooved ⅜-inch deep by ½-inch wide to receive the aluminum glazing frame sections. Make these cuts through the center using a dado head.

The six lower rails are rabbeted ¾″ × ¾″ along the lower inside edges. Although a dado head would readily make this deep rabbet, it is advisable to make the cut with two passes at right angles using a regular saw blade. The cross section of the rail is too small to permit safe handling over the dado head for such a deep bite.

Note that, when assembled, the ends of the rails should project about ⅛ inch beyond the edges of the plywood base. This clearance is necessary to permit the upright frame corners to butt without interference. Check this and remove any excess plywood before gluing on the rails. Use only a highly-water-resistant glue such as plastic resin for this project. Secure the rails to the bases with nails or screwdriver through the bottom. End and center notches are required on the surfaces of the rails but these are not cut until the stiles (upright frame members) have been cut to shape to permit accurate marking of the joint lines.

1. Three plywood base panels can be ganged and cut at the same time on the band saw.

2. Mitered cut-off waste is used as a stop to assure uniformly sized frame members. A total of twelve upper and lower rails is required.

3. Assembly starts at the bottom. Deeply rabbeted rails are glued to the plywood base sections.

The six end stiles are cut from 1½-inch stock and beveled 30 degrees on one edge. If you set the blade of the radial-arm saw or the rip fence of the table saw (you can use either one) for the width of two pieces including the thickness of the saw blade, you can save time and minimize waste. Alternately swing the stock end-for-end to obtain bevels on both edges. Later, a straight cut down the center will yield two stiles. Run a ⅜" × ½" groove down the center opposite the beveled edge for the sash frame.

The configuration of the center stiles is a bit more detailed but not difficult to cut. You'll need nominal 2-inch or ⁸⁄₄ stock for these parts. As for the end stiles, with the saw blade tilted 30 degrees, make two rip cuts, swinging the work end-for-end so you come up with a piece with a truncated triangular cross section with a base measuring 3½ inches in width. Make three pieces.

The remaining cuts are made on the table saw. Set the blade to the normal position to make right-angle cuts. Place the previously beveled surface face down to cut the outside flats. Repeat this on the other side. Next, lower the blade and shift the fence to make the straight cuts to form the 120-degree inside corners. This is also done with the bevel face down. Finally cut the grooves down the center of the beveled edges. You can switch to the dado head for this. The numbered diagram in the plan gives the sequential order of the cuts. While it will be more time consuming, the radial-arm saw can be used to make these cuts. As shown in the cutting diagram, the sequence will be: 1, 2, 5, 6, 7, 8, 3, 4, with appropriate blade adjustments.

Hold the stiles in position on the rails and mark

4. Radial-arm saw blade is tilted 30 degrees to rip the beveled vertical members.

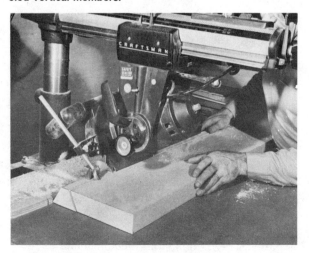

5. A dado head is used to cut the grooves to a width that will permit a slip fit of the aluminum storm-sash framing.

make up the three sections required. A triangular bracing block is used to reinforce the joint. This should be attached with glue and screws before the notches are cut. These notches are identical to the ones on the lower rails.

Final assembly of the lower framing (as well as the roof section) cannot be done until the sash panels have been completed. The details for making them will follow later. In order to continue with the woodworking phase, assume that the sash panels have been made for the following procedures.

Clamps cannot be used effectively for assembly; therefore, screws are used on all the glued joints.

Since it would be structurally unsound to drive a screw through the joint line, two screws are used to fasten the center stile to the rails, one on each side

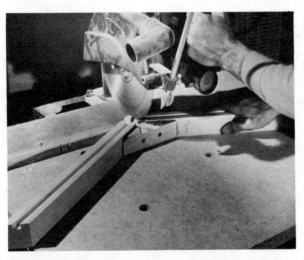

6. Upper-rail miter joint is reinforced with a glue block. The angled center recess is cleaned out with repeated kerf cuts, rather than with a dado head, which would cut too wide.

7. A pair of dummy sash sections is used to hold the stile in place while drilling screw pilot holes.

the rails for the ⅜-inch-deep lap or notch cuts. The radial-arm saw is ideally suited for this task because the cut can be fully observed. Another advantage is that the blade is moved rather than the work. The assembled base section in particular would be a bit awkward to handle on the table saw, but it can be done.

You can use a dado head on the radial-arm saw to cut only the end notches. Due to the keystone shape of the center notch, a wide dado blade would cut beyond the limits of the desired outline. A regular saw blade and repeated passes will do to make the recess.

Note that two upper rails are joined end to end to

8. The main frame members ready for assembly.

of the joint. One screw suffices for the end stiles. Use a portable drill to bore pilot holes; then dry-assemble the unit to check the fit of the parts. It will be helpful to tack-nail the bases of the three units to a scrap board to keep them in alignment during the drilling operation. Temporary triangular braces are also screwed into the upper rails between sections.

Begin the glued assembly of a side section by attaching the center stile to a base. End-grain soaks up glue, so you should apply a second coat to the end of the stile. Insert the sash panels into the grooves and add the end stile. If you work on sawhorses, you will have easy access to the screws from below. Complete the closure by adding the top rail section.

When the three side sections have been completed, again fasten them together temporarily, using the board at the bottom and the three cleats at the top. This is necessary to facilitate adding the pitched roof sections.

The roof-framing members are cut from 1¼″ × 1¹³⁄₁₆″ stock. The pieces are mitered at both ends. The bottoms have steep 60-degree miters while the top ends require 30-degree compound miters; single-faced on the two end members and double-faced on the center piece.

The compound miter is a combination of the miter and bevel made in one crosscutting operation. To make this cut, set the saw arm or the table saw miter gage for a 30-degree miter. Also tilt the saw blade to 30 degrees with either machine. Both left- and right-hand angles are required, so the machines must be adjusted accordingly.

Next, cut the grooves on the sides of the roof-frame members as indicated in the plan. Note that the lower edge of the grooves is beveled 20 degrees. This cut can be made with one pass of a regular blade after dadoing. The ridge bevels are formed by making two 15-degree tilt cuts.

Assembly of the roof is done in stages. Start by gluing only two outer members into place on one main section only. A 2-inch finishing nail can be driven into each lower end and into the rails. Nailing is not feasible at the top point so glue alone is used there. Mix the glue a bit thicker than normal consistency so it isn't too runny. Insert pieces of wax paper between the butted sections of the main frame below so glue runoff won't stick them together. Apply glue, then drive in the nail to secure the lower ends. Masking tape is used to hold the peak together. Allow the glue of this initial assembly to dry thoroughly before proceeding further.

With partial roof framing in place, the remaining members will be easier to install because they can rest against the peak. Apply glue, inserting wax-paper between all section joints, and install the other four outer framing members.

9. The three sections are temporarily joined with three angled cleats at the top, a flat board at the bottom, to facilitate accurate assembly.

10. Wax-paper barriers are inserted between section ends during gluing to prevent them from sticking together with glue runoff. A single 2-inch finishing nail is used to hold each piece in place. Note that three of the cleats are glued in place, the other three are temporarily secured with screws.

11. Center members have a compound angle at top. Test the fit but do not install until the glazing panels are ready.

12. Center piece and two glazing sections are assembled together. One screw at the top and a nail at the bottom provide glue pressure.

The center divider members are installed together with a pair of triangular sash panels. The three main lower sections are separated for this stage. This will allow driving a screw from the inside to secure the glued three-part junction at the top. Small pieces of triangular trim are used to snug the bottom of each sash panel. These must be cut to size to fit as required inasmuch as slight variations may occur.

Note that the outside ends of the lower, larger trim must be back-mitered 45 degrees to allow the individual sections to hinge fully open.

Paint the inside of the frame before installing the shelves. The shelf-support brackets are custom made by combining a 2½-inch flat corner iron with a 1½-inch angle bracket, as shown in the plan. A plain angle bracket is used at the center.

A simple latching device consists of one pair of hinges in which the regular pins are replaced with removable L-shaped brass rod.

GLAZING

Reynolds do-it-yourself aluminum storm-sash framing is available in 6- and 8-foot lengths, with rubber spline included. Waste will be negligible if you obtain a dozen 8-foot lengths. Special corner locks are used to join the pieces—you will need 30 of these.

The Plexiglas required for this application can be cut from four 3' × 5' sheets of the material in ¹⁄₁₀-inch thickness. You can purchase an acrylic scriber where you buy the plastic. This is an inexpensive tool used for cutting the material.

Start by cutting the aluminum frame members to length. Obtain the dimensions by measuring the space between grooves when the wood framing is dry-assembled with screws. Deduct ⅛-inch from the length and width; then mark the sash frames to length. Remove the rubber spline from the channels. Scribe 45-degree angles and cut miters at each end for the rectangular frames. You can make the cuts on the radial or table saw using a fine-tooth plywood

13. Fine-tooth plywood blade easily cuts miters in the aluminum sash. This miter jig for the radial-arm saw is a handy accessory.

blade, or you can cut the miters by hand with a hacksaw. After cutting, remove any burrs with a file or sandpaper.

Determine the size to cut the Plexiglas by measuring the width and height of the aluminum frame, outside to outside. Deduct 1 1/16 inch from each of these dimensions and cut the sheet accordingly. Using a straightedge as a guide, place the point of the scribing tool at the edge of the material, apply firm pressure, and draw the cutting point across the length four or five times. Place the scribed line face up over a broomstick and apply downward pressure with the fingers on both sides of the line. The plastic will break. On the long pieces, move the fingers to

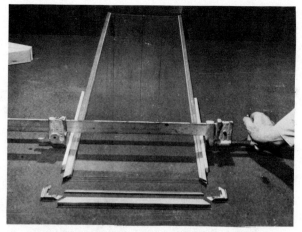

16. If some of the aluminum frame members are stubborn you might try this, but don't apply too much pressure.

14. Acrylic plastic glazing is easy to cut. Clamp a straightedge on the line and make several passes with an acrylic scoring tool. Place the scored line over a round stick and press down on each side of the line to snap a clean break.

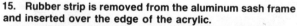

15. Rubber strip is removed from the aluminum sash frame and inserted over the edge of the acrylic.

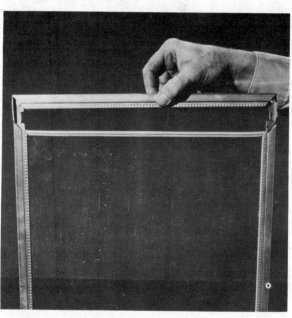

17. Mitered frame members are joined with corner-locking fasteners.

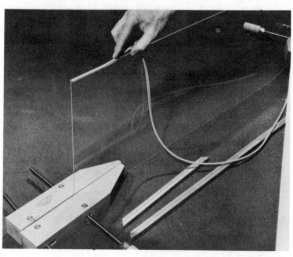

new positions as the break progresses. Lightly sand the sharp edges and form a slight radius at the corners. This step is important, as it will prevent the plastic from developing stress fractures.

Peel the protective masking from the acrylic sheet. Stretch the rubber spline over two long edges. Wet the rubber with water and press the sash sections into place. With a razor blade, trim the spline ends to match the mitered sash ends. Push the corner locks into both mitered corners of an end sash sec-

18.   View shows a completed glazing panel being inserted during initial assembly

19.   A wedge snipped out of the center of the corner lock permits making the required sharp bend for the roof panel.

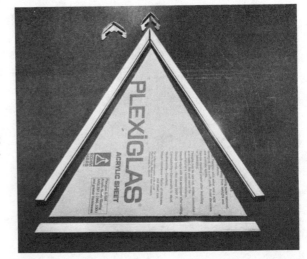

tion, then add to the assembly. Use a rubber mallet, if necessary, to obtain a good fit.

The corner-lock fittings are designed for right-angle applications. In order to adapt them for use on the upper triangular points, a wedge is cut out of the center portion. This allows the fitting to be bent to the required sharp angle. A tinsnip can be used to cut the wedge. Lock fittings are not used at the base ends of the triangle. Due to slight variations which may exist in your roof panels, it is advisable to cut cardboard templates for testing before cutting the triangular acrylic inserts.

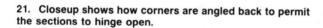

20. A set of four plate casters is screwed to the bottom of each section.

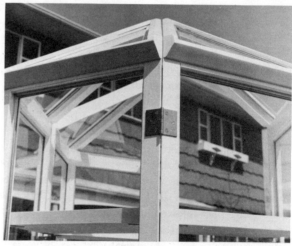

21. Closeup shows how corners are angled back to permit the sections to hinge open.

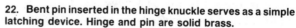

22. Bent pin inserted in the hinge knuckle serves as a simple latching device. Hinge and pin are solid brass.

33

Full-Function Wall

Enliven a humdrum wall with this handsome, multi-purpose, built-in storage unit. Books, accessories, and art objects on bountiful shelves glow by the light of fluorescent fixtures concealed behind an attractive, triple-arched valance. The base cabinet below features a drop-lid desk on one side and a drop-lid bar on the other. The midsection is compartmented to house a television set, a turntable, tuner/amplifier, and digital clock. The clock is optional; the space allotted to it is sufficient to contain an average-size tape deck, should you prefer. In addition there are four general-storage sections, two large record-storage drawers, and a pair of wide drawers for holding newspapers, magazines, or the usual clutter that collects in a living room.

The unit is unique, owing to the innovative use of wall paneling as the surfacing material over an ordinary plywood framework. Solid-colored Marlite paneling is applied to the back plywood panel and to both sides of the shelves and uprights. This results in inch-thick sections which are accentuated with solid-wood edging painted black. Marlite woodgrain paneling was used for the valance and to surface the cabinet doors and drawer fronts.

Construction entails butt joints mainly, some dadoes, rabbets, and half laps, and quite a bit of straight accurate sawing, so a table or radial-arm saw is practically a necessity for this job. Earlier projects involved two simple methods of bending wood. A third technique is utilized in this one for making the curved framing members of the valance.

This unit measures 18" deep by 8' high by 11'11" long. If your wall is a different size, alter the dimensions accordingly. But there is an important consideration: The cabinet doors and drawer fronts should not exceed 15½ inches in width. This is so because Marlite plank panels measure 16" × 8', and the width includes a tongue and groove which must be trimmed off. By keeping within this maximum width you will avoid the need for butting pieces together. Although the panels butt together nicely, a definite grooved joint line would be visible, thus interrupting the pattern. But certain other textured panels are available in 4' × 8', so the restriction would not apply.

One of the first things you should do is to make a simple layout on your wall indicating the location of the various compartments so that you can pinpoint the location for new electric outlets, TV antenna plug-in terminal, and lighting fixtures. Two 4-foot single-tube fluorescent fixtures are recommended on the ceiling, behind the valance. In addi-

tion to the outlets for the TV and sound equipment, you may want to include an outlet for a small lamp to illuminate the area between the bookshelves where you can display a painting. Attend to this before you close in any area of the wall and ceiling.

Floors are frequently out of level, so you must begin construction of the base cabinet by establishing a level working line on the wall 41 inches above the high point of the floor. Place a long strip of wood across the floor and check with a spirit level. If the floor is off, measure and draw a line 41 inches above the high point. Using the level and straightedge strip, continue this line on the side walls. Cut two ¾" × 16 ¼" pieces of plywood to fit from the line to the floor and attach them to the side walls. If the floor is level, both these pieces will be 41 inches in length.

THE BASE CABINET

If the length of your wall does not exceed 12 feet, you can make the top and bottom of the base cabinet with continuous panels by obtaining a ¾" × 4' × 12' plywood panel. This size may not be normally stocked by retail lumber dealers, but they can get it for you on special order.

If you must piece panels together to obtain the desired length, an end-to-end half-lap splice joint should be used. For maximum strength, make the length of the lap at least four times the thickness of the stock.

Use a portable saw with a guide to cut the large plywood panels down to manageable size. The apron (the strip across the front of the base) and one of the long cleats required can be gleaned from the cut-off of the large panel.

Three kinds of joints are used in the assembly of the base cabinet: plain butt, cleat, and edge half-lap. Since they are not visible, cleats are used to provide a simple, strong method for securing the top and bottom panels in place against the wall. Nailed butt joints serve to support the top panel over the two main dividers and the end panels. Edge half-laps are required to join the bottom panel to the dividers. This permits the use of continuous panels, which results in greater strength and stability.

Locate the studs in the back wall by probing with a nail. Then attach the four cabinet-support cleats; two on the back wall and one on each side-wall panel at the floor. Make sure that the lower cleats are equidistant from the 41-inch level line. Drive two 3-inch common nails into the cleats at each stud

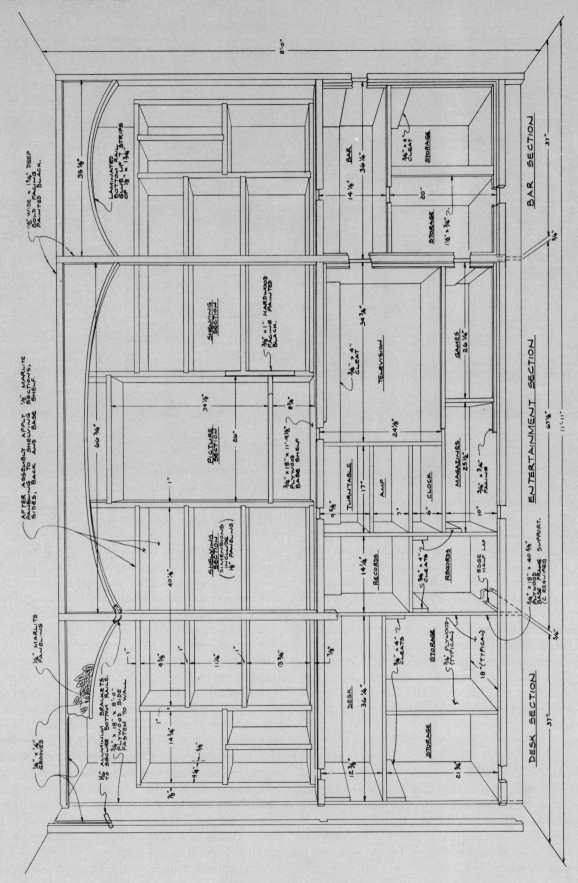

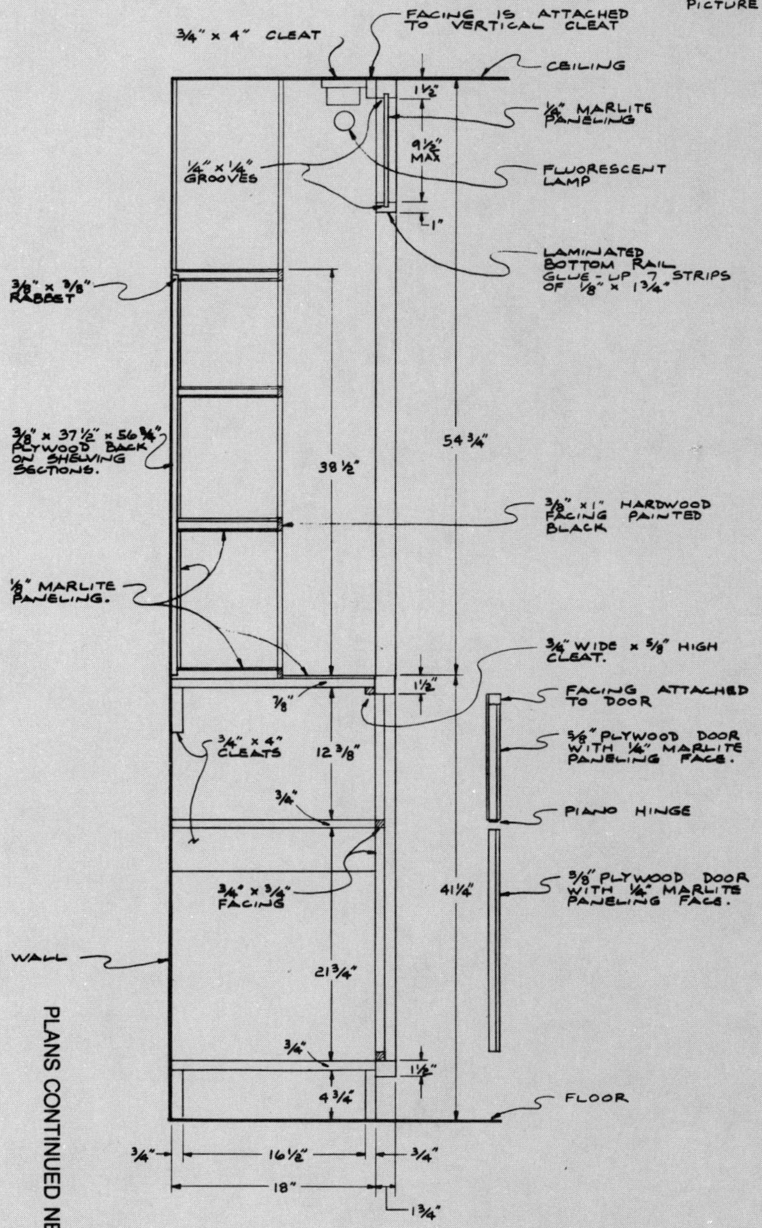
3/4" x 4" CLEAT
FACING IS ATTACHED TO VERTICAL CLEAT
CEILING
1 1/2"
1/4" MARLITE PANELING
9 1/2" MAX
1/4" x 1/4" GROOVES
FLUORESCENT LAMP
1"
LAMINATED BOTTOM RAIL GLUE-UP 7 STRIPS OF 1/8" x 1 3/4"
3/8" x 3/8" RABBET
3/8" x 37 1/2" x 56 3/4" PLYWOOD BACK ON SHELVING SECTIONS.
38 1/2"
54 3/4"
3/8" x 1" HARDWOOD FACING PAINTED BLACK
1/8" MARLITE PANELING.
3/4" WIDE x 5/8" HIGH CLEAT.
7/8"
1 1/2"
FACING ATTACHED TO DOOR
3/4" x 4" CLEATS
12 3/8"
5/8" PLYWOOD DOOR WITH 1/4" MARLITE PANELING FACE.
3/4"
PIANO HINGE
3/4" x 3/4" FACING
41 1/4"
5/8" PLYWOOD DOOR WITH 1/4" MARLITE PANELING FACE.
WALL
21 3/4"
3/4"
1 1/2"
4 3/4"
FLOOR
3/4"
16 1/2"
3/4"
18"
1 3/4"

SECTION VIEW AT DESK

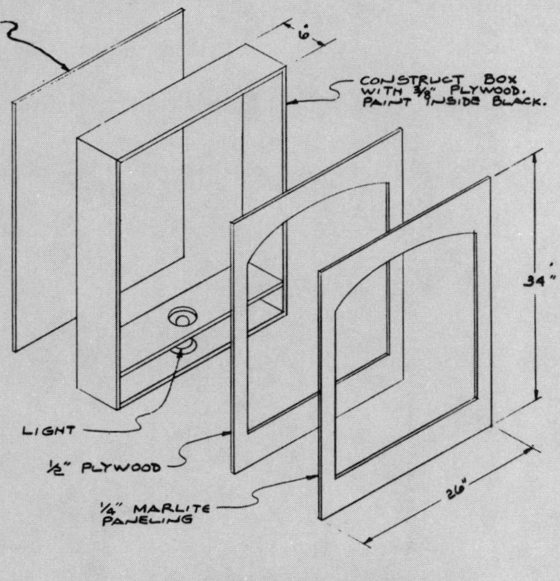
PICTURE
6"
CONSTRUCT BOX WITH 3/8" PLYWOOD. PAINT INSIDE BLACK.
34"
LIGHT
1/2" PLYWOOD
1/4" MARLITE PANELING
26"

PICTURE SECTION INSERT

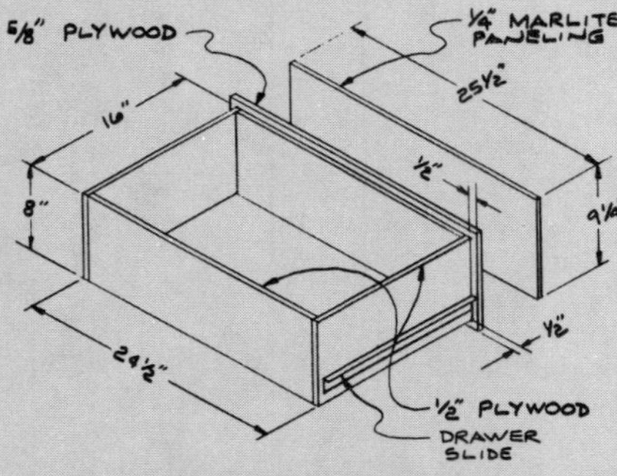
5/8" PLYWOOD
1/4" MARLITE PANELING
25 1/2"
16"
8"
1/2"
9 1/4"
24 1/2"
1/2"
1/2" PLYWOOD
DRAWER SLIDE

DRAWERS
(2 REQUIRED)

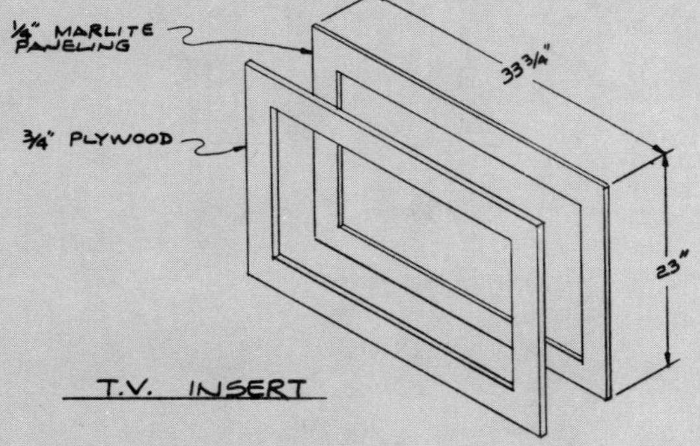
1/4" MARLITE PANELING
33 3/4"
3/4" PLYWOOD
23"

T.V. INSERT

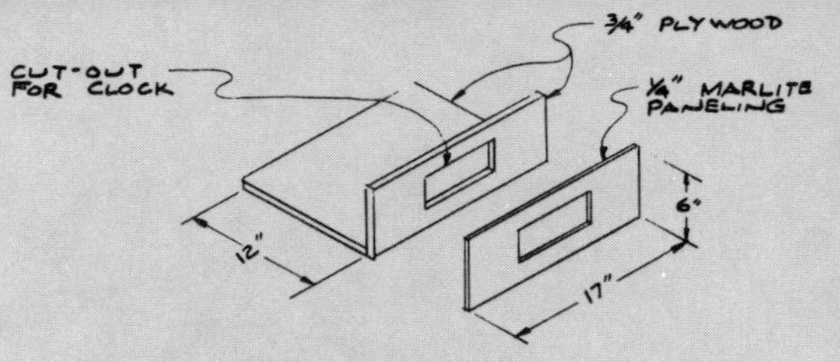
3/4" PLYWOOD
CUT-OUT FOR CLOCK
1/4" MARLITE PANELING
6"
12"
17"

CLOCK INSERT

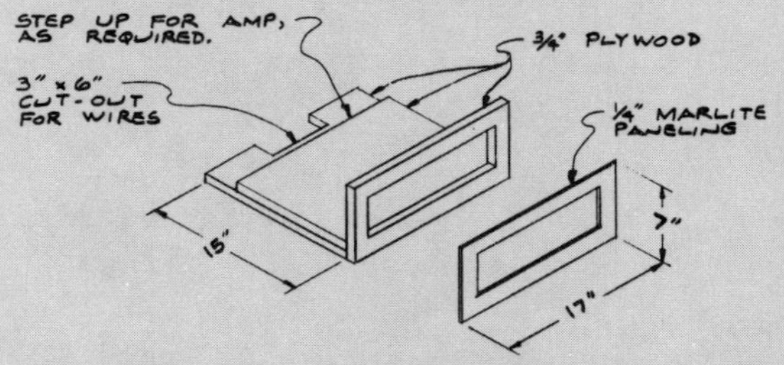
STEP UP FOR AMP, AS REQUIRED.
3/4" PLYWOOD
3" x 6" CUT-OUT FOR WIRES
1/4" MARLITE PANELING
7"
15"
17"

AMPLIFIER INSERT

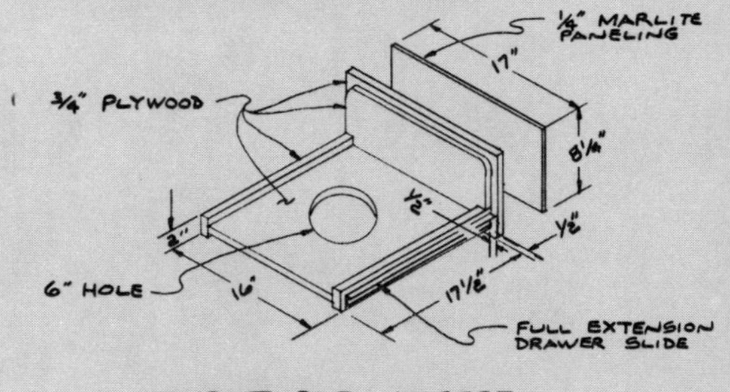
1/4" MARLITE PANELING
17"
3/4" PLYWOOD
8 1/4"
2"
1/2"
1/2"
6" HOLE
16"
17 1/2"
FULL EXTENSION DRAWER SLIDE

TURNTABLE INSERT
(2 REQUIRED)

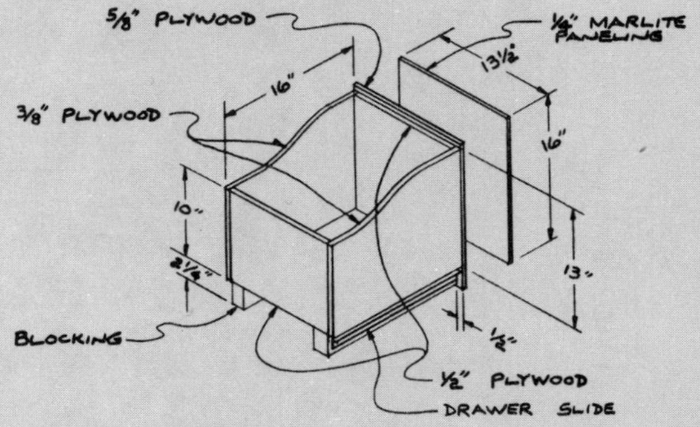
5/8" PLYWOOD
1/4" MARLITE PANELING
13 1/2"
16"
3/8" PLYWOOD
16"
10"
2 1/4"
13"
BLOCKING
1/2"
1/2" PLYWOOD
DRAWER SLIDE

RECORD DRAWERS
(2 REQUIRED)

PLANS CONTINUED NEXT PAGE

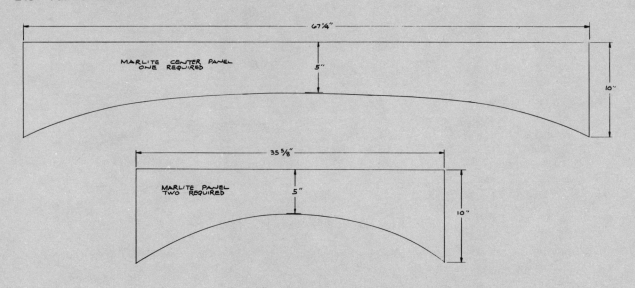

MARLITE CENTER PANEL
ONE REQUIRED

67 1/4"

5"

10"

MARLITE PANEL
TWO REQUIRED

35 5/8"

5"

10"

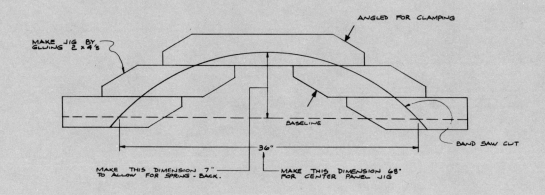

ANGLED FOR CLAMPING

MAKE JIG BY
GLUING 2 x 4's

BASELINE

BAND SAW CUT

36"

MAKE THIS DIMENSION 7"
TO ALLOW FOR SPRING-BACK.

MAKE THIS DIMENSION 68"
FOR CENTER PANEL JIG

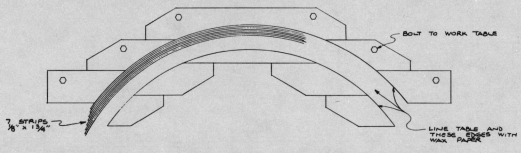

BOLT TO WORK TABLE

7 STRIPS
1/8" x 1 3/4"

LINE TABLE AND
THESE EDGES WITH
WAX PAPER

JIG FOR LAMINATING STRIPS
FOR ARCHED FRAME MEMBERS

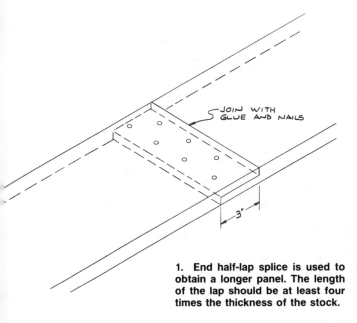

1. End half-lap splice is used to obtain a longer panel. The length of the lap should be at least four times the thickness of the stock.

2. The upper and lower base-cabinet members are secured by nailing into cleats that are attached to the wall. The partitions are preassembled with glued and nailed butt joints.

location on the back wall. Place the top panel onto the cleats and side panels and secure with 2-inch finishing nails driven into the edges of the cleats and the side panels (3-inch common nails driven into a plywood edge would split it).

Make the edge half-laps by notching the front edges of the dividers and the rear edge of the bottom panel. The panels are too large to be properly handled on a stationary saw, so use a portable circular or sabre saw. Attach a guide strip and make two cuts so the width of the notch equals the thickness of the stock, and the length of the notch equals one-half the width. It is important to lay out the notches on the dividers so their bottom edges line up with the top edge of the lower wall cleats.

Cut notches at the back of each divider so they will clear the rear wall cleats, then put them into place and secure with a few nails driven through the top panel.

Engage the notches and slide the bottom panel into position. It should come to rest on the lower wall cleats. Nail it into place.

The subdivisions for the three main lower compartments are assembled in separate units and inserted into the main structure. A combination of butt joints and cleats is used to make up these units. Nails and glue should be used on each joint.

FACE-FRAMING

The bold face-framing is made with 1½" wide × 1¾" deep solid hardwood of any closed-grain spe-

3. Slide the partitions into place; then nail through the top members into the edges of the verticals.

cies (poplar, birch, maple) that will take paint well. This framing is assembled flush with end, middle, and cross half-lap joints. These are all basically the same joint; the different terms merely describe their location. Three horizontals are required. You can cut them to size and form the notches using the same formula described earlier for the main dividers. For this you can use a stationary saw with a dado head.

Glue and nail the lower horizontal face-framing member to the apron strip which forms the front of the cabinet at the floor. Note that this projects ¾ inch above the top edge of the apron so it will be flush with the bottom panel of the cabinet. Nail the

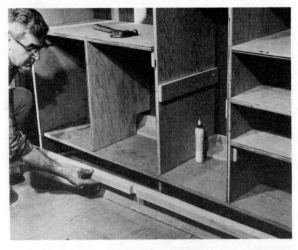

4. Bottom face-framing strip is dadoed for the half-lap joints, attached to nailed apron, and glued in place.

5. Dadoes are required for the open upper-shelving uprights. The radial-arm saw is ideal for this operation.

apron into place; then slide in the compartment assembly, nailing through the top panel into the vertical members to secure them at the top. Neat toenailing will hold them in place at the bottom. Use 1½-inch finishing nails for this.

The second horizontal face-frame member can now be added. This must project ⅛ inch above the top panel in order to be flush with the ⅛-inch-thick face paneling which will subsequently be added. A ⅝" × ¾" cleat (in three sections) is added to the rear bottom of this piece to obtain a reinforced butt joint. Use glue and 2½-inch finishing nails to attach this piece. Counterbore holes in advance so the nail heads will seat about ½ inch deep.

UPPER SECTION

Now you can proceed to work on the upper section. The bookshelves are made up as preassembled separate units. Cleats cannot be used to reinforce the shelves as was done in the base cabinet because they would be visible; therefore, dado joints must be employed. A ¼-inch plywood back is used to reinforce the overall assembly. This is set into a ¼ inch deep by ⅜ inch wide rabbet cut along the inside edges of the sides and top and bottom members.

Cut the four case sides to size. Then cut the rabbet on the back edges using a dado set or by making two passes at right angles using a regular saw blade. When making a rabbet with a saw blade, it is best to make the first cut into the edge of the stock and the second pass into the broad face. If the reverse order is followed, the progressively narrowed edge will be prone to inadvertent tilting. However, be

sure to adjust the fence so the second cut is made on the free edge of the work. This will allow the waste strip to separate freely. If the second cut is made inboard, the waste strip will be trapped between the blade and fence and could be kicked back with considerable force towards your body.

Next, cut the end rabbets and dadoes in the side members to receive the butt ends of the shelves. Also cut the dadoes for the vertical dividers. These cuts can be made with a dado head or a regular blade on the radial-arm or table saw. Or you can use a router. With a dado head you can make the cuts in one pass; the repeat-pass method will be necessary with a regular saw blade.

If the router is used to cut the dadoes, much setup time can be saved by doing gang cutting. Lay out the cutting lines, then group a number of pieces side-by-side and tack-nail a long straightedge across the lot to guide the router. To position the guide, measure from the cutting edge of the bit to the outside edge of the router base. Set the guide precisely this distance from the point at which the cut is to be made.

If you have a ¾-inch- diameter straight router bit and a heavy-duty router you can make the ⅜-inch-deep grooves in one pass. Otherwise, several passes and a shift of the guide strip will be necessary with a smaller diameter router bit. In either case, be sure to drive two nails partly through the guide and into each board to prevent them from shifting during the operation.

Due to the clockwise rotation, the thrust of the router is to the left as viewed from above and behind the direction of travel. Therefore, it is important to position the guide to the left in relation to the direc-

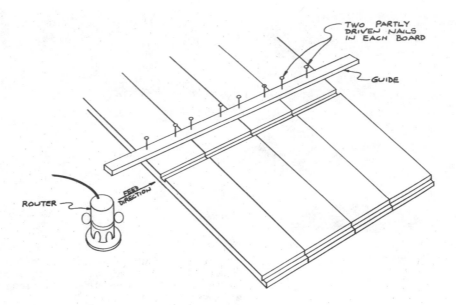

6.   Ganged boards can be dadoed or rabbeted at the same time. When using a router to cut dadoes or rabbets, you can gang the boards and route them in one pass.

tion of travel. Otherwise the router will have a tendency to drift away from the guide, resulting in a spoiled cut.

When all the pieces have been rabbeted and grooved, dry-assemble the sides and measure the spaces between the back rabbets to determine the size of the back panel. Cut the back panel to size, making sure the rectangle is perfectly true. This will assure a true assembly of the case.

7.   Preassembled shelving units are backed with ¼-inch plywood panels set into a ¼" × ⅜" rabbet.

Glue and nail the boards together, then lay the piece face down and insert the back panel into the rabbeted recess. If the assembly should be out of square, the fitted back will true it up. The bookshelf units are now positioned on the base cabinet and secured to the wall by nailing into studs. Measure the space between the outside edges of both cases and bridge them with two shelves.

SURFACING

The shelves and surrounds are now surfaced with the ⅛-inch tempered hardboard Marlite paneling. Install the back pieces first, then the tops and bottoms; the sides go on last. Measure the spaces carefully and deduct 1/16 inch from the width and length of each piece to allow for expansion. Work with a smooth-cutting blade on the radial-arm or table saw. Break all sharp corners by hand sanding with 180-grit paper wrapped around a wood block.

If the panel adhesive you're using is the flammable type, be sure to observe all safety precautions: no smoking, no pilot lights or open flame—and be sure to provide good ventilation. Use the cohesive procedure to make a quick, lasting bond. Spread a very thin full coating of adhesive over the wood surface and a combed layer, applied with the notched spreader, on the back of the panel. Allow the adhesive to set for about 15 minutes, then press the piece into place. A few blows over the entire surface with

8.   Thin layer of adhesive is spread fully over backing to install paneling by the cohesive method.

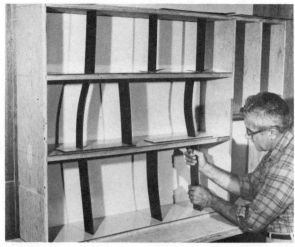

11.   Install the panels on the upper and lower faces of the shelves. Strips of scrap paneling wedged between the shelves will prevent the panel inserts from sagging until the adhesive sets.

12.   Side panels go on last. Here a cardboard template is cut to size to check the fit for an irregular shape.

9.   Adhesive is applied to the panel back with a notched spreader. When contact is made, the bond will be firm.

10.   Tap the panels with your fist or with a hammer and padded block to obtain good contact.

13. All sharp corners of paneling are lightly sanded with fine-grit abrasive paper before installation.

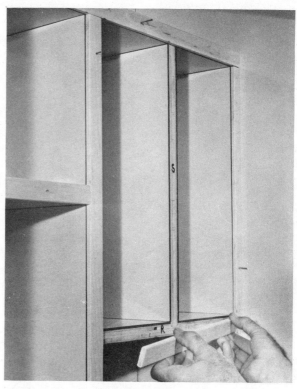

15. The shelf edges are faced with hardwood strips. Test the fit, then remove and paint them before final assembly.

14. A notched flooring-tile trowel is handy for spreading a combed layer of adhesive on the panels.

FINISHING THE FACE-FRAMING

Now the bold face-framing can be completed. A right-angle cleat attached to the ceiling will provide a bearing surface for the top horizontal member. If the cleat does not cross ceiling joists to permit nailing, simply use toggle bolts to attach it. Before you attach the frame member to the ceiling you must cut a ¼″ × ¼″ groove through the center of the underside. This will receive the edges of the valance panel inserts.

Cut the four vertical frame members to length, then hold them in place against the horizontals in order to mark them accurately for cutting the half-lap notches. Make the cuts; then groove the upper ends ¼″ × ¼″ × 11½″ for the insert panels. Bore and counterbore holes at each lap joint for 2½-inch flathead wood screws. Screw the verticals into place and conceal the holes with glued dowel plugs.

The arched valance-framing sections are made by laminating seven strips of ⅛″ × 1¾″ stock in a simple bending form. To make the form, glue several pieces of 2×4 stock together, edge-to-edge, as shown in the drawing. The offset arrangement permits the use of relatively small pieces of 2×4 stock for purpose of economy. The dimensions apply for

the side of the fist or with a hammer and padded block will assure good contact.

Scrap strips of paneling or wood cut to length for a tight fit are used to prop up the panels on the undersides of the shelves. These braces should be left in place for at least several hours; preferably overnight.

The front edges of the shelves and dividers are faced with ⅜-inch-thick solid wood. While the ¾-inch plywood and two thicknesses of ⅛-inch panel measure 1 inch, the actual thickness of the sections will measure slightly more due to the layers of adhesive in between. Cut the strips to size, sand, then glue and nail them into place.

17. **Forming jig made with 2×4s and lined with wax paper makes easy work of laminating strips for the curved frame members. Seven strips are joined for each member.**

16. **Mark and cut the dadoes in the vertical face-framing members only after the three horizontal pieces have been installed. A screw is set into a counterbored hole to secure each half-lap joint.**

the valance shown. If your situation differs, you'll have to alter the form dimensions accordingly.

Use three nails and a flexible stick to draw a curved line through the approximate center of the forming block. Note that while the curvature of the finished piece represents a 5-inch differential between the base line and apex, a 7-inch differential is figured for the form to allow for spring-back: the laminated piece will flatten slightly when it is removed from the form.

Cut along the curved line with a band or sabre saw so you have a two-part form. Lay a piece of wax paper down, then bolt the upper (concave) section to the work table. The paper will prevent the work from sticking to the table. Apply glue to both surfaces of the strips (except on the two outside pieces which are coated on one side only), and place the bundle on edge against the form. Butt the mating lower (convex) section of the form against the strips, then apply clamps to force the bundle together. When the glue has set use a plane or a belt sander to true and smooth the sides.

A groove ¼ inch wide by ¼ inch deep is cut across the length of the top of the piece to form the recess for the textured paneling. A shaper is the ideal tool for this cut, but it can also be made on the table saw with a dado head or a regular blade. To make the cut on the shaper you use a ¼ inch straight groove cutter with a collar that will limit the depth of cut to ¼ inch. On the table saw a hold-down block with a curved bottom is clamped to the rip fence, centered over the blade. The work is pushed through the space between the hold-down and saw table. When a little more than half the work has been cut, switch the hands to the back and pull the piece through the rest of the way. This will keep the fingers safely away from the blade.

Hold the curved piece up to the framing to mark the end cut-off lines. Use a hand, band, or sabre saw to trim the ends as required.

Cutom-made brackets of ¹⁄₁₆-inch aluminum sheet, fastened with screws from the rear, are used to secure the curved sections. Cut the textured panel to size, allowing ⅛ inch extra on all sides for recessing into the grooves. Bow the inset panel slightly to clear the sides of the frame, then move it upwards so it seats in the grooves at the top of the frame. Position the curved frame section and mark it for drilling the screw pilot holes for the brackets.

Solid ¾-inch-square stock is used to face the plywood edges and to trim the perimeter of the cabinet compartments. This is attached with glue and finishing nails. Note that the square strips should be omitted on the frame over the desk and bar openings because at these locations the trim is part of the lid edge banding.

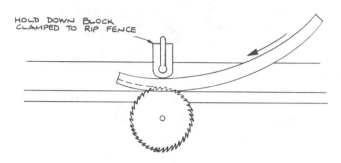

HOLD DOWN BLOCK
CLAMPED TO RIP FENCE

18. Hold-down block with a rounded end is clamped to the saw fence for cutting the groove on the curved surface of the arched frame member.

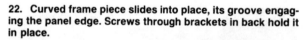

21. Valance insert panels, cut slightly oversize, are bowed to snap into the grooves in the frame.

19. Fine-tooth sabre-saw blade is used to cut the paneling. Cardboard template was made to check the fit; it can also be used to guide the saw.

22. Curved frame piece slides into place, its groove engaging the panel edge. Screws through brackets in back hold it in place.

20. View shows one of two flourescent lamp fixtures which are concealed behind valances. Note the aluminum bracket at the upper left which is used to secure the curved frame

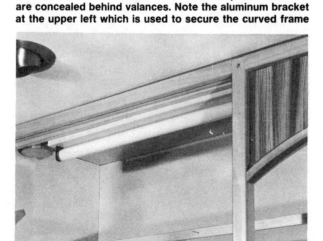

DRAWERS

Except where noted, ½-inch plywood is used for constructing the drawers. They're made up as simple boxes with four sides and a bottom butt joined with glue and nails. The decorative fronts are added on as separate plywood backed panels.

Earlier in this book, in the Bunk Bed Group project, projecting nail points were used to facilitate alignment of the drawer fronts. A slightly different approach is utilized here: Nails are driven through the front of the plywood backup pieces before attaching the decorative panels. Cut the backup pieces to size then install the sliding track hardware and set the drawers in place in the cabinet.

Use cardboard shims to space the backup onto the drawer front in accurate alignment, then partly drive four nails so they emerge on the back side of the drawer front. Withdraw the nails; the resulting holes will serve as alignment guides later when the nails are driven in again from the inside of the drawer during final glue assembly.

Although the panel adhesive holds exceptionally well, it is not used to join the decorative panel to the plywood backup because it would result in a fairly wide, spaced joint line. Contact cement is used instead to obtain a more attractive fine joint line on all exposed edges.

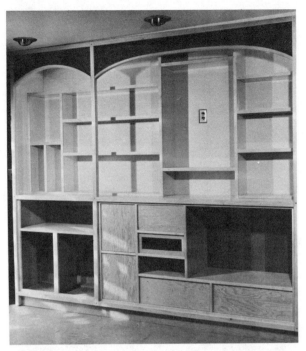

24. Here unit is ready to receive cabinet doors, drawer-front panels, and paint.

23. Backup panels are fitted accurately to drawers before facing is installed. Note spacing shims at bottom. Nail holes will help in realignment when gluing.

25. One coat of contact cement on the paneling and two coats on the plywood will make a lasting bond.

Cut the decorative panels about ¼ inch oversize in length and width and apply a coat of contact cement to the plywood only. When this has set (non-sticky to the touch), a coat is applied to both surfaces. Thus the more absorbent plywood will have a second coat and both surfaces will set and be ready for assembly within the manufacturer's prescribed time, which is usually about thirty minutes. Join the panel to the plywood backup.

Trim the overhanging edges flush with a router, then proceed to round the leading edge of the Mar-

26. Oversize panel is trimmed flush with plywood back with router and straight cutting bit. This is followed with a shallow cut with lower portion of corner-rounding bit.

lite panel slightly with a block plane, by sanding, or by taking a shallow cut with a corner-rounding bit in the router. The Marlite edges are brought to an unusually fine finish by sanding thoroughly, then polishing. After sanding with 220-grit paper, apply some polishing compound, such as DuPont 606 Extra Fine, to a soft cloth and burnish the panel edges by rubbing briskly, shoe-shine fashion. When the fronts are completed, glue and nail them to the drawers.

To wind up the project, add paneling to the door and lid fronts, face the inside surface of the lids, and the desk and bar interior, with white plastic laminate. Finally, construct the TV masking frame and art display box.

Use a good quality black enamel to paint the trim, and door and drawer edges.

34

Butcher Block

The massive, sturdy butcher block has become one of the most favored work tables in the American kitchen. Its rugged top is designed for hard use and abuse, and its bold design will fit into most kitchens.

Authentic butcher blocks are true heavyweights with tops usually made of on-end stacked maple at least 12 inches thick. While it might be desirable, such a thick top is really not required for typical kitchen chores. Nor is it feasible to construct such a top with average home-workshop equipment.

The table design presented here is a compromise —it has the appearance of the real thing but the thickness of the top has been scaled down to a workable size. The top is 2½-inches thick except on the perimeter where it is 9½ inches deep. The wall thickness at the sides is 3¼ inches and 1¾ inches at the ends. Resting on chunky 4-inch-diameter legs, this table is more than solid enough for any use in the home kitchen.

The top is made by joining 98 individual blocks of wood, end-grain up. This requires a considerable amount of precision cutting, jointing, and gluing. The gluing is done in stages, using the pinned butt-joint technique, which simplifies the process and assures good results.

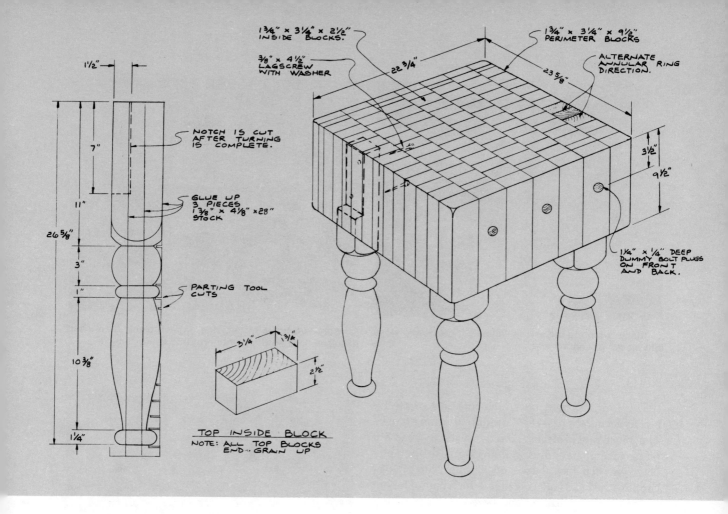

1¾" x 3¼" x 2½" INSIDE BLOCKS.

1¾" x 3¼" x 9½" PERIMETER BLOCKS

ALTERNATE ANNULAR RING DIRECTION.

⅜" x 4½" LAGSCREW WITH WASHER

NOTCH IS CUT AFTER TURNING IS COMPLETE.

GLUE UP 3 PIECES 1⅜" x 4⅛" x28" STOCK

PARTING TOOL CUTS

TOP INSIDE BLOCK
NOTE: ALL TOP BLOCKS END-GRAIN UP

1¼" x ¼" DEEP DUMMY BOLT PLUGS ON FRONT AND BACK.

23¾"

23⅝"

3½"

9½"

1½"

7"

11"

26⅝"

3"

1"

10⅜"

1¼"

3¼"

3¼"

2½"

Sugar maple, also known as rock maple and hard maple, is generally used for commercially made butcher blocks; but soft maple, also known as red maple, has working properties which are better suited for home-workshop tools. The latter species is certainly hard enough for this project.

All the pieces for the top can be cut from 50 lineal feet of ⁸⁄₄ stock. The leg squares are made up by gluing three pieces of ⁶⁄₄ stock. For this you'll need 28 running feet. Be sure to select the lumber carefully; warped or twisted boards will cause great difficulty in sawing and gluing.

Start with the top, which will require 60 blocks measuring 2½ inches in the direction of the grain and 38 blocks 9½ inches long, all 3¼ inches across. Hardwood is normally sold in random widths and lengths, so when you shop for the wood try to select widths that will give you one or two 3¼-inch cuttings with minimal waste. Set your saw for ripping and make a test cut on scrap to make sure the blade is cutting perfectly perpendicular. The importance of perfectly true right-angle edges cannot be stressed enough if your tabletop is to be successful. Cut all the stock to size with the same fence adjustment for uniformity. Next, clamp a stop block on the saw to cross cut the 2½- and 9½-inch pieces to size.

Now you can prepare the small blocks for gluing. Stand all the blocks on end and divide them into five groups of twelve blocks each, butted face to face. Rearrange individual blocks, if necessary, so the annular ring directions oppose each other. This will minimize any stress potentials and will result in a better appearance, as well. Number each block in sequence so they can later be reassembled in the same order.

1. Select lumber for this project with particular care. Warped boards will cause great difficulty in gluing. Rip the stock to width.

2. Clamp a stop to the saw table and cut the ripped stock into blocks of uniform size.

3. Bore two holes in one side of each block; then insert headless nails so the points protrude about ¼ inch.

The top is started by gluing five sets of twelve blocks each, face to face, to produce five long blocks. The most practical and effective way to keep the pieces in alignment during gluing is to use blind pins between each face. Make up a supply of pins by clipping the heads off 17-gauge 1-inch nails. Use one of the nails as a drill bit and bore two holes on one side of each block, about ¾ inch from two diagonal corners, to a depth of about ⅝ inch. This will allow the nail points to protrude about ¼ inch. Use a drill press or a portable drill with a guide, as these holes must be perfectly perpendicular.

Insert the nails, clipped ends first, into each hole, using pliers to grip and push them. Line up a set of twelve blocks between two boards clamped to the work table, spaced 3¼ inches apart. This will keep them in alignment. Place a bar clamp over the blocks and slowly take up on it to squeeze the blocks together, driving the nail points into the adjoining surfaces. Repeat the procedure for the other sets.

Mix up a sufficient amount of plastic-resin glue, following the manufacturer's directions carefully so you get the correct consistency. Too thin a mix will be weak; too thick a mixture may set too quickly to allow ample spreading time.

Pull the blocks apart and keep them in sequential order. Lay the first block down on its side (start with a block with holes, not points), apply glue to the surface. Apply glue to the surface of the adjoining block and join the two, locating the nail points into the holes. Repeat the step, gradually making a vertical stack twelve blocks high. Use two bar clamps to apply pressure to the stack. Allow the squeezed-out glue to become partially set before scraping it off.

4. Stack twelve blocks between two clamped boards to keep them in line. Apply a bar clamp to force the points into the back of each block. The last block in each group does not receive nails.

5. Number and letter each block of each group so they can be assembled in the same order for gluing.

6. Pull the stacks apart, apply glue to each surface, then restack them one atop the other, locating the nail points in the holes.

It'll come off much cleaner than it would if still wet. When the glue has dried, take the pieces to the jointer to dress the sides for gluing. Take small cuts and take off only as much stock as is necessary to remove all traces of glue from the surfaces.

The five blocks are not joined in line. Instead, the joint lines are alternately offset half the thickness of an individual block. This is done for two reasons: it makes a stronger construction and adds visual interest. When the five blocks are so aligned, mark the alternate projecting ends for cut-off. Make the cuts, then insert two headless nails in four of the blocks as was done with the smaller blocks, and glue them together. When dry, joint the four sides.

The end sections are made by gluing five 9½-inch blocks edge to edge. Nail pins are used again, but in addition to the endwise bar clamps, additional clamps and stout boards must be used on the broad faces in order to obtain a truly straight slab. Use a wax-paper barrier on the faces to prevent the clamp-

7. Two bar clamps are used to close the joints. Apply equal pressure to both clamps.

8. Scrape off all excess glue before it sets.

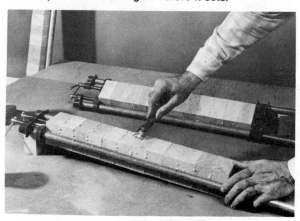

9. Joint two sides of each glued-up block. The end-grain will face up in the final assembly, so you joint only the easier cutting side grain.

10. When the five blocks are jointed, line them up so the joint lines are offset one-half block; then mark them for cutting off the waste at both ends.

11. Nail alignment pins are used again, two in each block. Then apply glue and clamp. Place clamps above and below to obtain even pressure throughout.

14. Plugs are cut from 1⅛-inch closet-pole stock. Insert them with the grain running horizontally.

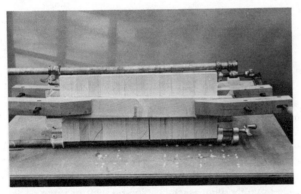

12. Fourteen 10-inch blocks are joined, face to face, to make up the sides. Note that the second block in this group is half-thickness. The glue pads on the sides are faced with wax paper so they won't stick to the work.

13. The end blocks are made up by gluing five pieces edge to edge. Here the block is being jointed on the portion that will butt against the top. The remainder need not be jointed. The blade guard must be removed for this operation.

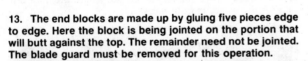

ing boards from sticking to the work. Apply only moderate pressure to the face clamps until the end bar clamps have been fully tensioned. When the glue has dried the upper section of the face, which is to butt against the top slab, can be dressed on the jointer. It will be necessary to remove the blade guard for this operation.

Bore the three dummy bolt holes ¼ inch deep and insert 1¼-inch-diameter plugs with the grain running crosswise.

Employ the same pin procedure to assemble and glue two sets of fourteen 10-inch blocks to make the sides. Note that one block in each group must be only half-thickness in order to correspond to the dimension of the top. Again, the upper butting surface can be dressed on the jointer, but the strips along the side faces will have to be handled with a hand plane. Use a sharp tool and take shallow cuts.

Surfacing hardwood end-grain on a slab of this size would normally be a most difficult task using a plane or even a belt sander. You can surface the top to perfection with relative ease, however, by using a router and a simple jig. This consists of a wood "bridge" that you place over the tabletop. It supports the router on a constant plane, allowing a mortising bit to ride over the slab, slicing away any irregularities. The opening in the top of the jig is wide enough to allow several passes to be made before the jig is moved to a new position. Two guide strips prevent the router from cutting into the sides of the jig top. Use the widest mortising bit possible for this procedure.

Follow this operation with a belt sander using 80

15. The sequence for assembly of the top: Glue together five 12-block sections . . .

19. Four bar clamps will suffice to join ends to top.

16. . . . make up two end sections of five blocks each, glued edge to edge; glue them to the top slab . . .

20. Use seven clamps in this manner to complete the gluing of the tabletop.

17. . . . make up two side sections of fourteen blocks each, glued face to face; add them to the assembly . . .

18. . . . to come up with this.

and 100 grit belts; then switch to a finishing sander working with 120, 150, 180, and 220 grit papers. All exposed corners are rounded with the router using a ½-inch corner-rounding bit.

LEGS

The legs are next. The overall length of the legs is 26⅝ inches, so the turning blanks should be made about 2 inches or so longer. Three glued lengths of ⁶⁄₄ stock are indicated for the turning blanks in order to permit jointing them down to 4 inches square for the finished size of the upper section of the legs. If your jointer has only a 4-inch capacity, be sure to rip the stock to be glued to a 4-inch width. The jointer can then span the width to square the block.

The turning is a simple one that can be shaped with four basic tools: the gouge, skew, spear-point,

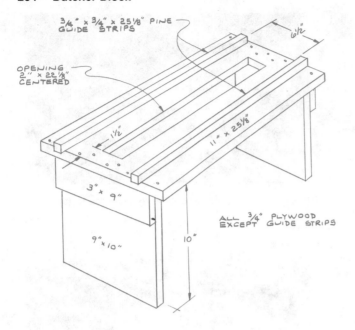

3/4" x 3/4" x 25 1/8" PINE GUIDE STRIPS

OPENING 2" x 22 1/8" CENTERED

6 1/2"

1 1/2"

11" x 25 1/8"

3" x 9"

ALL 3/4" PLYWOOD EXCEPT GUIDE STRIPS

9" x 10"

10"

21. This easy-to-make jig and a router can save many hours of tedious labor in surfacing the top.

22. Sides can be trued with a plane and belt sander, but the tough end-grain top surface is best handled with a router chucked with a mortising cutter. This jig maintains the cutter at a constant height.

23. Belt sander is used to smooth the top further after surfacing with the router. Keep the sander constantly in motion to prevent gouging.

24. Round all corners with a ½-inch corner-rounding bit.

and parting chisels. Use the skew first to cut a shallow nick at the shoulder in order to prevent splintering the square corners. Make the cut with the heel of the tool while holding it vertically. Then follow the procedures illustrated. Rough-round the cylindrical section with the gouge and make parting cuts to set the diameters at key points as indicated in the plan. Use the skew and spear point to form the contours, working to the limits set by the parting-tool grooves. It is important to leave a square portion in the waste at the tailstock end. This is necessary later in order to support the leg perfectly level on the saw table when cutting the notch at the top end.

You can use either the radial-arm or table saw to cut the deep notches on the legs. If you have the choice, the radial-arm saw is preferable. Clamp a

27.   Work the block to a full round with the gouge.

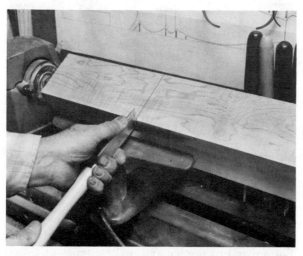

25. Begin turning the leg by nicking the corners at the square shoulder to prevent splintering. Use the skew, held on edge, for this. A gouge is used to rough-round the block.

28.   Go back to the head and complete the shoulder with the skew. Repeat these steps to this point on other legs.

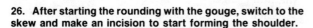

26.   After starting the rounding with the gouge, switch to the skew and make an incision to start forming the shoulder.

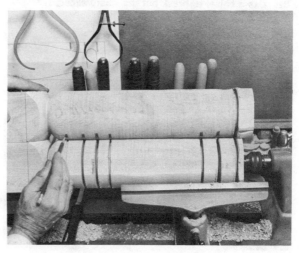

29.   Use the parting chisel to cut depth-sizing grooves in one leg and transfer the marks to the other legs. Check the diameters constantly with a caliper to assure uniformity.

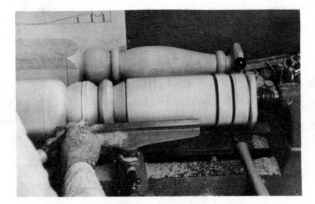

30. Complete one leg and use it as a sample to turn the others. The spear-point and skew chisels are used almost exclusively to form the final contours.

31. Waste end at bottom is left partially square in order to support the leg on a level plane for cutting a notch. First, make a series of kerf cuts, as shown. Here, a board is clamped to the saw table to support the end.

32. Use a chisel to break out the waste slices.

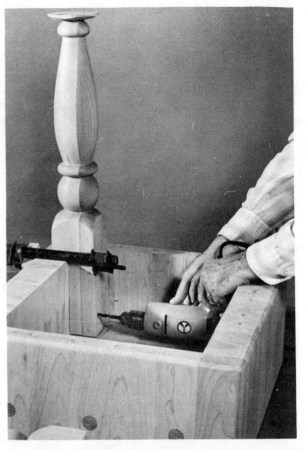

33. Clamp leg in place and drill body hole for the lag screw. Remove leg and enlarge the hole to ⅜-inch diameter. Install legs with lag screws and washers. Glue is optional.

board to the saw table to support the overhanging bottom end of the leg and make a series of closely spaced kerf cuts to clear out the waste. To use the table saw it will be necessary to provide a level surface at the side to support the bottom of the leg. It will also be necessary to attach an oversize fence to the miter gage.

When notched, clamp the legs in place on the tabletop and drill the holes for the lagscrews. Apply glue and mount the legs.

The type of finish you apply is optional. Three coats of semigloss, clear tung-oil finish were used on the prototype. However, surfaces for food should not be finished with conventional materials. If you plan to use the table for food preparation, you can finish it with several coats of mineral oil thoroughly rubbed in. Or you can apply a special salad-bowl finish which is available (see Sources of Supply). Another possibility is to apply a food-safe finish to the top surface only and a regular finish to the rest of the table.

35
Curved-Back Chair

Building a typical curved-back chair is usually a rather complex undertaking involving steam bending, time consuming, painstaking joining, and somewhat difficult assembly procedures. Not so with this chair.

While careful and skillful workmanship must be exercised in all phases of the project, innovative design elements and construction techniques are incorporated to enable you to turn out a quality piece with relative ease on your first attempt.

Let's examine some of the significant aspects of the design and methods involved.

Starting with the pedestal, a strong joint is achieved by nesting the post over the edge half-lapped base members. This necessitates cutting deep cross-notches in the bottom of the post. Following a normal procedure of first turning the cylindrical post, you would unavoidably be stymied in an attempt to cut those deep notches. A 10-inch table-saw blade will project sufficiently for the endwise cuts. But how would you guide a standing round post accurately and safely past the blade? Such an approach is simply not feasible. The solution to the problem is quite novel, however: the turning blank for the post is pre-notched before it is glued together and turned.

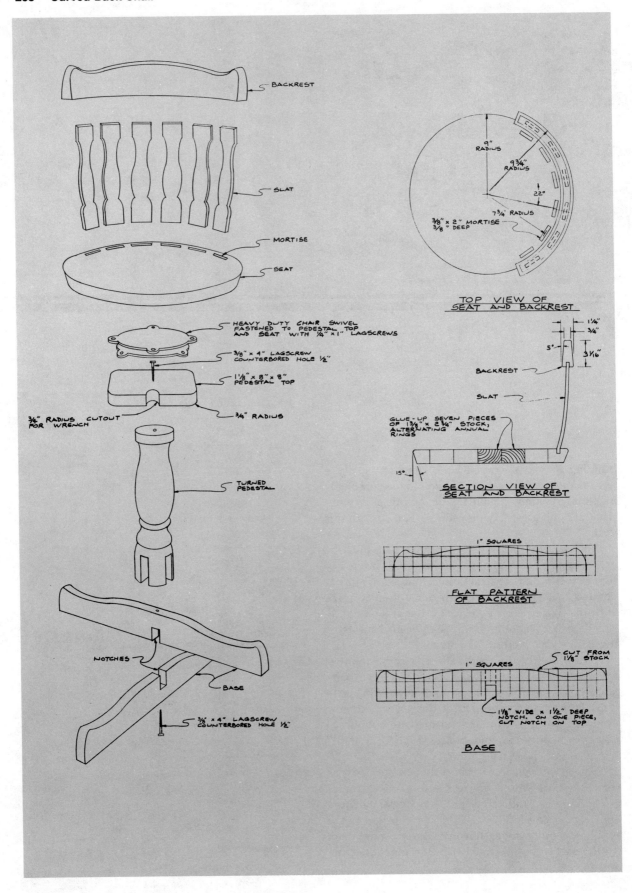

BACKREST

SLAT

MORTISE

SEAT

HEAVY DUTY CHAIR SWIVEL FASTENED TO PEDESTAL TOP AND SEAT WITH 1/4" x 1" LAGSCREWS

3/8" x 4" LAGSCREW COUNTERBORED HOLE 1/2"

1 1/8" x 8" x 8" PEDESTAL TOP

3/4" RADIUS CUTOUT FOR WRENCH

3/4" RADIUS

TURNED PEDESTAL

NOTCHES

BASE

3/8" x 4" LAGSCREW COUNTERBORED HOLE 1/2"

9" RADIUS

9 3/4" RADIUS

22°

7 3/4" RADIUS

3/8" x 2" MORTISE 3/8" DEEP

TOP VIEW OF SEAT AND BACKREST

1 1/4"
3/4"
5°
3 1/16"

BACKREST

SLAT

GLUE-UP SEVEN PIECES OF 1 3/4" x 2 1/4" STOCK, ALTERNATING ANNUAL RINGS

15°

SECTION VIEW OF SEAT AND BACKREST

1" SQUARES

FLAT PATTERN OF BACKREST

1" SQUARES

CUT FROM 1 1/8" STOCK

1 1/8" WIDE x 1 1/2" DEEP NOTCH ON ONE PIECE, CUT NOTCH ON TOP

BASE

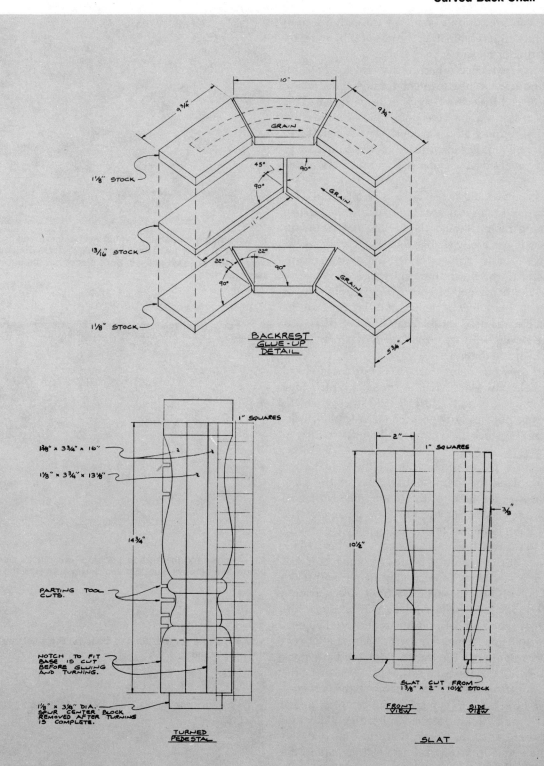

10"

9¾"   9¾"

GRAIN

1⅛" STOCK

45°   90°

90°   GRAIN

13/16" STOCK

11"

22°   22°

22°   90°

90°   GRAIN

1⅛" STOCK

5¾"

BACKREST
GLUE-UP
DETAIL

1" SQUARES

1⅜" x 3¾" x 16"
1⅛" x 3¾" x 13⅛"

14¾"

PARTING TOOL
CUTS.

NOTCH TO FIT
BASE IS CUT
BEFORE GLUING
AND TURNING.

1⅛" x 3¾" DIA.
SPUR CENTER BLOCK
REMOVED AFTER TURNING
IS COMPLETE.

TURNED
PEDESTAL

2"

1" SQUARES

10½"

3/8"

SLAT CUT FROM
1⅜" x 2" x 10½" STOCK

FRONT
VIEW

SIDE
VIEW

SLAT

The slats are cut on a band saw through a section of ⁶⁄₄ stock, thus eliminating the need for bending by laminating or steaming.

The tapered, curved back is also cut to shape on the band saw out of a segment-formed, glued blank made of eight pieces of stock in three layers. This results in a strong, staggered joint-line with the grain direction running advantageously nearly parallel to the curve. Pivot jigs are utilized on the band saw to cut the bevel-edged circular seat and the back member.

This comfortable swivel chair is ideally suited for a desk, or you can make several to use in the kitchen or dining room. Should the styling not suit your decor, you can easily change the design while maintaining the basic form and dimensions. For an example, refer to the illustration in Chapter 2.

Use any hardwood of your choice; maple, oak, or cherry are but a few of the possibilities. Soft southern maple was used for the chair illustrated. To duplicate it you will need ⁴⁄₄, ⁵⁄₄, and ⁶⁄₄ stock as indicated in the drawing.

Start construction on the base. Set up a dado head or a regular saw blade to cut the notches for the edge half-lap joint. Sand the faces of the stock, then cut dadoes or notches at the center, sized to the thickness of the stock in width and half the width in depth.

Cut three pieces of stock to length to make the turning blank for the post. Use stock of the same thickness as the base for the center and two pieces of 1⅜-inch stock for the outsides. Note that the center piece is shorter than the others by an amount equal to the width of the base stock (3 inches). Mark the ends of the two outer boards for notch cuts. Set the table-saw blade to maximum height and make two kerf cuts into the end of each piece, penetrating exactly 3 inches. The high blade will minimize the length of the radial kerf on the underside. The outside-to-outside dimension of the two parallel cuts should be equal to the thickness of the base stock (1⅛ inches). Use the band saw or jigsaw to make the crosscut to drop out the waste between the kerf cuts.

You now have two pieces with a notch and a shorter one without. Insert two headless nails into the face of two of the pieces, along the center, allowing the points to protrude about ¼ inch. Stand the short member centered on the base and place the outside pieces on the base with the notches engaged. Slide the outer pieces towards the center, pressing them firmly so the nail points make contact. Use a clamp to embed the nail points fully and make positive registration holes. When assembled this way, the block will automatically form a four-way notch

1. Deep notch for half-lap joint in the base is made by making a pair of saw cuts halfway through, then clearing out the waste with repeated passes. Both pieces can be cut at the same time.

2. Notches for the turned pedestal are cut in advance, before the block is glued up. Make two cuts with the blade set high.

3. A band or jig saw is used to clear out the waste between the parallel cuts.

4. Edge half-lap should mesh with a slide fit.

grooves at key locations as indicated in the drawing, using the parting chisel. Work with the round-nose, spear-point, and skew chisels to shape the profile. Sand the piece. Remove it from the lathe and cut off the waste ends on the band saw. Prop up the post with a piece of wood so it will be level and grip the end with a clamp, as shown, to make the cut.

Cut the swivel-support block, making sure to cut the wrench-access notch in line with one of the screw tabs on the swivel flange. This block is attached with glue and a lag screw. Counterbore the hole so the head of the screw will not project above

5. Three members for the pedestal are positioned over the base and pressed together so the nail points make alignment indents in the adjoining surfaces.

6. Scrap of hardwood is glued to notched end of the block to aid in mounting block on the lathe.

7. Start the turning with a sharp gouge. Work from the center outwards to form the cylinder. Make light thrusts in the area of the notches to avoid splintering.

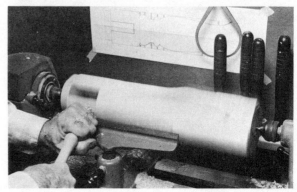

at the bottom. Pull the three pieces apart, apply glue and clamp. Take care to remove all excess glue from the inside of the notch area so a good fit will be obtained in the final assembly. Glue a disc of stock over the notched end to provide a surface for mounting the blank on the lathe.

Use the gouge to shape the post to a rough round. Feed the tool lightly in the area of the notches to avoid splintering the corners. Make diameter-sizing

8. View of the partially formed cylinder.

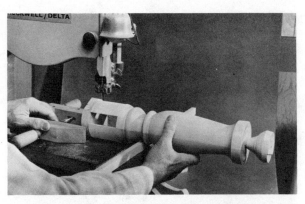

10A This is how the waste end is cut from the pedestal. Note the prop stick which serves to keep the piece level. Also note how a clamp is used to keep the fingers safely away from the blade.

9. Make diameter sizing cuts with the parting chisel as indicated in the pattern; then work the various chisels from groove to groove to form the profile.

10. Run lathe at high speed for sanding. Back abrasive paper with a soft pad.

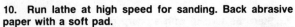

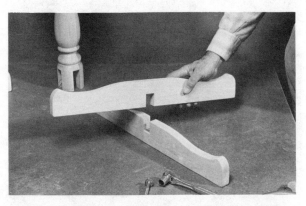

11. Assembly begins after all parts are shaped, sanded.

12. Prenotched pedestal fits neatly over crossed base.

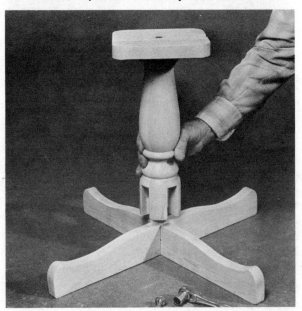

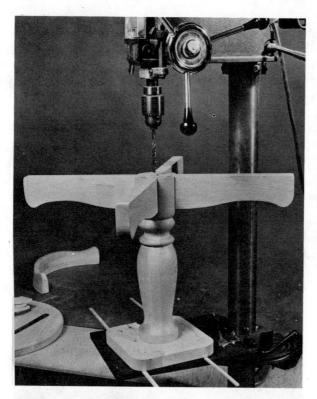

13. Hole for lag screw is bored with the parts assembled. First bore the large counterbore hole to recess the screw head. This hole must be of a diameter that will accept the socket wrench used to drive the screw.

14. Apply glue and secure the joint with a lag screw. Rub threads on a bar of soap if the screw offers resistance.

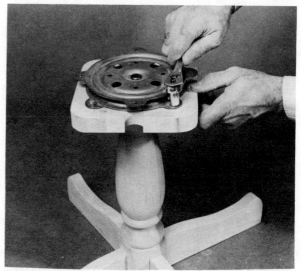

15. Swivel fixture is attached with lag screws. Note the hole in the block which permits access to the flange when joining the swivel to the seat bottom.

the surface. This hole must be of sufficient diameter to accept a wrench socket for driving the screw.

Insert the post over the base, stand it upside-down on the drill press and bore the hole for the lag screw. Again, the hole must be counterbored to receive the wrench socket. Bore the larger hole first, then the screw body hole. Finally, bore the screw-shank hole only through the base section. Apply glue and assemble the post and base. The swivel can be attached and the pedestal put aside.

THE SEAT

The seat is made by joining seven lengths of 6/4 stock, edge to edge. Since the contact area is relatively wide, a plain butt joint will prove adequate. Arrange the pieces so the annual ring directions alternate to counteract warping tendencies. Use the nail-pin method for assembly registration and be sure to position the nails so they will not be in the path of the circular cut. After gluing the pieces, clean and true the surface of the slab with a belt sander.

A pivot is used on the band saw to make the beveled circular cut for the seat. To do this drive a nail through the bottom of a flat board so the point projects slightly. Tilt the table 15 degrees; then clamp the pivot board to the saw table so the pivot is 8⅝ inches from the blade. Make sure the pivot is in exact right-angle alignment with the front edge of the blade. It is advisable to make a test cut in a scrap of cardboard to check the alignment of the pivot; if it is off, the resultant cut will be eccentric rather than perfectly circular. It will be necessary to start the cut freehand in order to get the blade into the wood. Withdraw the pivot from the backboard temporarily until the cut is started; then reinstate it into a pilot hole previously bored in the bottom center of the slab. The stationary disc sander works best for smoothing the beveled edge. A similar pivot arrangement can be used with the sander.

The slats are housed in mortises cut into the seat. The recesses are made by drilling a series of five holes, which are then trimmed with a chisel. A simple jig is used to drill the holes in line and evenly

18. Six bar clamps, three on each side, assure good overall pressure. If the slab assembles reasonably flat, crosspieces won't be necessary. If it bows, be ready with four wax-paper lined strips (in background), which can be clamped to the faces to true the slab.

16. Chair seat is made by edge-gluing seven blocks of 6/4 lumber. Concealed pin method is used to keep each piece in alignment during gluing. One of the nails is used as a drill bit to bore holes on one side of each piece.

19. Slab is sanded flat on both sides before sawing the curve. Start with a belt sander and course-grit abrasive and work down to a fine grit with a finishing sander.

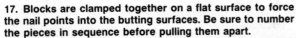

17. Blocks are clamped together on a flat surface to force the nail points into the butting surfaces. Be sure to number the pieces in sequence before pulling them apart.

20. Board with a pivot nail projecting is clamped to the band-saw table to make a perfect circular cut. Table is set for a 15-degree bevel.

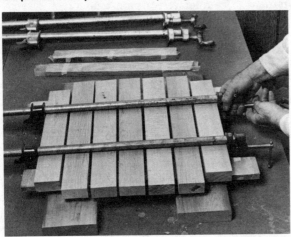

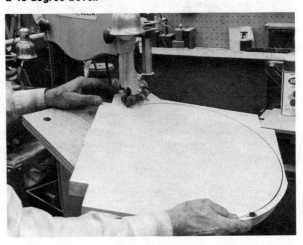

spaced. This consists of a stick with a hardwood block attached to one end, containing a series of guide holes. To make the jig, drill five ⅜-inch holes in the block, spaced so the edges of the outside holes measure exactly 2 inches. Cut a ¼" × 2" dado through the center of the block to recess a strip of wood ¼" × 1" × 12". Nail the strip in the dado, centered and just behind the holes. Note that the dado is cut wider than the strip to allow the wood chips to be readily expelled.

Find the center of the seat and place a protractor over it. Mark off and draw six radial lines from the center, spaced 22 degrees apart. These lines represent the centers for each mortise. Adjust a compass for a 7⁹⁄₁₆-inch radius and draw a circle to cross the radial lines. Reset the compass to 7¹⁵⁄₁₆ inches and draw another circle. Measure 1 inch on each side of the radial center line, mark, and draw a ⅜" × 2" rectangle centered over the guide marks. While you won't need the outlines when using the jig, you will need them to guide the chisel cuts to clean out the mortises.

To drill the holes, drive a nail through the jig strip 7¾ inches from the center of the center hole in the block. Partly drive this nail into the center of the seat. Center the block over a radial line; then start a second nail to keep the jig from shifting. Drill the series of ⅜-inch holes ⅜-inch deep using a brad-point bit. Withdraw the holding nail, pivot the jig to the next position and repeat the step. Use chisels to trim the walls of the recesses. To complete the seat, round the top edge with a router and a ¼-inch corner-rounding bit. Work on the slats next.

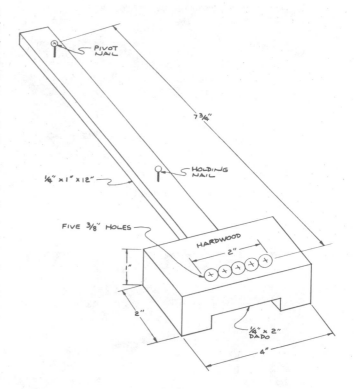

22. **Make this jig to simplify aligning and drilling the straight-line holes in a true arc.**

23. **The far nail is for pivoting the block from station to station; the other locks the jig in place. Note that the holes are in a straight line, not curved.**

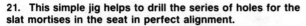

21. **This simple jig helps to drill the series of holes for the slat mortises in the seat in perfect alignment.**

24. Clean out the webs between the holes with a chisel.

26. Cut one slat to shape and use it as a template to outline the others. They're cut out of 6/4 stock.

27. Make two cuts on the back side of the slat first. Do not cut completely through until later. This will keep the waste intact, providing a safe grip for steering the work.

25. A router equipped with a ¼-inch corner-rounding bit is used to round the top edge of the seat.

28. Pivot block is used in this manner to guide the slat against the sanding drum.

THE SLATS

Mark the curved profile for a slat on the edge of a 1⅜″ × 2″ piece of stock. Make two band-saw cuts on the back of the slat, working from both directions. Leave a small portion uncut until the front curve is cut. The attached waste simply provides a place to grip the piece, as illustrated.

Use the drill press with a large sanding drum to smooth out the saw ripples on the front surface. This is done freehand. When all the front surfaces have been sanded, clamp a pivot block (a piece of wood with a rounded end) on edge, slightly more than ⅜ inch away from the drum. Pass the work through the space. Move the block to ⅜ inch from the drum and repeat the step. This will help to obtain parallel surfaces. Note that the flat area at the bottom of the slat must be sanded by hand.

29. Contours are cut on the band saw with the concave side down. Sanding is done in the same way.

30. Curved back-rail blank is made by gluing together three layers of segments. The joint lines are offset for greater strength. This arrangement orients the grain approximately parallel to the curve.

THE BACK

The chair back is next. Eight pieces of wood are required for this. Cut them as indicated in the drawing, observing the grain directions. The segments are held in position during gluing with nails driven into predrilled holes. Align the bottom row of three pieces, position the two center segments over them, and drill two nail holes in the waste area of each piece. Add the top row and repeat. Be sure to mark each piece for proper assembly. Apply glue and drive in the nails, starting with the bottom row. Clamp the block.

The back is tapered 5 degrees on each face. This can be band-sawed to perfection with a pivot jig. Nail a scrap of ⅛-inch hardboard or plywood about 12″ × 18″ to the block. Tilt the saw table 5 degrees to the right. Turn the block, with the thin panel attached, and drive a pivot nail through the radial center into a support board clamped to the band-saw table. The pivot nail must be positioned so its axis is 9¾ inches from the blade, where it meets the upper surface of the work. Use a square and rule to locate the point (this is done before the nail is driven into the backboard). Stand the square upright on the pivot board and shift the board until the edge of the square measures 9¾ inches from the blade. The front edge of the square's blade should of course be in alignment with the pivot center. Again, be sure the pivot is in right-angle alignment to the blade teeth. Make the cut.

The second cut is made by tilting the saw table 5 degrees to the left. The backboard remains where it is. The pivot board is now shifted towards the blade

31. Pilot holes for alignment nails are drilled into each segment. Match-mark each piece so they will be glued in the same position.

32. Ample supply of clamps is essential for a glue-up such as this. Two nails in each piece will prevent them from sliding apart, especially at the joint lines.

33. Controlled, curved cut is made by nailing a scrap of hardboard to the surface of the blank (see drawing). A pivot nail is driven through the panel and into a board clamped to the band-saw table. The table is tilted 5 degrees down on the left to make the outside cut.

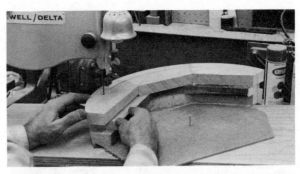

34. Table is tilted 5 degrees down on the right to make the inside cut. The pivot nail is moved ¾ inch closer to the blade for this second cut. The result is a curved piece with tapered sides.

so the second cut will be 1¼ inches away from the first, measured on the upper surface of the back. The amount of offset for the pivot will be ¾ inch plus the thickness of the saw blade. Check the accuracy of the new pivot location by making a starting cut into the waste area on the end of the block. Note that as this final cut progresses, the supporting pivot panel is also being cut off. Apply feeding pressure to

the work on both sides of the blade so the assembly remains intact until the blade cuts through. Feed slowly.

The mortises for the slats are made in the same way as for the seat, with the exception that the holes are bored without the aid of the jig. Make the layout by scribing three lines, one centered and the others ⅜ inch apart. The spacing between mortises here is

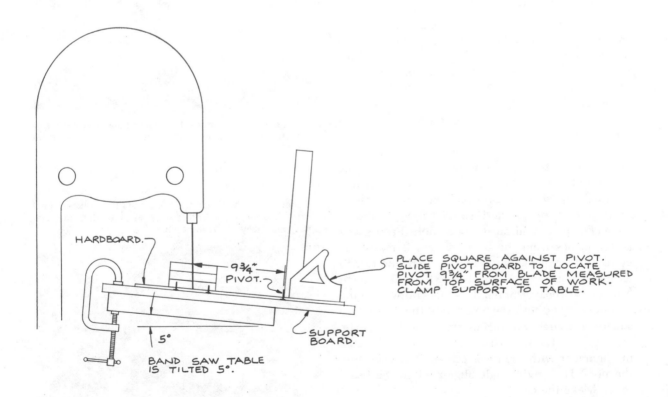

HARDBOARD.

9¾"
PIVOT.

PLACE SQUARE AGAINST PIVOT. SLIDE PIVOT BOARD TO LOCATE PIVOT 9¾" FROM BLADE MEASURED FROM TOP SURFACE OF WORK. CLAMP SUPPORT TO TABLE.

SUPPORT BOARD.

5°

BAND SAW TABLE IS TILTED 5°.

METHOD OF SETTING UP JIG FOR CUTTING TAPERED CURVED BACK

1¼ inches. Draw a straight line through each mortise location; then center-mark with an awl for five equally spaced holes starting 3/16 inch in from the end of each mortise border. Bore the holes and trim with a chisel.

The back contours are cut on the band saw. Draw the pattern on the inside surface and simply keep tilting the piece as the cut progresses, keeping the bottom of the work continually tangent to the table. Sand the back on a belt or disc sander and the inside curve with a sanding drum.

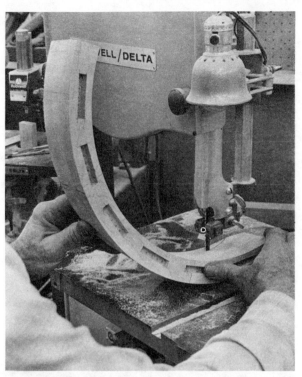

37. Contour on the seat back is cut on the band saw. Work slowly and keep tilting the piece continually so the curve is always tangent to the table.

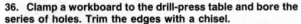

35. Lay out mortise holes for the slats with a rule. Draw a center line; then mark off 2-inch blocks equally spaced. Draw a straight line through each unit and use the awl to indent each series of five holes.

36. Clamp a workboard to the drill-press table and bore the series of holes. Trim the edges with a chisel.

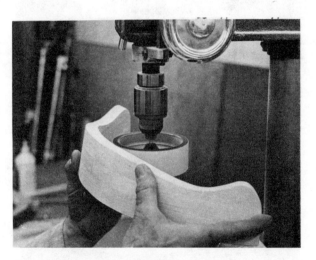

38. A large, padded sanding wheel is used to smooth the concave side of the back. The outside is best sanded on a stationary belt or disc sander.

ASSEMBLING THE CHAIR

Assembly is best done in two stages, simply to prevent messy glue runoff. Check the parts for proper fit, then apply glue to the seat mortises only

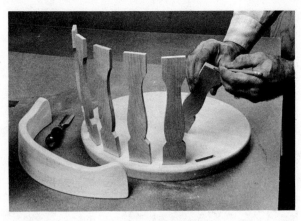

39. Custom fit each slat to a mortise; then match mark the pieces.

and insert the slats. Attach the curved back dry, without glue. This will hold the slats in alignment while the glue dries. When the glue has set, turn the seat upside-down, apply glue to the mortises and fit the slat ends into place.

The upper flange of the swivel is attached to the seat bottom by driving lag screws through the screw tabs. The notch in the support block allows access for the socket wrench. The pedestal is rotated to reveal the four screw positions. Steel button glides can be installed on the bottoms of the four base sections.

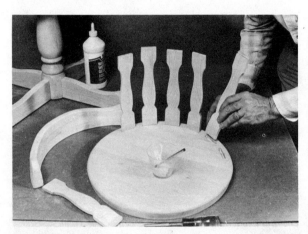

40. Gluing is done in two phases to avoid messy glue runoff. Glue the slats into the seat; then install the back piece dry, without glue. This will keep the slats accurately aligned.

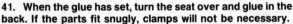

41. When the glue has set, turn the seat over and glue in the back. If the parts fit snugly, clamps will not be necessary.

42. The completed chair, ready for application of finish.

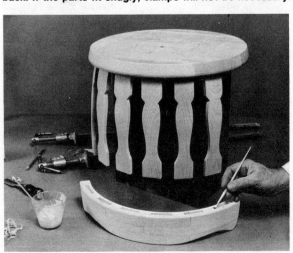

PART III

ON YOUR OWN: FURNITURE PLANS

36

Butler Table

This piece serves a dual purpose. With the flaps horizontal it's a handsome coffee table. When the flaps are folded up and the handles grasped, the novel top can be lifted off the base and used as a serving tray.

The underside of the top is cleated to provide a quick, positive means for aligning it over the base. The cleat arrangement also prevents the top from sliding off the base. Special spring-tensioned hinges are used for the flaps so they will stay put at any angle.

The hinges are set in mortises to mount flush with the top. The simple template jig shown will enable you to cut the mortises to perfection using a router with a straight or mortising bit. For additional data on making the template, see Chapter 49.

Note that while the bevels on the inside of the legs are 45 degrees, the insertion angle of the cross bracing differs since the leg relationship is not square but rectangular. Therefore the mortises in the legs are not perpendicular to the bevel surface. A practical method for cutting the mortises is as follows: Tilt the drill-press table to the required angle and clamp a board to the table to hold the work in position. Use a ⅜-inch brad-point spur bit and bore several overlapping holes ⅜ inch deep to rough form the mortise. Then clean out the waste with a chisel. The fit of the cross braces should be slightly loose to permit assembly without excessive forcing. A good gap-filling glue such as liquid hide will take care of the slight play.

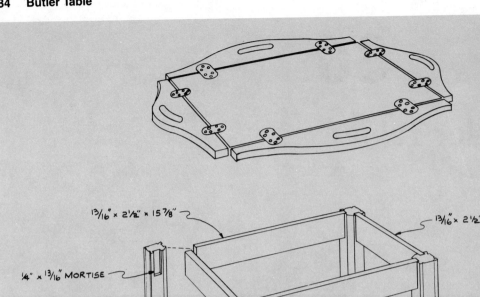

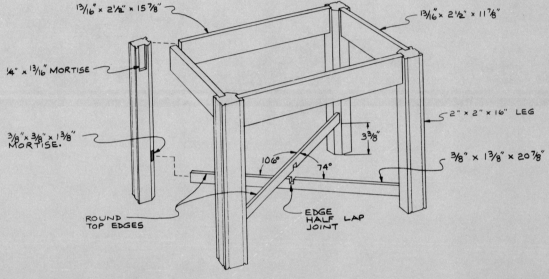

13/16" × 2½" × 15⅞"

¼" × 13/16" MORTISE

3/8" × 3/8" × 1⅜" MORTISE.

ROUND TOP EDGES

106°

74°

EDGE HALF LAP JOINT

3⅜"

13/16" × 2½" × 11⅞"

2" × 2" × 16" LEG

3/8" × 1⅜" × 20⅞"

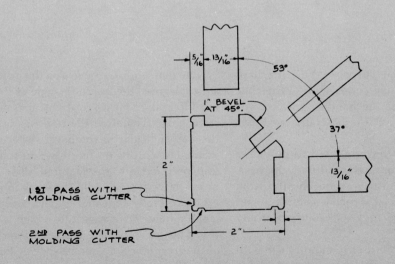

5/16"

13/16"

53°

1" BEVEL AT 45°.

37°

13/16"

2"

1 ST PASS WITH MOLDING CUTTER

2 ND PASS WITH MOLDING CUTTER

2"

LEG DETAIL

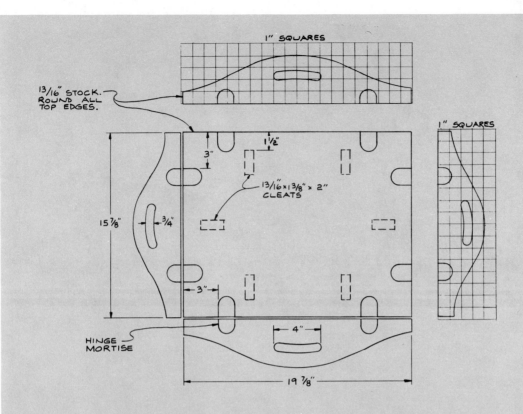

1" SQUARES

13/16" STOCK. ROUND ALL TOP EDGES.

3"

1½"

13/16" x 13/8" x 2" CLEATS

15 7/8"

¾"

3"

4"

19 7/8"

HINGE MORTISE

1" SQUARES

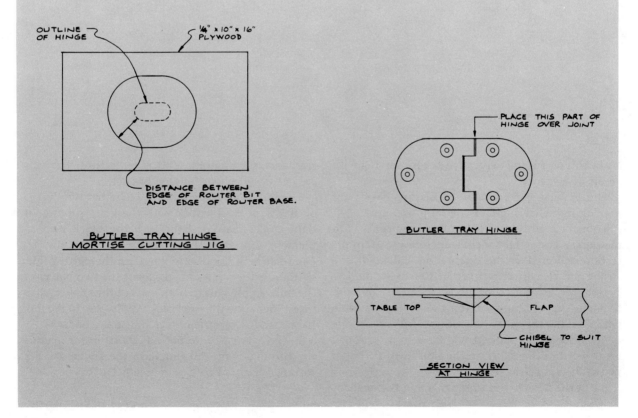

OUTLINE OF HINGE

¼" x 10" x 16" PLYWOOD

DISTANCE BETWEEN EDGE OF ROUTER BIT AND EDGE OF ROUTER BASE.

BUTLER TRAY HINGE MORTISE CUTTING JIG

PLACE THIS PART OF HINGE OVER JOINT

BUTLER TRAY HINGE

TABLE TOP

FLAP

CHISEL TO SUIT HINGE

SECTION VIEW AT HINGE

37

Tea Cart

Make this useful and decorative cart for serving with an air of elegance.

The general construction details are basic, but making the wheels entails special procedures.

To make a wheel, cut four curved segments with temporary gluing tabs included. Note the grain direction indicated, as this orientation will result in a strong and visually attractive rim. Retain the outside cut-off pieces after cutting the segments and use them to support the work on the drill-press table while drilling the spoke holes. If the drill-press table is not tiltable, the support will have to be propped up to position the work so the holes will be bored perpendicular to the arc.

Insert the dowels and clamp together two pairs of segments; then join these together in turn. The tabs are cut away when the glue has set.

The hub is made by screwing together two pieces of ¾″ × 4″ × 4″ stock with the grain running at right angles. Saw or lathe-turn the block to a 3″ diameter disc. Bore the spoke holes around the circumference of the disc centered on the parting line. Withdraw the screws to take apart the two halves of the hub. Apply glue to both ends of the spokes, then insert them into the rim holes. Apply glue to the hub halves and rejoin them over the spoke ends.

In the event you do not have a lathe for making the turnings, you can purchase the spoke and leg turnings readymade. See source list.

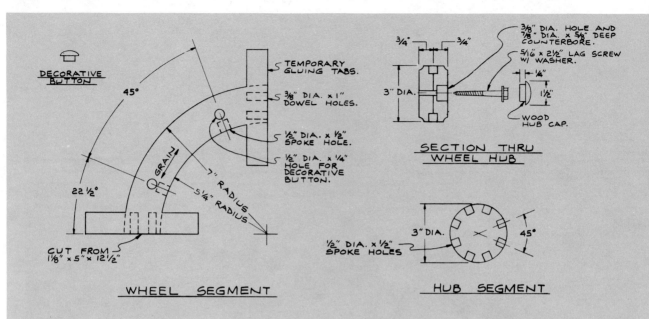

DECORATIVE
BUTTON

45°

TEMPORARY
GLUING TABS.

3/8" DIA. x 1"
DOWEL HOLES.

GRAIN

22 1/2°

1/2" DIA. x 1/2"
SPOKE HOLE.

7" RADIUS

5 1/4" RADIUS

1/2" DIA. x 1/4"
HOLE FOR
DECORATIVE
BUTTON.

CUT FROM
1 1/8" x 5" x 12 1/2"

WHEEL SEGMENT

3/8" DIA. HOLE AND
7/8" DIA. x 5/8" DEEP
COUNTERBORE.

3/4"   3/4"

5/16 x 2 1/2" LAG SCREW
W/ WASHER.

3" DIA.

1/4"

1 1/2"

WOOD
HUB CAP.

SECTION THRU
WHEEL HUB

3" DIA.

45°

1/2" DIA. x 1/2"
SPOKE HOLES

HUB SEGMENT

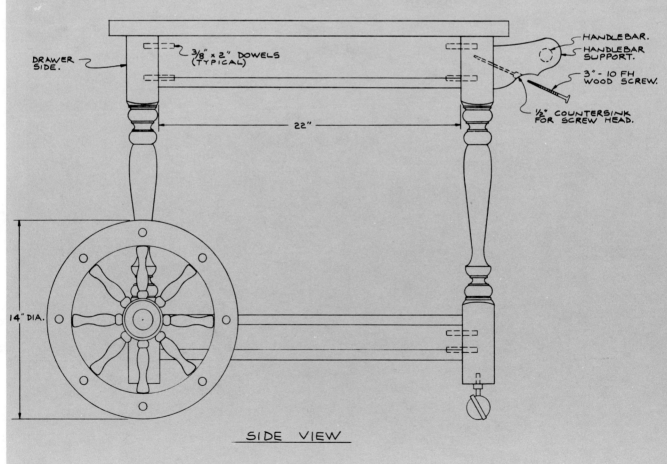

DRAWER
SIDE.

3/8" x 2" DOWELS
(TYPICAL)

22"

HANDLEBAR.

HANDLEBAR
SUPPORT.

3" - 10 FH
WOOD SCREW.

1/2" COUNTERSINK
FOR SCREW HEAD.

14" DIA.

SIDE VIEW

NOTE:
ALL LUMBER IS PINE.

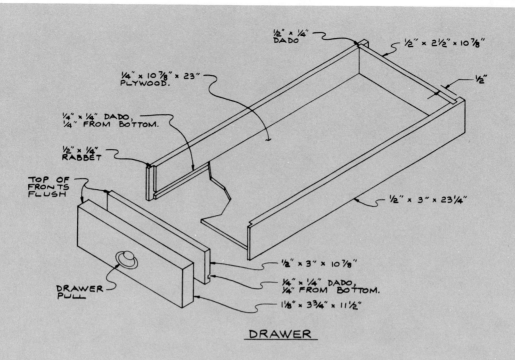

½" × ¼" DADO

½" × 2½" × 10⅞"

¼" × 10⅞" × 23" PLYWOOD.

½"

¼" × ¼" DADO, ¼" FROM BOTTOM.

½" × ¼" RABBET

TOP OF FRONTS FLUSH

½" × 3" × 23¼"

½" × 3" × 10⅞"

¼" × ¼" DADO, ¼" FROM BOTTOM.

1⅛" × 3¾" × 11½"

DRAWER PULL

DRAWER

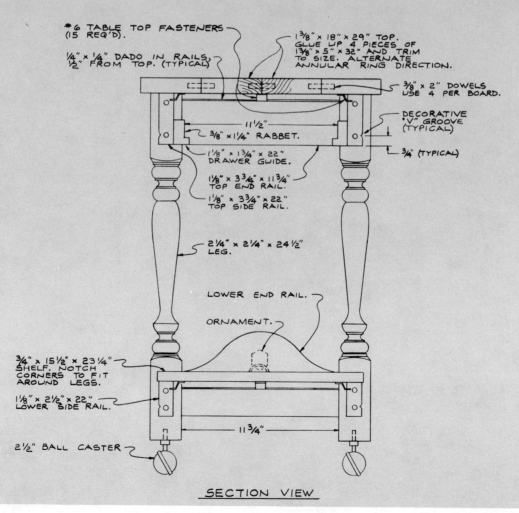

#6 TABLE TOP FASTENERS (15 REQ'D).

¼" × ¼" DADO IN RAILS, ½" FROM TOP. (TYPICAL)

1⅜" × 18" × 29" TOP. GLUE UP 4 PIECES OF 1⅜" × 5" × 32" AND TRIM TO SIZE. ALTERNATE ANNULAR RING DIRECTION.

⅜" × 2" DOWELS USE 4 PER BOARD.

DECORATIVE "V" GROOVE (TYPICAL)

11½"

⅜" × 1¼" RABBET.

¾" (TYPICAL)

1⅛" × 1¾" × 22" DRAWER GUIDE.

1⅛" × 3¾" × 11¾" TOP END RAIL.

1⅛" × 3¾" × 22" TOP SIDE RAIL.

2¼" × 2¼" × 24½" LEG.

LOWER END RAIL.

ORNAMENT.

¾" × 15½" × 23¼" SHELF. NOTCH CORNERS TO FIT AROUND LEGS.

1⅛" × 2½" × 22" LOWER SIDE RAIL.

11¾"

2½" BALL CASTER

SECTION VIEW

PLANS CONTINUED NEXT PAGE

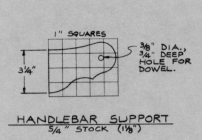

HANDLEBAR SUPPORT
5/4" STOCK (1⅛")

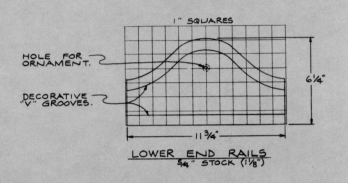

LOWER END RAILS
5/4" STOCK (1⅛")

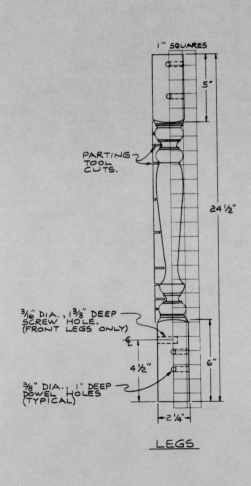

LEGS

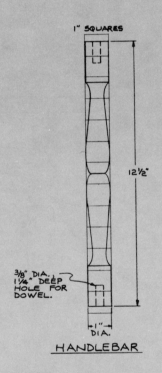

HANDLEBAR

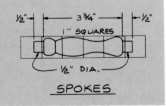

SPOKES

38

Cradle
Magazine Rack

While this unit is shown as a magazine holder, its overall dimensions will allow it to be used as an actual cradle. To adapt it for baby occupancy, the magazine divider assembly would simply be omitted. Also, the rocker bottoms would have to be shaped to a sweeping curve to allow the cradle to rock.

As a magazine rack the project can be given any kind of finish, but for use as a cradle only nontoxic materials must be used.

Common grade ¾-inch pine is the economical choice for this project. A table and band saw are the ideal stationary power tools to use for this job due to the numerous bevels and curves involved.

However, a portable circular saw and sabre saw can be used instead. The job will obviously take a bit longer to accomplish with portable tools, but the end result will be the same.

Note that the side members require left and right bevels. When using the table saw to make these cuts you need only to feed the pieces with alternate faces up: outside up for one, and inside up for the other. This will produce left and right bevels.

Screws and glue are indicated for assembly, but you can substitute nails. In either case, be sure to counterbore the holes for the decorative buttons in advance.

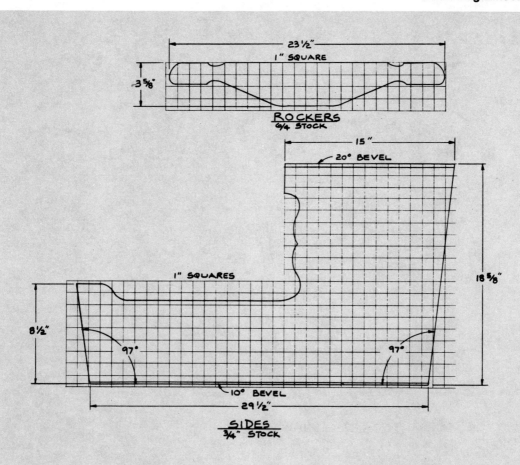

23 ½"
1" SQUARE
3 ⅝"

ROCKERS
4/4 STOCK

15"
20° BEVEL
1" SQUARES
18 ⅝"
8 ½"
97°
97°
10° BEVEL
29 ½"

SIDES
¾" STOCK

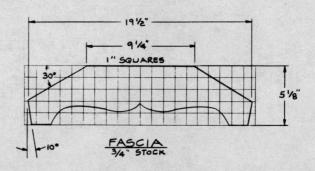

19 ½"
9 ¼"
1" SQUARES
30°
5 ⅛"
10°

FASCIA
¾" STOCK

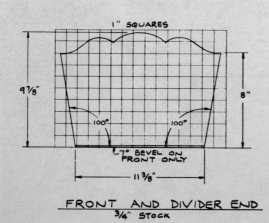

1" SQUARES
9 ⅞"
8"
100°
100°
7° BEVEL ON
FRONT ONLY
11 ⅜"

FRONT AND DIVIDER END
¾" STOCK

PLANS CONTINUED NEXT PAGE

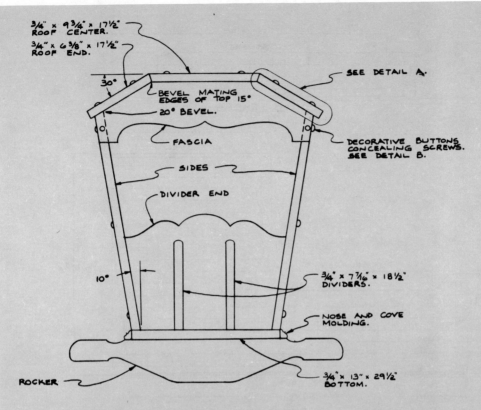

3/4" x 9 3/4" x 17 1/2" ROOF CENTER.
3/4" x 6 3/8" x 17 1/2" ROOF END.

30°

SEE DETAIL A.

BEVEL MATING EDGES OF TOP 15°

20° BEVEL.

FASCIA

DECORATIVE BUTTONS CONCEALING SCREWS. SEE DETAIL B.

SIDES

DIVIDER END

10°

3/4" x 7 7/16" x 18 1/2" DIVIDERS.

NOSE AND COVE MOLDING.

ROCKER

3/4" x 13" x 29 1/2" BOTTOM.

SECTION VIEW

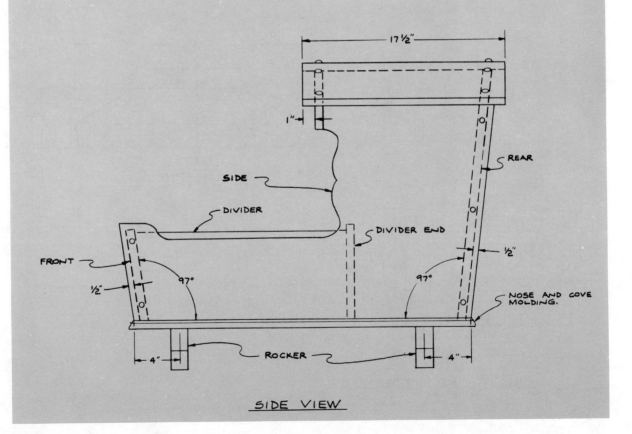

17 1/2"

1"

SIDE

DIVIDER

REAR

DIVIDER END

1/2"

FRONT

1/2"

97°

97°

NOSE AND COVE MOLDING.

4"

ROCKER

4"

SIDE VIEW

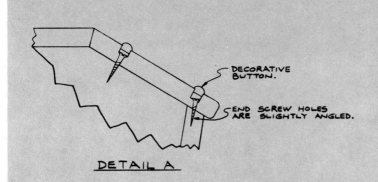

DECORATIVE BUTTON.

END SCREW HOLES ARE SLIGHTLY ANGLED.

DETAIL A

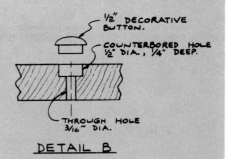

½" DECORATIVE BUTTON.

COUNTERBORED HOLE ½" DIA., ¼" DEEP.

THROUGH HOLE 3/16" DIA.

DETAIL B

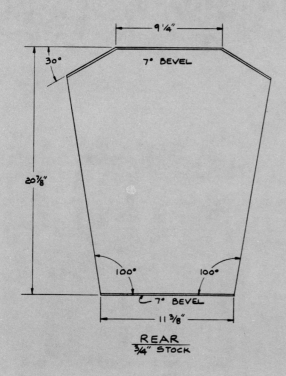

9 ¼"

30°

7° BEVEL

20 ⅛"

100°   100°

7° BEVEL

11 ⅜"

REAR
¾" STOCK

ALTERNATE ANNULAR RING DIRECTION.

LUMBER GLUING DETAIL

NOTE:
ALL LUMBER IS PINE.

39
Nautical Lamp

Here's a lamp that can be appreciated by nautical buffs and landlubbers alike. The massive pulley block, made by gluing up sections, features actual manila hemp for a realistic effect.

The pulley block is made up by combining $\frac{4}{4}$ and $\frac{5}{4}$ cutouts. The center section is slotted to eliminate the need for drilling the threaded pipe hole through the entire piece. The flats on the bottom of the spacers provide a firm mounting surface. Glue is used to assemble all parts except the base, which is attached to the sides with screws. This permits access for wiring after finishing.

The ropes are cut from a length of $\frac{3}{4}$-inch manila hemp. Make each piece 6 inches long and dip the ends into a thinned mixture of white glue to prevent them from unraveling. They are inserted into the openings after finishing. The electrical parts and ornaments are available as a kit. See source list.

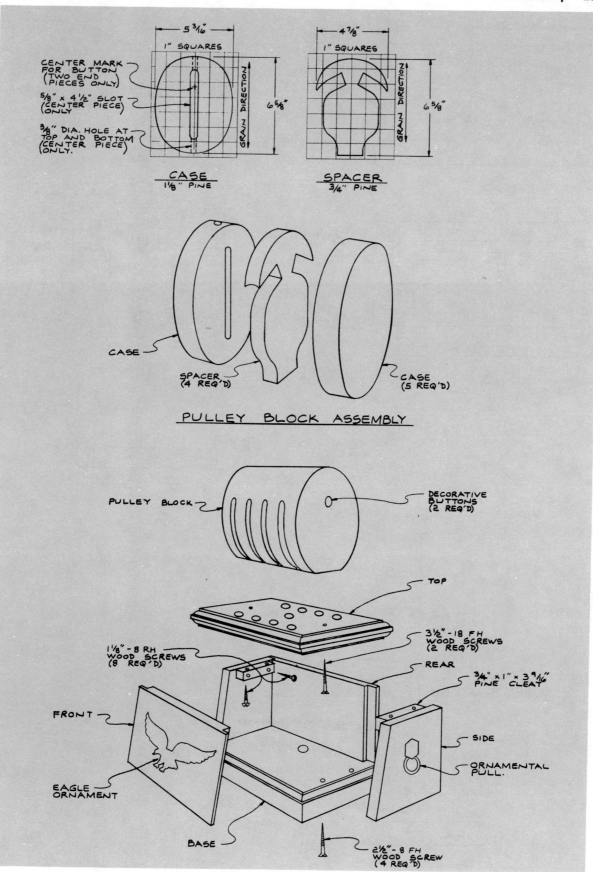

5 3/16"
1" SQUARES

CENTER MARK
FOR BUTTON
(TWO END
PIECES ONLY)

5/8" x 4 1/2" SLOT
(CENTER PIECE)
ONLY

3/8" DIA. HOLE AT
TOP AND BOTTOM
(CENTER PIECE)
ONLY.

GRAIN DIRECTION

6 5/8"

CASE
1 1/8" PINE

4 7/8"
1" SQUARES

GRAIN DIRECTION

6 5/8"

SPACER
3/4" PINE

CASE

SPACER
(4 REQ'D)

CASE
(5 REQ'D)

PULLEY BLOCK ASSEMBLY

PULLEY BLOCK

DECORATIVE
BUTTONS
(2 REQ'D)

TOP

1 1/8" - 8 RH
WOOD SCREWS
(8 REQ'D)

3 1/2" - 18 FH
WOOD SCREWS
(2 REQ'D)

REAR

3/4" x 1" x 3 9/16"
PINE CLEAT

FRONT

SIDE

ORNAMENTAL
PULL.

EAGLE
ORNAMENT

BASE

2 1/2" - 8 FH
WOOD SCREW
(4 REQ'D)

PLANS CONTINUED NEXT PAGE

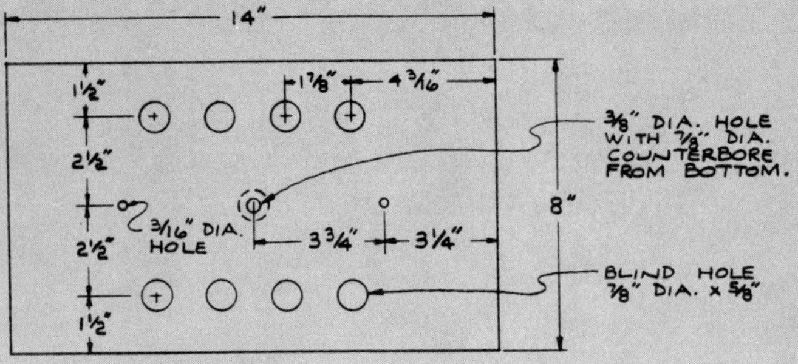
14"
1½"
1⅞"
4 3/16"
2½"
2½"
1½"
3/8" DIA. HOLE WITH 7/8" DIA. COUNTERBORE FROM BOTTOM.
3/16" DIA. HOLE
3 3/4"
3 1/4"
8"
BLIND HOLE 7/8" DIA. x 5/8"

TOP
1⅛" PINE

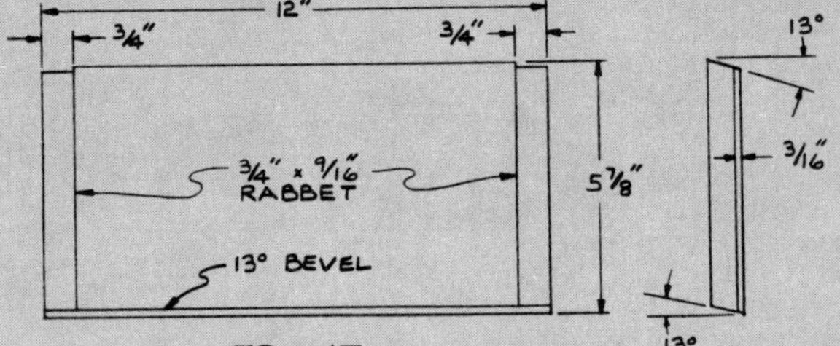
12"
3/4"
3/4"
13°
3/16"
3/4" x 9/16" RABBET
5⅞"
13° BEVEL
13°

FRONT
3/4" PINE

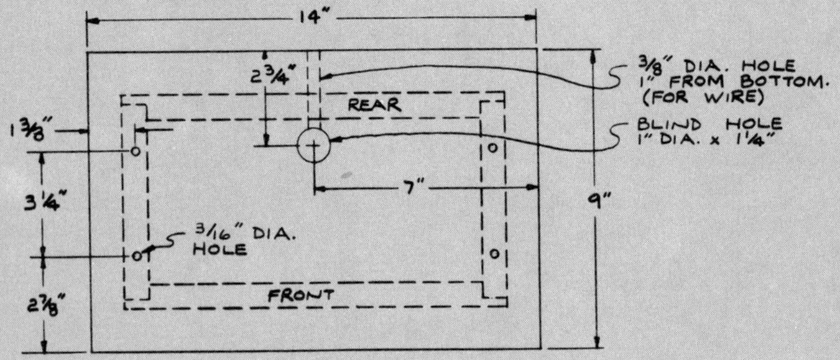
14"
2 3/4"
REAR
1 3/8"
3 1/4"
7"
9"
3/16" DIA. HOLE
FRONT
2 7/8"
3/8" DIA. HOLE 1" FROM BOTTOM. (FOR WIRE)
BLIND HOLE 1" DIA. x 1 1/4"

BASE
1 3/4" PINE

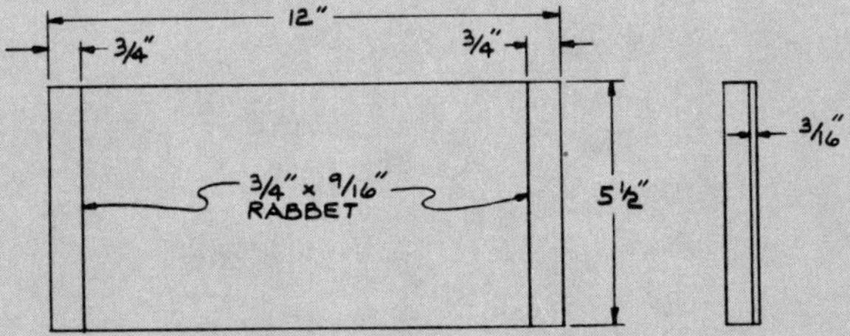
12"
3/4"
3/4"
3/4" x 9/16" RABBET
5½"
3/16"

REAR
3/4" PINE

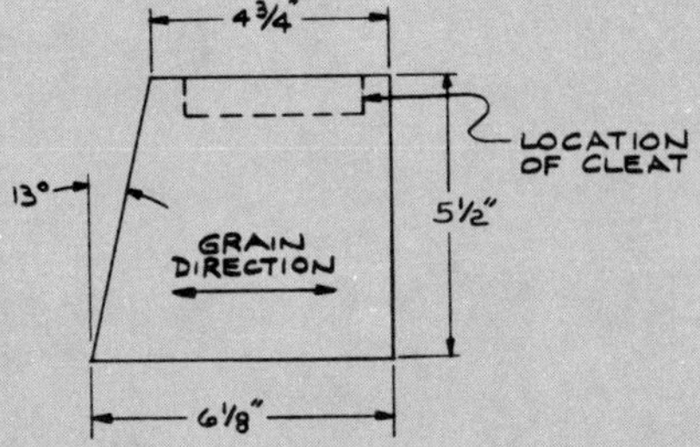
4 3/4"
LOCATION OF CLEAT
13°
5½"
GRAIN DIRECTION
6⅛"

SIDES
3/4" PINE

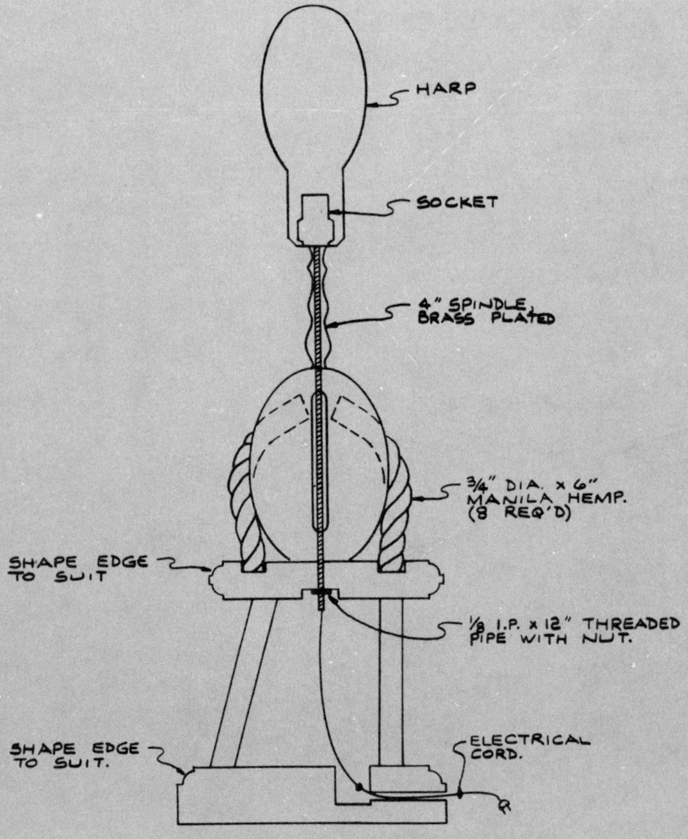
HARP
SOCKET
4" SPINDLE, BRASS PLATED
3/4" DIA. x 6" MANILA HEMP. (8 REQ'D)
SHAPE EDGE TO SUIT
1/8 I.P. x 12" THREADED PIPE WITH NUT.
SHAPE EDGE TO SUIT.
ELECTRICAL CORD.

SECTION VIEW

40

Molly Pitcher Clock

This is a smaller, or grandmother version, of the traditional tall grandfather clock—ideally suited, so the story goes, for those households where shorter grandmothers are assigned to set the clock.

The clock case consists of three subassemblies: hood, waist, and base. They are made as separate units to simplify construction. You will note that except for the 45-degree crown-molding miters and the rabbets to let in the various panels and glass, butt joints are indicated in the plans. Parts are fastened with glue, nails, and screws. Use the nails to position the parts, then reinforce with screws. In most instances the fastener heads will be concealed by the moldings.

The front frames of the hood, waist, and base are shown as plain butt joints, but this is not conclusive. Plain butt joints for these members would indeed prove structurally unsound. Stronger joints are essential and the choice is left up to you. You can reinforce the joints with dowels or you can utilize end half-lap joints. If you opt for the latter you must make certain to lengthen each member by twice the width of the adjoining member.

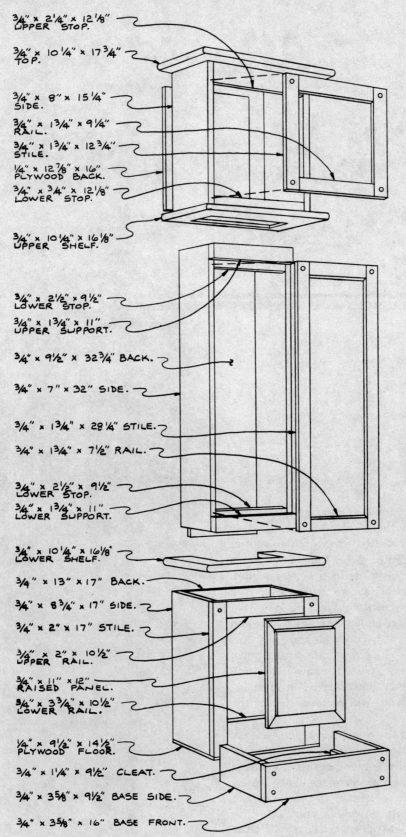

3/4" x 2 1/4" x 12 1/8"
UPPER STOP.

3/4" x 10 1/4" x 17 3/4"
TOP.

3/4" x 8" x 15 1/4"
SIDE.

3/4" x 1 3/4" x 9 1/4"
RAIL.

3/4" x 1 3/4" x 12 3/4"
STILE.

1/4" x 12 7/8" x 16"
PLYWOOD BACK.

3/4" x 3/4" x 12 1/8"
LOWER STOP.

3/4" x 10 1/4" x 16 1/8"
UPPER SHELF.

3/4" x 2 1/2" x 9 1/2"
LOWER STOP.

3/4" x 1 3/4" x 11"
UPPER SUPPORT.

3/4" x 9 1/2" x 32 3/4" BACK.

3/4" x 7" x 32" SIDE.

3/4" x 1 3/4" x 28 1/4" STILE.

3/4" x 1 3/4" x 7 1/2" RAIL.

3/4" x 2 1/2" x 9 1/2"
LOWER STOP.

3/4" x 1 3/4" x 11"
LOWER SUPPORT.

3/4" x 10 1/4" x 16 1/8"
LOWER SHELF.

3/4" x 13" x 17" BACK.

3/4" x 8 3/4" x 17" SIDE.

3/4" x 2" x 17" STILE.

3/4" x 2" x 10 1/2"
UPPER RAIL.

3/4" x 11" x 12"
RAISED PANEL.

3/4" x 3 3/4" x 10 1/2"
LOWER RAIL.

1/4" x 9 1/2" x 14 1/2"
PLYWOOD FLOOR.

3/4" x 1 1/4" x 9 1/2" CLEAT.

3/4" x 3 5/8" x 9 1/2" BASE SIDE.

3/4" x 3 5/8" x 16" BASE FRONT.

NOTES:
1. UNLESS NOTED, ALL LUMBER IS PINE.
2. DIALS RECOMMENDED: SM-69 OR AL-1010.
3. MOVEMENTS RECOMMENDED: HCS-2W, TW-9 OR TW-10.

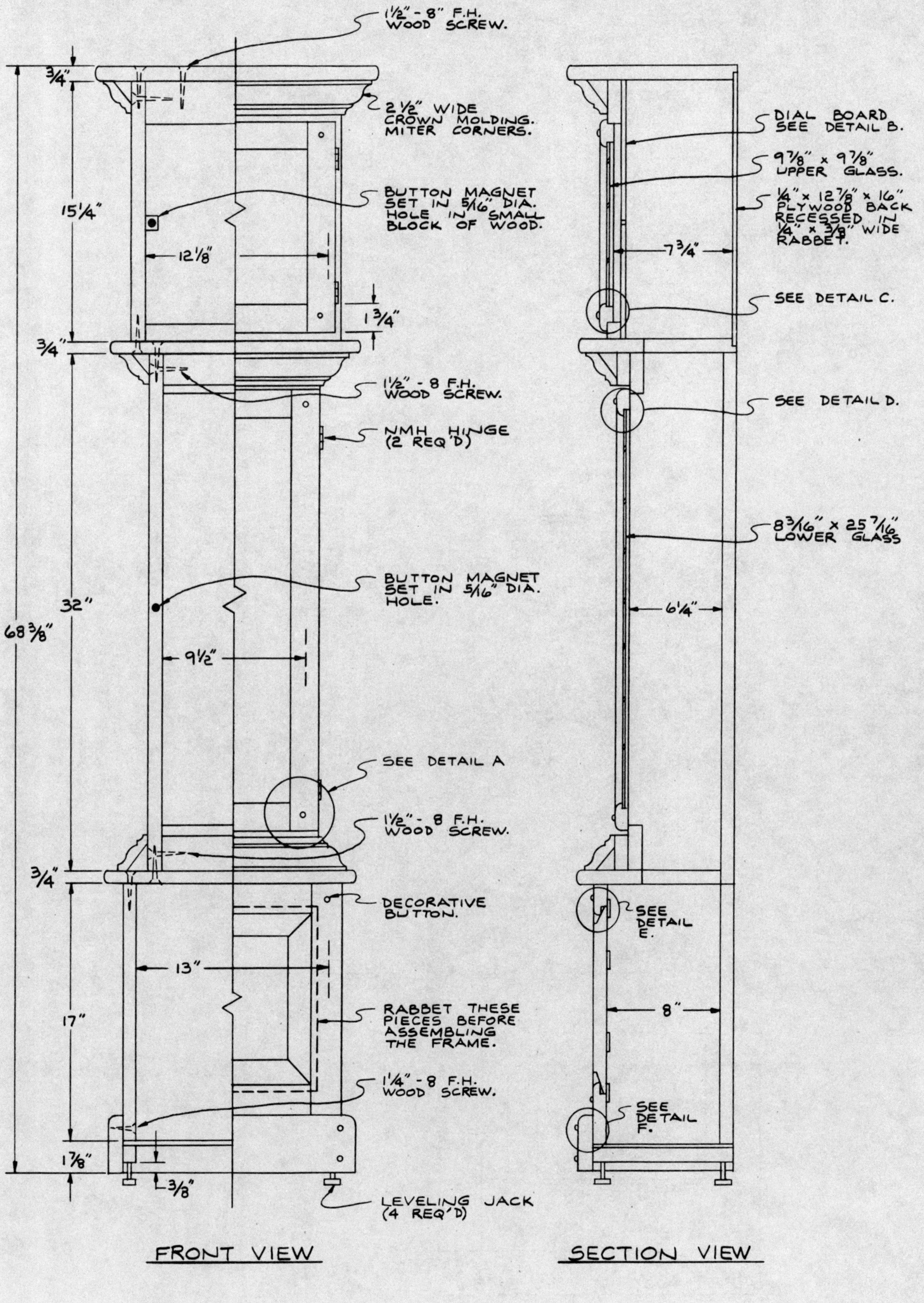
1½" - 8" F.H. WOOD SCREW.
3/4"
2½" WIDE CROWN MOLDING. MITER CORNERS.
15¼"
BUTTON MAGNET SET IN 5/16" DIA. HOLE IN SMALL BLOCK OF WOOD.
12⅛"
1¾"
3/4"
1½" - 8 F.H. WOOD SCREW.
NMH HINGE (2 REQ'D)
68⅜"
32"
BUTTON MAGNET SET IN 5/16" DIA. HOLE.
9½"
SEE DETAIL A
1½" - 8 F.H. WOOD SCREW.
3/4"
DECORATIVE BUTTON.
13"
17"
RABBET THESE PIECES BEFORE ASSEMBLING THE FRAME.
1¼" - 8 F.H. WOOD SCREW.
1⅞"
3/8"
LEVELING JACK (4 REQ'D)
FRONT VIEW
DIAL BOARD SEE DETAIL B.
9⅞" x 9⅞" UPPER GLASS.
¼" x 12⅞" x 16" PLYWOOD BACK RECESSED IN ¼" x 3/8" WIDE RABBET.
7¾"
SEE DETAIL C.
SEE DETAIL D.
8 3/16" x 25 7/16" LOWER GLASS
6¼"
SEE DETAIL E.
8"
SEE DETAIL F.
SECTION VIEW

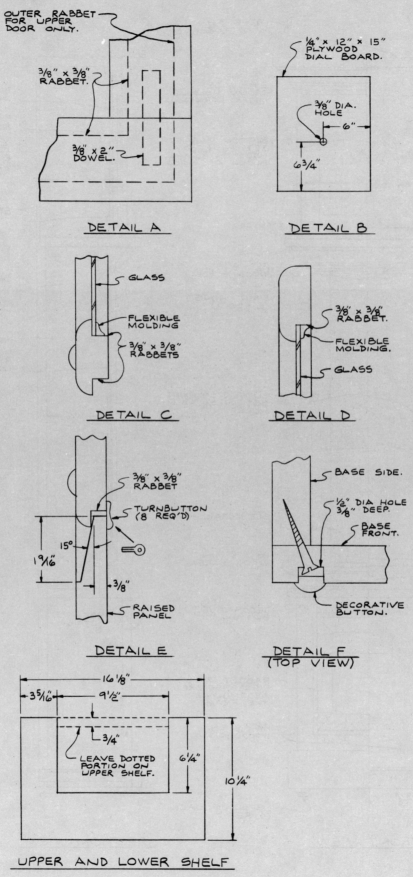

OUTER RABBET FOR UPPER DOOR ONLY.

3/8" x 3/8" RABBET.

3/8" x 2" DOWEL.

DETAIL A

1/4" x 12" x 15" PLYWOOD DIAL BOARD.

3/8" DIA. HOLE

6"

6 3/4"

DETAIL B

GLASS

FLEXIBLE MOLDING

3/8" x 3/8" RABBETS

DETAIL C

3/8" x 3/8" RABBET.

FLEXIBLE MOLDING.

GLASS

DETAIL D

3/8" x 3/8" RABBET

TURNBUTTON (8 REQ'D)

15°

1 9/16"

3/8"

RAISED PANEL

DETAIL E

BASE SIDE.

1/2" DIA HOLE 3/8" DEEP.

BASE FRONT.

DECORATIVE BUTTON.

DETAIL F
(TOP VIEW)

16 1/8"

3 5/16"

9 1/2"

3/4"

LEAVE DOTTED PORTION ON UPPER SHELF.

6 1/4"

10 1/4"

UPPER AND LOWER SHELF

HOOD

The rear edge of the hood members are rabbeted to receive the back panel. Do not run the rabbet to the ends of the top and shelf members; it should start and stop just short of the ends to avoid exposing the cut to outside view.

Assemble the hood door first, then use a router to cut the rabbets along the inner and outer edges on the back side. Neat, easy-to-install ornamental non-mortise hinges are used to attach the door. Due to the setback of the door, which limits space, a button magnet catch is mounted in a block attached to the inside of the hood frame.

WAIST

Note that the waist back and sides are flush at the top, but at the bottom the back panel projects ¾ inch beyond the sides. Glue and nails only, no screws, are used to join the sides to the back panel. Drive the nails at a slight angle from the rear edge of the sides into the back member. Do this carefully to avoid driving the nails into the surface of the waist compartment. Screws can be installed from the surfaces of the side panels in those areas that will be covered with molding.

The waist door is similar to the hood door except that only the inner rabbet for the glass is required.

BASE

The raised panel is made with the table saw. Set the blade for a 15-degree tilt and elevate it $1\frac{9}{16}$ inches above the table. Feed the work vertically against the fence to cut the bevel on the four sides. Turnbuttons are used to hold the panel in place.

Note that the decorative buttons in the front base member would be too close to the corners if the screws were installed in a normal manner. Therefore the holes are set in and the screws are angled as indicated in Detail *F.*

Leveling jacks are essential to set the clock case perfectly plumb if the clock mechanism is to function properly. The jacks are set into tee nuts installed in the bottom cleats.

Fasten the three assemblies as follows: Screw the lower shelf to the underside of the waist, then fasten the shelf to the top edge of the base with screws. The hood is fastened to the top of the waist in a similar manner.

Installing the crown molding with mitered corners requires making precise compound-angle cuts. This can stump you unless you know how to go about it. See Chapter 30, Cupola/Weathervane project, for the correct procedure.

Flexible molding is handy for installing the door glass. For this and other specialty items such as the dial and clock movement, see the source list.

41

Colonial Chair

This comfortable chair, made of cherry, will afford the opportunity to put a number of shop skills to use, such as: dowel joints, round mortise/tenon joints, lap joints, repeat turnings, and spokeshave shaping.

You can concentrate all your efforts on woodworking and not be concerned with upholstering. The chair is dimensioned to accommodate a set of standard-size, readymade seat and back cushions which are readily available from Sears Roebuck.

The parts can be cut from 12 feet of ⁵⁄₄ × 8" stock and 8 feet of ⁸⁄₄ × 8" stock. The seat frame, arm rests, and six of the turning blocks are cut from the heavier stock while the side panels, back framing and the spindle turning blocks are cut from the ⁵⁄₄ material.

To make the half-lap joint layout for the chair side, first make rough-cut oversize sections of the two pieces of stock. Note that if the grain direction indicated in the plan is followed, the 8-inch-wide stock will be sufficient. Place the sections one atop the other; then lay the full-size paper pattern of the side in place. Transfer only the lap joint to each piece. Use a dado head or router to remove half the

thickness from each piece to form the angled half-lap joint.

Be sure to make left and right sections for each side member to obtain opposite, symmetrical joint lines. Glue the parts together, then trace the pattern outline and cut the piece to shape.

To obtain true spindle holes in the side member, sandwich and clamp it between two straight boards. Positioned at the required angle, the supported workpiece can be drilled with accuracy on the drill press.

Cut the blanks for the arm rests and trace the cutting outlines, but do not make any of the curve cuts until the spindle holes have been bored because in the squared form the piece will lay true on the drill-press table. Also, bore the dowel holes after the back of the arm rest has been notched but before cutting the curves.

The arm rests are sculpted with a spokeshave. To save some time and effort, remove some of the waste beforehand by making beveled band-saw cuts. A scrap block of 2×4 screwed to the underside will permit gripping the workpiece in a vise for spokeshaving. The front end of the arm rest is made

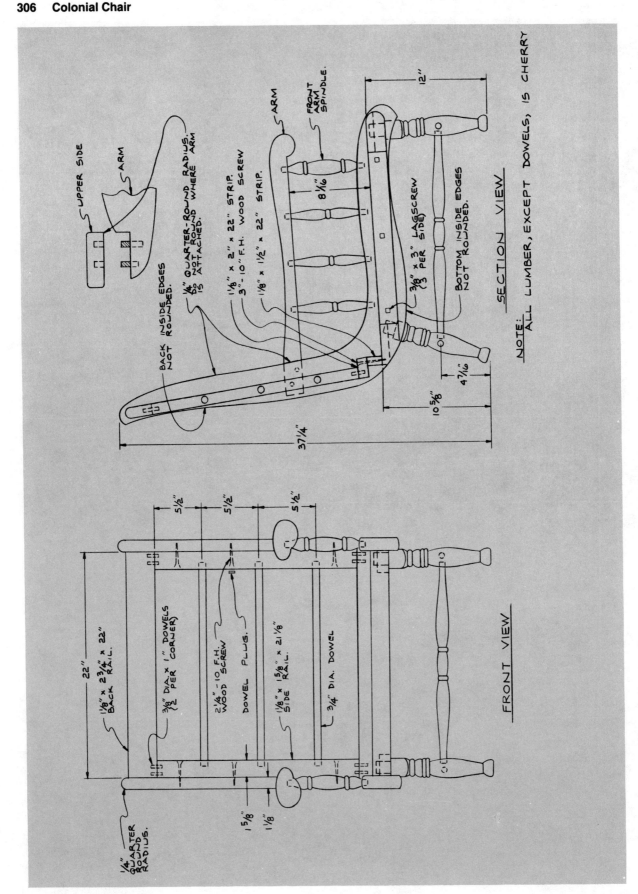

UPPER SIDE

ARM

BACK INSIDE EDGES NOT ROUNDED.

1/4" QUARTER-ROUND RADIUS. DO NOT ROUND WHERE ARM IS ATTACHED.

1 1/8" x 2" x 22" STRIP.

3"-10" F.H. WOOD SCREW

1 1/8" x 1 1/2" x 22" STRIP.

ARM

FRONT ARM SPINDLE.

8 1/2"

12"

3/8" x 3" LAGSCREW (3 PER SIDE)

BOTTOM INSIDE EDGES NOT ROUNDED.

37 1/4"

10 5/8"

4 7/16"

SECTION VIEW

NOTE: ALL LUMBER, EXCEPT DOWELS, IS CHERRY

5 1/2"

5 1/2"

5 1/2"

22"

1 1/8" x 2 3/4" x 22" BACK RAIL.

3/8" DIA. x 1" DOWELS (2 PER CORNER)

2 1/4"-10 F.H. WOOD SCREW

DOWEL PLUG.

1 1/8" x 1 5/8" x 21 1/8" SIDE RAIL.

3/4" DIA. DOWEL

1 5/8"

1 1/8"

1/4" QUARTER ROUND RADIUS.

FRONT VIEW

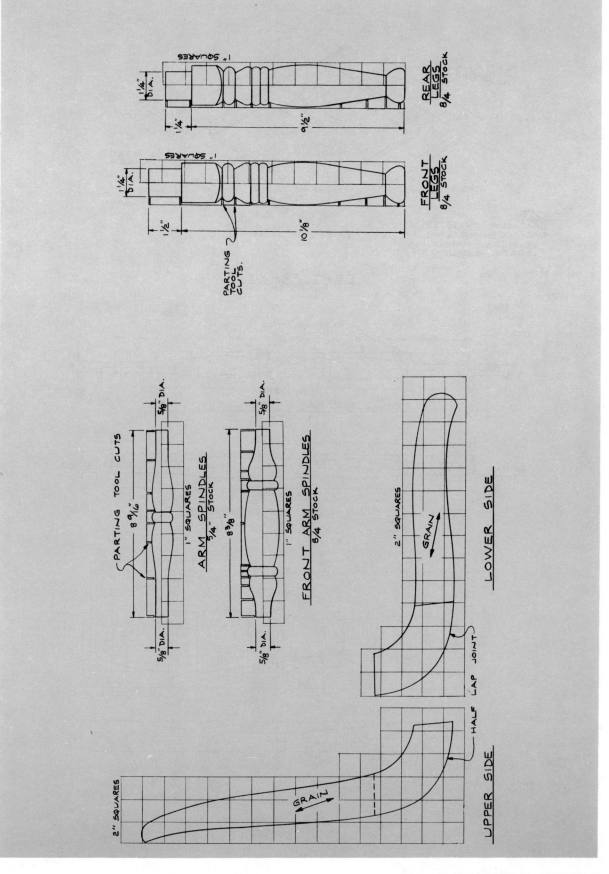

PLANS CONTINUED NEXT PAGE

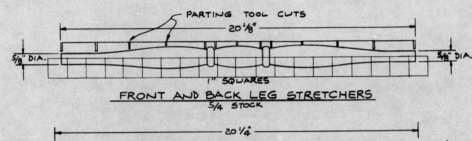

FLAT HEAD
UPHOLSTERY
TACKS.

CANVAS
WEBBING

FRONT

1¼" MORTISE
FOR LEG.

¼" x ¾" WIDE
RABBET FOR
WEBBING.

HALF LAP
JOINT

NOTE:
SEAT CUSHION: 22" x 23" x 4"
BACK CUSHION: 22" x 21" x 4"
(AVAILABLE FROM)
(SEARS ROEBUCK)

SEAT FRAME
8/4 STOCK

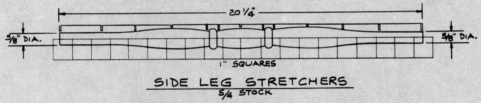

PARTING TOOL CUTS

20⅛"

⅝" DIA.

⅝" DIA.

1" SQUARES

FRONT AND BACK LEG STRETCHERS
5/4 STOCK

20¼"

⅝" DIA.

⅝" DIA.

1" SQUARES

SIDE LEG STRETCHERS
5/4 STOCK

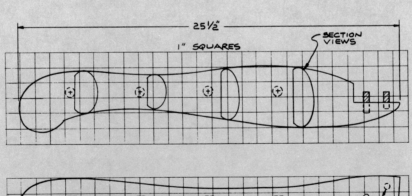

25½"

1" SQUARES

SECTION
VIEWS

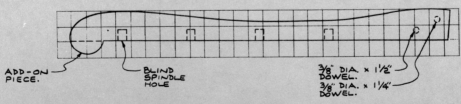

ADD-ON
PIECE.

BLIND
SPINDLE
HOLE

⅜" DIA. x 1½"
DOWEL.

⅜" DIA. x 1¼"
DOWEL.

ARMS
8/4 STOCK

thicker by gluing on a small block of wood.

Note that the legs appear to be angled. Actually, the front legs are fitted into perpendicular mortises (holes) in the seat frame. The angle is achieved because the seat frame slants downwards when assembled. The angled notches at the rear of the seat frame, with holes bored perpendicular to the slanted face of the notch, effect the angle for the rear legs.

An important tip: When turning the legs, leave a square section in the waste area beyond the actual leg bottoms. The flat areas at both ends will provide the only means to drill the holes for the spindles. The flats, resting on a board placed on the angled drill-press table, will hold the legs in the proper attitude.

Turn the ends of all legs and spindles a shade under the drill size used for their respective holes to allow a slight amount of play, which will be necessary to assemble the parts. Mix plastic-resin glue to a slightly thicker than normal consistency so it won't readily run out of the joints. Be sure to whittle small flats on all leg and spindle ends to prevent compressed glue joints, as explained in Chapter 5.

Assembly pointers: Insert the arm-rest spindles into the sides, then add the arm rests. The two dowels at the rear end of the arm rests should be tapered slightly to permit some twisting of the arm rest, so it can be worked into place over the spindles.

To assemble the base, start by inserting the spindles into the legs. Insert the front legs into the frame first. Then, with some prodding and twisting, work the angled rear legs into place.

42
White-Ash
End Table

White ash is most commonly used for tool handles and many types of sports equipment, such as oars and baseball bats. It is also widely used in manufacturing fine furniture.

This wood is a relative stranger in the home workshop but should not be. Though quite hard, it responds well to power tools. Its sharply defined grain pattern is quite attractive and is especially enhanced when topped with a light-toned clear finish.

Dowel joints are used in assembly, except for the base, where splines are used to join the mitered corners. Here you must be careful in the order of assembly; if you attach both ends to one of the side members at the onset, you will be unable to insert the other side member. The correct procedure is first to join one end to the front and the other to the back, then bring the diagonal corners together.

The tabletop and base shelf are secured with steel tabletop fasteners which insert into a $\frac{1}{8}$-inch groove. It is essential to cut these grooves before assembly. The decorative grooves on the outside of the base are best cut after the rectangle is assembled by passing the piece over a slightly projecting table-saw blade.

You need not disqualify yourself from this project for lack of a lathe with which to turn the front legs, as you can obtain them readymade. See Sources of Supply.

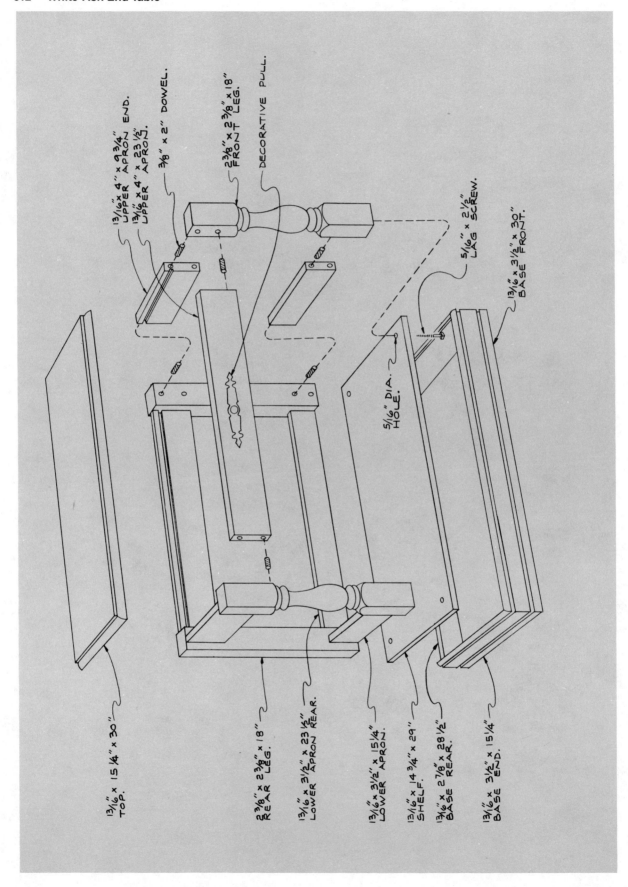

13/16" × 15 1/4" × 30" TOP.

13/16" × 4" × 9 3/4" UPPER APRON END.

13/16" × 4" × 23 1/2" UPPER APRON.

3/8" × 2" DOWEL.

2 3/8" × 2 3/8" × 18" FRONT LEG.

DECORATIVE PULL.

5/16" × 2 1/2" LAG SCREW.

13/16" × 3 1/2" × 30" BASE FRONT.

5/16" DIA. HOLE.

2 3/8" × 2 3/8" × 18" REAR LEG.

13/16 × 3 1/2" × 23 1/2" LOWER APRON REAR.

13/16 × 3 1/2" × 15 1/4" LOWER APRON.

13/16" × 14 3/4" × 29" SHELF.

13/16" × 2 7/8 × 28 1/2" BASE REAR.

13/16" × 3 1/2" × 15 1/4" BASE END.

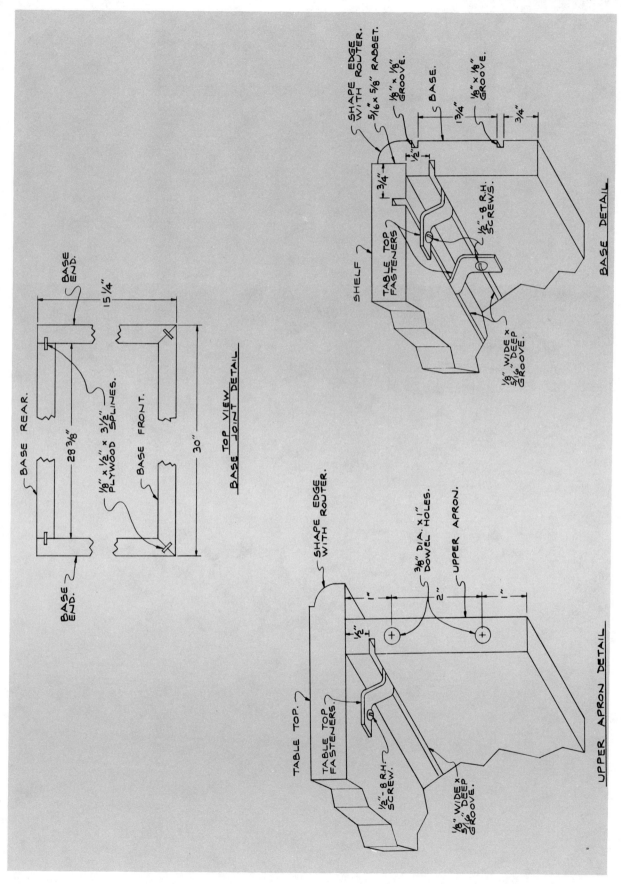

BASE TOP VIEW JOINT DETAIL

BASE DETAIL

UPPER APRON DETAIL

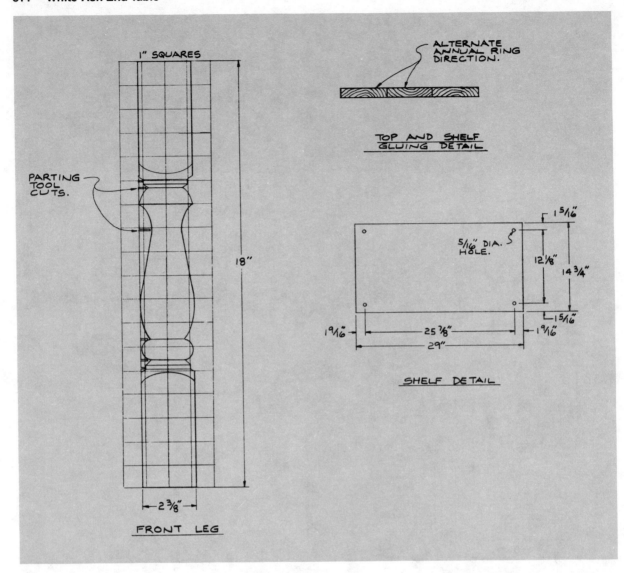

1" SQUARES

PARTING
TOOL
CUTS.

18"

2 3/8"

FRONT LEG

ALTERNATE
ANNUAL RING
DIRECTION.

TOP AND SHELF
GLUING DETAIL

1 5/16"

5/16" DIA.
HOLE.

12 1/8"

14 3/4"

1 5/16"

1 9/16"

25 7/8"

1 9/16"

29"

SHELF DETAIL

43

Book Trough Table

The plan for this dainty table specifies the use of lumber-core plywood. This type of plywood has a solid-wood core, usually poplar, of a quality that permits leaving the edges exposed. Veneer-core plywood, on the other hand, would not be suitable for this clear-finished project because its inner veneers, usually fir plies, would present a poor appearance. A word of caution about plywood: Corner-cutting is widely practiced in the manufacture of off-brand materials. You can't see inside a panel, of course, but you can check the outside. A reputable manufacturer imprints the brand name and grade. When this is not present either on the edge or back of the panel it is usually a sure sign that the core fillers will be of exceptionally poor quality. Unusually large voids, disintegrated knots, loose splintery scraps and the like are what you'll find in so called "bargain" plywood in both the veneer- and lumber-core variety.

Construction of this table is rather basic, but note the novel use of large, 5-inch screws which extend through the entire top assembly to simplify joining the subtop, end and back panels, the top and rails. Glue is used with this and the other screw-assembled joints.

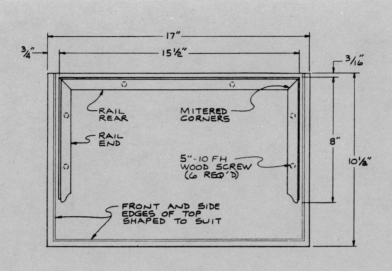

TOP VIEW

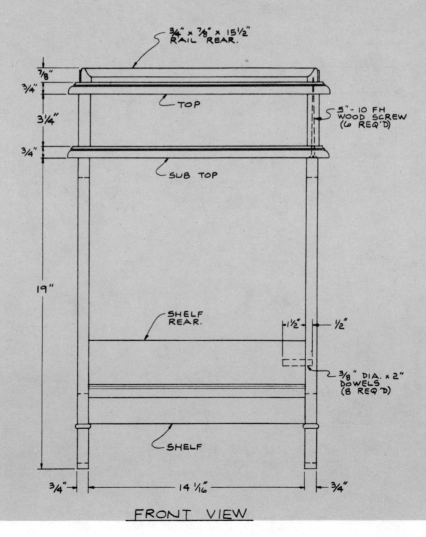

FRONT VIEW

PLANS CONTINUED NEXT PAGE

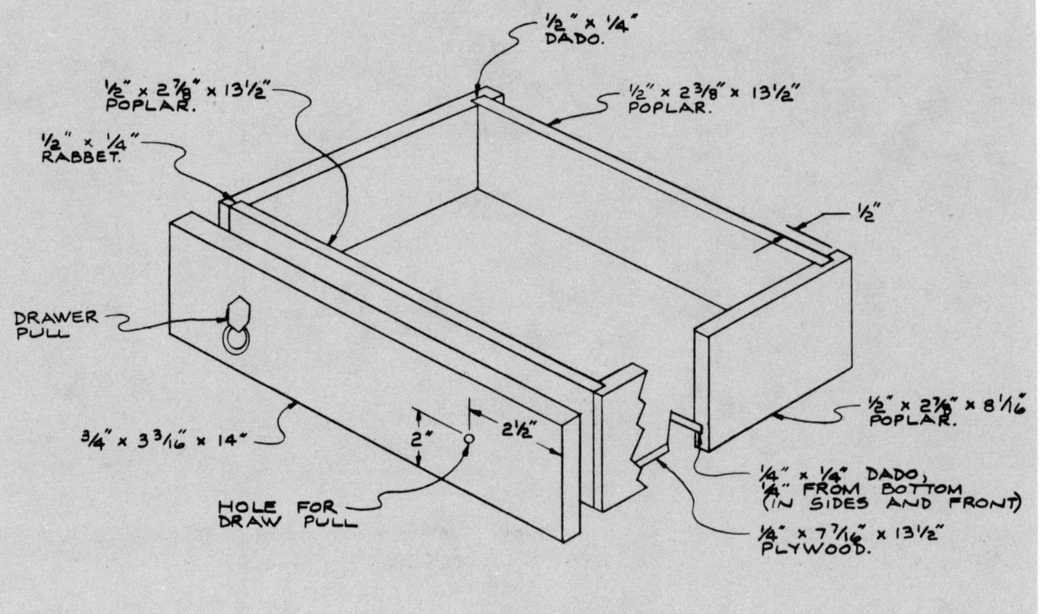
1/2" x 1/4"
DADO.
1/2" x 2 7/8" x 13 1/2"
POPLAR.
1/2" x 2 3/8" x 13 1/2"
POPLAR.
1/2" x 1/4"
RABBET.
1/2"
DRAWER
PULL
1/2" x 2 7/8" x 8 1/16"
POPLAR.
3/4" x 3 3/16" x 14"
2"
2 1/2"
1/4" x 1/4" DADO,
1/4" FROM BOTTOM
(IN SIDES AND FRONT)
HOLE FOR
DRAW PULL
1/4" x 7 7/16" x 13 1/2"
PLYWOOD.

DRAWER

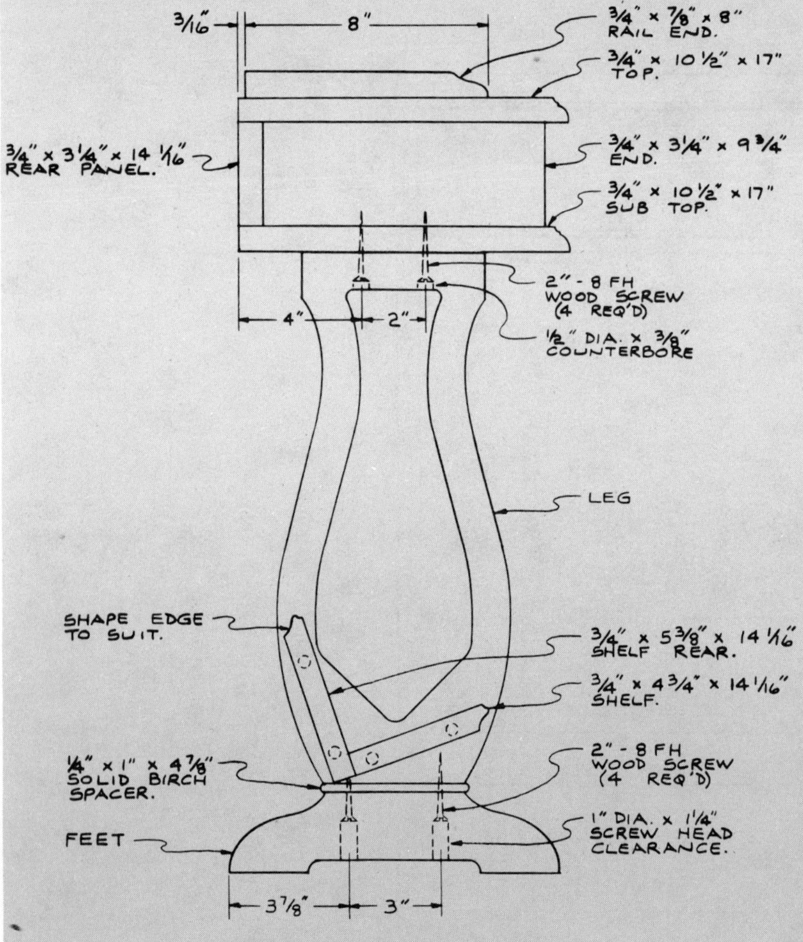
3/16"
8"
3/4" x 7/8" x 8"
RAIL END.
3/4" x 10 1/2" x 17"
TOP.
3/4" x 3 1/4" x 14 1/16"
REAR PANEL.
3/4" x 3 1/4" x 9 3/4"
END.
3/4" x 10 1/2" x 17"
SUB TOP.
2" - 8 FH
WOOD SCREW
(4 REQ'D)
4"
2"
1/2" DIA. x 3/8"
COUNTERBORE
LEG
SHAPE EDGE
TO SUIT.
3/4" x 5 3/8" x 14 1/16"
SHELF REAR.
3/4" x 4 3/4" x 14 1/16"
SHELF.
1/4" x 1" x 4 7/8"
SOLID BIRCH
SPACER.
2" - 8 FH
WOOD SCREW
(4 REQ'D)
FEET
1" DIA. x 1 1/4"
SCREW HEAD
CLEARANCE.
3 7/8"
3"

CROSS SECTION

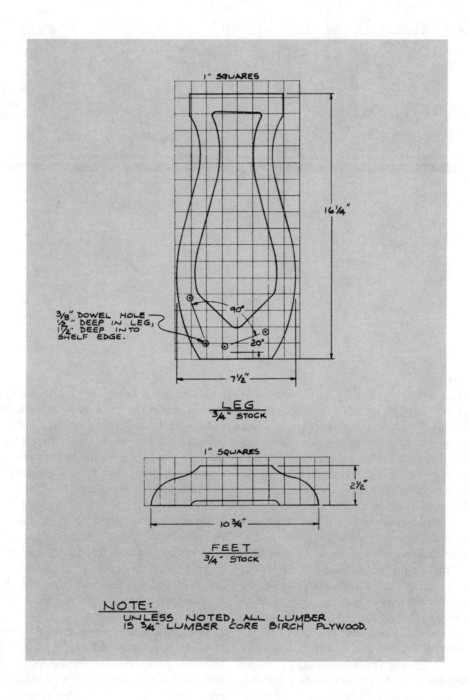

1" SQUARES

16¼"

3/8" DOWEL HOLE
½" DEEP IN LEG,
1½" DEEP INTO
SHELF EDGE.

90°

20°

7½"

LEG
¾" STOCK

1" SQUARES

2½"

10¾"

FEET
¾" STOCK

NOTE:
UNLESS NOTED, ALL LUMBER
IS ¾" LUMBER CORE BIRCH PLYWOOD.

44
9-to-9
Gateleg Table

This versatile gateleg table will comfortably seat twelve when expanded to its full 9-foot length but it takes up a mere 9-inch width of floor space when folded. The table can be set up in several in-between modes to seat three, six, or seven persons.

White-oak veneer plywood and solid-oak legs are used in the table shown. The top panels are cut with the grain direction running parallel to the longer dimension to avoid butting mismatched grain patterns end-to-end.

There are several ways to conceal the raw plywood edges. You can apply matching flexible wood-veneer trim or $\frac{1}{8}$" $\times$ $\frac{3}{4}$" solid wood edging. To obtain a really professional result, use the method detailed in the plan. While the groove can be cut on the table saw, the radial-arm saw will prove easier. Or, if you have a shaper, use it with a V-groove cutter. Whichever means you employ, do not make the cut so deep that it will form sharp edges. Instead, adjust the depth of cut so that flats of about $\frac{1}{16}$ inch remain on each edge.

Sectioned piano hinges are used to join the top panels to the dividing strips. The spaces between the hinges permit the gatelegs to swing into place without obstruction. Rabbets are cut along the tops of the leg-support frames to clear the thickness of the hinge leaves. Do not glue the frames to the divider strips until later, after the leg assemblies have been completed. This will allow the frames and gatelegs to be clamped together for accurately drilling the holes for the steel pivot pins at top and bottom. Cut the pins from $\frac{1}{4}$-inch-diameter rod. Bevel the lead ends of the pins slightly to facilitate insertion. Avoid driving in the pivot pins until all the parts have been finish-coated, as this will simplify the task. This applies throughout; apply the finish before final assembly.

The locking strip serves to fill the gap between the two main sections and keeps them together when the table is in the folded mode. Wood dowels glued into the strip and slightly tapered on the exposed ends serve as retainers. The strip is lifted out to expand the table.

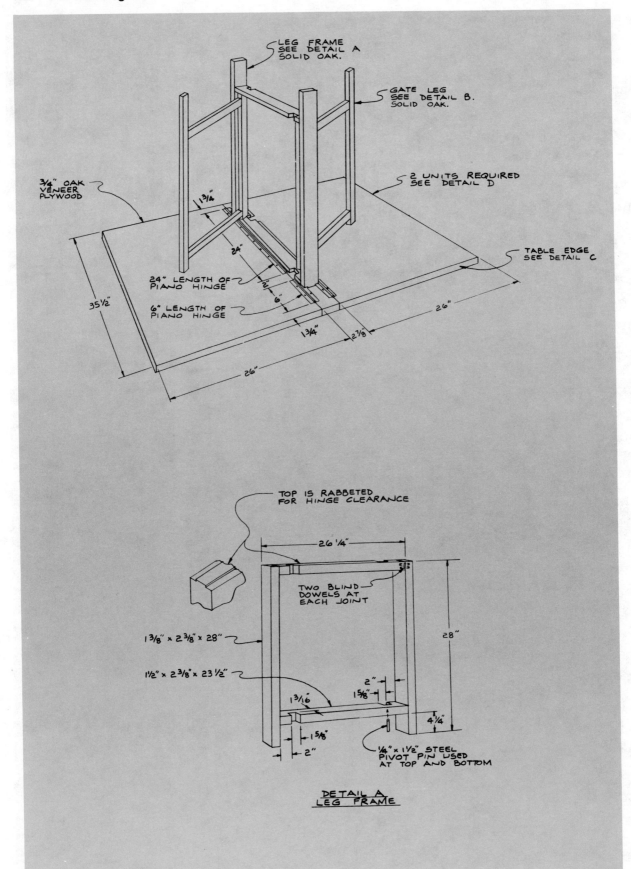

LEG FRAME
SEE DETAIL A
SOLID OAK.

GATE LEG
SEE DETAIL B.
SOLID OAK.

3/4" OAK
VENEER
PLYWOOD

2 UNITS REQUIRED
SEE DETAIL D

1 3/4"

TABLE EDGE
SEE DETAIL C

24"

24" LENGTH OF
PIANO HINGE

2"

6"

6" LENGTH OF
PIANO HINGE

35 1/2"

1 3/4"

2 7/8"

26"

26"

TOP IS RABBETED
FOR HINGE CLEARANCE

26 1/4"

TWO BLIND
DOWELS AT
EACH JOINT

1 3/8" × 2 3/8" × 28"

1 1/2" × 2 3/8" × 23 1/2"

28"

2"

1 5/8"

1 3/16"

1 5/8"

4 1/4"

2"

1/4" × 1 1/2" STEEL
PIVOT PIN USED
AT TOP AND BOTTOM

DETAIL A
LEG FRAME

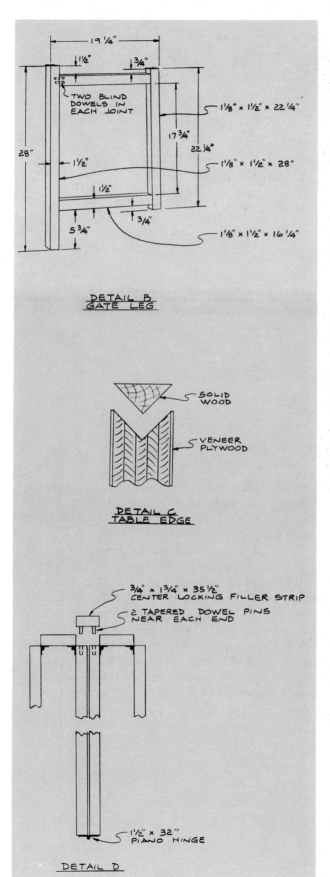

DETAIL B
GATE LEG

- 19 1/4"
- 1 1/2"
- 3/4"
- TWO BLIND DOWELS IN EACH JOINT
- 28"
- 17 3/4"
- 22 1/4"
- 1 1/2"
- 1 1/2"
- 5 3/4"
- 3/4"
- 1 1/8" × 1 1/2" × 22 1/4"
- 1 1/8" × 1 1/2" × 28"
- 1 1/8" × 1 1/2" × 16 1/4"

SOLID WOOD

VENEER PLYWOOD

DETAIL C
TABLE EDGE

3/4" × 1 3/4" × 35 1/2"
CENTER LOCKING FILLER STRIP

2 TAPERED DOWEL PINS
NEAR EACH END

1 1/2" × 32"
PIANO HINGE

DETAIL D

With one leg swung and one leaf lifted, the table will seat three.

Two legs swung and two leaves up, the table seats six.

Retainer strip is removed to allow the table to be fully extended.

With the four legs swung to support it, the fully extended table will seat twelve.

45

Chest Table

This attractive piece will serve nicely in a den, living room or bedroom. Make it with hardwood if you prefer, but common pine will do fine and certainly will keep cost to a minimum. Select warp-free stock with small-to-medium-sized sound, tight knots.

If you plan to cut the dadoes in the cabinet sides on the table saw, be sure to do so before you cut the bottom curves. This will preserve the solid edge to ride against the saw's rip fence. If you use a router, it won't matter if you cut the curves before or afterwards.

The drawer-frame sections are reinforced with two blind dowels at each corner. This is optional, depending upon the finish you plan to use. You can use through dowels driven from the outside to sim-plify the task, but this method will be suitable only if an opaque finish is to be applied. With a clear finish the dowel ends would be visible on the front edges between the drawers.

The best way to cut through mortises in the pedestal is with a sabre saw using the guide technique described in Chapter 48. Dimension the mortises carefully to achieve a slip fit of the tenons. The holes for the dowel pegs should be located so they do not project fully; if about $\frac{1}{16}$ inch of the holes are beyond the surface of the pedestal, the desired forced fit of the pegs will assure a solid joint. A slightly tapered flat sanded on the dowel will allow it to get started in the hole.

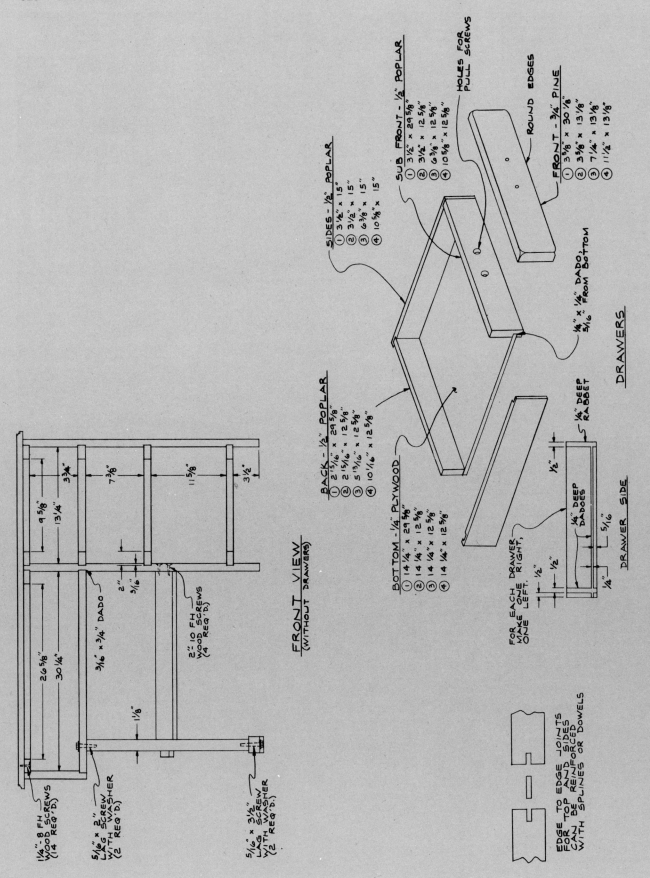

FRONT VIEW
(WITHOUT DRAWERS)

1¼"- 8 FH
WOOD SCREWS
(14 REQ'D.)

5/16" × 2"
LAG SCREW
WITH WASHER
(2 REQ'D.)

5/16" × 3½"
LAG SCREW
WITH WASHER
(2 REQ'D.)

3/16" × ¾" DADO

2" 10 FH
WOOD SCREWS
(4 REQ'D.)

26 5/8"
30 ¼"
1 1/8"
2"
5/16"

3 ¾"
9 5/8"
13 ¼"
7 7/8"
11 5/8"
3 ½"

SIDES - ½" POPLAR
① 3½" × 15"
② 3½" × 15"
③ 6 3/8" × 15"
④ 10 5/8" × 15"

SUB FRONT - ½" POPLAR
① 3½" × 29 5/8"
② 3½" × 12 5/8"
③ 6 3/8" × 12 5/8"
④ 10 5/8" × 12 5/8"

HOLES FOR
PULL SCREWS

ROUND EDGES

FRONT - ¾" PINE
① 3 5/8" × 30 1/8"
② 3 5/8" × 13 1/8"
③ 7 ¼" × 13 1/8"
④ 11 ½" × 13 1/8"

BACK - ½" POPLAR
① 2 15/16" × 29 5/8"
② 2 15/16" × 12 5/8"
③ 5 13/16" × 12 5/8"
④ 10 1/16" × 12 5/8"

BOTTOM - ¼" PLYWOOD
① 14 ¼" × 29 5/8"
② 14 ¼" × 12 5/8"
③ 14 ¼" × 12 5/8"
④ 14 ¼" × 12 5/8"

1/8" × ¼" DADO,
5/16 FROM BOTTOM

DRAWERS

¼" DEEP
RABBET

¼" DEEP
DADOES

½"
½"
½"
5/16"
¼"

DRAWER SIDE

FOR EACH DRAWER
MAKE ONE RIGHT,
ONE LEFT.

EDGE TO EDGE JOINTS
FOR TOP AND SIDES
CAN BE REINFORCED
WITH SPLINES OR DOWELS

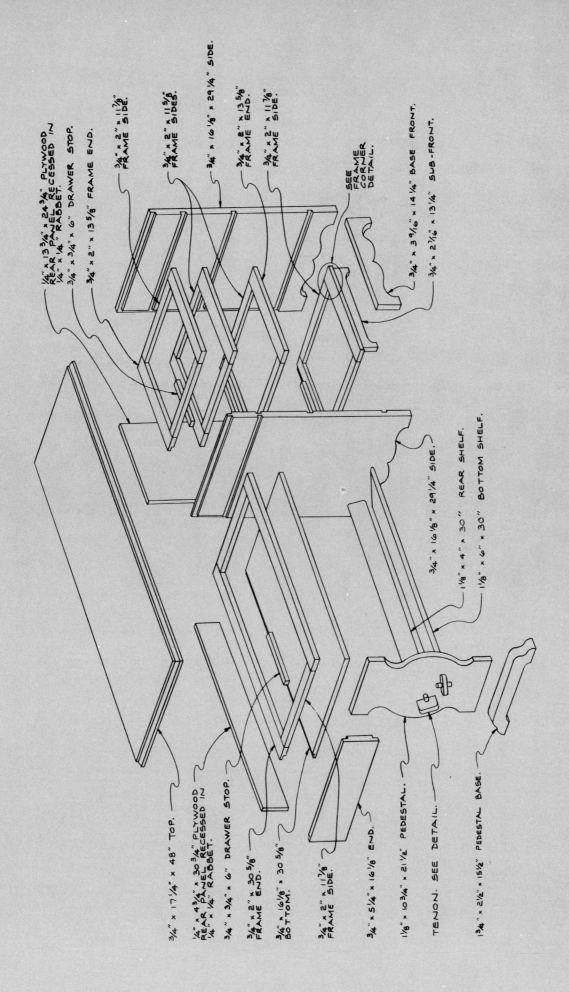

1/4" x 13 3/4" x 24 3/4" PLYWOOD REAR PANEL RECESSED IN 1/4" x 1/4" RABBET.

3/4" x 3/4" x 6" DRAWER STOP.

3/4" x 2" x 13 5/8" FRAME END.

3/4" x 2" x 11 7/8" FRAME SIDE.

3/4" x 2" x 11 5/8" FRAME SIDES.

3/4" x 16 1/8" x 29 1/4" SIDE.

3/4" x 2" x 13 5/8" FRAME END.

3/4" x 2" x 11 7/8" FRAME SIDE.

SEE FRAME CORNER DETAIL.

3/4" x 3 9/16" x 14 1/4" BASE FRONT.

3/4" x 2 1/2" x 13 1/4" SUB-FRONT.

3/4" x 16 1/8" x 29 1/4" SIDE.

1 1/8" x 4" x 30" REAR SHELF.

1 1/8" x 6" x 30" BOTTOM SHELF.

3/4" x 17 1/4" x 48" TOP.

1/4" x 4 3/4" x 30 3/4" PLYWOOD REAR PANEL RECESSED IN 1/4" x 1/4" RABBET.

3/4" x 3/4" x 6" DRAWER STOP.

3/4" x 2" x 30 5/8" FRAME END.

3/4" x 16 1/8" x 30 5/8" BOTTOM.

3/4" x 2" x 11 7/8" FRAME SIDE.

3/4" x 5 1/4" x 16 1/8" END.

1 1/8" x 10 3/4" x 21 1/2" PEDESTAL.

TENON. SEE DETAIL.

1 3/4" x 2 1/2" x 15 1/2" PEDESTAL BASE.

PLANS CONTINUED NEXT PAGE

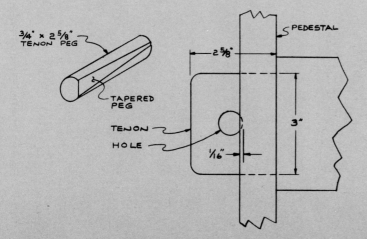

3/4" × 2 5/8" TENON PEG

TAPERED PEG

TENON

HOLE

PEDESTAL

2 5/8"

3"

1/16"

TENON DETAIL

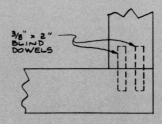

3/8" × 2" BLIND DOWELS

FRAME CORNER DETAIL

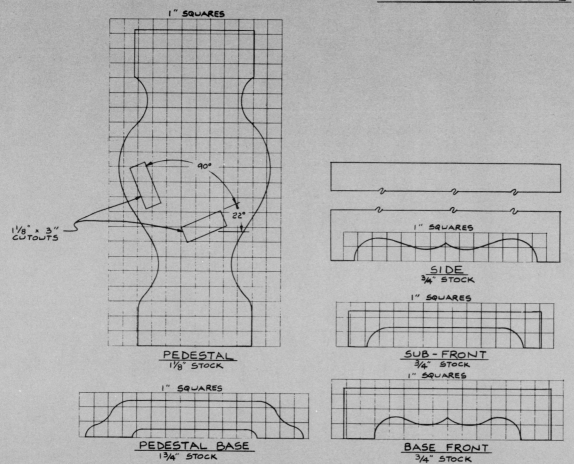

1" SQUARES

90°

22°

1 1/8" × 3" CUTOUTS

PEDESTAL
1 1/8" STOCK

1" SQUARES

SIDE
3/4" STOCK

1" SQUARES

SUB-FRONT
3/4" STOCK

1" SQUARES

PEDESTAL BASE
1 3/4" STOCK

1" SQUARES

BASE FRONT
3/4" STOCK

46
Campaign Desk

This piece is styled after the British military desk used by field officers during the 19th century. The campaign desk of bygone days usually had a leather top embellished with gold-leaf border designs. This version utilizes plastic laminate sheet with a distinctive leather-like embossed texture. Water-applied decals are used in lieu of gold leaf to produce a very attractive border design.

Three kinds of wood are used for this project: ⁴/₄ cherry, ½-inch and ¾-inch fir plywood for the top and bottom, and ½-inch poplar for the drawer sides and back. Hardboard, ¼ inch thick, is used for the drawer bottoms.

The top is a spline-reinforced mitered frame with a ⁹/₁₆" deep × ¾" wide rabbet on the inside. This houses the ½-inch plywood panel with ¹/₁₆-inch-thick plastic laminate so it's flush with the top surface of the frame. This design permits the laminate to be applied easily to the plywood and, very important, it permits the plywood edge to be trimmed cleanly before installation.

Note that the exposed edges of the ends and drawer partitions are faced with ⅛-inch strips to conceal the end-grain. Be sure to anticipate the added dimensions when cutting the four cross members to length.

The steel line-up pins for the trestles are cut from a length of ¼-inch-diameter rod. One end of each pin is secured with epoxy. If the desk is to be mounted permanently, two screws through the cleats will secure the trestles.

Economical nylon self-adhesive drawer-slide tape is used instead of metal or wood drawer slides. The tape is applied near the fronts of the drawer compartments and to the bottom rear of the drawer sides.

When making the desk-top insert, cut the plywood to size for a slip fit into the frame rabbet. Cut the plastic-laminate sheet about ¼ inch oversize on all sides, then trim it flush with the plywood edge after bonding. Use contact cement to apply the laminate. A router with a straight piloted bit is used to

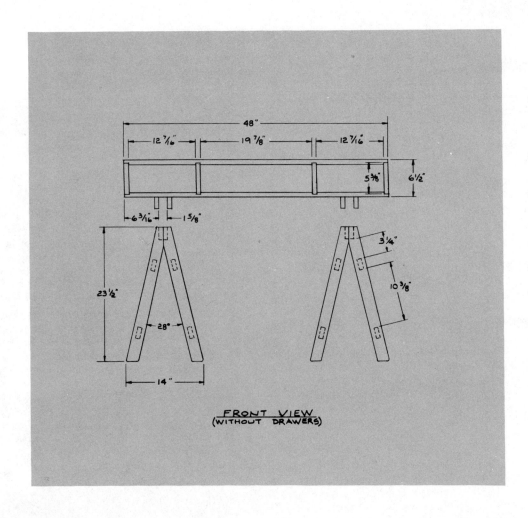

FRONT VIEW
(WITHOUT DRAWERS)

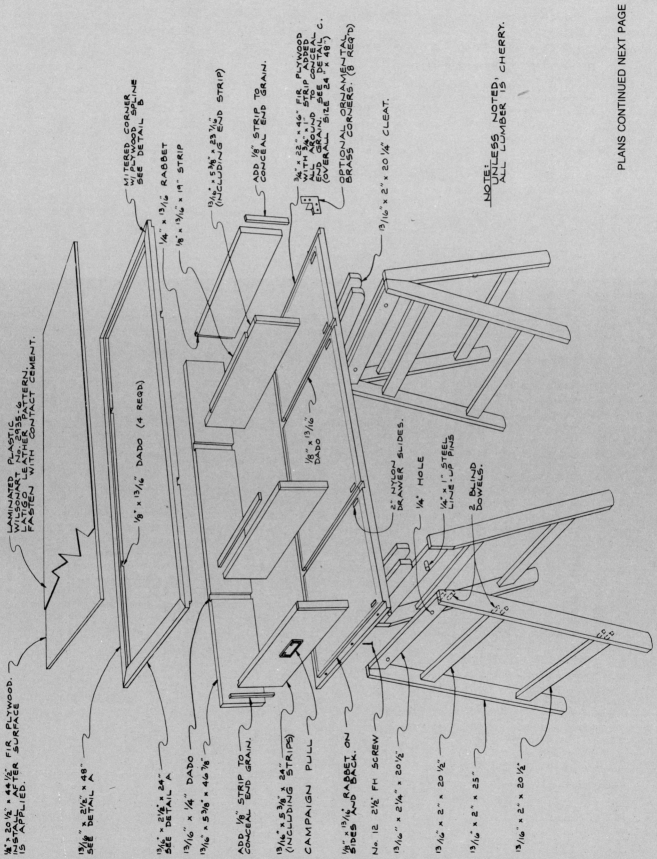

1/8" x 20½" x 44½" FIR PLYWOOD.
INSTALL AFTER SURFACE
IS APPLIED.

LAMINATED PLASTIC
WILSONART No. 2935-6
LATIGO LEATHER PATTERN.
FASTEN WITH CONTACT CEMENT.

13/16" x 2½" x 48"
SEE DETAIL A

MITERED CORNER
W/ PLYWOOD SPLINE
SEE DETAIL B

¼" x 13/16" RABBET

1/8" x 13/16" x 19" STRIP

13/16" x 5⅜" x 23 1/16"
(INCLUDING END STRIP)

ADD 1/8" STRIP TO
CONCEAL END GRAIN.

¾" x 22" x 46" FIR PLYWOOD
WITH ¾" x 1" STRIP ADDED
ALL AROUND TO CONCEAL
END GRAIN. SEE DETAIL C.
(OVERALL SIZE 24" x 48")

OPTIONAL ORNAMENTAL
BRASS CORNERS. (8 REQ'D)

13/16" x 2" x 20¼" CLEAT.

13/16" x 2½" x 24"
SEE DETAIL A

1/8" x 13/16" DADO (4 REQ'D)

13/16" x ¼" DADO

13/16" x 5⅜" x 46⅞"

ADD 1/8" STRIP TO
CONCEAL END GRAIN.

13/16" x 5⅜" x 24"
(INCLUDING STRIPS)

CAMPAIGN PULL

1/8" x 13/16" RABBET ON
SIDES AND BACK.

1/8" x 13/16" DADO

2" NYLON
DRAWER SLIDES.

¼" HOLE

¼" x 1" STEEL
LINE-UP PINS

2 BLIND
DOWELS.

No. 12 2½" FH SCREW

13/16" x 2¼" x 20½"

13/16" x 2" x 20 ½"

13/16" x 2" x 25"

13/16" x 2" x 20 ½"

NOTE:
UNLESS NOTED,
ALL LUMBER IS CHERRY.

PLANS CONTINUED NEXT PAGE

331

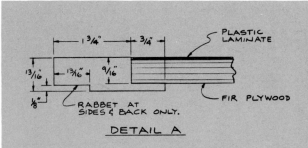

1 3/4"   3/4"

PLASTIC
LAMINATE

13/16"   13/16"   9/16"

1/8"

FIR PLYWOOD

RABBET AT
SIDES & BACK ONLY.

DETAIL A

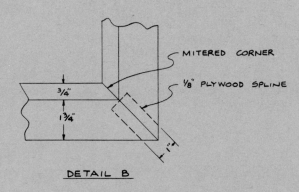

MITERED CORNER

1/8" PLYWOOD SPLINE

3/4"

1 3/4"

1"

DETAIL B

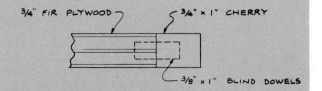

3/4" FIR PLYWOOD   3/4" x 1" CHERRY

3/8" x 1" BLIND DOWELS

DETAIL C

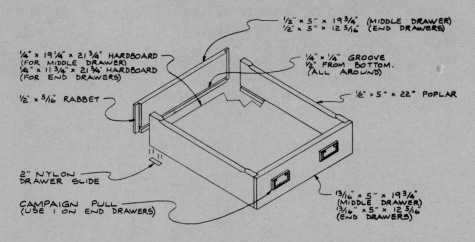

1/2" x 5" x 19 3/4" (MIDDLE DRAWER)
1/2" x 5" x 12 5/16" (END DRAWERS)

1/4" x 19 1/4" x 21 3/4" HARDBOARD
(FOR MIDDLE DRAWER)
1/4" x 11 3/4" x 21 3/4" HARDBOARD
(FOR END DRAWERS)

1/4" x 1/4" GROOVE
1/2" FROM BOTTOM.
(ALL AROUND)

1/2" x 5/16" RABBET

1/2" x 5" x 22" POPLAR

2" NYLON
DRAWER SLIDE

13/16" x 5" x 19 3/4"
(MIDDLE DRAWER)
13/16" x 5" x 12 5/16"
(END DRAWERS)

CAMPAIGN PULL
(USE 1 ON END DRAWERS)

DRAWERS

Closeup of the ornamental top. The gold
and red border adds a nice touch to the
simulated leather surface.

trim off the overhang. The top panel need not be
glued in until the woodwork has been finish-coated.

Cut-apart portions of Meyercord # 1539-A water-applied decals are used to make the decorative
border on the laminate, or you can choose from a
selection of border-design decals which are generally available.

In order for the decal to "take" on the textured
surface of the laminate, you must first apply a size.
Brush on a coat of Aqua Podge or similar latex-based
decoupage finish, which is available at handicraft
and hobby shops. Allow the coating to dry.

Dip the decal strips in warm water for about ten
seconds, then place the decal, face up, on a damp
towel. Wait for the design to release, then slide the
decal off the backing paper and into the desired position on the laminate. Place a piece of clean, unruled
writing paper over the decal and press firmly with a
small rubber roller. When the decals have dried,
apply a final coat of the decoupage finish over the
entire surface of the laminate.

Water-applied decals, a rubber roller, scissors, and decoupage glaze are what you'll need to decorate the top. The glaze
serves as a size to allow the decals to adhere to the textured
laminate surface.

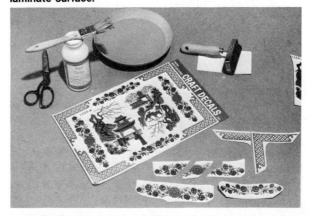

Border strips are soaked in water until they come off the
backing. They are positioned, then pressed with the roller
with paper in between.

47

Rolltop Desk

The rolltop, a common desk at the turn of the century, is back in style. Now as popular as ever before, reproductions modeled after 19th century antiques are available but quite costly. These plans, adapted through the courtesy of Furniture Designs, will enable you to build your own charming heirloom at a fraction of current prices. If you prefer to work from full-size plans, they may be obtained from this company (see address in the source list).

The desk is made of veneer plywood and matching solid wood. Cherry is indicated, but pine, oak, maple, or any wood of your choice may be used. Note that the solid wood thicknesses are given as ¾ inch. These dimensions will apply if you substitute pine, which is commonly dressed to exactly ¾ inch thickness. It will be necessary to make minor dimension adjustments if you use hardwoods, which are generally dressed to $^{13}/_{16}$ inch thickness. However, solid cabinet hardwoods in ¾ inch thickness can be obtained from woodworker's supply outlets such as Constantine.

The desk is built as two separate parts: the pedestal base and the rolltop. Note that the top can be made with either a single or double curve outline. Both configurations are shown in the plan.

The plywood top is shown attached to the pedestal bases with blind dowels. This will require great care in laying out and drilling matching dowel holes. A simpler alternative is to attach the top with screws driven from the surface. Set in counterbored holes, the screw heads can be concealed with wood plugs. Here's a foolproof technique:

Set the top onto the pedestals, then draw pencil lines on the bottom of the panel to outline the location of the pedestal wall edges. Remove the panel and drill $^{1}/_{16}$-inch-diameter pilot holes for each screw location. Do this from the back of the panel using the pencil outline as a guide. When the preliminary pilot holes have been drilled through the top, position it onto the pedestals again and drill through the pilot holes from the top to make corresponding pilot holes in the top edges of the pedestals.

Work with a drill guide such as the Portalign to control the depth and to assure perpendicularity of the holes. Bore ½-inch-diameter holes ⅛ inch deep into the top to allow the use of matching wood plugs. Next bore the screw body holes and the larger shank clearance holes. This order is important, particularly if you use the preferred brad-point spur bit

to make clean-cut holes for the wood plugs. If the larger screw-clearance holes are made first, the spur bit point would not center properly.

The drawer fronts are shaped by tilting the table saw blade 8 degrees. Be sure to slice the ends first, then the sides, to avoid chipping the end-grain.

The ends of the rolltop unit are made of solid stock. The ⅜″ deep × 9⁄16″ wide curved groove for the slat curtain is cut with a router using a straight or mortising bit. A 9⁄16-inch-diameter bit, which would permit cutting the groove in one pass, is not available; therefore, a ¼-inch bit is used with a two-part template, such as the one shown in the plan. Two passes are made using one template for each pass. This will result in two ¼-inch-wide parallel grooves with a 1⁄16-inch waste strip in between. This is easily cleaned out by making a freehand pass with the router.

Note that the template dimensions given are suitable only when using a ¼-inch bit in a router with a 5-inch-diameter base. For other combinations you will have to alter the dimensions.

To make the templates, draw the patterns onto paper, making sure to include the alignment line on template *B*. Rubber-cement the patterns to hardboard and carefully cut them to shape. Sand the edges smooth and free of any saw ripples. Tape both templates together with the baselines in exact alignment and with the smaller form centered side to side over the larger one; then bore two small registration holes through them.

To cut the groove, center one of the templates on the workpiece with the baseline even with the bottom edge of the work. Drive in a pair of nails through the predrilled holes, then clamp the assembly to the work table and make the first pass with the router. Remove the first template and install the other, using the same nail pilot holes to assure exact registration. Make the second pass with the router.

The top is assembled but is not attached to the base unit until the tambour curtain has been completed and installed. To make the curtain slats, cut a sufficient number of wide boards to length, then rabbet the ends with a dado cutter. Next, tilt the table-saw blade 10 degrees and rip the strips to width. Run each piece through twice to obtain the double bevel. Work with two push sticks for safety in this operation. Sand and apply the final finish to each strip prior to assembly. Be careful to keep the finish off the bottom surfaces so the glue will adhere properly.

To assemble the curtain, work on a flat surface lined with kitchen wax paper to avoid having the canvas stick to the work table. Tape the canvas to the table to hold it taut, then brush slow-setting hide glue to the canvas, not to the wood, working about 8 slats at a time. Clamp cleats crosswise over the slats to obtain even pressure throughout. To assure accurate alignment of the slats it is advisable to nail a guide strip to the table at one end before gluing. Add another strip at the other end before applying the clamps.

Wax the grooves, then insert the curtain. Secure the top to the base with dowels, as shown in the plan, or attach it with four 1″ × 1″ brass angle brackets on the inside.

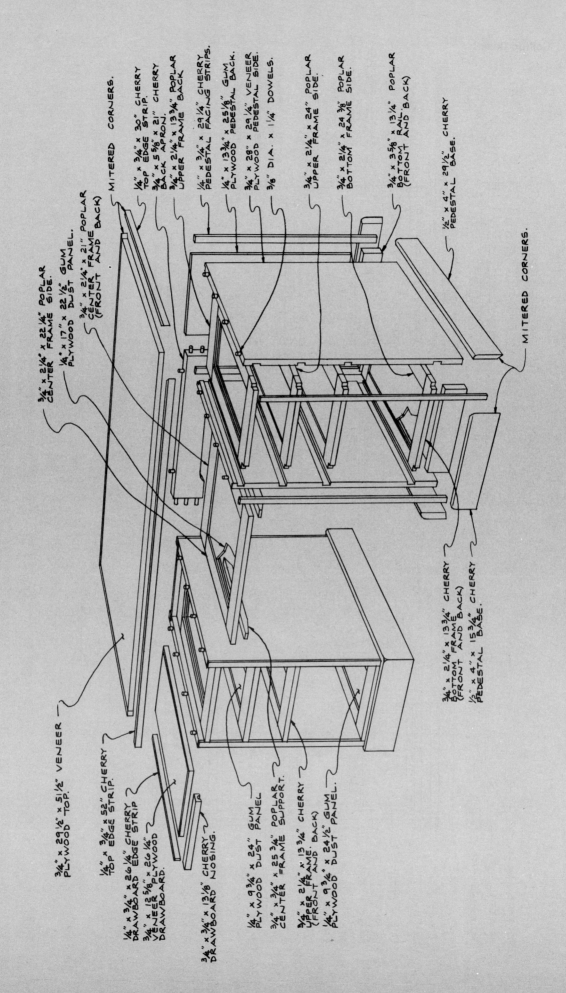

3/4" x 2 1/4" x 22 1/4" POPLAR CENTER FRAME SIDE.

1/4" x 17" x 22 1/2 GUM PLYWOOD DUST PANEL.

3/4" x 2 1/4" x 21" POPLAR CENTER FRAME (FRONT AND BACK)

MITERED CORNERS.

1/4" x 3/4" x 30" CHERRY TOP EDGE STRIP.

3/4" x 5 5/8" x 21" CHERRY BACK APRON.

1/4" x 2 1/4" x 13 3/4" POPLAR UPPER FRAME BACK

1/4" x 3/4" x 29 1/4" CHERRY PEDESTAL FACING STRIPS.

1/4" x 13 3/4" x 25 1/8" GUM PLYWOOD PEDESTAL BACK.

3/4" x 28" x 29 1/4" VENEER PLYWOOD PEDESTAL SIDE.

3/8" DIA. x 1 1/4" DOWELS.

3/4" x 2 1/4" x 24" POPLAR UPPER FRAME SIDE.

3/4" x 2 1/4" x 24 3/8 POPLAR BOTTOM FRAME SIDE.

3/4" x 3 5/8" x 13 1/4" POPLAR BOTTOM RAIL (FRONT AND BACK)

1/2" x 4" x 29 1/2" CHERRY PEDESTAL BASE.

MITERED CORNERS.

3/4" x 29 1/2" x 51 1/2" VENEER PLYWOOD TOP.

1/4" x 3/4" x 26 1/4" CHERRY DRAWBOARD EDGE STRIP

3/4" x 12 5/8" x 26 1/4" VENEER PLYWOOD DRAWBOARD.

1/8" x 3/4" x 52" CHERRY TOP EDGE STRIP.

3/4" x 3/4" x 13 1/8" CHERRY DRAWBOARD NOSING.

1/4" x 9 3/4" x 24" GUM PLYWOOD DUST PANEL

3/4" x 3/4" x 25 3/4" POPLAR CENTER FRAME SUPPORT.

3/4" x 2 1/4" x 13 3/4" CHERRY UPPER FRAME (FRONT AND BACK)

1/4" x 9 3/16" x 24 1/2" GUM PLYWOOD DUST PANEL.

3/4" x 2 1/4" x 13 3/4" CHERRY BOTTOM FRAME (FRONT AND BACK)

1/2" x 4" x 15 3/4" CHERRY PEDESTAL BASE.

PLANS CONTINUED NEXT PAGE

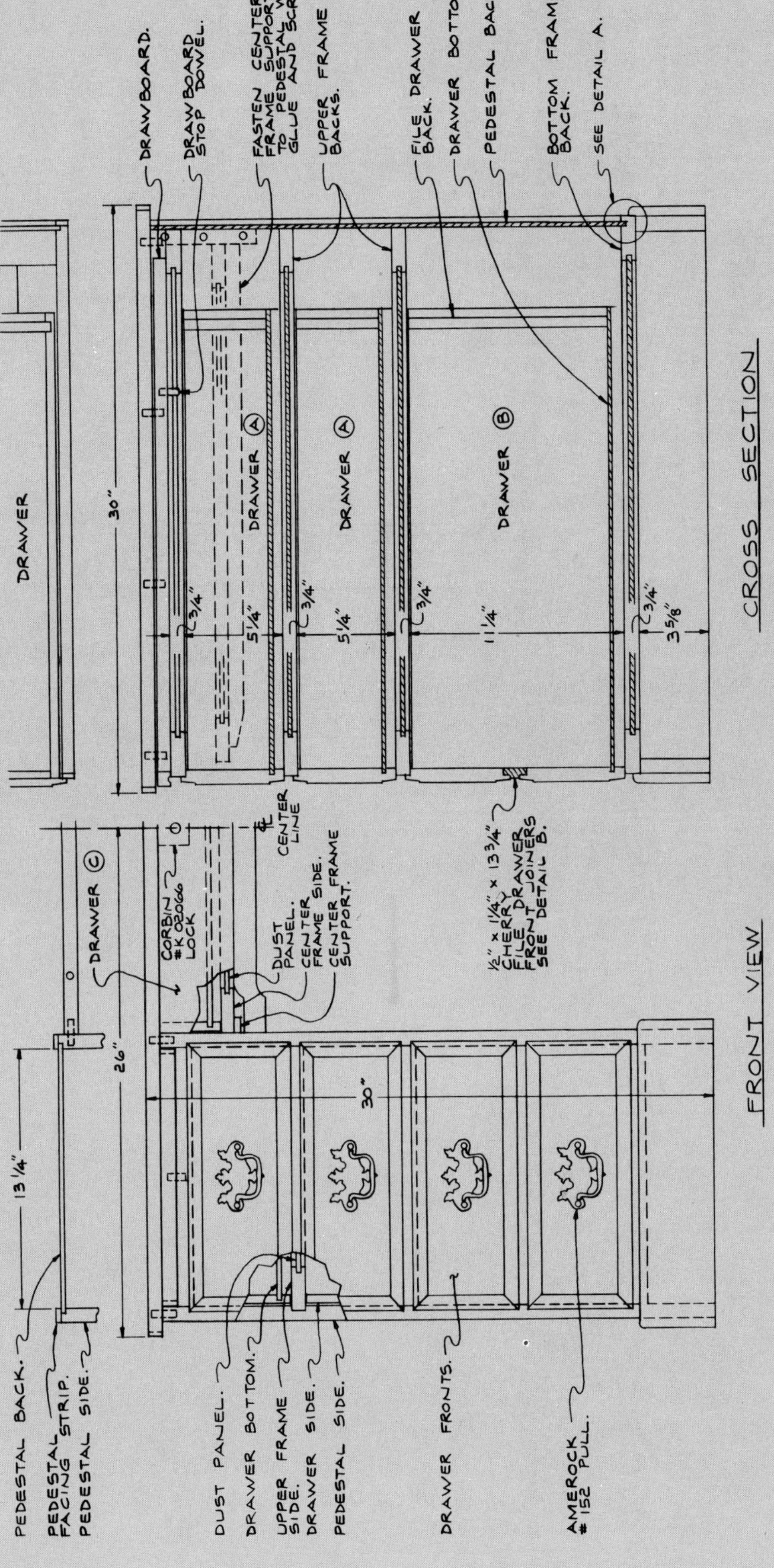

CROSS SECTION

FRONT VIEW

DRAWBOARD.

DRAWBOARD STOP DOWEL.

FASTEN CENTER FRAME SUPPORT TO PEDESTAL WITH GLUE AND SCREWS.

UPPER FRAME BACKS.

FILE DRAWER BACK.

DRAWER BOTTOM.

PEDESTAL BACK.

BOTTOM FRAME BACK.

SEE DETAIL A.

DRAWER

30"

DRAWER (A)

DRAWER (A)

DRAWER (B)

3/4"

5 1/4"

3/4"

5 1/4"

3/4"

11 1/4"

3/4"

3 5/8"

DRAWER (C)

CORBIN #K00000 LOCK.

CENTER LINE

DUST PANEL. CENTER FRAME SIDE. CENTER FRAME SUPPORT.

1/2" x 1 1/4" x 13 3/4" CHERRY FILE DRAWER FRONT JOINERS. SEE DETAIL B.

26"

30"

13 1/4"

PEDESTAL BACK.

PEDESTAL FACING STRIP. PEDESTAL SIDE.

DUST PANEL. DRAWER BOTTOM. UPPER FRAME SIDE. DRAWER SIDE. PEDESTAL SIDE.

DRAWER FRONTS.

AMEROCK #152 PULL.

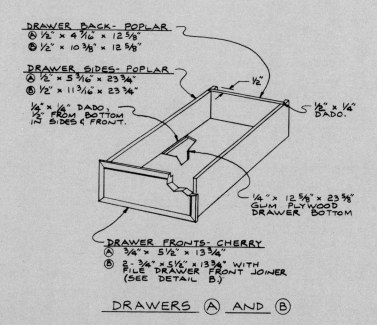

DRAWER BACK- POPLAR
Ⓐ ½" × 4 ⁷/₁₆" × 12 ⁵/₈"
Ⓑ ½" × 10 ³/₈" × 12 ⁵/₈"

DRAWER SIDES- POPLAR
Ⓐ ½" × 5 ³/₁₆" × 23 ³/₄"
Ⓑ ½" × 11 ³/₁₆" × 23 ³/₄"

¼" × ¼" DADO,
½" FROM BOTTOM
IN SIDES & FRONT.

½"

½" × ¼"
DADO.

¼" × 12 ⁵/₈" × 23 ⁵/₈"
GUM PLYWOOD
DRAWER BOTTOM

DRAWER FRONTS- CHERRY
Ⓐ ¾" × 5½" × 13 ¾"
Ⓑ 2- ¾" × 5½" × 13 ¾" WITH
FILE DRAWER FRONT JOINER
(SEE DETAIL B.)

DRAWERS Ⓐ AND Ⓑ

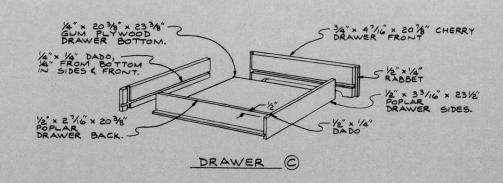

¼" × 20 ³/₈" × 23 ³/₈"
GUM PLYWOOD
DRAWER BOTTOM.

¼" × ¼" DADO,
¼" FROM BOTTOM
IN SIDES & FRONT.

¾" × 4 ⁷/₁₆" × 20 ⅞" CHERRY
DRAWER FRONT

½" × ¼"
RABBET

½" × 3 ³/₁₆" × 23 ½"
POPLAR
DRAWER SIDES.

½"

½" × 2 ⁷/₁₆" × 20 ³/₈"
POPLAR
DRAWER BACK.

½" × ¼"
DADO

DRAWER Ⓒ

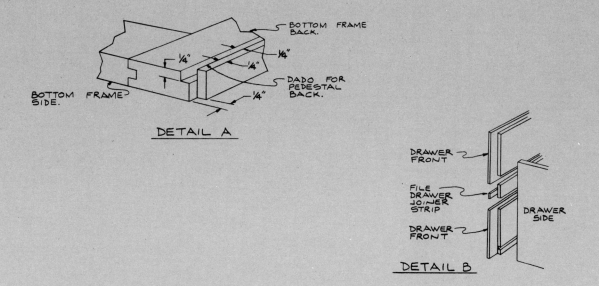

BOTTOM FRAME
BACK.

¼"

¼"

¼"

DADO FOR
PEDESTAL
BACK.

BOTTOM FRAME
SIDE.

¼"

DETAIL A

DRAWER
FRONT

FILE
DRAWER
JOINER
STRIP

DRAWER
FRONT

DRAWER
SIDE

DETAIL B

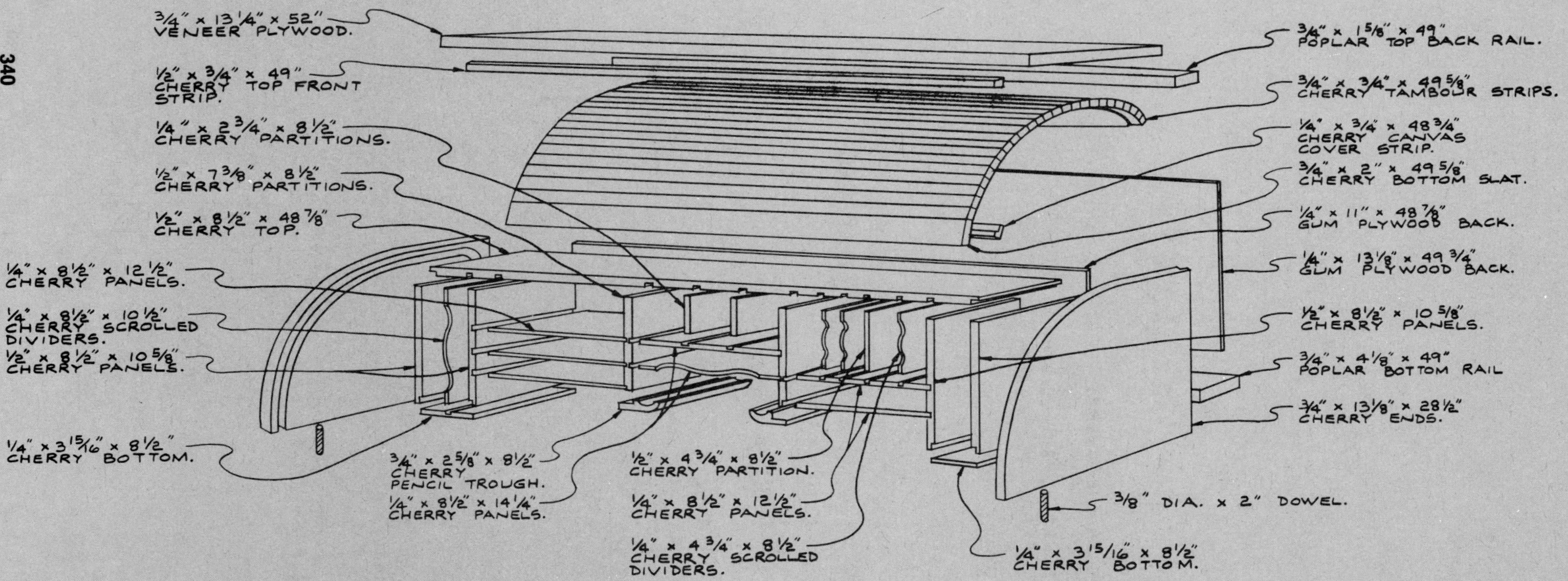
3/4" x 13 1/4" x 52" VENEER PLYWOOD.
1/2" x 3/4" x 49" CHERRY TOP FRONT STRIP.
1/4" x 2 3/4" x 8 1/2" CHERRY PARTITIONS.
1/2" x 7 3/8" x 8 1/2" CHERRY PARTITIONS.
1/2" x 8 1/2" x 48 7/8" CHERRY TOP.
1/4" x 8 1/2" x 12 1/2" CHERRY PANELS.
1/4" x 8 1/2" x 10 1/2" CHERRY SCROLLED DIVIDERS.
1/2" x 8 1/2" x 10 5/8" CHERRY PANELS.
1/4" x 3 15/16" x 8 1/2" CHERRY BOTTOM.
3/4" x 2 5/8" x 8 1/2" CHERRY PENCIL TROUGH.
1/4" x 8 1/2" x 14 1/4" CHERRY PANELS.
1/2" x 4 3/4" x 8 1/2" CHERRY PARTITION.
1/4" x 8 1/2" x 12 1/2" CHERRY PANELS.
1/4" x 4 3/4" x 8 1/2" CHERRY SCROLLED DIVIDERS.
1/4" x 3 15/16" x 8 1/2" CHERRY BOTTOM.
3/8" DIA. x 2" DOWEL.
3/4" x 13 7/8" x 28 1/2" CHERRY ENDS.
3/4" x 4 1/8" x 49" POPLAR BOTTOM RAIL
1/2" x 8 1/2" x 10 5/8" CHERRY PANELS.
1/4" x 13 1/8" x 49 3/4" GUM PLYWOOD BACK.
1/4" x 11" x 48 7/8" GUM PLYWOOD BACK.
3/4" x 2" x 49 5/8" CHERRY BOTTOM SLAT.
1/4" x 3/4" x 48 3/4" CHERRY CANVAS COVER STRIP.
3/4" x 3/4" x 49 5/8" CHERRY TAMBOUR STRIPS.
3/4" x 1 5/8" x 49" POPLAR TOP BACK RAIL.

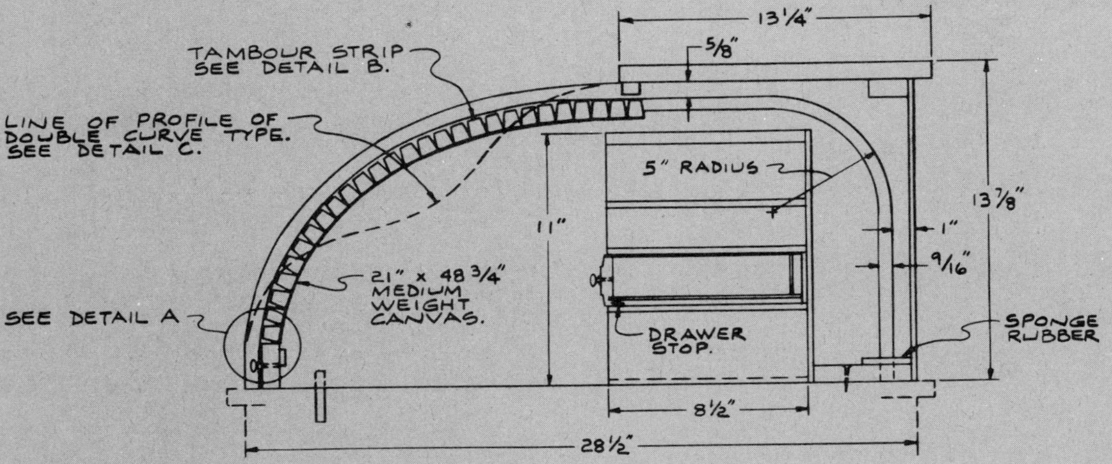
13 1/4"
5/8"
TAMBOUR STRIP SEE DETAIL B.
LINE OF PROFILE OF DOUBLE CURVE TYPE. SEE DETAIL C.
5" RADIUS
11"
13 7/8"
1"
9/16"
21" x 48 3/4" MEDIUM WEIGHT CANVAS.
SEE DETAIL A
DRAWER STOP.
SPONGE RUBBER
8 1/2"
28 1/2"

CROSS SECTION

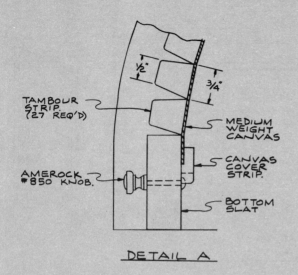

TAMBOUR
STRIP.
(27 REQ'D)

1/2"

3/4"

MEDIUM
WEIGHT
CANVAS

CANVAS
COVER
STRIP.

AMEROCK
#850 KNOB.

BOTTOM
SLAT

DETAIL A

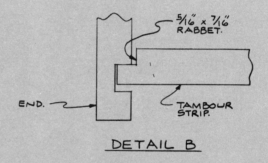

5/16" x 7/16"
RABBET.

END.

TAMBOUR
STRIP.

DETAIL B

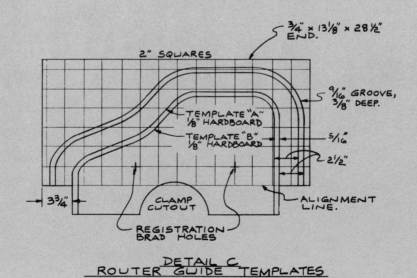

2" SQUARES

3/4" x 13 1/8" x 28 1/2"
END.

9/16" GROOVE,
3/8" DEEP.

TEMPLATE "A"
1/8" HARDBOARD

TEMPLATE "B"
1/8" HARDBOARD

5/16"

2 1/2"

3 3/4"

CLAMP
CUTOUT

ALIGNMENT
LINE.

REGISTRATION
BRAD HOLES

DETAIL C
ROUTER GUIDE TEMPLATES
SUITABLE FOR USE WITH 1/4" DIA. BIT
AND 5" DIA. ROUTER BASE.

PLANS CONTINUED NEXT PAGE

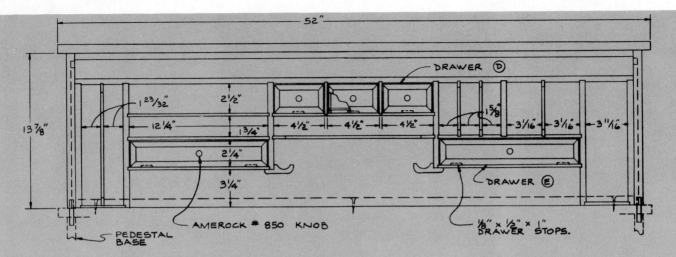

FRONT VIEW

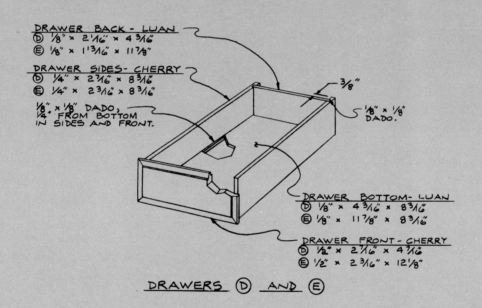

DRAWER BACK - LUAN
Ⓓ 1/8" × 2 1/16" × 4 3/16"
Ⓔ 1/8" × 1 13/16" × 11 7/8"

DRAWER SIDES- CHERRY
Ⓓ 1/4" × 2 7/16" × 8 3/16"
Ⓔ 1/4" × 2 3/16" × 8 3/16"

1/8" × 1/8" DADO,
1/4" FROM BOTTOM
IN SIDES AND FRONT.

3/8"

1/8" × 1/8"
DADO.

DRAWER BOTTOM- LUAN
Ⓓ 1/8" × 4 3/16" × 8 3/16"
Ⓔ 1/8" × 11 7/8" × 8 3/16"

DRAWER FRONT- CHERRY
Ⓓ 1/2" × 2 7/16" × 4 7/16"
Ⓔ 1/2" × 2 3/16" × 12 1/8"

DRAWERS Ⓓ AND Ⓔ

PART IV

JIGS, AIDS AND SPECIAL TECHNIQUES

48

Power-Saw
Helpers

PORTABLE CIRCULAR SAW

Plunge cuts

When plunge cuts are done freehand with a portable saw, the results are not especially precise. You can make accurate, controlled cuts with this saw in one of two ways, depending upon the type of base it has. If your saw has a wrap-around base, use a high straightedge guide such as a 2 × 4 on edge. Since the motor housing usually extends beyond the wide side of the base, you work with the unobstructed blade side of the base against the guide.

Clamp the guide in place. Tape or hook the blade guard out of the way. Place the saw into position with the front of the base firmly on the work, with the back of the base tilted so the blade is clear of the work surface. The side of the base should touch the guide evenly. Switch on the power and slowly lower the saw into the work, pivoting it on the front of the base. When the base is flush with the surface, push the saw forward to continue the cut. Switch off the power and wait until the blade stops before withdrawing the saw. Provided you start with the base firmly on the work surface and the side snug against the guide, your saw will enter the work perfectly in line.

If your saw's base extends from one side of the blade only, a different method is required. Here a low guide fence is clamped to the work, allowing clearance for the projecting motor. Again tape the blade guard out of the way. Adjust the saw for a zero depth of cut (fully retracted blade). Place the saw into position, hold it firmly with one hand on the grip and the other on the lock knob that adjusts the depth of cut. Switch on the power. Then loosen the lock knob slightly so the saw can be depressed into the work. When the blade has penetrated, tighten the lock knob and push the saw forward to continue the cut. Always be sure to reinstate the blade guard when the cutting has been completed.

Miter jig for portable saw

You will obtain excellent results in cutting 45-degree miters for frames or molding trim work with this handy jig. It is quite simple and is easy to construct but extra care must be taken to make sure that the channel sides are parallel, and spaced so the saw fits properly without side play. Drive nails only part way when installing the 45-degree fences. Make test

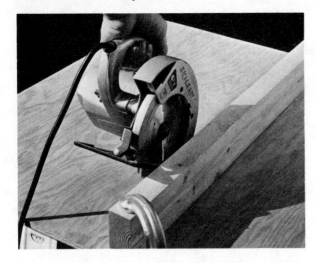

Using a high fence to guide the saw for a perfect entry into the work when making an internal cut. The blade guard is retracted for this operation so you must work with care.

The saw is advanced after the base has touched down. Note how the motor-housing projection necessitates working on the blade side of the base.

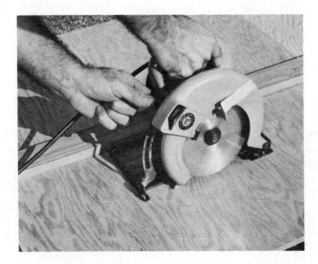

Shallow guide must be used with saw with non-wrap-around base. Power is switched on, then depth-of-cut adjustment nut is loosened and the blade is depressed into the work. Nut is tightened and the saw advanced after the blade has penetrated.

This jig lets you cut left and right 45-degree miters with consistent accuracy. A shallow kerf cut in the platform, near the side wall, guides the saw accurately.

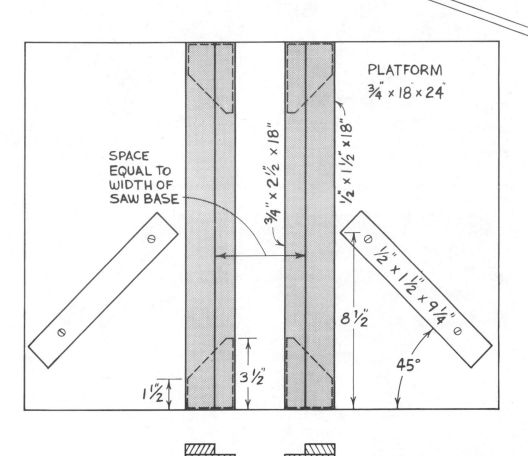

PLATFORM
$\frac{3}{4}$" × 18" × 24"

SPACE
EQUAL TO
WIDTH OF
SAW BASE

$\frac{3}{4}$" × $2\frac{1}{2}$" × 18"

$\frac{1}{2}$" × $1\frac{1}{2}$" × 18"

$\frac{1}{2}$" × $1\frac{1}{2}$" × $9\frac{1}{4}$"

$8\frac{1}{2}$"

45°

$3\frac{1}{2}$"

$1\frac{1}{2}$"

FRAME MITERING JIG FOR PORTABLE CIRCULAR SAW

cuts to be sure they are in perfect alignment; then glue and nail them in permanently.

Aligning tilted saw

Setting up a straightedge guide to do precision bevel cutting is extremely difficult because the tilted blade does not permit a positive reference point for measuring the offset to the edge of the saw base. When a job requires that the cut be made precisely on a marked line, here's how you can do it:

Tilt the saw to the required angle. Tack-nail a strip of wood to the edge of a scrap of wood to serve as a temporary fence. Make a rip cut so you come up with a beveled piece. Remove the strip. Now place the beveled scrap on the work and flip it over so the leading edge of the bevel is on the work surface. Align this edge to the line to be cut. Hold it in place and clamp the guide against the back edge. Make the cut, and it will be precisely on target.

Location of bevel cut can be pinpointed by first cutting a bevel in a scrap to which a temporary fence is nailed.

Flip the beveled scrap up-side-down and place the bottom edge precisely on the line which is to be cut. Move the guide strip into position against the back edge.

Nail in the guide strip, remove the scrap and make the cut. The bevel will coincide with the line. No other method is as accurate.

SABRE SAW

Ripping guide

Accessory ripping guides that come with portable circular and sabre saws have a tendency to allow the saw to wander in or out because their bearing surfaces are too small to keep the saw tracking parallel to the work edge. You can avoid the problem by attaching a long piece of wood to the guiding edge.

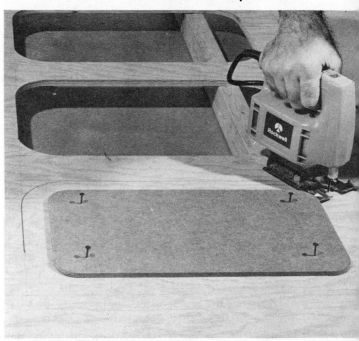

An arrow on the saw base, opposite the blade, is kept in constant contact with the template to achieve a perfectly true, controlled cut.

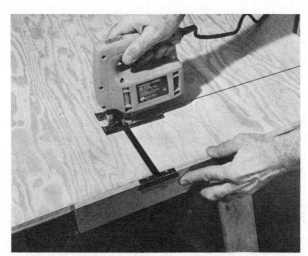

A strip of wood added to the sabre-saw ripping guide provides a greater bearing surface, prevents the saw from swinging off course.

Bore two holes in the top edge of the guide and attach a straight piece of wood about ½″ × 2″ × 12″. Center it on the guide and secure it with two round head screws. The added length will also insure the proper attitude of the saw at the start of the cut.

Pattern sawing

It is possible to make precisely guided irregular cuts with a sabre saw with the use of a template. Draw the desired pattern full size, then reduce it on all sides by an amount equal to the offset distance between the edge of the saw base and the blade. Trace the outline onto a piece of ⅛-inch or ¼-inch plywood or hardboard. Cut it out and smooth any irregularities.

Cut a triangular piece of masking tape and attach it to the top of the saw base so a point is at the edge and directly in line with the front edge of the blade. Attach the template to the work. Saw, keeping the arrow point continually in contact with the template edge.

Inside cutouts

When you want to make clean-edged inside cutouts with a sabre saw, be sure to make the blade entry and turning holes of large enough diameter so the blade can be started tangent to the hole. Otherwise you will have depressions in the edge which will require much work to level off.

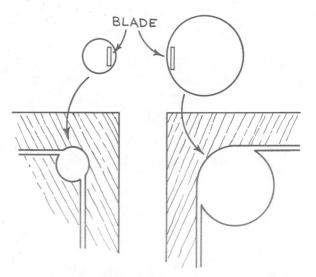

How the size of the sabre-saw blade-entry hole affects the internal cut.

Sabre-sawing joints

If you consider the alternatives, you'll agree that the sabre saw is the most practical and efficient tool among all the others for cutting large edge cross-laps and mortises in bulky workpieces. These cuts, common in trestle tables as well as many other pieces, are easily accomplished with this saw. In the example shown the workpiece is 1½-inch plywood (two pieces glued together). Uniformity and accuracy are achieved with the aid of a simple jig: a piece of ¼-inch plywood cut in the form of a U. The width of the slot in the jig is critical. You can determine this by measuring but you'll do better by making and using a pair of measuring blocks. Make them by cutting into a scrap of wood with the saw base edged against a temporary fence. Cut one from each side of the blade. The reason for this is that sabre-saw blades are never in the dead center of the base.

To lay out the width of the slot in the jig, first lay out the notch in the work that you want to cut. Position the blocks precisely on the outside of the lines; then measure the distance between the *outside* edges of the blocks. This will be the width of the cutout in the jig.

To simplify alignment, draw a center line on the jig and also measure the distance from the front of the saw base to the front of the blade and draw a corresponding line across the jig, set back this amount from the end of the slot. This will indicate how far in to set the jig from the edge of the workpiece. Clamp the jig into place on the work. If you clamp a strip of wood across the bottom of the overhanging ends of the jig it will support the base of the saw during the start of the cut.

Make two parallel cuts, guiding the saw alternately against each side of the jig slot. Remove the jig and cut across the end of the parallel cuts to drop out the waste.

The same jig is used to cut a through mortise. For this it will be necessary to bore blade entry holes (you can bore only one if you have a bit with a diameter equal to the width of the mortise). Clamp the jig into place and tack-nail it to the work in a few places.

Remove the jig temporarily while the waste is cut away, then reinstate it (using the nail holes). Slide-saw the forward end of the mortise square. To square and trim the back end where the holes were bored, it is necessary to reverse the saw blade so the teeth face backwards. This is because, as stated earlier, the blade is not centered in relation to the saw base. Thus it is not possible simply to turn the saw around and saw in the opposite direction; the blade would not line up with the original cuts. By reversing the blade and pushing the saw backwards, the relationship of base to jig is maintained.

Clamp a piece of wood in place for a backstop when making the cuts to square the end.

As you can see, the procedure is not really difficult and with it you will be able to turn out notches and mortises of excellent quality with minimal effort. Note that it is best to use a set-tooth blade when sawing thick stock, and feed the saw slowly.

Cut measuring blocks.

Method for dimensioning width of slot in jig.

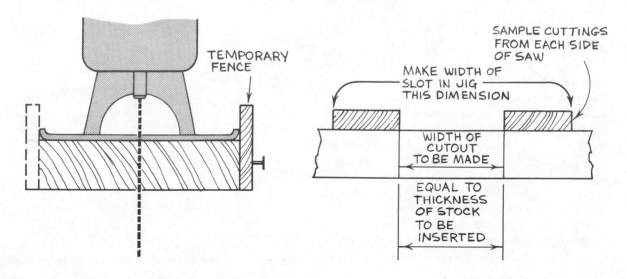

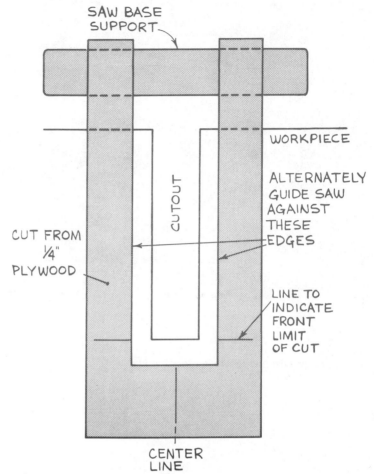

Jig for cutting slots with sabre saw.

SAW BASE SUPPORT

WORKPIECE

CUTOUT

ALTERNATELY GUIDE SAW AGAINST THESE EDGES

CUT FROM ¼" PLYWOOD

LINE TO INDICATE FRONT LIMIT OF CUT

CENTER LINE

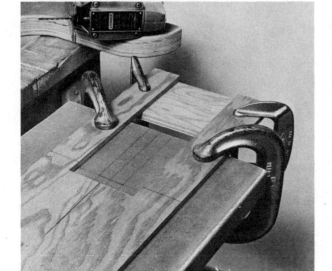

Align the jig on the work and clamp it in place. Saw support is clamped to overhanging ends.

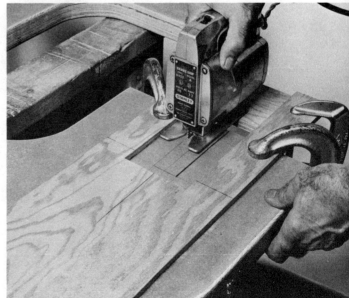

Make two parallel cuts, alternately guiding the saw against each edge of the jig.

Remove the jig and make a freehand cut across the end to drop out the waste.

Bore two blade-entry holes and secure the jig in this manner to cut the through-mortise.

After the two parallel cuts are made, the rounded corners must be squared.

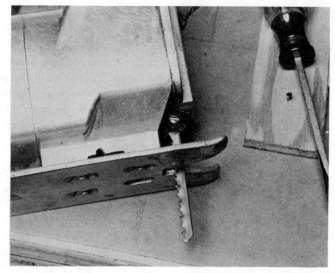

First, reverse the blade so the teeth point backward.

Push saw backwards in each kerf to square-cut the round corners. Remove jig and make two freehand cuts to drop out the waste. Then replace the jig and move saw sideways to true the ends.

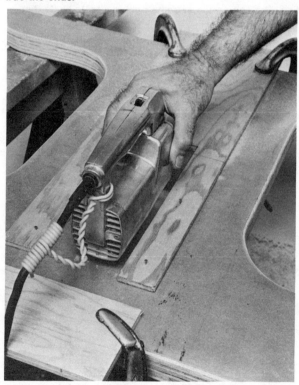

Completed cuts are quite precise. No other shop tool could do the job as well as the sabre saw.

Cutting circles

The sabre saw excels in cutting circles with speed and accuracy. Leashed to a pivot, the narrow blade can be made to travel a perfect circle—provided you set it up properly. The important factor is blade and pivot alignment. In order for the blade to track true so it ends the cut exactly where it started, the pivot point must be in exact lateral alignment with the front edge of the teeth.

Some accessory pivot guides for sabre saws have fixed pivots while others have adjustable pivots. The latter type is better because it permits making allowances for blade width variations. The pivot support bar is the reference for measuring the alignment of blade and pivot. If there is misalignment, the cut will spiral in or out, depending upon whether the blade is forward of the pivot point or behind. If you have a fixed guide and experience difficulty in obtaining a true circle, it will be necessary to select a blade that is compatible.

To make a circular cut, bore a blade entry hole on the waste side of the line to be cut. The hole must be of large enough diameter to allow the blade to start off tangent to it. If the nature of the work permits, you can bore the hole centered over the line.

The feed rate is important in cutting circles. In general you will have no difficulty when using a set-tooth blade, but if you force feed a smooth-cutting tapered or hollow-ground blade it frequently will drift off the vertical plane, resulting in a lop-sided edge. This is particularly true when cutting thick hardwood stock.

Most circle guides have the capability to cut diameters up to about 24 inches. If you require a greater diameter you can make your own guide. Use mild steel stock of a width equal to that of the original guide bar; thickness need not match exactly. Fold and hammer one end over to form a right angle. Drill a hole and use a nail for a pivot.

A variety of sabre-saw blades. Three on the left are for metal cutting. The one on the extreme right is a knife blade that can be used to cut cardboard, cloth or leather.

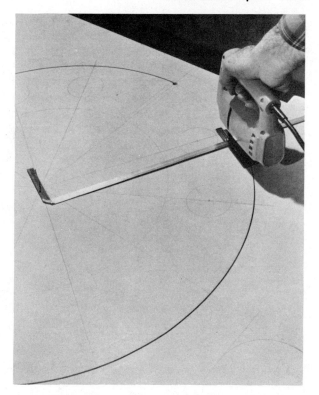

Making a large circular cut with a homemade pivot guide.

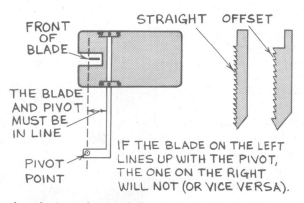

In order to track properly for circular cutting, the blade teeth and pivot point must be in alignment.

This is what happens when the blade and pivot point are out of alignment—a spiral cut results.

TABLE AND RADIAL-ARM SAWS

Checking saw for square

Any power saw that has tilting-blade capability presents the problem of possibly being slightly out of true even if the indicator reads zero, the setting for a right-angle cut. You can check this with a simple test. Cut through a scrap of wood so you come up with two pieces. Place them on a perfectly flat sur-

To make bevel cut on table saw, cutting mark on work is aligned with bevel in scrap which is positioned against the blade. The fence is then moved to meet the workpiece.

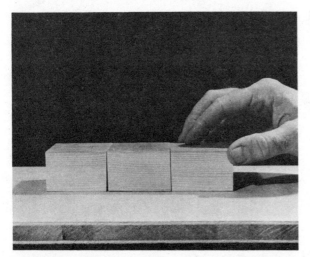

To check any saw's zero setting, make a cut and flip over one piece front-to-back. If the blade is not true a wedge space will show as at left. Second cut, right, indicates a perfect right-angle setting.

Dressing an edge

Hardwood is frequently sold with rough edges, or the edges may be dressed but crooked. The latter also applies to softwood. In any case, if the edge is irregular, a straight rip cut cannot be made. A simple solution is to tack-nail a straight strip of wood to the

face, then flip one piece upside-down, front to back. Press the cut surfaces together and observe the joint line. A good, snug fit indicates the saw is adjusted true. A tapered space at the top or bottom proves a left or right tilt, thus requiring an adjustment.

Adjusting fence for bevel cut

Adjusting the fence of a table saw for making a bevel cut precisely on a predetermined line presents a problem, due to the difficulty of making a positive measurement from blade to fence. Eye alignment by sighting along the blade edge is the usual approach, but for exacting work there is a better way.

Cut the bevel in a scrap of wood which is a few inches longer than the diameter of the saw blade. Position this strip against the tilted saw blade so it rests against the teeth at both ends. Line up the workpiece so the marked angle on its front edge coincides with the beveled edge of the scrap which represents the line of cut. Slide the rip fence against the work and lock it.

Straightedged strip is tacked over a crooked edge to make a straight rip cut.

surface of the board, allowing it to overhang the edge slightly so it will ride against the fence. Then you have a straight edge for ripping the board.

Cutting deep bevels safely

Cutting a deep bevel on the face of relatively narrow stock could be dangerous and erratic. The high blade leaves little gripping space on the wood, and as the cut progresses, the base of the stock becomes thinner and prone to tipping.

If you are making more than one identical piece, back both against the rip fence and bridge them with a piece of wood temporarily nailed. This will allow a safe and accurate feed. The assembly is simply rotated to cut the second bevel. If making only one beveled piece, use the same arrangement nevertheless.

Here's how to handle pieces that are too small to guide safely with the miter gage.

Use this simple procedure to make deep bevel cuts safely.

Cutting angles in wide boards

When an edge overhangs the front of the saw table, start the cut with the miter gage in the reverse position against the back edge of the work. When the cut has progressed sufficiently, stop the saw and move

the gage to its normal position; then continue the cut.

Another way to handle angle cuts in very large boards is with a nailed-on strip. Cut a piece of wood dimensioned to fit the saw's miter-gage slot. Nail it to the bottom of the work, angled as required. This method is also useful for truing an edge of a large board that has no straight edge.

Sawing a chest lid

The best way to construct a chest with a perfectly fitting deep lid is to make it in one piece, then cut the lid apart on the table saw. Besides obtaining a good fit, the grain pattern of the sides will match, since they are cut from the same piece of wood.

There is a definite procedure to follow to insure good results in cutting. Adjust the fence so the

A strip that fits the table slot is tacked to the underside of the work to guide large pieces for angled cuts.

Before making the final cut, insert shims in the upper kerf and tape them firmly to both sections.

Circular cuts with table saw

It may seem impossible, but you can make perfect circular cuts on the table saw. A special accessory called Circ-L-Cut ⓉⓂ makes it possible. It is a rather simple device consisting of a clamp which seats in the saw's miter-gage groove, an adjustable track and a sliding pivot.

The clamp is secured in the groove directly opposite the blade center. The track is attached to the clamp; its T shape supports the work in an even plane. The pivot is positioned at any point along the track for the desired radius of the circle to be cut.

The saw blade is retracted below the table surface. A hole is drilled in the center of the stock, which is then placed over the pivot. The power is turned on and the blade is slowly elevated until it penetrates about $\frac{1}{16}$ inch into the underside of the work. The work is then slowly rotated about the pivot to make a full 360-degree circuit. The blade is then elevated another $\frac{1}{16}$ inch or so and another pass is made. This operation is repeated until the saw cuts through the top. The result is a perfectly circular cut with a square edge. The edge of the cut-off waste will have a concave shape.

The accessory has a circle-cutting capacity from 3 to 48 inches. A special knob is used to rotate small-diameter work to keep the fingers safely away from the blade. When working on very large diameters, it is advisable to tape $\frac{1}{4}$-inch blocks near the outer corners of the table to keep the work from tipping.

greater part of the chest will be between it and the blade. Cut through the shorter ends first, then one long side. Before making the final pass on the fourth side, insert cardboard spacers into the upper saw kerf, of a thickness equal to the space. Apply masking tape to secure the spacers and also over a bit of the kerf. If you don't take this precaution, the lid may tilt or drift sideways as the cut nears completion, scraping against the blade and marring the edge.

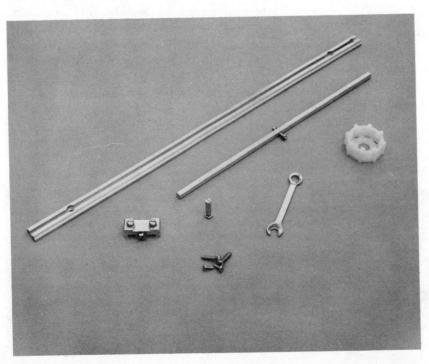

Circle-cutting jig for a circular saw.

Pivot track is held by a clamp that seats in the table-saw groove. The pivot slides in the track and is locked at any desired position with a screwdriver.

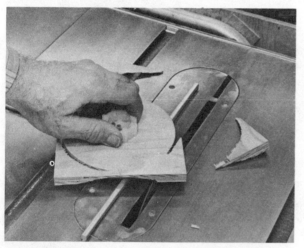

Gripping knob is used to permit safe handling of small work. Blade is elevated about 1/16 inch after each full rotation.

The completed cut. Edge is perfectly true and smooth.

Partially cut disc shows concave shape in waste area.

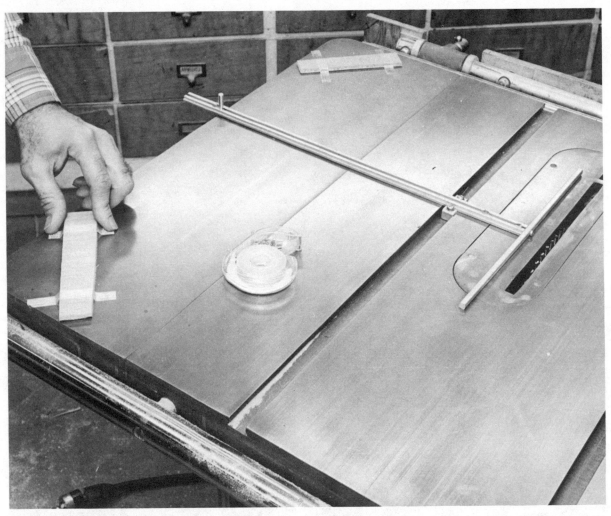

Wood standoff strips are taped near the corners of the saw table to help keep a large workpiece from tipping.

Making the final rotation to cut through the stock.

A perfect 36-inch-diameter disc is easily cut with the device. As the pivot can be positioned remotely, there is no limit to the size of the disc that can be cut.

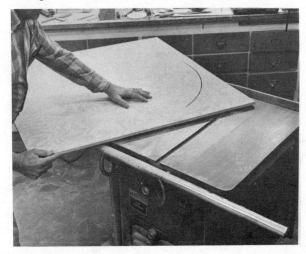

Setting miter angle

The miter scale on a radial-arm saw is accurate, but sometimes the eye is not capable of making a fine adjustment with accuracy by sighting on the relatively small graduations. You can make a fine adjustment by aligning the blade directly to the work. Draw the required angle on the work (in this illustration a pattern is taped to the work). Hold a rule against two teeth of the blade; then swing the arm of the saw until the rule lines up with the angle on the work.

Ripping support

A dowel inserted between two blocks which are clamped to a saw horse will support long boards as they emerge from the saw. If you make the dowel slightly loose-fitting and wax the ends it will rotate freely as the stock moves past.

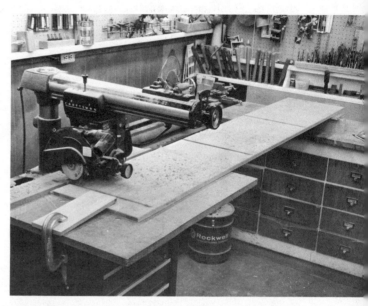

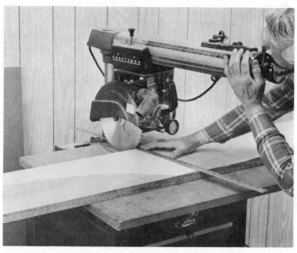

Adjusting the saw for a miter angle with a steel rule as a guide assures pinpoint accuracy.

Support the work. Large workpieces that overhang the radial-arm saw table should always be supported, particularly when cutting dadoes. If unsupported, the work could lift up, the blade cutting a groove that is too deep. Note how a board is used to clamp the work to the table.

Deep crosscut

Cutting through a piece of 4×4 stock with a 10-inch radial-arm saw requires two passes, one from each side. If the piece extends beyond the saw table, clamp an L-shaped stop to the table as shown. This will assure perfect alignment for the second cut.

Make this simple device to support long workpieces when ripping on the table saw.

The setup for making a deep crosscut in two passes.

Tenoning jig

If you don't own a regular tenoning jig, you can easily make your own. You should never attempt to cut a tenon freehand by feeding the work on end along the rip fence. This is dangerous. This jig can be made with a few scraps and will work as well as a commercial one. If you use screws to attach the stop block, you can vary its position to a 45-degree angle to permit cutting mitered tenons.

Using a homemade tenoning jig.

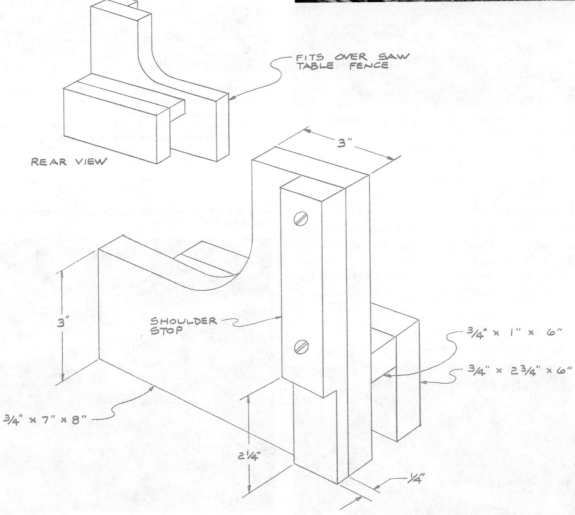

FITS OVER SAW TABLE FENCE

REAR VIEW

3"

SHOULDER STOP

3"

3/4" x 1" x 6"

3/4" x 2 3/4" x 6"

3/4" x 7" x 8"

2 1/4"

1/4"

Feather board

A feather board is useful for applying side pressure to the stock during ripping or shaping operations. The close slots render the fingers springy. Make it by cutting a series of slots about $\frac{3}{16}$ inch apart in the end of a $\frac{3}{4}$-inch-thick board. In use it is important to position it so the pressure bears just ahead of the blade, never against the side of it, otherwise binding and kickback may occur.

To avoid injury, use a feather board and push stick when ripping narrow stock.

This adjustable taper jig will simplify the cutting of tapers. Stop block at the end grips the work, which moves along with the jig past the blade.

Plan for taper jig.

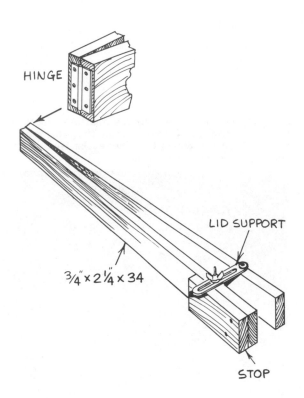

HINGE

LID SUPPORT

$\frac{3}{4}$" × 2$\frac{1}{4}$" × 34

STOP

When you want to cut a number of triangles or pieces with equal angles on both sides,   use the first cut piece as a stop block. Clamp it to the table so it just clears the blade. Alternately flip the work to obtain identical pieces.

Board on left was cut with a hollow-ground planer blade; the one on the right with a rip blade. It should be noted that the excessive roughness is due in part to unevenly set teeth.

Several types of circular-saw blades, from top: crosscut, rip, hollow-ground planer and combination. The planer is a combination blade but differs from the regular type in that it makes an extremely smooth cut.

49

Router Aids

The router is a versatile and practically indispensible tool in any home workshop. Basically a portable shaper, it is used to cut decorative edges and surfaces, to form depressions and to make numerous types of joints.

The variety of cutting bits available is quite large but you can meet the needs for most woodworking projects with a selection among the most commonly used shapes that are shown.

A variety of cuts can be made by running several different cutters over the same edge. Or a single cutter can frequently be adjusted with differing projections to produce several varied patterns.

Router edge guides. An edge guide is available as an accessory with most makes of routers. This is simply a fence that attaches to the base to guide the router in a cut parallel to the work edge. Some types include a trammel point to permit circular routing and edge shaping. Two rods secured to the base hold the fence in position. The rods are relatively short, generally about 10 or 12 inches in length. Therefore the distance from the work edge to the bit is limited. The use of longer substitute rods is not recommended because a pivoting action could occur, caus-

ing the router to swing off course and spoiling the work. As a matter of fact, any surface routing more than a few inches or so from the edge presents this possibility, so be very careful when using this device.

A straightedged strip or board clamped to the

work surface provides the safest and most positive method for guiding the router, without piloted bit, along an edge or on the surface of the work. This is the method most widely used for cutting wide rabbets for lap joints and for forming dado grooves.

Templates. There are two methods of guiding the router against a template to cut irregular shapes: either with the use of a template bushing or by direct contact of the outer edge of the router base with the template.

The template bushing is required when the pattern is intricate and contains small radii. It is locked into the sub-base of the router and projects around the bit just below the base. It is essentially a pilot that rides against the template. Various templates are available as accessories such as the dovetail fixture shown in the chapter on joints, or you can make your own. The bushings are available in several sizes to match specific router-bit diameters relative to the readymade template requirements.

To make a template for edge contact, you must first draw a full-size pattern of the desired shape, which is then modified to allow for the offset distance from the bit to the base edge. This is easily accomplished with a compass in this manner: Measure the offset and adjust the compass to that dimension. Place the compass point on the outline and

ROUTER BITS

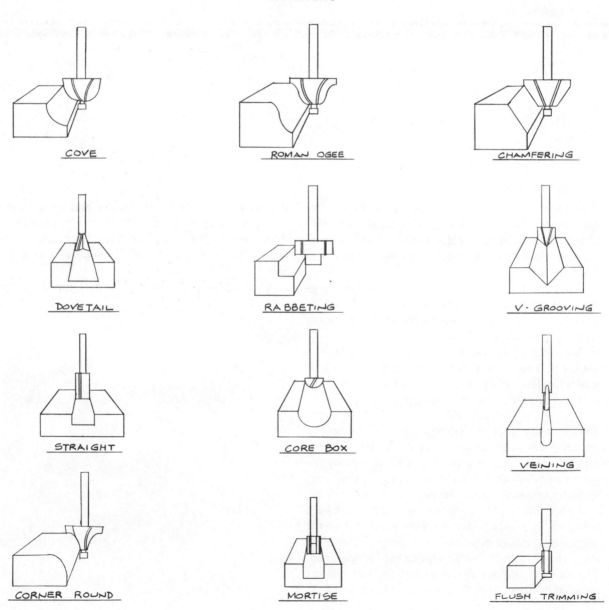

COVE

ROMAN OGEE

CHAMFERING

DOVETAIL

RABBETING

V-GROOVING

STRAIGHT

CORE BOX

VEINING

CORNER ROUND

MORTISE

FLUSH TRIMMING

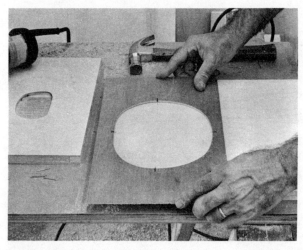

Positioning a custom-made template to rout a recess for a chest handle.

The router base rides against the template edge to duplicate the contour in reduced size.

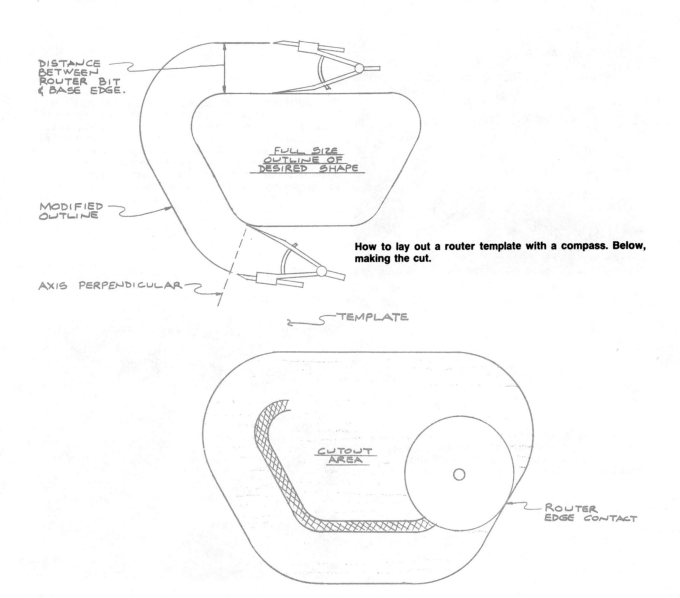

DISTANCE BETWEEN ROUTER BIT & BASE EDGE.

FULL SIZE OUTLINE OF DESIRED SHAPE

MODIFIED OUTLINE

AXIS PERPENDICULAR

How to lay out a router template with a compass. Below, making the cut.

TEMPLATE

CUTOUT AREA

ROUTER EDGE CONTACT

trace completely around it, allowing the pencil to draw a parallel line. It is important to keep the compass point/pencil axis always perpendicular to the outline. Transfer the revised outline to a piece of ¼-inch hardboard or plywood and cut it out with a saw. Sand it smooth and tack-nail or clamp it to the work. Note that this method is practical for patterns with sweeping curves and with radii equal to, or larger than, the radius of the router base when guiding against an inside curve.

Router dado guide
Straight or mortising router cutters capable of making a ¾-inch-wide dado groove in one pass, as well as a router powerful enough to drive such a cutter, are rare in the home workshop. Consequently, when

it is necessary to cut the common ¾-inch and $^{13}/_{16}$-inch dadoes, the usual practice is to make one pass against a straightedge guide. The guide is then shifted to a second position for an additional pass to widen the cut. You can save time in setting up for dadoes by making and using one of the guides shown.

Rolltop grooving
Routing the grooves for a rolltop desk tambour is easily done with a shaped template. A problem frequently arises, however, when the available bit is too small to permit routing a groove of sufficient width in one pass. The solution is to make two passes, using two templates; one dimensioned for the first cut, and one for the second. Proper align-

This router guide can be adjusted for bits of varying diameters. The four strips of wood are joined with bolts and wing nuts. To determine the space between the parallel strips you simply add the width of the desired dado to the diameter of the router base, then subtract the diameter of the cutter in use. Check to make sure the strips are parallel and clamp the jig on each side. The router is then guided against each side to produce a groove of the desired width.

You can make a fixed guide for a specific bit. Nail two long boards to two short ones, spaced according to the method described for the adjustable guide. Partial cuts in the end boards are used to align the jig with guidelines on the work.

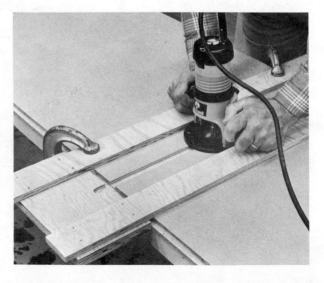

ment of the templates is essential for this operation.

You will be assured of accuracy in alternately positioning the templates on the work by making registration holes. To do this place one template atop the other, then position them and drive a few nails through them and partly into the work. Remove them and use the nail holes to align each template for the separate passes.

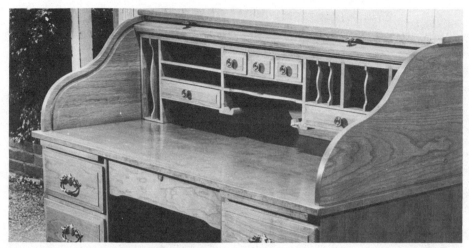

The router is the only home-workshop tool capable of cutting the contoured groove for a roll-top desk tambour.

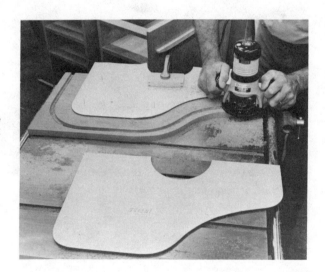

A pair of matched templates is used to cut the wide groove in two passes. Nail holes in both templates and the work assure exact alignment.

When the router is used with a template guide, it is essential that the base is absolutely centered in relation to the cutter. You cannot take it for granted that the base is centered; as the connecting screw holes are slightly oversize, the base can go out of adjustment. Centering rule shows this router's base to be almost 3/32 inch off center.

Closeup shows what happens to a groove which was made with the off-center router guided by a template. The belly was caused by the tool being rotated during a pass, allowing a different section of the base to come into contact with the template. It is advisable to check for this problem occasionally, especially before doing important work.

Mortising a butler table hinge

Mortises for round ended butler table hinges must be cut to perfection since they are so prominently featured in the table top. The only practical way to make the recesses for the hinges is with a router and a homemade template. The template is made by tracing around the hinge with a compass.

Hinges are an important feature of this table.

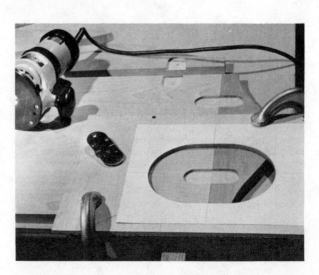

Template is made as described earlier, tracing around the hinge with a compass. It is centered over the tabletop and leaf so both are cut at the same time.

A straight or mortising bit can be used for this operation. Make the perimeter cut first, then rout in between to clear out the waste.

Hinge with adjustable tension feature has a double thickness on one leaf. To simplify matters, the mortise is cut to the depth of the thicker portion and a thin plywood shim inserted in one of the recesses.

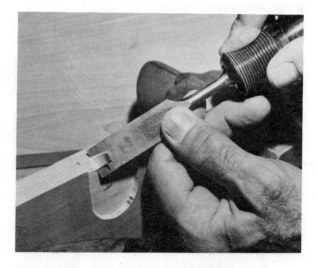

Some handwork cannot be avoided. The chisel is used to cut a clearance bevel for the hinge knuckle. The bevel is down for this cut.

Lettering template

Lettering template kit including two sizes of letters, a template holder and two matching bushing inserts makes easy work of routing letters and numerals. This one is available from Sears Roebuck.

Holder has built-in clamps, is shifted to new positions and locked into place to rout each figure.

Router is simply moved about to follow the template. It is not removed from the work until the bit stops turning.

Auxiliary shaper

There is a way you can enjoy the advantages of a stationary shaper at relatively low cost—convert your router to a shaper by mounting it to the underside of an accessory table.

This accessory table will accept either a router or sabre saw. Two adjustable fences guide the work. Table permits you to perform many operations without special guides or setups.

Router is easily attached to the table with several screws. It is readily accessible for vertical adjustment of the cutter projection.

Fences are removed to shape irregular edges with a piloted bit. Safety guard flexes vertically to accommodate work of varying thickness.

Fences permit shaping an entire edge. Forward fence is off-set to meet the new edge for this operation.

Ends of rounded stock can be shaped by rotating the piece against the miter gage, which is held in a fixed position.

Blade guard is retracted to permit surface shaping. Workpieces of unlimited size can be handled comfortably if the tabletop is set into an opening in a large workbench.

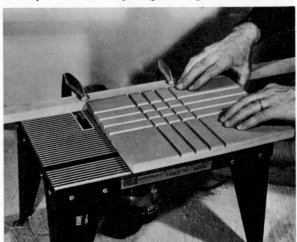

50

Hole-Making Techniques

Practically any woodworking project will require the boring of holes. Usually they will have to be made with precision—the nature of the job dictating the degree of accuracy required. When a hole is part of the design or if it simply will be visible in the finished product, the smoothness of the wall and edges are of major importance. How well you succeed in making holes will depend upon the tools at your disposal and the way you use them.

Boring holes for a blind dowel joint requires a high degree of precision in order to obtain holes that are perfectly perpendicular and identically located in the mating pieces. A lesser degree of accuracy can be tolerated in boring through dowel holes whereby they are made from the outside of the first piece and continued into the second. They must be in alignment, of course, but they can be slightly off the perpendicular. All screw holes are made in this manner.

The drill press is the ideal machine for precision boring but you can do quite well with a portable electric drill with the aid of several accessories that are available including a doweling jig, a drill guide such as the Portalign® or by converting it into a miniature drill press by attaching it to a table drill stand.

BIT SELECTION

There are many kinds of bits and cutters available for boring holes in wood. The ones most commonly used are the twist drill, machine spur bit, single spur, spade, masonry, countersink, combination bit, hole saw and circle cutter. A plug cutter is not used for making holes but is nevertheless a form of drill bit.

Twist drills for metal are frequently used for boring holes in wood but those made specifically for wood, having an included point angle of 60 to 80 degrees, work more efficiently and produce smoother holes. Some drill bits have reduced shanks to permit drilling holes larger than a drill's normal capacity. Fractional-size twist drills commonly used for woodworking are available in diameters from $\frac{1}{16}$ inch to $\frac{1}{2}$ inch in $\frac{1}{64}$-inch increments.

Brad-point machine spur bits are preferred for precision boring in wood. They cut fast and clean. The sharp brad point makes alignment on the work's center mark easy and accurate. Sizes range from $\frac{3}{16}$ inch up to $1\frac{1}{4}$ inches in $\frac{1}{32}$-inch increments; shanks are $\frac{1}{2}$ inch in diameter.

The spade bit, also called speed and flat bit, can handle almost any routine boring job. It cuts fast and clean and expels shavings readily. Its depth capacity can be increased considerably with the use of an

375

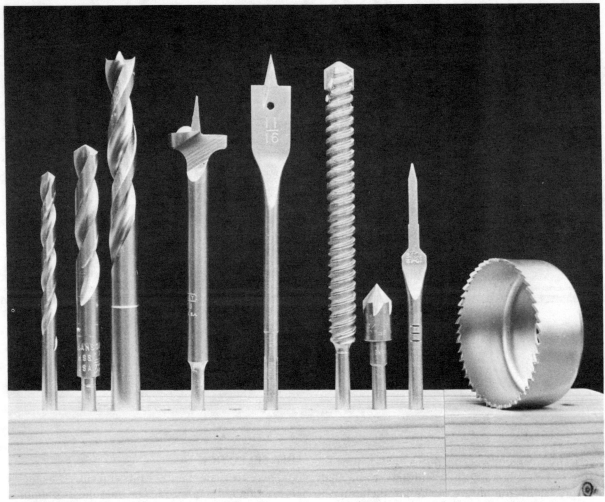

Some of the common boring tools, from left to right: twist drill, reduced-shank twist, brad point, single spur, speed bore, masonry, countersink, combination, hole saw.

extension. Due to the plain cutting edges, sharpening is readily accomplished with straight-line filing.

The countersink forms a beveled hole to allow a flathead screw to be driven flush with the surface or slightly below. Two holes must be bored for installing a regular wood screw, the shank clearance hole and the pilot or lead hole for the threaded section. If the screw has a flat head, a countersink hole will also be necessary to set the screw flush with the surface. To set the screw farther below the surface, to permit it to be concealed with a wood plug, a counterbore hole is required. The Screw-Sink ⓉⓂ is a combination bit that will perform all these steps in one operation. The Screw-Mate ® will do the first three in one operation. These bits, made by Stanley, can be purchased individually or in sets. They are identified by screw length and gage number. A set of

these bits in the most commonly used screw sizes can save lots of time in drilling screw holes.

Large holes from 1 inch to 2½ inches in diameter can be cut with the hole saw. It cuts a rotary kerf on the perimeter only so it is useful for through-holes only. Sizes increase by ¼-inch increments. Very large holes up to 8 inches in diameter are made with a circle cutter. It has a single stout blade that is secured to an adjustable cross arm. Like the hole saw, it can cut only through-holes because the waste remains intact until the blade cuts through the bottom surface. *This tool is designed for use in a drill press only and should never be used with a portable drill of any kind.* Any attempt to do so will surely result in a broken wrist or much worse. The single cutter exerts a powerful side thrust; therefore the work must always be clamped to the drill-press table. When it is necessary to bore large blind holes up to 3 inches in diameter, an adjustable expansive bit is used. Two types are made: screw point and brad point. The screw point is for use with a hand brace and should never be used with a power drill. The brad point is used exclusively with power equipment.

The plug cutter is used to make short plugs or dowels used for concealing screws in counterbored holes. It is available in sizes from ⅜ inch to 1 inch in 1/16-inch increments.

Drilling speeds for wood range between 600 to 3000 rpm. The choice depends upon the diameter and depth of the hole and the hardness of the wood. In general, you should run bits up to ¾ inch diameter between 1800 and 3000 rpm; those over ¾ inch diameter at 600 to 1300 rpm. Expansive bits, hole saws, and circle cutters will overheat, lose their tem-per, and burn the wood at speeds greater than 600 rpm.

BORING HOLES

Start by accurately laying out the hole center and use an awl to indent it. Always use a scrap of wood below the work to prevent splintering on the underside when boring through holes. Maintain a steady, even pressure, allowing the bit to cut without forcing, and slack off the pressure as the bit approaches the breakthrough point. If the hole is deep, retract the bit frequently to clear out wood chips and prevent jamming and overheating.

Whenever a hole is to be counterbored, the larger hole should be bored first. If the smaller hole is made first it will remove the center, thus making it difficult to center the larger bit.

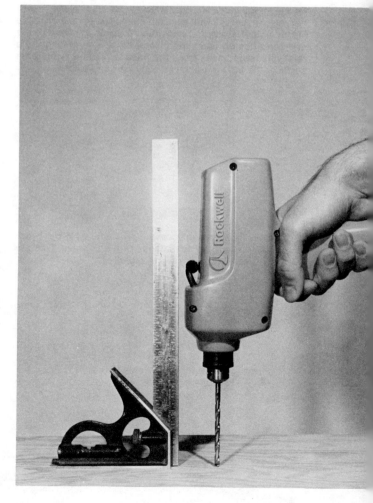

Boring straight. When more sophisticated guiding devices are not available, this method of visual alignment will offer some degree of accuracy for jobs with tolerance.

Portalign drill guide will enable you to bore holes with a high degree of accuracy with a portable drill. The concept is quite simple and effective: A removable trolley is attached to the drill and rides on two upright rods which are attached to a relatively large base. When the base is planted firmly on a surface, the bit will track perfectly perpendicular.

Rods project below the base to center unit. When rods are pressed against the sides of the stock, as shown here, the hole will automatically be centered on the edge.

A relatively inexpensive accessory drill stand for the portable drill gives you the advantages of a drill press. This unit features a small auxiliary tilting table.

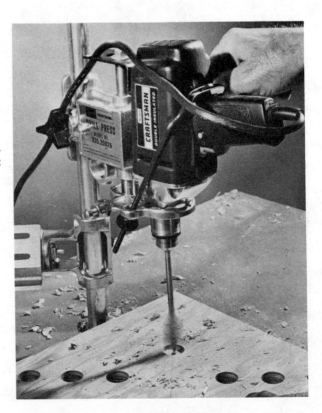

Through doweling is easy and accurate even if the holes are drilled not precisely perpendicular. Actually, a stronger joint will result if the dowels are canted slightly, as this would have a locking effect.

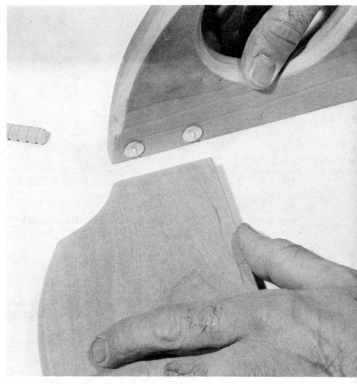

Locating dowel holes. Dowel centers provide an accurate method for marking matching holes for a dowel joint. Drill the holes in one of the pieces and insert the centers; then bring the two members together in alignment. The second set of holes is drilled in the marks made by the center points.

Doweling jig makes it possible to bore holes accurately. It can be finely adjusted for precise edgewise spacing, but the lengthwise location is not automatic; it must be set visually.

Any construction, large or small, should be assembled with clamps and adjusted for squareness before drilling holes for screws. Freehand drilling usually will do, but if the screw heads will be exposed in the finished project, use some form of drill guide.

A drill-bit extension is useful for boring deep holes with spade bits of any diameter greater than the diameter of the connecting bushing.

This heavy-duty circle cutter is capable of making holes 8 inches in diameter in stock up to ⅞ inch thick, or 1¾ inch thick by drilling through both sides. If the pilot drill doesn't penetrate extra-thick stock, you simply bore completely through with a ¼-inch bit to provide a centering hole on the second surface.

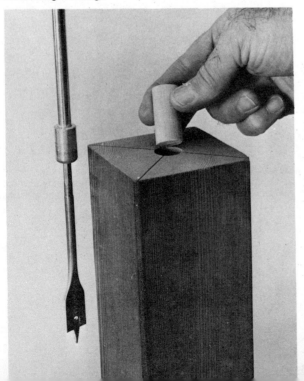

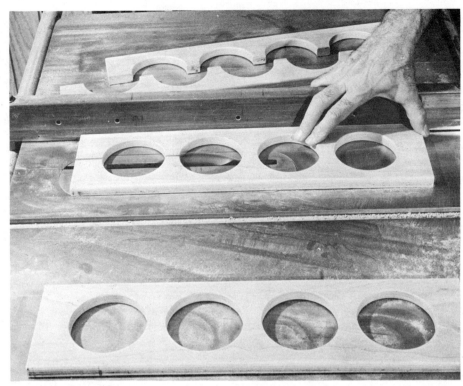

Much painstaking sawing work can be avoided in cutting scallops if you cut the stock to the required width, bore a series of holes, and cut down the middle.

This is another example of how you can use a drill to obtain clean, curved sections with minimal sawing. Bore holes of the appropriate diameter in the key locations, using an adjustable cutter.

A few severing cuts quickly complete the task.

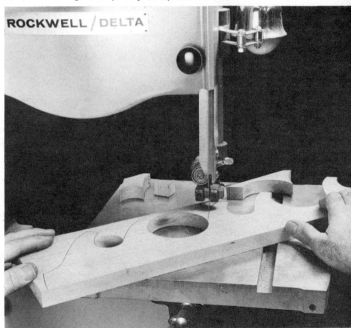

Plugs are normally cut with a plug cutter chucked in a drill press. They are cut to the required length, then pried out with a screw driver.

While the plug cutter is designed for use in a drill press, it can be used with a portable drill. To prevent the cutter from skipping about on the surface, first drill a slight depression in the surface of the stock with a countersink.

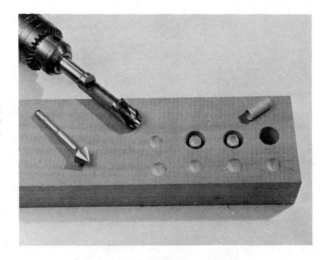

The spur bit bores clean and fast. Note how it can be used to cut partially off the edge. A backup pad must always be used to prevent splintering the back surface.

Blind holes with a hole saw. The hole saw cannot be used to bore blind holes because it cuts only a circular kerf. But the task can be accomplished with relative ease by teaming up the saw and router.

After the circular kerf is cut to the required depth, a router with a mortising bit is used freehand to rout out the stock up to the kerf line.

Supporting work in drill press. There are a number of ways to support work for other than flat-on boring. If the table is tiltable, a clamped block will hold the work for boring into a corner. This method can be used for round stock as well.

A tilting drill-press vise is a useful accessory for quickly setting up small workpieces at any angle.

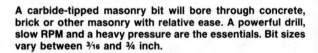

A carbide-tipped masonry bit will bore through concrete, brick or other masonry with relative ease. A powerful drill, slow RPM and a heavy pressure are the essentials. Bit sizes vary between 3/16 and 3/4 inch.

Right-angle drive is a handy accessory that permits drilling in tight quarters. The handle on the drive must be held to provide downward pressure while drilling.

51
Concealing Plywood Edges

While plywood has many advantages, it does have one shortcoming: its edges are unattractive. In projects where the edges will be exposed, and particularly if they are to be finished with clear coatings, they need to be concealed. There are several ways this can be done easily. The same methods can be applied to concealing the end-grain of solid wood.

VENEER BAND

Perhaps the simplest way to conceal edges is with veneer edge-banding, which is available in a variety of wood species to match face veneers commonly used on plywood. This is a very thin flexible trim that comes in rolls 1 inch and 2 inches wide, usually 8 feet long. Since it usually is only about $\frac{1}{48}$-inch thick, don't use it on edges of furniture that will be subject to normal abuse, such as chairs, beds, doors, and most tables.

Several types of banding are available. Some are self-adhering and pressure-sensitive; you merely peel off the protective backing and press the veneer into place. Others are thermo-setting; the adhesive is already applied and is activated when heated with an electric iron. The plain kind, which you apply

with contact cement, is the one that will probably bond most permanently.

When working with contact cement you must be very careful with alignment because permanent bond is immediate. Since contact cement doesn't ad-

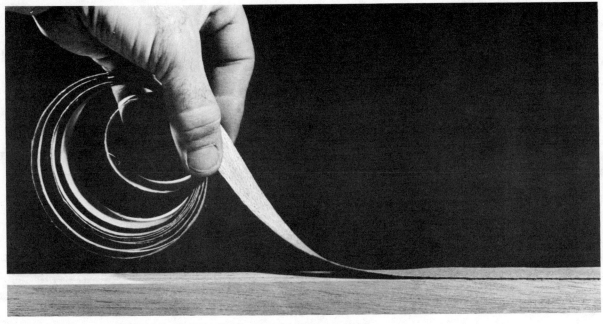

Plywood edges on work that is to be clear-finished need to be concealed.

When applying contact cement to veneer tape, work on scrap paper and tape the ends down to prevent curling.

After the veneer strips are in place, tap them firmly over the entire surface, using a mallet and softwood block, to assure good contact.

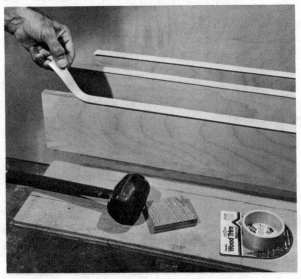

here until both cemented surfaces are dry, alignment errors can be avoided by using paper slipsheets between the surfaces. When the veneer is properly positioned on the work, the paper is pulled out to allow the surfaces to come into contact. Plywood edges soak up cement readily, so apply two coats. One coat is usually sufficient on the veneer.

The veneer strip should be applied slightly oversize in width so it can be trimmed flush with the mating surface. You can use a sharp knife or razor blade for this, or you can use a router with a flush-trimming bit. When trimming with a knife, be especially careful to cut with the grain, not against it, to avoid splits. Since the veneer surface is usually quite smooth, sanding will be required only along the edges. Work with fine-grit abrasive and be sure to ease the corners. Always sand away from the edge, never into it.

SOLID-WOOD EDGING

Solid-wood edge-banding has several advantages over veneer. It is stronger and can be shaped. In addition, should it ever become dented or otherwise damaged in use, it can be planed or sanded to effect a repair.

In assemblies where many exposed edges are involved it is sometimes advantageous to band each component before assembly. This will allow easier flush-trimming and sanding. The procedure calls for careful planning in dimensioning the major parts to allow for the increased thickness of the added band. Generally, however, you can obtain equally good results in applying the edging after assembly. An advantage of this approach is that you can miter the corners where edges meet at right angles to obtain a pleasing grain pattern. Whichever method you choose, always apply the edging with a slight overhang to permit trimming. Use regular glue, not contact cement, and apply it sparingly to avoid excessive runoff, but do be sure to coat the entire surface of both parts. Edges requiring shaping should be assembled first to permit proper utilization of clamps. Edging in thicknesses of $\frac{1}{8}$" or so can be held in glue contact with brads or masking tape provided the parts fit together properly. When feasible the tongue and groove is a good joint to use.

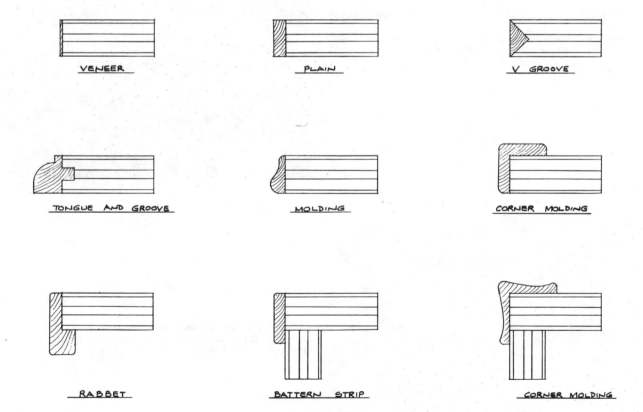

METHODS OF EDGE-BANDING PLYWOOD

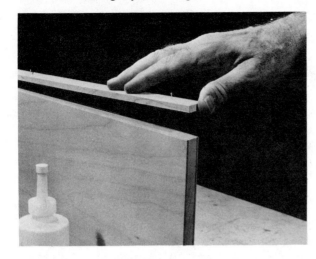

When concealing edges with solid wood strips, start several nails to make alignment holes before applying glue. Use a brush to spread the glue evenly on both surfaces.

You can use masking tape to apply pressure when gluing solid-wood edging. Round toothpick standoffs are used to keep the tape off the glue line and prevent gumming, which occurs when the glue mixes with the adhesive in the tape. A router with a trimming bit will trim these edges.

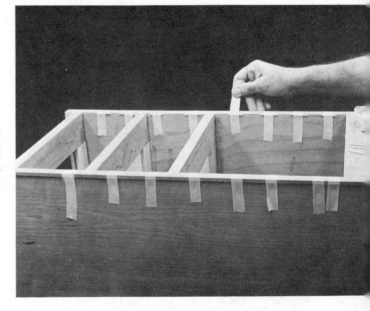

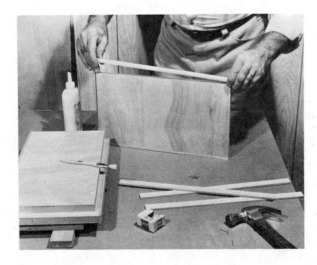

Applying solid-wood edging in advance makes it easier to obtain good results. You must anticipate the added dimension and cut the basic parts accordingly smaller.

If grain of plywood and edging don't match, block plane can be used for preliminary trimming, but sanding should take over before reaching the main surface. Otherwise plane will gouge the plywood.

V-groove edge-band treatment is more difficult.   45-degree bevel cut is made halfway into the edge, then repeated on the other side to form the V-groove.

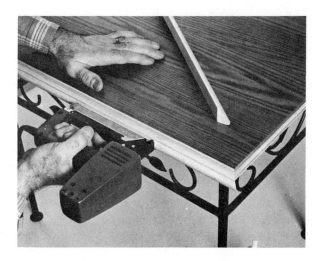

Ready-made molding can be applied to conceal a plywood edge. Glue and a nail gun make a good combination. This tool drives the nail head slightly below the surface.

A raised panel effect on a door is easily accomplished by adding plywood rectangles to the surface. Molding is applied to trim and conceal the plywood edges.

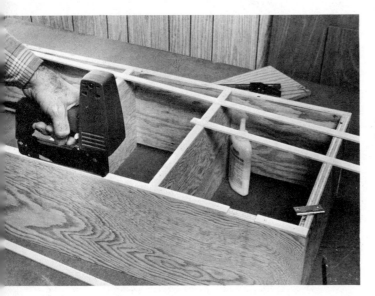

You can avoid cutting a gain for a hinge when edge-banding with solid wood by leaving gaps at the hinge locations.

Use a router with a trimming bit for plastic-laminate edges.

Sources of Supply

Armor Products
Box 290
Deer Park, NY 11729   (Catalog $1.50)

Brass knob; Butler Table hinge; Campaign Desk ornamental corners, pulls; candle cup, dish; coffee mill; corner mount casters; decorative wood buttons; Molly Pitcher Clock movement, dial face, flexible molding for glass, non-mortise hinge; Nautical Lamp eagle ornament, pull, threaded pipe, socket, spindle; Rotating Centerpiece Server swivel bearing, gallery spindles; Saltshaker/Peppermill hardware; tabletop fasteners; Tea Cart wheel spokes, legs, handlebar, wheel hub cover; White-Ash End Table turned legs. Also available are the following large-scale plans: Book Trough Table, Chest Table, Cradle Magazine Rack, Molly Pitcher Clock, Nautical Lamp, Tea Cart, White-Ash End Table.

Constantine
2050 Eastchester Road
Bronx, NY 10461   (Catalog $1.00)

Cabinet woods, solid and plywood; center-finding rule; chair swivel—heavy duty; Circ-L-Cut, fly circle cutter; drawer slide—full extension; inlay border strip; drill guide—Portalign; hinge—ornamental brass; veneers; veneer sample pack; Veneering tools and supplies.

Additional mail-order sources for woodworking supplies. Write for catalog prices.

Brookstone Company
127 Vose Farm Road
Peterboro, NH 03458

Frog Tool Company, Ltd.
541 N. Franklin Street
Chicago, IL 60610

Garret Wade Company
302 Fifth Avenue
New York, NY 10001

John Harra Wood & Supply Company
511 W. 25th Street
New York, NY 10001

Furniture Designs
1425 Sherman Avenue
Evanston, IL 60201

Full-size plans Rolltop Desk. Ask for price of catalog listing 175 full-size plans.)

The following project materials are generally available at local lumberyards and building-supply centers. If you have difficulty in obtaining them write to the manufacturers for source listings in your area:

Marlite paneling, moldings, man-made stone

Masonite Corporation
29 N. Wacker Drive
Chicago, IL 60606

Plexiglas acrylic glazing

Rohm and Haas Company
Independence Mall West
Philadelphia, PA 19105

Reynolds aluminum storm sash and fittings

Reynolds Metals Company
6601 W. Broad Street
Richmond, VA 23261

Waddell hardwood moldings

Waddell Manufacturing Company
1115 Taylor Avenue NW
Grand Rapids, MI 49503

Index

unearthed rather flowery accounts of Taos Pueblo life in periodicals going back as far as 1885.

In a used-book store in Santa Fe, I stumbled upon a huge portfolio of fifty full-color drawings by natives of San Ildefonso and Zia Pueblos. They are stunning examples of art done during the 1920s and '30s, when the Dorothy Dunn school became popular. (She taught Pueblo Indian art students to tap into their roots by producing simple, uncluttered paintings of tribal life and mythological subjects.) A number of these paintings are published for the first time here, including the painting of a water serpent on the front jacket of the book.

Trips to the Indian Pueblo Cultural Center, the Laboratory of Anthropology, the Museum of New Mexico, the Institute of American Indian Art, and the School of American Research yielded unexpected numbers of art slides, meticulously cataloged and captioned. The staffs of these places went out of their way to be helpful to me. At the end of the research phase, I had more than one thousand pages of text and nearly four hundred illustrations, enough for many books. Karen Lotz and I cut and revised during a four-day marathon editing session in Santa Fe. We not only selected on the basis of literary merit but also considered diversity, complexity, and originality. Either we loved a piece, or we didn't. The art struck us, or it didn't.

Readers will recognize, I hope, that this book is meant to be a tribute to a great native culture, a work painstakingly gathered and lovingly presented.

Nancy Wood
Santa Fe
1997

Endless testimonies . . . prove the mild and pacific temperament of the natives. . . . But our work was to exasperate, ravage, kill, mangle and destroy; small wonder, then, if they tried to kill one of us now and then. . . .

—Bartolomé de Las Casas, *History of the Indies*, Book Two (1548)

You might as well try to convert Jews without the Inquisition as Indians without soldiers.

—Captain–General and Governor don Diego de Vargas Santa Fe, New Mexico (1693)

Cliff-perched Acoma (1904)
Edward S. Curtis

Historians have found the first treaty the United States government ever signed. It states that the Indians can keep their lands for "as long as the river runs clear, the buffalo roam, the grass grows tall"—or ninety days, whichever comes first.

—**Frank Marcus, Taos fire chief (1987)**

When mountains die, we die. When rivers run backward into time, our spirits will travel along. All is a circle within us. What ends here begins in some other place. What begins here has no end.

—**Traditional Tiwa prayer**

INTRODUCTION

In the Days of the Ancestors

The Pueblo Indians of New Mexico believe they came from a murky underworld, so long ago that the time cannot be measured in ordinary years. According to one of many legends, they knew neither death nor illness there, but they were not happy in such a dark and watery place.

One day they climbed up a spruce tree and emerged through the Shipapu, a sacred hole in the ground. The ancestors were sightless, so they turned toward the rising sun, and their eyes opened. They grew quickly into people of all ages, both male and female. A powerful spirit came with them from the underground, common to people and animals alike. Through this spirit, children learned how stars are connected to snakes, how trees are related to moths, and how rain comes from the Cloud People, the oldest ancestors. By imagining the underworld, the Shipapu, and the blind ancestors acquiring sight, people connected themselves to the spirit world.

This connection, this belief in the spirit world, was all the Pueblo Indians needed to survive. Tribes do not accept the idea that their ancestors crossed the Bering Strait land bridge and moved southward during the Ice Age. We have always been here, they insist. Our world came with us.

For countless generations, time stirred slowly under the hot New Mexico sun. Tribes moved from place to place, leaving few clues about their lives. Prehistoric memory evolved into tradition, which became the basis for legend and ritual. Pueblo religion stems from all of this, and more. Pueblo religion is life itself. Without it, the underworld would not have yielded the ancestors.

The Land and Its Lessons

The land of the Pueblos is magical. Crystal-clear light, olive-hued, plays across the vast red earth. Dark blue shadows dance long and changing paths. Mountains, covered with thick forests, rise toward a searing blue sky. On a clear day one can see a thousand square miles from a mountaintop. At night stars blaze across a black velvet sky. Sunsets, with their rich burst of magentas, ochers, oranges, and deep purples, are said to be the Sun Father dressing himself to go out.

Sunrise, according to legend, is when the Magpie Sisters part the Sky Curtain so the Sun Father can rise. Clouds form in the shapes of buffalo, coyotes, bears, eagles, sheep, and turtles. Our ancestors, the Indians say, are keeping watch over our people. To the west the desert shimmers with tantalizing mystery. Apache, Navajo, and Hopi live there. To the Pueblos, the land represents harmony between earth and sky. Their entire history belongs there. It is the Center Place.

Early on, the landscape and the people were one. It was their church, their cathedral. It was like a sacred building to them, but one without walls, tithes, or dogma. Nature had no need for sin, guilt, or redemption. Why should it? No Bible was necessary to mete out justice, form ties to the community, or force people to behave. The Indians knew right from wrong; they honored their elders, loved their children, and lived within a communal framework of work, cooperation, and tribal hierarchy. Prayer and observation were part of everyday life. Everything in the sky or on the earth was either male or female, because that was what the Old Man of the Sky and the Old Woman of the Earth taught them. If a man connected himself to the spirit of the land, he was said to be "living the right way." From the earth women learned about medicinal plants and herbs; earth provided food, shelter, clothing, and tools. The seasons reflected change, and women invented songs about their mystery. They watched men perform incredible feats based on superhuman physical strength and a holy alliance with their sacred land.

Serpent bird
Miguel Martinez

At Chaco Canyon, near Farmington, men carried from the distant mountains fifty thousand huge logs to build the town; they constructed four hundred miles of graded roads, the equivalent of four-lane highways. The ancestors knew about irrigation and crop rotation; they were masters of astronomy, architecture, plant science, and herbal medicine. But they did not invent the wheel or develop a written language. They had no need for them.

Something brought the life of these people, now known as the Anasazi, to an abrupt end—drought, disease, warfare, or a shift in religious power. By the mid-1300s most of the villages were abandoned, and the former residents moved to new sites along or near the Rio Grande. They left scant clues about themselves, but on the canyon walls they made pictures of animals, birds, mythical figures such as Kokopelli the flute player, clouds, corn, warriors, spirals, and other cryptic symbols of their lives. Archaeologists have spent their careers trying to learn what these drawings mean.

The Spanish Invasion

Many years before the Spaniards arrived, elders learned of them through Aztec traders, who reported the fall of Tenochtitlán and its great leader, Montezuma. Prophecies were told about A-wan-yu, the plumed serpent deity, who had retreated to the sky to prepare himself for the Time When Blood Flowed Alongside Water. Shamans took a solar or lunar eclipse to mean that drastic change was upon them. But despite the prophecies, the Pueblos were unprepared for what happened.

During the summer of 1540, the Indians of Hawikuh, today called Zuni Pueblo, were going about their timeless chores, singing as they worked, the smoke of countless fires wafting lazily into the clear blue air. They were unaware, until a lookout spotted them, that a column of soldiers in armor suits, riding splendid horses and carrying the twin banners of Spain and the Catholic Church, was marching northward toward them. By this time Hernán Cortés had wiped out the Aztec civilization in central Mexico, while in the swamps of Florida and Mississippi Hernando De Soto, with six hundred heavily armed troops and vicious war dogs, had slaughtered the native populations. De Soto's men, devout Catholics and trusted servants of the Spanish king, showed no mercy. (Nor had Christopher Columbus in 1492, when the peaceful Arawak, living on present-day

Haiti, failed to produce the required gold. He killed them by hanging, burning, unleashing his war dogs, or hacking off their hands so they bled to death.) Now the agrarian Pueblos were the target of religious and military fanaticism.

When the Hawikuh saw the Spanish troops approaching, they laid down a cornmeal line to indicate to them they were not to cross it. The Spaniards stormed the village, demanding gold, while an interpreter read the Requerimiento, which had been written in Latin. This specious document, a joint proclamation of church and state, set forth the uncompromising rules: henceforth the Hawikuh and their land, lives, and religion belonged to the Spanish king and to Holy Mother Church. If the Indians did not agree, the interpreter warned, "We shall forcefully enter your country and shall make war against you.... We shall take you and your wives and your children and shall make slaves of them . . . and shall do you all the harm and damage that we can." The Hawikuh were puzzled. They thought the Spaniards were gods—until twenty Hawikuh men were shot dead.

Next to be invaded by Spanish troops, with their powerful weapons and war dogs, were the twelve villages of Tiguex, near present-day Bernalillo. The village of Alcanfor was ordered vacated so Spanish troops could move into it for the winter. Men were forcibly stripped of their shirts, made of cotton and yucca fiber, in which strips of rabbit fur were twisted. The soldiers stole stores of corn, beans, and dried meat that the Indians had put away for the winter. One man complained that his wife had been raped. After the Indians killed a number of Spanish horses in retaliation, the conquistador Coronado sacked the villages. A forty-day battle ensued, after which two hundred Indians lay dead. A hundred others were burned at the stake. The villages fell to ruin.

Genocide began then, in 1541, in peaceful New Mexico. Blood dripped from the rooftops of Tiguex, and in the ashes of human fires only a blackened hand or twisted foot remained. Genocide in North, South, and Central America would continue for more than four centuries as native people, most of them unarmed, became the objects of greed and savagery by men who staunchly believed in a Christian God. As many as thirty million Indians were killed during those centuries--through warfare, disease, and starvation—by Spanish, English, French, Dutch, and American invaders.

At the time of the Spanish conquest, about twenty thousand Indians were living in seventy villages along the major river drainages of New Mexico. They spoke five mutually unintelligible dialects. Their lands stretched for thousands of square miles, across river valleys, mountains, and mesa tops. Coronado did not find gold in New Mexico, but there were thousands of souls to be converted, which meant that the Spanish king was eager to send both priests and colonists to that remote frontier. Forced to assist in their own "colonization" during the late sixteenth and seventeenth centuries, the Indians, usually women and children, built sturdy mission churches. Men grew crops and hunted game for their Spanish masters. With everyone busy making sure the Spaniards were fed, housed, and clothed, Indian families often went hungry themselves. Disease took its toll.

The Pueblo Revolt of 1680

For 140 years, from the time that Coronado left a bloody trail across New Mexico to the greatest Indian revolt in history, little changed in the pueblos. Indians were seen as pagans, beasts of burden, items of trade, commodities, savages, or animals, but never as men and women. In 1599, following a fierce mesa-top battle at Acoma, Don Juan de Oñate, the first territorial governor, cut off the left feet of rebel warriors. Countless more Acoma were put in chains and sold into slavery in Mexico. Eventually Oñate himself was removed from office in disgrace, but the Indians were demoralized.

The friars, no strangers to the whip, forced Catholicism on the pueblos. Those who refused baptism were routinely hanged; others were sold into slavery. Kivas were filled with sand and religious objects smashed. Medicine men were hanged in the plaza. Church and state fought over who had authority over the Indians; the state needed slaves, the church needed converts in order to justify Rome's outpouring of money into the far-flung frontier churches. The Indians survived this brutal period by pretending to accept the alien faith, but they practiced their own religion as well. Detection, they knew, meant certain death. Until well into the twentieth century, neither church nor state accepted the Indian religion. Kivas were raided as late as the 1920s. But when priests looked inside those native hearts, they saw something primordial and frightening.

Throughout much of the seventeenth century the pueblos seethed with resentment. There were numerous attempts at rebellion, but the powerful Spanish knew how to cure disobedience—with whip, noose, or sword. For generations, the Indians had dreamed of freedom. On Catholic feast days they sang about it in their own language, unfathomable to the Spaniards. Clan leaders from different tribes met secretly at trade fairs, wondering how to rid themselves of their hated masters. Their pueblos were scattered over thousands of square miles, and both civil and religious authorities watched their every move. The Indians called upon the spirits to help them. Leaders moved into the mountains to pray to their old, dependable gods.

A controversial San Juan medicine man named Popé masterminded a plan. Plotting for four years in the kivas of Taos, he devised a scheme of knotted yucca cords, one knot for each day, to be delivered by runners to each pueblo. When all the knots were untied, the Indians, from Taos to San Juan, from Acoma to Zuni and Hopi, would attack simultaneously on a given day. From a military stand-point, the plan seemed impossible. Distance alone was an insurmountable problem; so was the language barrier, the utter reliance on the runners. What else can we do? Popé asked. They had only to look at their decimated villages to know they could not last much longer. Many villages had perished during those 140 years. The irony was that the Golden Age of the Pueblos was over and nothing, not even revolt, could bring it back.

On August 10, 1680, the Pueblos struck in one great united effort over an area the size of Massachusetts. Four hundred soldiers and twenty-one priests were killed, though the Indians suffered a loss of three hundred warriors themselves. The great mission churches, built with Indian slave labor, were destroyed brick by brick; wooden statues, crucifixes, and altars were demolished. Many Indians ran to the river to wash the hated baptism from their souls; others scalped the fallen enemy and waved the scalps from poles. After a fierce battle at Santa Fe, where the Indians cut off the Spaniards' water supply to their stronghold inside the Palace of the Governors, the Spaniards surrendered. The Pueblos allowed them to leave peacefully, though they easily could have killed them all. The exit from Santa Fe ended in El Paso, on the Mexican border. The Indians burned the Span-ish furniture and turned the Palace of the Governors into a pueblo, quartering their animals there, burying their dead, and installing baking ovens. This historic building is still standing; many believe that Indian spirits continue to live there. Every renovation turns up artifacts from that era.

Despite their common beliefs and origins, the Pueblo Indians were unable to live in harmony for very long. Popé, who had led the rebellion, insisted that the people give up everything Spanish, including the new crops and implements, and exacted his own tribute as dictator. Bitterness erupted, with each tribe reclaiming its former independence. Factions split into smaller factions. Greatly weakened by battle, hunger, drought, and smallpox, the Pueblos were easy prey for Comanche and Apache attacks. Leaders knew that without the Spaniards to protect them, life was almost as bad as it was under their former masters. When Don Diego de Vargas returned in 1693, many tribes bitterly fought the Spaniards as they had before, but, weakened and divided as they were, the Pueblos eventually succumbed. Vargas had come, he said, only to bring Christ to the natives, who were required to wear small wooden crosses around their necks.

In the eighteenth century the Pueblo Indians began to enjoy some of the things Spanish colonists brought along. Foremost was the horse, equal in value to two women. A splendid array of new crops—wheat, apples, peaches, pears, apricots, tomatoes, and chiles—added variety to the old diet of corn, beans, and squash. Cattle, oxen, donkeys, goats, pigs, sheep, and chickens eventually appeared in Indian villages. Metal tools such as hoes, shovels, knives, needles, and axes became indispensable. Gunpowder and European clothing and food also were introduced. The Pueblos learned the Spanish language in addition to their own dialects. The padres

Horse in the Wind
Ian Carlisle, age 11, Tewa

who baptized them gave them their own surnames—for instance, Martinez, Trujillo, Archuleta, Sánchez—which they retain to the present day, along with a number of secret Indian names. Intermarriage became more frequent, though the two cultures remain distinct and separate. Churches were painstakingly rebuilt. The Indians were known to put their own fetishes inside the thick adobe walls.

Swarms of colonists arrived; huge rancheros were established through land grants by the king, who assumed he now owned all the property that had belonged to the Indians and could dispense it to his friends.

Conquest, Change, and Conflict

In 1821, following the successful revolt of the Spanish colonists of Mexico against the Spanish crown, New Mexico became part of the Republic of Mexico. The opening of the Santa Fe Trail the following year provided a route by which Anglos could penetrate even more Pueblo country. Still, the Indians were little affected by any change in leadership until 1846, when New Mexico became part of the United States. As the new regime took over, rumors flourished about what would happen to Indians and Mexicans alike. They would lose all their land. They would have to report to the authorities. They would be forced to work for the Americans. One winter night in Taos, a group of angry Taos Indians and Mexicans rode into town and scalped Territorial Governor Charles Bent. More murders followed; then the Indians fled to the thick-walled mission church of San Geronimo at Taos Pueblo and hid there. A mostly volunteer army stormed the church with guns and howitzers; when fifty-one unarmed men tried to escape, the soldiers killed them. The army moved into the pueblo. Nearly two hundred Indian men, women, and children were killed; seventeen Taos leaders were hanged in the plaza. This was the last revolt of the Pueblo Indians, though the assault on their lives, lands, and religion was far from over.

After the American Civil War, opportunists, merchants, and settlers swarmed into the territory, demanding land for towns, ranches, and railroads. Unable to read or write English, many Indians simply scratched an X on a piece of paper and lost their land and water rights forever. They had no advocate within the government itself; the churches, far from actively seeking to defend Indian rights, offered salvation through Christ. The Indians turned to their old gods and prayed.

A generation later, the United States government began to remove Indian children from their homes and send them to boarding schools. Torn from their mothers' arms, the children were beaten, shut up in closets, forced to march to class to military music, and forbidden to speak their native languages or sing their old tribal songs. Their hair was cut short, their Indian clothing destroyed along with whatever sacred objects they might have brought with them. They were compelled to receive more Christian teachings from Protestant instructors. Some captives died in this hostile environment; others ran away; but most adapted, learning to read, write, and obey. After years of indoctrination, some students merged into the mainstream and never went home. Others returned and practiced their new skills. Many began to see education as a way of improving their lives. They became lawyers, teachers, skilled leaders, and craftspeople. Others took up an activist role. Though Indians were not granted the vote until 1948, many began to examine the legal documents that had deprived them of their land and water. They fought back with a different sort of weapon.

Victory

No symbol of Indian triumph over government injustice is more poignant than Taos Pueblo's struggle to regain their sacred Blue Lake. They believe they emerged from the underground via this lake and it is there the spirits reside, watching over them. High in a dense, unspoiled forest in the Sangre de Cristo Mountains, the lake is a pristine jewel, lying at eleven thousand feet. Every August the tribe goes there to celebrate its origins, to speak with the spirits, and to offer prayers of thanksgiving. To the Taos, Blue Lake is as sacred as St. Peter's Basilica is to Catholics.

It is not surprising that the government had long coveted this lake. Through executive fiat President Theodore Roosevelt made the lake and thirty thousand acres of Indian land part of the National Forest System in 1906. The Indians had not been told, and they became furious when they found their sacred lake closed to them, surrounded by a fence. The federal government issued grazing permits for sheep and cattle; they allowed hunting, camping, and fishing for non-Indians. The lake and surrounding area were quickly trashed; logging was planned, as well as mineral exploration. The Taos were allowed three days a year to use the lake themselves, and then only with the permission of the Forest Service. A legal battle, led by the Indians themselves, commenced.

After sixty-four years of relentless effort—lobbying Congress, blitzing newspapers, and a massive letter-writing appeal—the Taos forced Congress to return Blue Lake to them in 1970.

Not only was Blue Lake a symbolic victory for Indians pitted against an unsympathetic government, it had religious significance as well. After four hundred years of persecution, the Pueblos had proven, once and for all, their right to their sacred lands and rituals. They had defied the government through peaceful means and won. Federal officials would never again threaten to destroy the All Pueblo Indian Council, which had existed for centuries as a means to give common voice to Pueblo issues such as land, water, and religious rights. They would never again raid the kivas or drag children off to boarding schools. The Pueblos took charge of their lives.

Today, through profits from their gambling casinos, Indian leaders are pouring millions of dollars into education, housing, economic development, and visitors' centers. They effectively market their arts and crafts; the Indian Market, held every August in Santa Fe, is the biggest in the country. Indian writers have written movingly of their experiences growing up in the pueblos.

The connection to the ways of their ancestors remains strong in New Mexico's nineteen pueblos. When mountains die, we die, goes a Tiwa prayer. When rivers run backward into time, our spirits will travel along. All is a circle within us. What ends here begins in some other place. What begins here has no end.

CONTENTS